FURLOUGH

a novel

JACOB MOON

ISBN: 978-1-7361642-0-4 (ebook)
ISBN: 978-1-7361642-1-1 (paperback)
ISBN: 978-1-7361642-2-8 (hardcover)
ISBN: 978-1-7361642-3-5 (audio)

Furlough is a work of fiction. Names, characters, places, and incidents are the products of the author's imagination or are used fictitiously. Any resemblance to actual events, locales, or persons, living or dead, is entirely coincidental.

Published in the USA.

For my mother, Lois, there since the beginning.

ONE

EDDIE GRASSLE LEANED his bicycle against the One-Stop's facade and walked inside, grateful to be out of the late afternoon Florida heat. He felt even more grateful for simply being free to come and go as he pleased. As he perused the aisles, searching for the items he'd come for, he relished the feeling of the blowing air conditioning—a luxury he'd gone without for the better part of the past five years. Prison walls had ways of changing a person's perspective. No longer did he have to lie on a metal bunk, staring at the peeling ceiling while listening to the collective groans of those imprisoned with him. No longer were watchful eyes upon him as he performed even the most basic of human functions. And finally gone was the near-constant slamming of doors, the clank of keys shutting him away for hours on end, like a specimen in a human zoo.

Three weeks of freedom was a nice start, but it hadn't been enough time to keep from sometimes pinching himself just to make sure he wasn't dreaming.

Eddie found the items he'd come here for—a small bottle of chocolate milk and two packages of Jolly Ranchers—and placed them on the counter. Both were things Clarissa had said the boy liked most. She'd told him that just after Eddie landed in prison, during her final visit. He remembered her voice trembling with hurt and rage as she gripped the phone receiver, her eyes tear-streaked and bloodshot through the inch-thick glass as she'd accused him, among other things, of not even knowing his own son's favorite snacks. And Eddie had silently sat on the other side of the glass, feeling like an asshole as he watched her fight back more tears. Then in a torrent, the tears *had* come, and with a shout of years-old frustration she'd slammed home her receiver and hurried away.

Then again, it was easy to walk away from someone who had never truly been there at all.

The clerk's voice broke Eddie's daydream.

"Excuse me?" he asked, blinking.

"Would you like a bag?" the Hispanic clerk repeated in his heavy accent. He stood quite a bit shorter than Eddie's six-foot-two frame, looking upward at him from behind the counter, offering an affable smile that suggested he'd become accustomed to customers like Eddie caught in the trappings of their own busy lives.

"Yes, please," Eddie said, returning the clerk's smile. He glanced at the electronic date displayed behind the counter—April 25, 2016—feeling amazed at how fast five years could fly by. He paid for his items and walked back out into the blazing late-April sun. Climbing onto his used ten-speed, he began pedaling toward his apartment, taking in the scenery around him. The sky seemed bluer than he remembered, the palm fronds lusher as they waved lazily at the air. Springwood, one of many small cities in this part of southwestern Florida, seemed like it had aged twice as fast as he had in the time he'd been away. The vehicles cruising down the roads looked different. Sleeker. Not as blocky as he remembered them being. Even the clothes people wore had changed. Businessmen no longer wore squared-off dress shoes. Young mothers pushing exercise baby strollers down the sidewalks had exchanged sweatpants for new Dri-fit material that clung a little more closely to the body. He took it all in, breathing air that no longer came stale and putrid from the combined smells of sixty grown men packed together in an area the size of the average family's home. Three weeks since his prison counselor had arranged an apartment for him with the thousand dollars Eddie had saved over the last five years. Located two miles ahead in the worst area of town, the complex lay claim to shady characters and more than a few cockroaches; but none of that mattered, because he could walk up the stairway with its chipping railing and rickety stairs knowing he would fall asleep poor and half-hungry, but at least free.

He came to a street sign that read Humboldt and for a reason he didn't quite understand, he turned suddenly onto it. Ten minutes later he stopped in front of a salmon-colored stucco home on the east end of town. Digging in his pocket, he uncrumpled a scrap of paper and double-checked the address before knocking on the door. *Just five minutes to break the ice,* he thought to himself. *It might make the boy nervous going to the park with a total stranger.* After detouring from his apartment, Eddie had felt confident on the way here. But now as he heard voices from inside, one of them an adult male, he considered hopping on his bike and riding away. He didn't recall Clarissa having any male family members living locally. The thought of the voice belonging to someone romantically connected to her caused old feelings of jealousy to creep into him. He could just come back tomorrow as expected, he reasoned. Besides, that might give him more time to get used to the idea that when the door opened, he'd see another man standing in the place Eddie had always felt he should be.

But he'd hesitated too long. The door swung open to reveal a man in his early thirties with a prematurely receding hairline and a slight gut. Several inches shorter than Eddie, the man gave him a once-over before glancing past him toward the bicycle in the driveway. Confusion showed in his eyes before sudden understanding dawned in them. "You must be Eddie."

Eddie extended his right hand. "Yes sir, I'm Liam's dad."

The man regarded Eddie's offered hand but made no move to accept it. Just then, the door opened more fully, and a woman appeared. Clarissa. Her dark brown hair sat tied back in a simple ponytail, and she wore a pair of cut-off shorts and an old t-shirt that hugged her shapely body. Seeing Eddie, and with annoyance flashing in her eyes, she whispered something into the man's ear. The man gave Eddie another once-over, this one more disapproving than the first, before disappearing into the house. Clarissa stepped out onto the stoop, leaving the door cracked. When she turned to face him, her eyes burned into him. Eddie felt like he'd definitely made a mistake in stopping by unannounced.

"You're not supposed to be here until tomorrow," she said, keeping her voice low. "Do you know how something like this looks?"

Eddie looked into Clarissa's eyes for the first time in almost five years, unable to believe it had been that long. Tilting his head, he gave her that same sidelong grin he'd given her so many times before, when she'd ultimately folded her anger away over one of his many transgressions, and allowed him to lead her into the bedroom where not long after her fists had gripped the bedsheets. He'd always been able to soften her frustration and anger with that grin; but when she responded this time by folding her arms across her chest and setting her mouth firmly in a line, he stood up straight and cleared his throat.

He motioned toward the door. "Who was that?"

"That," Clarissa said, "was my fiancé. His name is Roger. He lives here, not that it's any of your business." She brushed a strand of hair from her face, agitation causing her cheeks and ears to flush red.

Eddie shook his head. "Your fiancé?"

"Yes, Eddie," she snapped. "Did you expect me to sit around and twiddle my thumbs waiting for you to get out?"

He huffed. "I didn't mean it like that. I guess I'm just surprised. He doesn't seem like your type."

She laughed a humorless little laugh. "Not my type? I suppose you consider my type men who take the fall for their best friend and get sent to prison just weeks before their son is due to be born."

Eddie dropped his eyes to the concrete stoop. "Look, I thought I'd stop by on my way home and say a quick hello. Just so tomorrow wouldn't be awkward for him. But you're right, I should have called first to see if it was okay. And it isn't my business who you're dating." He sighed, realizing for the first time how it must have felt to be in her shoes all those years. "It's just that I've never seen you with anyone else before."

"Eddie ten, Clarissa one," she said with a hint of satisfaction in her voice. "And yes, you should have called ahead first. You're putting me in a difficult position here, Eddie, and I don't appreciate it."

He sighed. "I guess I'm just excited to see him. I've had five years to think about what an idiot I've been." He dug into the convenience store bag and showed her the chocolate milk and candy. "I brought him his favorites."

Clarissa huffed. "I'm shocked you remembered."

Eddie placed the items back in the bag and took a step closer to her. On reflex she stepped backward, her backside pushing the door slightly open. Flustered, she closed it to just a crack again. When she turned to meet his eyes, her expression betrayed some long and painful memory that until now had lain dormant.

"I want to be a part of his life, Clarissa. I know you've moved on, and I can't blame you for that, but a boy needs his father and— "

She raised a hand to cut him off. "You had a choice, Eddie, and you chose your friend over Liam and me. Life is about doing things right the first time. I used to sit and fantasize about you being able to go back in time and choose us. But I realized, you would just do the exact same thing. That made me feel like a fool, Eddie. I refused to lose you *and* myself at the same time."

Eddie shook his head. It was as if his life, like a pot of soup, had been left to slowly simmer during his five years away, leaving nothing but a charred and inedible lump. Five years—nearly one-fifth of his life up to this point—and all he had to show for it was a bag of sweets he couldn't even give to his son when he wanted to. Looking at the sky, he spied a hawk circling high above. He watched as it glided in the airstream like some graceful avian sentinel. As it disappeared into the clouds, Eddie felt his own insignificance fall over him like a shroud. He knew then he'd never get her back.

"You're one hundred percent right," he finally said. "I fucked up. I wish like hell I could go back and make it right."

Despite being almost a foot shorter and seventy pounds lighter than Eddie, Clarissa had always shown a fiery spark that had more than made up for it. It had been what attracted him to her the most, more so even than her good looks. And if he hadn't already known that he'd blown any chance with her, what she said next only confirmed the fact.

"It really doesn't matter," she said. "I've moved on. I raised Liam the best way I knew how, and I finally met someone who was willing to be there. You're a passionate person, but your passion is unfocused. Jules is a perfect example. You went to *prison* for him, for God's sake. Even I knew those drugs weren't yours."

Eddie silently stared at the ground. He could sense what was coming next and didn't want to see the look in her eyes when she said it.

"I made a promise to myself I'd never bring him to see you in that place, and I kept it. Know that if you ever choose anyone else over him again, especially Jules, you'll lose him forever."

Hearing this caused him to meet her gaze. "Just give me one chance," he pleaded. "I won't let you down again."

She cemented her eyes onto him, consideration showing in her furrowed brow. After some time, she brushed away tears that burned fresh in her eyes and said, "I promised him he'd get to see you and I won't go back on that. But you need to know I talked to a lawyer, and he said you'll never get full visitation rights if I don't agree to it."

Outwardly, Eddie kept his expression even and nodded. But inwardly, he felt like doing backflips.

"Tomorrow, ten o'clock," she said. "I work at one and need to drop Liam off at the sitter's by noon. Don't be late."

"Okay, I won't," he promised, his heart racing. As he turned to leave, she called out to him.

"Eddie, wait. There's something I'd like to say to you. I waited five years to say it and it's important I finally get it out of my system."

He turned back to face her, the smile on his face faltering a bit.

"After Liam was born and I was still in the hospital, I started bleeding that first night," she said. "They checked me and said I'd have to have an emergency hysterectomy. I almost died. When I woke up the next day, I remember you called me from jail. It was a Sunday morning. I remember because there were church bells ringing somewhere close by. You asked how the baby was, but you didn't even think to ask about me. I hung up and told myself I'd never talk to you again. That I'd never let you see Liam. He was my angel, and since I'd never be able to have any more children, I wasn't going to let you put a stain on the one I did have." She drilled her eyes into him. "Don't make me regret letting you see him, Eddie. Don't make me feel like I did in that hospital room. Most of all, don't ever let

Liam down like that. If you aren't serious about this, please just turn around and don't look back."

Eddie felt something lurch inside of him, like a piece of him had just broken free and had floated away into a hidden recess of himself. He realized that Clarissa meant every word. Remembering what she'd said earlier about undoing the past, he imagined stepping into a time machine right then and going back to the night he and Jules had been stopped by the police, when the cop had found the bags of dope in the glovebox. How Eddie had immediately claimed them as his, despite the fact he hadn't known a thing about them. Eddie felt if he were able to undo that, he would see her smiling at him now, proud of her son's father, instead of looking so skeptical. But he knew that wasn't possible. No time machine existed. Even if it did, he'd probably find a way to fuck that up as well. The simple reality was he stood on the wrong side of the front door, and all the regret in the world would never change that. He wasn't just a stranger to his son—he realized he barely knew even himself.

"I won't let you down," he managed, his voice seemingly not his own. "I don't deserve it. Thank you for giving me a chance with him."

"Don't thank me, Eddie," she said with a sigh. "I'm not doing this for you. And you're right, you don't deserve it."

The sound of Roger's raised voice came from somewhere inside the house. Clarissa sniffled. "I have to go," she said. As she slipped through the door, a high-pitched giggle rose from a nearby room, and then there was nothing but a closed door and Eddie standing there on the stoop, his hand extended toward it. Toward the only important thing he had left in his life.

Tomorrow.

TWO

A SILVER MERCEDES convertible pulled into a riverfront gated community and parked in the circular brick driveway of a sprawling Spanish-style home. Alan Ashford, wearing a suit and carrying a leather briefcase, stepped from the car and stood beneath the shade of a royal palm. Removing his sunglasses, he regarded the mansion before him and sighed. How in the world the man he had come here to see could afford such a lavish home was beyond him. Public servants received notoriously low salaries, even such a high-ranking attorney as his soon-to-be host. Prior to making the trip, Ashford had done his homework. He'd been unable to identify any other source of income or investments for the enigmatic homeowner—Mathias Hood, appointed State Attorney for Florida's 21st Circuit, rumored to be in contention for higher state or even federal office—other than his publicly listed salary of one hundred forty-two thousand dollars. Yet somehow, the man had managed to buy the sprawling riverfront property for three million dollars cash just the year before. Champagne taste on a beer budget.

The two-story home sported an expansive red tile roof that protected its four thousand square feet. Even though Ashford had never visited the house before, he knew from those who had that a large custom swimming pool in the shape of an eagle head sat in the backyard. The pool alone, built after Hood purchased it, had reportedly cost a cool two hundred thousand.

Ashford stood on the stoop for several moments, pondering how he would begin his speech. He'd been given orders to have no mercy, and that under any circumstances Ashford was to end the meeting having either willingly received Hood's resignation from office or forcing it. It would be tricky, but Ashford held faith the job could be done. Once the governor wished to have a thing done, be it officially or not, he expected it to be executed without deviation.

Taking a deep breath, Ashford rang the bell. Mechanical chimes sounded through the house's interior. When no one answered, he rang it again. Finally, a looming shape approached from behind the beveled glass door. It opened to reveal a towering, well-built man in his late fifties. So, this was Hood. He had never seen him in person, and despite already knowing the stories of him being a physically imposing person, Hood proved even more so in the flesh. He stood bare-footed, his bathrobe hanging open to his navel to reveal a surprisingly chiseled chest and abdomen. A towel hung in one hand, and Hood used it to wipe beaded perspiration from his perfectly bald head. Standing before him, the man regarded Ashford with eyes so black and cold the latter felt an instant uneasiness pass over him, a feeling he wasn't at all accustomed to as the chief aide to the most powerful man in state government.

"Alan Ashford, Governor's office," Hood said. "You're early." He held out a hand. Ashford accepted it, surprised by the power behind it.

"Traffic from Tallahassee was lighter than I expected," Ashford explained. "Is this a good time?"

"Of course," Hood said, showing Ashford inside. "You'll have to excuse my lack of formality. I just got out of the pool—the doorbell sounds out back also. Swimming is such great exercise, I think. Care to join me? I've got some spare trunks you can borrow."

Ashford blinked, unsure of how to respond. But then Hood's expression softened, and he laughed good-naturedly, leading Ashford down the corridor to the study at the rear of the house. "We can talk here," he said, sitting behind a large desk and offering his guest a seat opposite it. "This is my favorite room in the house." A smile touched his eyes, brightening them briefly. As Ashford settled into his seat, he looked out toward the oversized, eagle-shaped swimming pool, and to the sparkling river beyond. Moving his eyes around the room's interior, he observed a man's painted portrait hanging on the wall directly behind Hood's desk. He detected a strong resemblance between the man in the portrait and his host.

Hood noticed his guest's appraisal and was seemingly pleased by it. "My father," he said without turning to look behind him. "The greatest man I've ever known. He taught me many things, most of all conviction." Emphasizing this, Hood placed a plaintive hand over his heart. A whimsical expression washed over his face before it disappeared as quickly as it had appeared.

Ashford's confidence had been high during his drive here. Now it wavered. Effectively firing a man in such a lofty position—one that held such esteem and political clout —would not be an easy thing to do. He would have sympathized with anyone else in his position. Yet the state attorney had to know this visit was not a social call. Hood appearing so relaxed and in such good spirits only increased Ashford's trepidation over the job he was about to perform.

"Care for a drink?" Hood asked, motioning to a bar against the near wall.

"No thank you," Ashford said, deciding to get straight to the point. "Mr. Hood, concerning the fact you failed to provide—"

"Special aide to Governor Braxton for the past two years," Hood said, the interruption flowing naturally, as if Ashford had requested it. He stood and fixed himself a glass of scotch served neat. "Harvard School of Law with dual master's in business and political science. Most people would assume someone in your position would aspire to national politics. My money says you wish to remain at the state level, no?"

Ashford waved his hand, passing on the question.

"I could only afford state law school myself," Hood continued, retaking his seat. "I find the Ivy League a bit limiting—snobbery is almost a prerequisite for admission. But I won't hold your choice of schools against you."

Ashford shifted uneasily in his seat. He searched his mind for the next part of his speech—something he had rehearsed many times during the drive—but drew a blank. Why he had become suddenly nervous, he didn't know.

"Where are my manners?" Hood said, smiling graciously. "I interrupted you. You were saying I have failed in something."

Ashford cleared his throat. "Yes. Well—as you know, the deadline has passed for you to provide litigation data to the governor's office. Yours is the only circuit in the state to fail in this mandate. You were even given a sixty-day extension, something not normally granted. The governor is frustrated, to say the least."

Hood calmly sipped his drink. Warmth spread through his chest as his eyes moved past his guest to the river and its shimmering surface. After a moment of silence, he nodded to himself, as if finally deciding among a selection of courses to take. "I am a man of few trifles, Mr. Ashford. Life is short, and I believe we must take seriously those things that are pleasurable to us. Does that make sense?"

Ashford offered a polite smile but said nothing. He had heard of Hood's proselytizing, his philosophical speeches on law and life in general. Several colleagues in the capitol had spoken of being held hostage by one or more of these sessions. Ashford had laughed at the stories. He did not laugh now.

"I know the reason you've been sent here," Hood said, his smile disappearing. "Governor Braxton has instructed you to ask for my resignation from office. Perhaps *ask* is too soft a word."

Ashford shifted in his seat. "Well, to be quite direct, Mr. Hood, yes. But not until the end of the legislative session several months from now. As you know, the outgoing state attorney is still on official suspension, which of course is how you came into the position. Since state law permits the governor to appoint a replacement either temporarily or permanently, the length of that replacement is entirely at his discretion. The governor values your time in office. It has been nearly two years, far longer than most attorneys will ever see at that position during their lifetimes. The governor is prepared to offer a generous severance of sorts, even though he has no obligation to do so."

The sun turned the pool's surface into a twinkling blanket of light. Hood kept his gaze fixed on it, his expression betraying no emotion. As he sipped his scotch, he allowed what his guest had said to settle in the air. After some time, he sighed and said, "Please show me what you have."

Hood watched Ashford reach into his briefcase to first remove a file, then set it on the desk. He read its contents twice while his guest waited patiently, before placing the file back on the table. "This is very generous of the governor. And you are correct on two fronts. He does in fact have the authority to approve or, in my case, rescind my appointment. He also is under no obligation to offer a severance." Without realizing he did so, he began to twist a large ring on his right ring finger.

Ashford took note of the ring's center-mounted, cheap red stone and judged it to be of little value. Surprising, considering the opulence that surrounded every other aspect of the man's persona.

What Hood said next caught Ashford off guard. "And what if I choose not to resign my position?"

"Then...then you will be immediately removed by the governor's order," Ashford responded. "Your office will be cleared out first thing Monday morning. Worse, you will never receive the support of the governor or any of his officers again. Call it the difference between a nasty divorce and an amicable one. The choice is yours."

"The choice certainly does seem to be mine, doesn't it?" Hood said. He held up an exploratory finger, the way a man might do when suddenly discovering a way out of an impossible trap. "But what if I had a *third* choice?" He continued turning the ring around his finger. "Do you want to know how I came into possession of this ring, Mr. Ashford? I believe you may appreciate the history behind it—if you will indulge me."

Accepting his fate, Ashford bowed his head.

"When I was ten years old my life changed forever. My father had been returning home from work when he stopped at a drug store to buy my mother a set of sewing needles that she'd asked him to get the day before. Unbeknownst to him, the store was being robbed."

Ashford glanced at the portrait. "And he was killed in the process."

"Indeed," Hood said matter-of-factly. "Thirty-four years of honest living and caring for his family in God's name, and his life was extinguished in an instant. The robber was a junkie looking for quick cash. Thirty-four dollars is what he got. A dollar for every year of my father's life. They caught the man several blocks away and he went on trial, which I attended. I'll let you guess how it ended."

Ashford understood where this was going. "He was acquitted."

"Correct again. I take back what I said about you Harvard boys." Hood clapped his hands. "'Not guilty,' said the jury. They were unwilling to send a man to prison on flimsy evidence. No gun was found. The many storm drains in the area were swollen with summer rains and could have easily carried it away. The only witnesses had been the elderly clerk who died the following month from a heart attack and an old woman who'd forgotten her bifocals at home."

"Did the robber make a statement?" Ashford asked, irritated at himself for being sucked into the story.

"Even better—he confessed. But the police failed to read him his Miranda warning. This occurred in the early days of the law's passing, and the local police did not figure it to be an issue. How wrong they'd been. The jury never heard his confession since it had been thrown out. Ten minutes after the verdict was read, the man who gunned my father down walked right past me, a free man. As he did, he winked and tossed me this—" Hood held up his hand, showing Ashford the ring on his finger. "My mother didn't see the exchange. I pocketed the ring and later crept to the barn and hid it. That next summer, when my father's grave had grown over with grass and the worst of my mother's tears had dried, I removed it from its hiding place and slipped it onto my finger. It was much too large at the time, but boys grow into men." Hood's eyes moved from the ring to his guest. "Call it morbid fascination for my father's death. From that day forward, I knew where my life would lead."

Unsure why, Ashford felt his pulse quicken. Hood leaned forward in his chair, his black eyes flashing like daggers as they moved to the rhythm of the story.

"Before you leave, Mr. Ashford, I'd like to show you something that may add clarity to our situation." Hood reached into a desk drawer and removed a manila envelope. He placed it on the desk in front of Ashford and motioned for his guest to open it.

Ashford's imperious expression melted away as he opened the envelope and began to look through its contents. At first, he'd been confused as to the nature of the photographs inside the envelope. They'd captured a man and woman in fairly innocuous frames—holding hands at a cozy restaurant, riding together in a gondola down a Venetian canal, embracing in a secluded park. As Ashford continued looking through the photos, sudden recognition dawned on him. His eyes widened as he flipped through the photos more rapidly, his mind racing. How could it be? He recognized the man in the photos as being none other than Governor Braxton himself. Worse, Ashford also recognized the red-headed beauty with him. As he should. The governor had paid Ashford a generous bonus over the past six months to keep the woman a secret, after all. He had gone to great lengths to ensure the governor's wife, the press, and anyone else who may have an interest in knowing about the risky affair remained completely in the dark. A politician engaged in a romantic relationship with a woman other than his wife was nothing new in the annals of politics. But complicating the issue was precisely *whom* the governor had chosen to have his affair with— the wife of his own lieutenant governor.

Aside from the photos, the envelope contained printed cell phone logs and text message screenshots. Ashford read through the first few pages, feeling increasingly nauseous. There existed no doubt in his mind these came from the governor's own private account. Using false identification and a disguise, Ashford had taken the extreme measure of activating the phone line himself, honoring the governor's wish to have him personally take care of the matter in hopes of eliminating as many connections as possible. All that planning had now been rendered useless. Because of a woman. Or more precisely, because of the governor's insistence on continuing his affair with this *particular* woman. As Ashford continued to read, his disbelief turned to panic. Not only was the governor now poised to suffer a scandal of epic proportions, but Ashford himself would certainly be dragged into it. His sights set on an eventual appointment to a coveted state cabinet position, he'd be ruined if the affair, and his involvement in it, came out. His two children thrived in private school, and his wife had become accustomed to a lifestyle the Tallahassee political scene provided. Ashford himself enjoyed golfing with society elites and had recently smoked smuggled Cuban cigars with several state Supreme Court judges. All of it would evaporate if the newspapers and political talk shows had their way with him.

"What...what is this?" Ashford asked, his voice sounding weak.

"I think you know perfectly well what this is," Hood responded, his voice that of a parent scolding a child. "This is a business meeting between two men who each have something the other wants. Tell me, Mr. Ashford, what is the price one would pay to keep every personal and political achievement they had ever worked for, or ever hoped to achieve?"

Ashford stared back, speechless.

"An extremely talented woman, from all accounts," Hood continued, relishing in his guest's anguish. "Former model and once runner-up in her state's beauty pageant. Smart too, seeing as she is currently head of her husband's Public Relations committee. Ironic, don't you think?"

Had Hood not clearly been the bigger, stronger man, Ashford could have reached across the desk and strangled him.

"I've taken the liberty of gaining access to the cell phone application you installed," Hood went on. "Or should I say, the application your *alter ego* installed. Unfortunately, you weren't able to alter your fingerprints, either physical or digital. They connect you to the application, and the application connects you to the user of the account."

Hood smiled a mischievous sort of smile, his perfectly white teeth like a row of alabaster tombstones in his grave of a mouth.

"How on earth did you get this information?" his guest managed.

"I've found that information is much easier to obtain by being the eagle in the sky rather than the rabbit on the ground."

Despite a gust of warm air blowing in through the open French doors, Ashford shivered. "What do you want?"

"Not too much that should trouble the governor. I need only to retain my position in this circuit as state attorney, for the duration of Braxton's term and the next should he be re-elected in November. In the unlikely event he is defeated, I will require he give his expressed written endorsement of me to the incoming governor. As my father once said, 'The winds of destiny blow strongest for those who set their own sails.'"

Ashford looked to the portrait that hung behind Hood and noted the subject's resolute countenance. It seemed to him then that even from beyond the grave the elder Hood appeared to inhabit his own painted form. "I will pass along your proposal to the governor," he said. "Given the circumstances, I am sure he will consider a compromise."

A ladybug fluttered through the air and landed on a desk-mounted cigar humidor, complete with Hood's vast collection of lighters and butane fuel canisters. Extending his hand, Hood allowed the tiny creature to crawl onto his finger. Bringing his finger up to eye level, he pressed his thumb firmly onto it. An audible popping sound could be heard in the near-silent room. When he lifted his thumb, he studied the insect's smashed remains before pulling out a silk handkerchief and delicately wiping his fingers.

"I'm afraid a compromise will not do, Mr. Ashford. Governor Braxton will withdraw all plans for my replacement at once. There will be no deviation from my demands. I will require an answer in the next half hour."

Ashford's mouth hung open. He sat speechless, ruined, and utterly defeated.

"These are changing times," Hood went on. "One must resort to methods not conceived of by our forefathers as they huddled in candlelit rooms, scribbling laws with sharpened goose feathers. If Lady Justice becomes lost in the dark, Mr. Ashford, it is up to others to step forward and light her way."

Five minutes later, after completing his phone call with the governor and assuring Hood his demands would be met, Ashford gathered the contents of the envelope and stashed them despairingly into his briefcase.

"Excellent," Hood said. "Now I'll continue my swim. Please be so kind as to show yourself out."

Hood stood and untied his bathrobe. It fell to the flagstone floor, revealing his exquisitely chiseled body covered only in a red speedo swimsuit. Ashford stared, feeling himself blush as he averted his eyes toward the darkening river that lay beyond his tormentor's towering form.

Hood walked out the doors and dove into the pool, his body gliding beneath the surface for half its length before resurfacing. He backstroked to the far end before switching to a breaststroke on the return lap. Ashford watched him for several minutes, unable to make his legs move. When he did manage to find his feet, he hurried down the corridor and out the front door as if chased by a ghost. As he sped away past the manicured lawns and expensive homes that stood behind them, he gripped the steering wheel much more tightly than he had when he'd arrived not thirty minutes before.

THREE

EDDIE CLIMBED BACK onto his bicycle and pedaled away. He made it home ten minutes later. The one-bedroom apartment went for seven hundred a month, half of what he made at his job at a printing factory a mile from where he lived. He'd saved nearly every penny that he'd made at his prison job (at a rate of two dollars a day) in order to secure a roof over his head. Most newly released inmates weren't so lucky—if you counted a roach-infested rat trap lucky. And since thieves in this neighborhood were notorious for cutting bicycle locks, he did as he had since buying the bike and carried it up the single flight of stairs. Parking it just inside his front door, he flipped the deadbolt and collapsed onto the cheap recliner he'd recovered from the side of the road the week before. Intending on taking a short nap, he instead fell into a deep sleep.

He dreamed he was a kid again, playing a video game in his bedroom, when his mother entered. She'd been crying recently. Walking to the window, she pushed aside the curtains and stared out in silence. When Eddie asked her what the matter was, she told him she could never be happy again until he won the game he was playing. The character in the game had to search a maze for his father, who had left them just months before. Yet the harder Eddie searched, the further he got from finding him. He'd been in the middle of an especially difficult level when the ringing telephone startled him awake.

He rubbed his eyes and checked his digital watch—five past ten.

Instantly, his heart froze inside his chest. Panicked, he jumped to his feet and ripped open the drapes. Streetlights glowed fluorescent orange and the moon hung in the night sky. Relief washed over him as he realized he hadn't slept into the next morning. He picked up the relic of a cordless phone and read the caller ID: Restricted. Probably Jules again. Apparently, he hadn't gotten the clue. He'd called over twenty times in the almost three weeks Eddie had lived here. How he'd gotten his number, Eddie had no idea. And each time Eddie had let the call go to voicemail. On each message he had left, Jules had doled out one of his trademark offerings:

Hey retard, drop your dick and answer the phone. I wanna hang!

Really, Eddie, I'm starting to get the impression you're avoiding me. Don't make me stalk you. I'm an excellent stalker.

So, is it the prison thing? Damn, man, that was way cool of you to do that. Epic how you never snitched on me. I don't even know if I could have done that for you. The fucking truth, bro. Now come see me so I can buy you a drink and tell you about all the girls who've been asking about you, you big handsome devil!

Jules. The only true friend Eddie had ever had in this world, despite the fact the guy had stupidly agreed to transport a large amount of pre-scription pills for his dealer. That fact had only been eclipsed by the fact he'd decided to run a stoplight *after* picking Eddie up.

The phone stopped ringing. Eddie set it down and prepared to listen to the voicemail when it rang again thirty seconds later. Same restricted number on the ID. This time, and for a reason even he wasn't sure of, Eddie answered.

"Hello?"

"There's my favorite person in the world. I thought you'd fallen off the edge of the earth!"

Eddie rolled his eyes. "Hey, Jules. Um—what's up?" With a sigh, he sat back down on the recliner.

"What's *up*? It's been like five fucking years since I've talked to you, and all you can say is 'what's up?' Let me come see you so we can catch up."

Eddie groaned. "I don't think that's a good idea, Jules. It's a long story, but I'm sort of in a difficult position now that I got out."

A short pause from the other end, then, "Let me guess, does the reason start with a 'C' and rhyme with Blarissa?"

"Look, Jules, I'd really love to have you over, but—"

"I'll pick you up and we'll hit the Nest then. Problem solved."

Eddie winced, knowing Jules's well-practiced habit of talking his way around obstacles had just boxed Eddie into a corner. He started by telling him that he couldn't do that either, that there were a hundred different reasons why, but before he knew it he'd been talking on the phone for a half hour, even laughing several times. Jules was good for that. A natural gabber, and hilarious to boot. When Jules asked again if he could pick Eddie up so they could grab a couple beers, Eddie finally found the courage to tell him no.

"So, it *is* Clarissa," Jules said, his voice casual and loose. "I get it. If I were in her shoes, I'd say the same thing."

"Thanks for understanding, man," Eddie said, expelling an audible sigh of relief.

"It really is too bad we can't meet up one last time," Jules said through a mouthful of food. "You know, to formally say goodbye after being friends for so long. But I get it, Clarissa has the final say."

Eddie shook his head. "Clarissa doesn't run my whole life. I can do what I want. It's just that I have a huge day tomorrow and need to wake up early."

"Next you'll be telling me you need to stay in to watch *Wheel of Fortune* while your dentures are soaking. Your loss. If Clarissa changes her mind and lets you choose your friends, you know where I am."

Before Jules could hang up, Eddie blurted out, "Hold on." He paused. "I suppose it wouldn't be that big a deal to meet up for a beer or two. For old time's sake."

"Now you're talking. Want me to scoop you up?"

"Thanks, but I'll catch a cab. Just got my first paycheck from my new job yesterday."

"Gotcha," Jules said good-naturedly. "Meet you there in twenty."

Hanging up, Eddie looked dumbly at the phone, wondering how Jules had done it. A queer feeling came over him, a faint sense of dread that drew itself along the edge of his conscience like an icy finger. Staring at his apartment wall, he shook the feeling away. "He's the best friend you've ever had," he said to the wall, his face stoic. "You're allowed to tell him goodbye in person."

He showered and threw on a pair of jeans and a t-shirt. As he opened the door to leave and checked for his wallet, he spied the worn black and white photo he'd carried with him while in prison. An old snapshot of his father and grandfather, from when his dad had been a boy. Carrying the picture had become an unconscious habit of sorts, so much so that Eddie had already forgotten about it as he tucked it into his back pocket and bounded down the flight of stairs to wait for the cab. When it arrived, he slid into the back seat and enjoyed the drive through cozy Springwood streets he hadn't seen in years. They passed the city water tower, onto which he and Jules had once climbed with bottles of beer stuffed into their pockets; the old drive-in theater; the familiar eateries and shops Eddie had visited more times than he could remember. He missed Springwood—too big to be called a town, too small for a city—and told himself he'd never leave willingly.

Five minutes later, the cab deposited him at the Rat's Nest, a loveable dive to its many local patrons. Fronted by a flickering green neon sign, its exterior brick walls and blacked-out windows stood evidence to countless graffiti artists who had used them as a canvas over the years. Inside fared little better. The wood paneled walls were bare in spots, most of the barstools didn't sit straight, and the felt on both pool tables was stained with beer and Lord knew what else. The restrooms had doors that wouldn't lock properly, forcing users to hold the door closed with one hand while they did their business with the other. Finishing off the dive tableau, a smudgy print hanging just inside the front door depicted a scantily clad woman bending over a race car, a lollipop hanging seductively from her mouth.

Eddie knew the place well. He'd seen more wild nights inside the bar than he could count, albeit drinking illegally. Even underaged he'd frequented the place, and because he'd kept quiet and never caused trouble he'd been served. The waitresses, two of whom he had dated, all knew him on sight. Most of the regulars treated him like their adopted family member, a big reason the Nest had felt like his second home over the years.

As he stepped into the smoke-filled space, his previous concerns over Jules melted away. Clarissa's words of warning were quickly replaced by a collection of sights and sounds he hadn't experienced since he'd gone to jail. Winking waitresses, clinking glasses, groups of bar patrons—some familiar, some not—and the mixed aroma of peanuts and beer hit him strongly. Music from the jukebox pumped a rhythmic classic rock beat. Feeling a familiar adrenaline surge through him, he scanned the crowd for that most familiar of faces.

Eddie caught sight of him at the furthest corner of the bar. Jules had his back turned, spun around on his stool as he chatted with a pair of women. Even from a distance he looked skinnier than Eddie had remembered. Other than that he looked pretty much the same, down to his sleeveless t-shirt and spiky haircut. Although it had been half a decade since he'd seen him in the flesh, Eddie felt like it had only been a few days.

Eddie plopped down on the stool next to Jules and waved for the waitress, a short-haired brunette he'd briefly dated. Rhonda. She'd been working the last night he'd been here, the day before the 'incident.' Walking toward their end of the bar, a faint look of recognition in her eyes, she asked him what he was drinking.

"The usual," Eddie said above the music, not acknowledging his friend beside him. Hearing Eddie's voice, Jules spun around on his stool but kept his gaze straight ahead. He calmly sipped his beer, the hint of a grin appearing at the corners of his mouth. Rhonda, for her part, smiled in full recognition now and began pouring a beer from the tap. She sat the foaming mug down in front of Eddie and rested her elbows on the bar, her breasts blossoming from her low-cut shirt.

"Long time no see, handsome. You just get out?"

"Yeah. The slammer wasn't for me, and I wasn't for the slammer," he said in his best Italian wise guy impersonation. "By the way, you seen a skinny, rat-lookin' fucker around here lately?"

Grinning and playing along, Rhonda shook her head.

"This guy, he's a real asshole, you know," Eddie continued. "But I feel sorry for the schmuck 'cause he has a little dick and he's kinda slow upstairs. I promised I'd drop by and have a beer with him since nobody else can stand him." Eddie gave Rhonda a wink.

Beside him, Jules still hadn't flinched. He continued to sip his beer and stare straight ahead, unmoved.

"I do believe a gentleman who fits that description came in a while ago," Rhonda said, her voice playful. "He's around here some-where..." Her eyes made a dramatic sweep of the place until they fell squarely onto Jules. She looked at him expectantly, but he continued to sip his beer as if nothing were amiss. Lighting a cigarette, he took a luxurious drag and said in an aristocratic British accent, "What a coincidence, my dear, for I too seek a certain gentleman with whom I am to imbibe. You know, whet the whistle, share a bevvy with an old chum sort of thing." He gave Rhonda a wink. She rolled her eyes and giggled, clearly enjoying the charade.

"Perhaps you've seen the poor fellow. He's tall, well-built, and enjoys servicing strange men in darkened alleys. Not particularly intelligent either. Like any noble Englishman, I offered the poor chap a bit of charity by meeting him here. Have you by chance seen him?"

Rhonda looked between them both, stifling her laughter as best she could. For a moment both Eddie and Jules continued to ignore each other, until Jules suddenly jumped from his stool and embraced Eddie in an enthusiastic, bony bear hug. Eddie had just taken a drink, the contact causing beer to splash onto the bar top and across his lap. He slapped Jules's back and Jules slapped his. Remembering the elaborate handshake they'd created during middle school, Eddie performed the ten-part routine flawlessly. This elicited an impressed laugh from Jules, who plopped his hands atop Eddie's shoulders and gazed into his eyes as if his old friend had just rescued him from a deserted island.

"You guys are too much," Rhonda said with a laugh. "Where'd you come up with those voices? They're really good."

The two sat on their stools and took long pulls from their beer.

"When you grow up poor like we did, you have to invent your own games," Eddie explained. "One of ours was trying to see who could do the best impressions. We did lots of them, and I got good at it. But Jules is better, sad as it is for me to admit."

Jules made a showy bow, complete with an exaggerated hand flourish. "It's not easy being so awesome," he said, his expression smug.

It wasn't until now that Eddie noticed Jules's heavy metal t-shirt hanging over his thin frame much more loosely than it would have five years ago. His trademark hole-filled black jeans, usually tight, had a certain bagginess Eddie didn't remember seeing before, and even the boots on his feet appeared to be a size larger than needed. His normally tan skin seemed more fallow, and his eyes sunk into his face a bit deeper than they once had. Eddie *had* seen him this way before, in the year before Eddie had gone to prison, when he'd graduated from weed to pills, and ultimately to meth. Eddie began to say something about his old friend's appearance but decided against it. Surely Jules had learned his lesson. Besides, he wouldn't be hanging out with him again anyway, so he figured it wouldn't really matter.

Ignoring another patron hollering for a drink, Rhonda lowered her eyelids as she leaned even further across the bar toward Eddie. "I've missed seeing your face here. Maybe I can see it at my place after I get off work."

"I'd love to," Eddie said, "but I have plans in the morning and need to get to bed." He smiled meekly at her, feeling his cheeks and ears redden. It had been almost ten years since he'd felt himself blush. "I've missed seeing your face too," he said. "It's weird. Even after five years, this place seems the same. The people too. Except you—you're even prettier than I remember."

Rhonda pointed to Eddie as she addressed the collection of bar patrons. "Take note, gentlemen. *That's* what a woman likes to hear. Not that she has nice tits." She winked at Eddie then left to tend to the waiting patron down the bar.

Jules slapped a hand on the back of Eddie's neck. "Jesus, I really thought you'd broken up with me," he said, grinning. "I thought I was gonna have to start leaving boiling rabbits on your stove."

Eddie took a long pull from his beer and wiped foam from his lips. He stared down at the stained and scratched oak bar top, feeling that sense of faraway dread rise inside him again. "Jules, you can't say anything to Clarissa about meeting up with me. She's serious about it. You're a big reason she's so upset."

"Little old me?" Jules shot back, placing a hand over his heart. "Clarissa is hot-blooded. Cuban *and* Irish. Those kinds of chicks have it baked in their genes to get mad. But it does make for a good screw. Christ, I really did envy you. But she's a control freak, man. A woman shouldn't make a man choose between his friends and his kid. It isn't right. This is America, the land of opportunity. We have drive-thru restaurants, computers in our phones, and websites where people meet up to piss on each other. Stand up to a woman or she'll never respect you."

Rhonda passed by and overheard the last part of what Jules had said. When she gave him a playful sneer, he crossed his eyes and stuck his tongue out at her.

"Yeah, I guess," Eddie said, only in half agreement. "Clarissa is letting me take Liam to the park tomorrow. It's kind of a big deal."

Jules almost fell off his stool. "Holy shit! What happened, the ice queen finally thawed out? I didn't think she'd ever let you see the little bastard."

"I told you, I had to promise to get my life in order. I told her I cut off all my old contacts. Shit, I even admitted that I haven't had sex with anyone since her."

"Regrettable. The sex part."

"I'm serious, Jules. I have a job and a place of my own now. It takes most people like me twice as long to get that squared away, but my prison counselor was a big help. Maybe someday Clarissa will trust me to take Liam for a whole weekend. I signed up to work overtime so I can save for a car."

"And in order to see Liam you told her you'd stop being friends with me," Jules said, resignation in his voice. "That was part of the deal. You had to break things off with me for good, not just for a while. Me, the only person you have left in the world who's ever been there for you. Jesus Christ, your own dad walked out on you when you were, what, twelve years old?"

"Ten."

"Whatever."

"I just want a normal life for a change."

"And you deserve that," Jules said, raising his glass in a toast. "I respect the shit out of you for what you did. They should make a movie. With my priors, I woulda done twenty years. I remember the cop raising his eyebrows like he was asking me if I was gonna let you do that. I felt so bad afterward I couldn't bear to look you in the eye. That's why I never came to see you. The worst thing is, I know I couldn't have done the same for you. You're a stronger person than me, bro. I've always thought that."

Eddie turned to Jules and suddenly wondered how life would be without him. The guy had been right about one thing—he *had* been there for Eddie. Despite the trouble they'd found, with no other living relatives for Eddie to count on and only random flakes posing as friends, through it all Jules had been rock steady at his side. He'd been like the old man in Rocky Balboa's corner, the one who listened to Rocky's shit but stood by him no matter what. Eddie eyed the large scar that started above Jules's right ear and angled harshly across his cheek. Seeing it always brought up feelings of guilt. To his credit, Jules had never thrown the cause of the scar in Eddie's face. Nonetheless, Eddie still felt tremendous shame over the years-ago fight he'd gotten into with a drifter, how he'd gotten the better of him until the guy had pulled a knife and started slashing. How Eddie had become pinned on his back with the knife only inches from his throat, when out of nowhere Jules had come running and tackled the guy. And finally, as Eddie had picked himself up off the ground, breathless, he'd seen Jules lying in a heap next to a garbage dumpster, his face a bloody mess but the drifter running away down the street with his own knife stuck in his side. Jules. That goddamned Jules, sitting up and laughing like a madman, his face slashed open and bleeding like a faucet.

Eddie blinked the memory away and drained his beer. "You've been my only family, Jules, and I can't thank you enough. Don't think this is easy for me. But I stay awake at night wondering what my own son looks like. I just don't want to wake up one day and realize I missed my last chance."

Eddie removed the aged black and white photo from his pocket and placed it on the bar top. In it, a grinning man of about thirty knelt next to a boy who looked not much older than three. "My dad, the kid in the picture," Eddie said, showing Jules. "It's the only picture I have of him. My mom got rid of all the other ones after he left. About a year later, I was looking through an old shoebox in the attic and found this one tucked away in a notebook. She must have missed it. I hid it in my bedroom until the day she died. I think she would've torn it up right in front of me if she'd found it."

Jules motioned to Rhonda and pointed to their empty glasses. "This really sucks for me, but I get it. Remember that girl I was seeing right before you went away, the one with the nose piercing?"

"Which girl with the nose piercing?"

"Touché. Okay, the one with the blue hair and the tattoo of her ex-boyfriend's face on her ass. Don't tell me you forgot that story."

"Her eyes rolled back in her head when you guys had sex and you'd make funny faces at her without her knowing. Yeah, I remember."

Jules turned ninety degrees on his stool so that he faced Eddie directly. He placed one hand on Eddie's shoulder and gave it a good squeeze. All around them, the bar livened up even more than when Eddie had arrived. From the jukebox, Mick Jagger crooned about needing shelter, and patrons hollered and laughed as the combined drunkenness of the place seemed to double in the space of just a few minutes. "Well, the day she broke it off with me, she told me she'd only dated me because she was trying to get over her ex-boyfriend. She actually told me that. Said she thought of him every time we screwed, even bought me clothes the dude used to like wearing."

Eddie turned to look into his friend's eyes. "Damn, bro, that's shitty."

"It's okay, I'm used to people using me then throwing me away."

"But do you see what you're doing?" Eddie said, becoming annoyed now. "I'm talking about my kid, and all you can talk about is some chick you used to screw."

Jules hung his head and smiled sardonically. "Jesus, bro, I'm pouring my heart out here and all you can do is ram your Dear John speech down my throat. I get it. You and I are through being friends. I can accept that. I kind of resent you for it, but I'm a grown man and I don't need to be preached to."

Eddie nodded. "I'm sorry. You're right. That's the second time I've been an asshole today."

"Thanks for saying that," Jules said, appreciative. "That part about you being an asshole. Because you can be, you know. The whole world doesn't revolve around Edward Grassle. You're not the fucking sun."

"I said I was sorry."

"Apology accepted." He pulled out an empty pack of cigarettes and groaned. "Anybody got a smoke?" he asked several nearby patrons. When none of them said they did, he rolled his eyes. "I was born in the wrong generation. Fifty years ago, everyone smoked. You go for a check-up and the doctor is sitting there with a Marlboro in his mouth. I can only imagine." He looked dreamily toward the ceiling and sighed. "Anyway—my story. So this chick breaks up with me and is telling me about how she'd used me to get over her ex, blah blah blah. Like a dummy, I offered to walk her to her car, and do you know what she says to me?"

"She offered to fuck you one last time?"

"Yes!" Jules exclaimed. "Told me we were still through but wanted me to fuck her really good one last time."

Eddie pushed away the gnawing feeling that had begun to grow inside him. He wasn't sure if the beer or the entire mood of the conversation was to blame for the creeping uneasiness. But just the act of talking with Jules distracted him from all that, as it always had. For all his faults, the guy had a disarming nature he achieved through basic conversation. Despite everything he'd gone through, including missing five years of his life because of the guy, Eddie already knew he'd miss talking with Jules the most, that good conversationalists didn't grow on trees. "Did you do it?"

A look of self-righteousness spread across Jules's face. He seemed to have been waiting for the question. "Of course not! I told her to look in the mirror while she fucked herself with a dildo, then she'd sort of be fucking her ex-boyfriend. She just stared at me with her mouth open. I laughed as she drove away." Jules beamed proudly, appearing like someone remembering their first kiss or some other pleasant, long-ago memory.

"What's it supposed to mean?" Eddie asked.

"You still don't get it, do you?" Jules responded with a shake of his head.

Eddie shrugged. He suddenly felt very tired. He wished he were home on his recliner, drinking the last beer in his refrigerator and falling asleep to ESPN. He couldn't get home fast enough.

"I told you that story because that was the only time in my life where I felt good about myself," Jules said. "You and me, we're not that different. Your dad skipped town and your mom croaked a few years later. My mom put me up for adoption and never cared two shits about ever finding me. My dad could've been a hundred different schmucks. Then I meet you and I see we're not that different at all. Except for my much larger dick, of course."

Eddie gave his friend a light-hearted punch to the shoulder. They both laughed.

"We did so much together," Jules continued, his voice dreamy. "I know we got in some trouble over the years and that some of it was my fault." Eddie gave him an incredulous look. "Okay, maybe most of it was. But I'm really not a bad guy. I wish Clarissa could see that."

There it all was in a nutshell. For the first time in his life, Eddie understood just how much doing the right thing could feel good and bad at the same time. Signaling for the tab, he watched Rhonda saunter over and set the bill in front of him. Before he could pick it up, Jules placed his hand over it.

"Nuh-uh, buddy. This is on me. Besides, you've got your son to worry about now. And from what I've been told, the little fuckers arc expensive these days."

"Thanks," Eddie said, feeling something stick in his throat. "For everything. I'm glad you understand. Once I get back on Clarissa's good side and there's a little water under the bridge, maybe things will change."

"Say no more, old chap," Jules proclaimed, snapping back into his British accent. "As we Englishmen say, a man must know when to grasp the nettle. A fair crack of the whip, I do say, is all we ask in life. One last toast, old boy?"

They clinked glasses. Jules performed the salutation. "To love and to lose, 'tis better than to never have loved at all."

After each of them drained their beers, Jules dug into his front jeans pocket. He produced several bills, as well as a small, cylindrical object that he quickly concealed in his fist. Eddie eyed him and started to ask what the object was when he changed his mind. *Stop it already*, he thought. *He's a grown man, so treat him like one.* As soon as Jules paid the tab, he stuffed the object back into his pocket. Telling Eddie he needed to use the bathroom, he returned five minutes later with a noticeable bounce in his step.

"Let's beat it," he said, leading Eddie out into the parking lot. Eddie lingered behind, having detected something different in Jules's eyes, something off. The usual liveliness in them had been replaced by a strange urgency, as if something alien now inhabited them, something bad. But he pushed the thought away, remembering the glazed looks in his fellow inmates' eyes. Loneliness mixed with depression and the knowledge of a wasted life. Deciding to let Jules be, that it wasn't worth hassling the guy any more than he had, Eddie waved goodbye to Rhonda and pushed his way out the tinted double doors. He climbed into the passenger seat of Jules's ragged out Mustang, content to enjoy the last few minutes he felt he'd ever have with his old friend. As they cruised along familiar-looking streets, he took in the sights and sounds of his old stomping grounds. A host of memories flooded back to him as they drove in silence, the radio providing a melodic backdrop to the Mustang's grumbling engine. Shops and eateries that he and Jules had visited since high school. An old neighborhood where an ex-girlfriend of his had once lived. All of it brought him a sense of peace and belonging, something he'd gone without for the past five years. Soon they pulled into a parking lot, and it wasn't until Jules said something about popping inside for a pack of smokes that Eddie realized they were at the same convenience store he'd been at earlier in the day.

Eddie ruminated on friends coming and going from a person's life, sometimes like a leaf on a glass-smooth lake, gently floating away from shore. Other times, their exit felt akin to a submerged seashell violently uprooted by a wave and pulled away by the current. Eddie wasn't sure which of these applied to his own relationship with Jules. Although it was over, a bittersweet feeling swept through him as he realized the death of one relationship made possible another. Enveloped in his reverie, he noticed Jules reach behind the passenger seat and fumble through an old duffle bag, but he thought nothing of it.

"Look at the moon," Jules offered, keeping his hand inside the duffle. "It always looks so much bigger when it's full."

Eddie craned his head to look up at the moon, half-shrouded in clouds. As he did, from the corner of his eye he noticed Jules quickly bring his hand from behind the seat. When Eddie turned back to look at him, Jules was smoothing his t-shirt over his waistband. And despite the cool evening, he'd begun to sweat profusely since they'd left the bar, Eddie thought. Even at night, this part of southwest Florida could feel like a veritable swamp, but tonight prevailing winds from the Gulf forty miles away had brought with them the final vestiges of the northern winter. He actually felt a bit chilly, but he reasoned this away as well, knowing he'd just spent five years languishing in housing units that had regularly reached ninety degrees due to most of Florida's prisons not having air conditioning. But tomorrow was forecast to be a great day, with highs in the seventies. Perfect weather for a father to take his son to the park, he thought.

A smile touched his lips.

"Be back in a jiffy," Jules said, jumping out of the car. The front of his shirt read *'One Sexy Mofo,'* and as he got to the store's front door, he adjusted the hem of the shirt once more before slipping inside.

His mind on tomorrow, Eddie turned the radio volume up. A favorite Zeppelin song of his, "Ten Years Gone," blared from the car's speakers. His smile grew, despite an old memory that resurfaced in his mind just then. One of a ten-year-old boy, having just thrown a baseball against the side of an old shed.

Shading his eyes from the blazing summer sun, he leaned in from the makeshift pitcher's mound and shook off a sign offered by his imaginary catcher. The boy's target—a square box etched in chalk on the side of the storage shed, located twenty yards from the house. With an imaginary right-handed batter standing at the plate, the boy's last pitch had been about four inches outside.

Coming to a set position, he glanced over his left shoulder to check the imaginary runner on first base. The boy had walked him on five pitches. Winding up, he hurled a fastball. The ball slammed just inside the upper portion of the chalked box—a strike. A puff of white dust floated into the air as the ball rolled halfway back toward the mound. The batter, a real bruiser who had hit a double his last at-bat, connected with the pitch in the boy's mind, sending the ball into the right-center field gap. The boy raced into the outfield (a half-acre-wide lawn which extended from one side of the unattached garage into an open field beyond) and screamed at the imaginary centerfielder to throw him the ball. 'Cut off, cut off!' he hollered, holding out his mitt as he waited for the relay throw.

'Cut off! Cut off!' he screamed again, and unlike last inning when the centerfielder had made a throwing error, this time he hit the boy with a perfect throw. With the game tied, the baserunner rounded third. Spinning, the boy unleashed a fake-throw home. Without breaking stride, he sprinted to home plate where he became the catcher. He imagined the runner sliding feet-first, kicking up a cloud of dirt as the throw came in on one bounce. Swiping his mitt in a looping, downward arc, the boy placed the tag. The likewise imaginary umpire stood off to the side to get a good look at the play, and for a moment he made no call. The boy turned to show the ump the ball in his glove. Nodding, the ump made a downward punching motion, signaling the runner out. The boy raised both arms in triumph, his imaginary teammates mobbing him in celebration. The crowd—thirty thousand strong in his mind—went wild.

The celebration over, the boy looked back toward the house. He'd been waiting for over an hour for his father to come out and pitch to him, but the screen door had remained closed, nothing but the sound of the television coming from the living room. His father had promised to play for several days now, and each time he'd either been too tired or his back ached from a long day of work.

Just as the boy turned to head back to the mound, the screen door screeched open and banged shut. Heavy footfalls coming down the front steps—his father, he knew the footsteps anywhere. The boy felt excitement surge through him, figuring his father had finally decided to join him. A baseball bat would be propped over one shoulder and he'd be wearing that sideways grin of his. 'Sorry there, Eddie,' he would say, handing him the bat. 'Had to let the old back loosen up a bit first. I'll pitch. Try not to hit it too far, huh?' And then he'd ruffle Eddie's hair like he always did, before taking his place on the mound.

Instead, Eddie turned and saw something strange. Instead of walking toward the field where Eddie stood, his father walked toward his truck parked on the gravel driveway. Instead of holding a baseball bat over his shoulder, he held a suitcase in one hand and a duffel bag in the other. He tossed them both onto the truck bed and stood there for a moment, as if deciding something. Eddie frowned. Today was Sunday, and Eddie had heard of no plans for the family to make a trip. Even if his parents had decided to travel on such late notice, surely his mother would have already called him inside to pack his things and wash up. As Eddie stood watching his father climb into the driver's seat and start the engine, the sound of the screen door opening again caused him to look back toward the house. Another curious sight. His mother stood in the doorway looking toward the driveway, one hand covering her mouth. Was she crying? From this distance, Eddie couldn't tell. Either way, his gut told him none of it was good.

As his father put the truck in gear he turned and made eye contact with Eddie. He raised one hand in a sort of half-wave. It seemed to Eddie as if he were saying hello and goodbye at the same time. And then, almost as if those waving fingers themselves had thought, they folded into his palm one at a time, and then his father looked away. Eddie's gut fell further. Unlike the many times before when his parents had fought and his father had stormed out of the house, not returning until the wee hours of the night, this time seemed different. Eddie opened his mouth to yell out, to protest— you were supposed to pitch to me, can't you just pitch one inning to me and then you can leave and I won't even say a word, I promise—but no sound escaped him. His mind spun with a thousand different thoughts and emotions. Yes, his parents had been fighting much more often lately. And yes, several times Eddie had glimpsed fresh bruises on his mother's face, her shushing him when he'd asked what had happened to her. And each time Eddie would lay awake in bed, listening to the sounds he'd become accustomed to—the settling house, the crickets in the darkened fields, his mother's soft weeping coming from her room down the hall.

Now, after his father's truck disappeared down the long gravel driveway, Eddie sat down cross-legged on the pitcher's mound. He did not move. He did not speak. After two hours of watching for his father's truck to return, he heard the screen door open and close. His mother came and sat down next to him in the dirt. Her arm slid around his waist and she hugged him close to her body and they stayed that way, silent except for his mother humming an old nursery rhyme she'd used to help Eddie sleep when he'd been a baby. She didn't speak for some *time, but when she did her words came like a whip across his very being. 'Your father will never come back. Maybe when you get older, I'll tell you more. Now it's just you and me, and you're just going to have to be a man quicker than I imagined.'*

The air smelled of ragweed and orange blossoms. Late afternoon gave way to dusk, and mother and son sat that way until the sky faded into deep blues and violets in the west.

At one point, Eddie said he felt funny inside, like something was missing from where it should have been. His mother said she felt the same way, but that it wouldn't last forever. She would have been worried if he didn't feel that way, she said. Then she kissed the top of his head and went inside, where she made him his favorite homemade blueberry pie for dinner. Told him it would be the only time she'd allow such a thing. With his mother silently watching, Eddie ate the entire pie himself, washing it down with a half-gallon of milk. When he finished, he helped wash the day's dishes then played in his room until his mother came to tuck him into bed. She stayed longer than usual, smoothing out his rumpled hair. When she left, Eddie lay awake for hours. He listened to those same night sounds, watched the way the moonlight made shadows dance across his ceiling. He wondered many things. Why had his father decided to leave, and where had he gone? He wondered if he would ever want to play baseball again, and if it would ever feel the same to him if he did. But most of all, he wondered what his life would be like when he woke the next morning, if the sun itself would look somehow different as it streamed through his bedroom curtains.

When sleep finally came to him, he dreamed of a giant train in the sky that went on as far as the eye could see.

Eddie blinked the memory away, returning to the present scene as he sat alone in the Mustang's passenger seat. The song continued its rhythmic beat and melody. It had always made him think about life, about missed opportunities, about how a person could gain perspective after missed time.

Most of all, it reminded him of how a person could *change*.

FOUR

Ten Years Gone...

THE CAR STEREO pumped out the classic Zeppelin tune, its melding of guitars, drums and vocals sending Eddie into a dreamlike state. It felt good to be in fresh night air again, finally free from walls and gates, where even his mind had been fair game to be shut away. With his head swimming from the beer, Eddie lost himself even further in the song's lyrics.

Save for an older sedan several spaces away, the parking lot sat empty of vehicles. But soon a pair of headlights swept into the lot, a light green Jeep pulling in two spaces to their right. Opening his eyes, Eddie watched as a young Hispanic woman hopped out. He did a double take, noting her long, tanned legs and jet-black hair that flowed nearly to her waist. As she made her way to the front door she glanced back and flashed Eddie a smile. Lifting his chin in acknowledgement, he returned her smile. As the woman slipped through the front door, she took a longer glance backward, brushing her hair away from her neck. Something stirred inside of Eddie as he watched her disappear inside the store. His pulse surged and a familiar rush of adrenaline, one decidedly different than the one he'd experienced at the bar, flowed through him. He placed his hand on the car's door handle, instinct instructing him to follow her inside and introduce himself, but another instinct made him pause. *Now isn't the time for that. Just stay in the car and mind your business.* As the music continued to blare, the feeling inside him—so much like a drug itself—only increased, and before he knew it he was telling himself, *what the hell, go talk to her, tell her she should take you for a ride in her Jeep sometime. Just say anything to get her talking.*

The song's lyrics he most identified with, about changes a person experiences over time, crooned from the car's speakers.

He'd just reached over to cut the ignition when a muffled, cracking noise accompanied the final word in the lyric. It sounded like a firecracker set off inside a closed room. Still lying across the front seat, Eddie first looked out the car's rear window, believing the noise had come from behind him. Nothing there but a darkened strip mall. He looked down both directions of the street but noted no other cars or pedestrians. He frowned. Turning down the radio, he finally looked toward the store and saw Jules through the large glass windows, standing at the counter with his arm raised at a peculiar angle. Then a flash of movement—the Jeep girl—now coming suddenly into Eddie's field of vision from behind one of the end displays. She stopped several feet from where Jules stood, and by her body language she had apparently rushed forward to investigate some strange sight or sound. But instead of an expression that denoted a question over a store item, her face was frozen, her mouth and eyes wide as she stared at something behind the counter. Even above the music and the car's still-rumbling engine, Eddie heard what came next—her bloodcurdling scream.

As his mind ticked off the possibilities of why the girl could have been screaming, Eddie looked back to Jules's form and for the first time realized what had seemed so unnatural about his position. With his feet bladed, Jules held a metallic looking object in his right hand. Eddie's eyes widened as it sunk in what was happening. He shook his head, willing the scene he was witnessing to somehow disappear. This wasn't happening. This *couldn't* be happening.

Jules, who should now be pumping Eddie's hand, and with his typical shit-eating grin saying something like *see you around, old boy* in that British accent. He'd offer a comical salute which Eddie would dutifully return. Then Eddie would say something like *keep your head down and your dick up*, in his own wise-guy voice, one of many he had perfected during their numerous play acts. Good old Jules, who just moments ago had breezily walked into the store for a pack of smokes, now stood holding a gun. Frozen in his seat, Eddie recalled the glazed look in Jules's eyes as they'd left the bar, and how he'd pushed the thought out of his mind, refusing to believe what a part of him had already been sure of. And now, as he sat staring through the windshield at the impossible image he was witnessing, Eddie imagined how the scene should be playing out. Jules exiting the store and lighting up a smoke, driving Eddie the last two miles to his apartment before they shook hands one last time. Then Jules peeling away into the night, his high-pitched cackling rising above the Mustang's squealing tires. Eddie would offer a final wave as he watched the car's taillights fade into the night, before climbing the stairs up to his apartment to drink the last beer in his refrigerator, going down cold and reassuring. He would sink into the recliner he'd salvaged from the side of the road two days before, feeling like a kid on Christmas Eve because in the morning he'd be knocking on Clarissa's front door, smiling nervously as she told him to wait on the stoop. When Liam appeared, Eddie would kneel and hug the boy, gazing into his eyes for the first time and ruffling his hair, and then they'd walk to the park where they'd swing, play tag or just sit on a bench and talk about race cars and their favorite television shows and other things fathers and sons spoke of. All while Liam sucked on Jolly Ranchers and drank the chocolate milk Eddie had bought him. The sky above would be clear and blue, and Eddie would take it all in, the mere act of being *present* making him feel content. In his mind's eye, Eddie saw it all. But then he blinked, and the image of tomorrow's scene irrevocably switched to the impossible scene playing out before him.

Eddie moved before his brain commanded him to. Springing from the car, he burst through the front door so quickly the force of it knocked over a display of two-liter soda bottles. Several of them rolled across the tiled floor, making intermittent plastic-y sounds as they went. A cap on one of the bottles broke partly off, causing the rolling bottle to mist orange soda onto a nearby shelf of potato chips. Eddie approached Jules slowly, keeping both palms extended in a combined calming and protective gesture. Sweat poured from Jules's face and his lips formed silent words. His pale face appeared frozen in a trance. Gripped in his outstretched hand was a chrome revolver he pointed in the direction of the unoccupied register. The air smelled of burnt carbon, reminding Eddie of the times he and Jules had taken his foster father's rifle into the fields and shot jugs filled with water. To Eddie's left the woman stood wide-eyed, clutching the sides of her face. For one crazy moment, Eddie thought she was auditioning for a part in a horror movie, practicing the part where she had just discovered a dead body. But then Eddie glanced behind the counter and saw the lower half of a man's body lying still on the floor. The upper half of the man's body lay obscured by the side entrance's ledge, having fallen partially into one of the aisles. Disbelief racking his brain, Eddie looked back to Jules, who still stared blankly ahead and from all appearances seemed unaware of anything or anyone else around him.

"Jules, what the *fuck* is this?" Eddie asked, his heart hammering in his chest. Amid his own rising panic, he forced himself to remain calm. "Jules, buddy, look at me. Look at me, man."

Jules turned his head slowly toward Eddie. The old scar on his face glowed a sinister red against his ashen complexion. His constricted pupils were mere pinpricks in his shock-blue irises.

"He pulled a fucking gun on me," Jules said, incredulous. "I told him to give me a carton of smokes for free, just lifted my shirt and showed him the gun in my waistband. He should have just given me the smokes, man, but he reached under the counter. What was I supposed to do?"

Eddie tried to think of something to say but couldn't. He stepped cautiously to his right to where he could see the man's upper body lying halfway out of the register entrance. Recognition hit him like a sledgehammer. It was the same clerk who had waited on him earlier. Even from the bad angle Eddie could see the lids of the man's eyes fluttering. His lips, bluish and peeled back against his teeth, moved wordlessly. A pencil-sized hole stood out in the center of the man's uniform shirt, and beneath him a growing pool of blood spread out toward a row of nearby coolers. Offering his hands toward Jules, Eddie approached him slowly.

"Give me the gun, bro. There's no need for anyone else to get hurt."

Jules lowered his arm, the gun dangling in his useless hand. Eddie took it from him and stuffed it into his waistband for safekeeping. "Thank you, buddy. Now, I'm going to go check on him. You stay right there and don't move."

Jules nodded and didn't move.

"Good." Eddie looked to the woman. Her terrified eyes moved between Eddie, Jules, and the dying man on the floor. "Tell me your name," he said to her, keeping his voice as even as possible.

The woman frowned. "Jessica—my name is Jessica."

"Okay, Jessica. I'm Eddie. You're going to be okay. I promise no one is going to hurt you."

Her eyes, wild with terror, blinked in disbelief. "I'm just a stupid *Honeybee* waitress," she said, a humorless laugh escaping her. "I called in sick tonight to go to a party. I don't want to die."

"You're not going to die," Eddie insisted, checking to make sure Jules hadn't moved. The guy still stood where he'd been, a zombie expression on his face.

A look of understanding seemed to flicker in the woman's eyes when Eddie looked into her eyes, a sort of inane belief conveyed in his expression that told her what he'd said must be true despite the horror show playing out before her.

Eddie stepped around the edge of the counter and stared down at the man on the floor, noting the ever-growing pool of blood beneath him. An overpowering smell of copper struck him, as if a giant bag of pennies had spilled onto the floor. Kneeling, Eddie pressed the tips of his first two fingers against the side of the man's neck. He'd learned to take a person's pulse during a summer lifeguarding class during high school. A faint heartbeat. Lowering his ear to the man's mouth, he watched for a rise and fall of his chest. Only a pair of faint breaths until a sort of rattle came from the man's throat and then nothing. Eddie checked for a pulse again. Nothing now. Looking into the man's eyes, he watched them glaze over, the lids having gone still and unmoving.

Quickly, Eddie folded his hands one over the other and began delivering a series of chest compressions while counting to himself—*one and two and three and four.* As he counted past twenty, he felt a sickening breaking sensation in the man's chest, accompanied by a sharp cracking sound. He remembered from his lifeguard class that this could happen, then continued until he reached thirty. Pinching the man's nose shut, he tilted the head backward and pressed his lips against the man's bloody mouth. Eddie gave two full breaths, observing the man's chest rising slightly each time. Transitioning back to compressions, Eddie resumed another round of thirty before switching back to breaths. He repeated this process once more and checked for a pulse. Still nothing.

Somewhere in the distance, the sound of wailing sirens.

Eddie drew a hand across his mouth to wipe away the man's blood. He stared into the man's ashen face, into those half-open eyes. Then hands were on Eddie's shoulders, shaking him. A voice, yelling in his ear. Jules's voice.

"He's dead, Eddie! We gotta go! Now!"

Eddie shook him off, hot tears burning in his eyes. He checked again for a pulse but still found none. His heart pounded in his ears, a drumbeat that grew louder and louder to the point he felt that it would explode inside of him if he didn't do something to stop it.

"Eddie, stop doing that to him. He's gone. Let's go!" Jules's voice, urgent over his shoulder. The wailing sirens growing nearer, just blocks away now.

What is happening oh my God why is this happening why Jules why did you do this—

Jules grabbed Eddie by the shirt and pulled him to his feet with such force that they both nearly slipped backward in the clerk's blood. And then Eddie saw himself racing past Jessica, a wide-eyed statue with her hands over her mouth. Their eyes met again, and even in that flash Eddie wasn't sure who was more afraid. Then Jules crashing through the front door, screaming for Eddie to get in the car for fuck's sake, the cops were almost here. Eddie next, kicking aside a spilled soda bottle before bursting through the door, every other step making a smacking sound due to the sole of his left shoe being covered in blood. Then sliding over the front corner of the Mustang, terror in his eyes, like one of the Duke boys in that old television show, and a surreal feeling seizing him as he tore the car door open and dove into the passenger seat.

The engine still running, Jules threw the shifter in reverse. He swung the Mustang backward so fast he clipped the Jeep parked next to him, the impact leaving a streak of black paint across the Jeep's left rear quarter panel. Eddie hollered for Jules to *stop goddammit, we need to figure this out!* but he either didn't hear him or didn't care. As Jules rammed the shifter into drive, Eddie turned to see a pair of police cruisers—emergency lights blazing—roaring in from just a block away. He considered jumping out of the car right then, feeling that anything would be better at this point than remaining inside it, but as quickly as the thought crossed his mind, Jules stomped on the gas and rocketed the Mustang hard over the curb, hurling them down the empty street.

Burning rubber. Eddie had smelled it plenty of times in his life. Mostly from drag racing out on the rural highways. But now, as Jules floored the accelerator, the black-rimmed tires leaving long lines of rubber on the blacktop, Eddie had one paralyzing thought: what if he never smelled burning rubber, or any other smell for that matter, ever again? A flash of sensibility made him wrest the seat belt across his chest and try to fasten it, but it wouldn't click home. Then he remembered none of the front belts worked, that Jules had joked a while back that one day the two of them would accidentally drive into a tree and be left as vegetables.

Blue and red lights swirled angrily behind them, accompanied by the shrieking sirens. Eddie checked the passenger mirror and counted three of them now, all closing fast. They'd arrived on scene so quickly that Eddie figured the clerk must have set off a silent alarm before being shot. Not that it mattered now. Panic overtaking him, Eddie turned in his seat and saw the lead cruiser had cut the distance to several car lengths. "You have to stop, Jules!" he yelled over the roaring engine. "You can't outrun them!"

A traffic light ahead turned red and Jules shot through it at seventy miles per hour. "Fuck that, man!" he yelled. "I'm not going back to prison!" And then, almost as an afterthought, he turned to Eddie with a crazed grin and added, "Besides, my asshole is too precious to get poked by those big-dicked brothers!" He faced the road again, cackling like a hyena. The Mustang fishtailed, taking out a newspaper stand as the right-side wheels hopped a curb. Eddie felt sure they'd crash into one of the storefronts, but Jules righted the pony back onto the road before taking two consecutive right turns. One of the cruisers clipped a parked car and fell behind but the other two stayed close on their tail. Eddie realized it would only be a matter of time before they managed to block them off, that this circus couldn't last much longer.

Fuck me, just motherfuck me...

Jules hooked a hard left. Before the cruisers made the turn, he deftly slipped the car down an alley. Braking to a point where he could coast at low speed, he lifted off the pedal and killed the headlights. For a moment Eddie allowed himself to believe the ploy might actually work. The first two cruisers flew by the alley entrance, their lights flashing in the pitch darkness as they screamed past. But the third, either through communication with the others or by the driver's own intuition, stopped shortly after passing the alley, only to back up and turn into the alley after them. The cruiser's spotlight bathed the blacked-out Mustang in white light and immediately sped forward after them.

Eddie grabbed Jules by the arm and shook him. "Stop the car, Jules! Stop the car!"

Ignoring him, Jules floored the accelerator. They hit a metal garbage can and sent it flying into the side of a nearby garage. "I told you, Eddie, I can't—"

And then it happened. As Jules overcorrected, the car veered hard to the right and slammed headlong into a power pole. In an instant, the Mustang went from nearly thirty miles an hour to a dead stop, hurling both its inhabitants forward like rag dolls. Jules let out a grunt as his chest hit first the wheel, then the windshield. Eddie flew sideways into the dash, the force of his two-hundred-ten-pound body forcing open the glovebox and spilling its contents onto the floorboard. He heard the air escape him before he felt the impact; and as the car settled back down onto its rear tires, both men inside flopped back into their seats and remained motionless for a moment, the event so new to each of them their brains had yet to register the shock.

The cruiser screeched to a halt, its siren cutting off but the overhead lights still swirling. The deputy jumped out and positioned himself behind the open driver's door. He announced something into his shoulder-mounted radio mic while training his drawn pistol on the Mustang. "Driver!" he yelled. "Place both hands out the window! Do it now!"

Eddie felt his world swim by in alternating waves of light and darkness. The pain in his side swelled like a live thing, and before he knew it, he bent forward and threw up onto the floorboard. Next to him, Jules groaned and placed a hand over a fresh gash on his forehead.

The deputy again. "Driver! Show me your hands and *do not* make any sudden movements, or I *will* shoot you dead!"

Eddie heard a chorus of approaching sirens. He looked over the dash at the Mustang's crumpled hood. Steam hissed from the shattered radiator. An audible ticking came from somewhere inside the engine compartment. He turned toward Jules and saw blood pouring down his face and into his mouth. When Jules spoke next, Eddie knew in his heart his friend's time on earth would be short-lived.

"I'm sorry, bro. I didn't mean for it to end like this."

Before Eddie could respond, Jules leaned over and yanked the revolver free from Eddie's waistband. In an instant he was out of the car and standing with the gun outstretched in his hand, and even though Eddie screamed at him to stop, that it didn't have to end this way, he still saw the cop's bullets rip into Jules's chest and abdomen, five of them in all, with two of them punching out his back and through his t-shirt where they clattered against a nearby industrial roll door.

Surprise in his eyes, Jules looked down at his riddled midsection. The gun slipped from his hand and struck the pavement, and a moment later he crumpled to the ground in a heap. Trying to open his door but finding it jammed shut, Eddie slid over the console and spilled through the open driver's door to where Jules lay in a growing pool of his own blood. Frantic, Eddie cradled his friend's head in his arms. Jules smiled up at him with his broken, bloody mouth. As his lips struggled to form words, he struggled to keep his eyes open.

The lids fluttered, and finally he found his voice between wheezing breaths. "I'm floating, Eddie. I feel like I'm floating away."

Eddie brushed away a spatter of blood that had gotten into Jules's eyes, concentrating on holding him that way and ignoring the officer's demands for him to lay face down, that he would shoot him too if he didn't, but Eddie didn't care. And then Jules's eyes did roll back in his head and his mouth slung open, and Eddie knew that he was gone. Eddie shook him hard, more out of his own despair than any hope of actually bringing him back, but it wasn't any good.

Other voices now. Ordering him to lie on the ground. Telling him to give up, that there was no hope for him to get away.

And then something solid striking Eddie across the back of the neck and him collapsing atop his lifeless friend, where he slipped into an unconsciousness so complete and black, he himself seemed to float toward some unseen otherworld.

FIVE

THE CELL PHONE rang, and amid her ecstasy Alice Riggins had half a notion to ignore it altogether. She'd chosen the ringtone—a plain yet shrill bell—as an homage to the lone rotary telephone that had sat in her family's living room for most of her childhood. She'd picked it to lessen the morbidity surrounding her job, to assuage a bit of the sadness that came with it. And now, as she rolled off her husband's naked body, whispering for him not to go anywhere, she knew before answering that the caller brought bad news. Be it that of a victim, a suspect, or a witness, it could at times include innocuous business talk.

But always death.

As the phone continued its urgent trill, she snatched it off the dresser and sat on the edge of the bed. Her husband, Chet, rolled over and traced an ebony finger down the length of her bare back. She shivered at the touch, looking back at him and mouthing the words 'I'll make it quick' before she pressed the phone's 'accept' button.

"Riggins, Homicide."

The voice on the other end came in that same cold, professional tone she'd become accustomed to over the years. "Hope I'm not disturbing you, Alice, but I had no choice on this one."

Riggins sighed. "Story of my life, Lieu. What you got?"

"Signal-50, times two. One of them is at the original crime scene.

At, um—" Riggins heard a rustling of papers from the other end. "At the One-Stop on Meadow Drive. You know where it is?"

Riggins folded one arm beneath her still-sweaty breasts and searched her memory. She felt her husband's finger trace itself longingly down the curve of her bare back to her naked hip. The lids of her eyes half-closed as she felt another tingle pass through her. "Yes, I know it. I worked a case there last year. Robber enters store. Robber pulls gun. Clerk also pulls gun. Robber sent to morgue."

"Well, same store, same clerk, same gun. Except backward this time. Clerk is Signal-7 at the scene. One of our perps also, about a mile away. Vehicle pursuit ended in a shooting. The surviving perp is at Memorial receiving treatment for non-life-threatening injuries. Units are standing by. Start at the store first then work the alley. Last time I checked, perp two was out cold, so you probably won't get to him until morning. Grab some coffee on your way. This'll be an all-nighter by the looks of it."

Riggins turned to Chet, and through the room's semi-darkness mouthed the words '*I have a case*' to him. He reached out and cupped one of her breasts in his large, muscled hand. Even in the low lighting, his jet-black hand stood in contrast to her much lighter, cocoa complexion. He mouthed the words '*so do I*' and smiled the sort of smile that said he had long accepted this part of her work but still didn't like it.

"Give me thirty mikes," she said, suddenly wishing some freak accident in space had rendered whatever satellite controlling her cell phone inoperable. As if sensing the consternation within her, the lieutenant's voice came to her softer now, warmer than before.

"I know it's your anniversary. Ten years already. If I could assign this to anyone else I would. I have Sanchez meeting you there to assist."

"It's okay, sir," Riggins said. "At least we got to finish dinner. Chet took me to that classy seafood place on the river. El Pescado-something."

Lieutenant Heinke muttered a comment about how much fish disgusted him, then added, "Five months to go, kid. I can barely believe you're already up for retirement, and only forty-three? I'm jealous. I wish I'd started as young as you did. I'll be fifty-five when I leave. That is, if my wife doesn't kill me first."

Riggins laughed despite her disappointment and hung up. She turned to her husband, who now lay on his back with both hands clasped behind his head. She lay across his muscular, dark brown chest, planting soft kisses across the skin there.

"I thought you had a case," Chet said, his baritone voice thick with passion.

"I told you when I took this job that it would never come first over you," she answered. Then, coyly, "Speaking of coming over you—"

Before he could respond, she took him in her hand and straddled him in one deft, well-practiced move.

RIGGINS HAD PROMISED to be there in a half hour; she made it with three minutes to spare. The scene reminded her of the one from the year before. Now, just as had been the case then, a dozen cruisers blocked off the surrounding streets, their swirling emergency lights turning the night into an angry swarm of blue and red. Yellow crime scene tape extended around the store and parking lot. A small crowd of onlookers stood on the opposite sidewalk conversing with one another, watching with wide, curious eyes.

After parking against the near curb, Riggins stepped out of her unmarked agency vehicle and stretched. Her navy-blue pantsuit felt a bit stiff, having just come from the cleaners today. Around her neck hung a lanyard with a gold, five-pointed star attached to a leather holder. **Calusa County Sheriff's Office** stood out above the star, and **Senior Detective** across the bottom. On her hip, accessible beneath her short suit jacket, sat a holstered .40-caliber Glock G27 pistol.

A uniformed deputy saw Riggins approaching and lifted the crime scene tape for her. "Good evening, detective," he said.

Riggins offered him a grim smile. "Not anymore it isn't."

The deputy nodded knowingly and escorted Riggins to the store's front door. A crime scene technician with blue booties on her shoes crouched at the propped door, alternatively applying and removing clear tape from different areas of the glass and both sides of the metal door handle. A fresh-faced uniformed deputy stood guard with a notepad and pen. Riggins gave her name for the required crime scene log and stepped around a trail of bloody, left-footed footprints. Yellow, numbered crime scene markers stood beside each print. Once inside the store, Riggins made eye contact with a patrol sergeant who stood over the body of a man on the floor. "Our victim?" she asked rhetorically.

The sergeant acknowledged her presence with a slight nod of his head. "In the flesh, so to speak."

Riggins crouched, taking care not to step in the now-coagulated pool of blood. Tilting her head, she looked into the man's lifeless, half-open eyes. "What time did Fire Rescue declare him?" she asked.

The sergeant scanned through his notes. "Eleven twenty-three."

Riggins sighed. "I know him. I worked a shooting here last year. He killed a robber. Shot him right in the face when the guy looked away for a second. Guess his luck ran out." She stood and glanced up to a series of globed surveillance cameras positioned in the ceiling.

"Do we know if these cameras are active?"

"I think so," the sergeant said. "Looks like they have an older surveillance system in the office. Probably the same one you saw last year. We didn't go in, but it looks like VHS. Can't believe people are still running those."

"What about witnesses?"

"The place was empty when the units rolled up, and nobody has come forward. So far, our only witness is the victim, but he hasn't said a word since I got here." The sergeant chuckled to himself. When Riggins didn't join in his laughter, he quickly resumed his official air.

"Blood smears next to the body," Riggins noted. "Looks like someone knelt next to him. Probably looking for valuables." She looked up and pointed to a ceiling camera behind the counter. "If I remember correctly from last time, that one will be our winning pony, as long as the tape is clean."

Just then, a dark-suited Hispanic man of about thirty stepped through the door. A Sheriff star, this one silver, hung on a lanyard around his neck. His jet-black hair lay combed in an immaculate sideways sweep across his olive-complexioned brow. As he approached where Riggins and the sergeant stood, he looked down at the body and frowned.

"Is that a dead person?" he asked, pointing. "Because I don't do dead people anymore. I'm boycotting them. My therapist told me they're starting to take away from my love life."

Riggins smiled despite herself. "Glad you could finally join us, Detective Sanchez. And if I remember correctly, you once picked up a girl at a funeral. While the casket was literally being lowered into the ground."

Sanchez ran a hand through his hair, a good-natured grin spreading across his face. "Fair enough."

"You really need to stop opening the door for me, Sanny," Riggins said playfully. "But if you've changed your mind and still feel like dealing with dead people, I need you to notify the ME, pronto. Then have the tech get those prints back from AFIS. I recognize him from an old case, but I want prints before we make a positive. The media will be all over this one, and I'd like to notify his next-of-kin before they get here."

Detective Sanchez nodded, snapping into official mode. "Yes, boss. Anything on our perp?"

"*Perps*." Riggins stressed the plural. "Both carried IDs that matched their prints. Julius Sanders and Edward Grassle. Sanders is deceased at our alley scene. Grassle is under guard at the hospital. Both did prison time." Almost as an afterthought, she added, "We'll finish this scene first, then do the alley."

Sanchez's lips formed a rigid line. "Could have had an easy wrap if the uniforms had capped the second guy too. A trial could take five years. Guy will probably live to a ripe old age watching TV and playing ball in the yard, while us working stiffs get cancer in our forties or get creamed by a drunk driver. It always happens like that. I could buy a place on South Beach for what it'll cost to house this guy for life."

This last part fell on deaf ears to Riggins. She surveyed the scene with a resigned eye. She'd seen this many times before, with only the faces and circumstances changed. Be it a single victim or multiple ones, the results had invariably been the same. Someone always ended up dead. When did it all end? When did people stop killing one another for such trivial reasons? In her decade as a detective, Riggins had only encountered a handful of homicides she had deemed justified—self-defense being the prevailing issue. Nonetheless, in all those cases a dead body had lain at the center of the case. A body that had once been a living, breathing human being with a heartbeat and a working brain. And those former human beings had all wound up going through the same stages of death. It had been eerie at first; but as the years went on and the body count increased, her revulsion had given way to a sort of detached curiosity, and finally a darkened sense of humor.

Sanchez placed a short phone call before stashing his phone inside his jacket pocket. "ME said he'll be here when he can. And something about our victim being very inconsiderate to be killed after ten o'clock at night."

Riggins looked from the body to the growing crowd on the sidewalk outside. "We need those prints before the news crews get here. They're going to tie this to last year's shooting. Once that happens and word gets out, the vic's family is going to put two and two together since he'll be missing. The last thing we need are hysterical family members trampling our crime scene."

Detective Sanchez checked his watch—quarter after midnight. A uniformed deputy peeked his head inside and announced the store owner had arrived and had given his consent for them to search the surveillance tapes. Riggins went over her mental checklist: step one, positively ID the victim; step two, view the surveillance tapes and gather any potential evidence from them; and step three, begin the process of identifying potential witnesses. The last part on her initial list would no doubt be the most difficult. Witnesses were everywhere, and yet with the unreliable nature of them, and with the street code often being what it was, they were nowhere at the same time.

What they did have was the possibility of DNA evidence, with all the blood at the scene. Once forensics completed their task, the chance that either of the perps had left any could greatly tilt the odds in their favor. Although the FDLE lab would likely take weeks to finish their profile, they only needed a single drop of the victim's blood found on the surviving perp's clothing or body to greatly increase the likelihood of a conviction.

But first things first.

A black BMW pulled into the parking lot, the driver waiting several minutes for a stark white van with the words **MEDICAL EXAMINER** printed in black block lettering on the side to arrive. When the van parked and shut off its headlights, a balding man of about fifty stepped from the BMW and approached the deputy guarding the front door. He wearily showed his ID then carefully stepped around the numerous evidence tags on the floor. The county medical examiner shook hands with both detectives, who led him to the body. Crouching beside it, the ME performed an initial visual inspection before speaking something into a hand-held digital recorder. Donning a pair of latex gloves, he began his physical inspection of the body, beginning at the top of the head and working his way down. After performing a series of routine examinations, he brought his full attention to the bullet wound in the center of the victim's chest. As he rolled the body over to inspect the exit wound, a black .38 caliber revolver revealed itself.

"Last to fire, situation dire," the ME intoned, stone-faced.

Riggins waved for a forensics tech, and after the gun had been photographed in place she slapped on her own latex gloves and carefully picked it up. All six chambers held unspent rounds. Unloading it, she handed it to a forensics member who dusted it for prints and swabbed it for DNA matches. Sanchez removed a wallet from the clerk's back pocket and compared the driver's license to the clerk's face. A match. When the tests on the gun had been completed, the tech handed the weapon back to Riggins for further evidence handling. After a series of examinations on the body, the ME stood and motioned to his assistants waiting inside their van. A pair of well-built men hopped out and wheeled a gurney into the store. After more pictures of the victim were taken and the forensic techs finished gathering their evidence, the assistants collapsed the gurney and rolled the body into a white plastic body bag. With this grim task completed, they zipped the bag closed, expanded the gurney, and wheeled it out into the awaiting van.

For a moment, neither of the detectives nor the ME said anything. An audible hum from the overhead fluorescent lights remained the only manufactured sound in the store. Detective Sanchez eyed the nearby food warmer and deadpanned, "Hot dog, anybody?"

Riggins shook her head. "You're a sick man, Sanny."

"Just a product of my environment, Rig. I grew up in the projects, so this stuff is in my blood. When I was a kid my friends and I found a homeless guy dead in an alley. Not a scratch on him. Just laid down one day and died leaning up against a dumpster. One of my friends had a Polaroid camera and we took turns posing with him. Guy sat there for three days. We all took turns shooing rats away until someone finally called it in. It may be twisted, but where I'm from weird shit like that happens all the time. I guess you could say I was born for this job."

After forensics finished their work, Riggins called for the store's owner to be escorted inside. A smallish man with unsure, beady eyes ushered the detectives into an office in the rear of the store, where he began tinkering with the surveillance equipment.

"Have you added any angles since last time?" Riggins asked him, recalling that only two had existed from last year's shooting—the interior front door and an angled side shot of the front of the counter.

"Same ones," the man responded, his voice apologetic.

Figured. But she understood most of these businesses couldn't afford lavish video upgrades. Asking him to load whatever he had, she and Sanchez waited patiently for the split screen image to forward to the time just prior to the robbery. Pausing the video to ensure the man wouldn't view it, Riggins asked Sanchez to escort him back out of the store. When Sanchez returned, Riggins rewound the tape thirty minutes as a starting point, then pressed the 'play' button.

The image on the left showed the store's interior front door from a distance of about ten feet. The glare from the interior fluorescent lights made it impossible to get a clear view out the door or adjoining windows. On the right, the counter shot appeared. Riggins pressed the 'fast-forward' button, and for the next several minutes they both watched as three separate sets of headlights could be seen pulling up to front of the store, several minutes apart. Three individuals, none matching their suspects' descriptions, walked into the store at different times. Each bought items before leaving without incident. Then, at the 10:56 PM mark on the tape, another set of headlights could be seen pulling into the parking lot. A lanky, Caucasian man in his mid-twenties entered the store. Riggins stopped the tape, noting the man's clothing and spiked haircut. Even through the tape's graininess, the man's eyes appeared glazed, the pupils constricted. Removing a photo of their dead suspect from a folder, Riggins held it up beside the frozen image on the screen.

"Bingo," Sanchez said, nodding.

Pressing 'play' again, they both watched as the suspect began wandering the store aisles. As he did, a second set of headlights could be seen pulling into a parking space directly next to what had presumably been the suspects' car. A young Hispanic woman could be seen opening the door and pausing to look behind her before entering.

"Can I get a witness?" Sanchez asked evangelically, tapping the screen. "Let's hope mama stuck around for the show."

Riggins kept her eyes glued to the screen, watching the woman move toward the coolers before leaving the camera's view. The suspect gave a furtive glance around, then approached the counter. He appeared to engage the clerk in conversation, and then the clerk could be seen reaching beneath the counter for something. The suspect immediately pulled a gun from his waistband and fired a single shot.

Riggins paused the video and jotted the information down in her notepad. Starting the video again, they watched as the clerk crumpled to the floor, falling so that only his legs remained in camera view. Riggins made careful notes about the suspect's positioning, the details of the shooting, as well as the exact time it had occurred, before allowing the tape to play again.

"So, our girl must have stuck around for the show after all," she said, watching as the woman they'd seen enter the store suddenly appeared back in the counter camera view. Looking in the direction of where the clerk had fallen, the woman clasped both hands to her face and appeared to scream.

"Not the show you were looking for, was it, mama?" Sanchez quipped, staring transfixed at the screen.

Seconds later, another man—taller and better built than the shooter—could be seen bursting through the front door. Riggins didn't need to consult her other suspect photograph; she clearly recognized the second man as Edward Grassle, their living suspect. His clothing and shoes had been seized as evidence and bore an exact match. Same close-cut brown hair, same ruggedly handsome face. Riggins paused the tape. "Posture suggests he's surprised," she said, frowning. "You see the way he's holding his hands out?"

Sanchez leaned in closer and shook his head. "To me he's telling the girl not to move. And giving the shooter directions. He's in charge of the whole thing. He sent his partner in to do the dirty work, but the partner fucked up and capped the clerk. It was supposed to be a quick in-and-out until the fireworks started."

Riggins let the tape play, and each of them watched as Lookout took the gun from Shooter, shoved it into his own waistband, and knelt beside the counter. Due to the camera angle, he remained mostly out of view, with only his head partly visible above the countertop. He remained that way for a full minute, all while Shooter and the woman stood frozen in place.

"He's robbing the guy," Sanchez said, tapping the monitor with one finger.

"But we found his wallet. And he still had a gold chain on his neck," Riggins pointed out.

"Tunnel vision. He's in a rush. Since they didn't get anything from the register, he's trying to get something off the guy."

"Why not just rob the girl?" Riggins asked.

"True," Sanchez conceded.

"Lookout doesn't just enter the store when he hears a shot, he *runs* in. His body language suggests he's non-aggressive, which is strange. He takes the gun from Shooter and safeguards it. Then instead of concentrating on the register, he kneels next to the clerk for almost a minute. I've seen a hundred robberies on video, and in each one the bad guys attempt to collect the score, even when things go south. Shooter almost looks like he's high on something from the way he's frozen there. Lookout is the active one here. He's got to know he's putting himself at tremendous risk remaining at the scene for that long."

They continued watching until both suspects ran from the store, leaving the woman standing on her own. The first set of headlights they'd seen now spun away, followed immediately by three sets of swirling blue and red lights. About ten seconds after they passed, the woman herself ran from the store, the second set of headlights disappearing into the night.

As Riggins rewound the tape so they could watch it again, Sanchez offered his insight.

"Armed robbery, clerk and Shooter both die. Lookout is the only one left standing. Easy peasy."

"Pretty much," Riggins agreed, although her eyes narrowed as she watched the scene play out again. "Lookout just seems—I don't know, almost like a bystander. If we hadn't caught them both in the getaway car, I'd have thought he wasn't involved."

Sanchez frowned. "They both ran out together. And even though it's not definitive, you can safely presume they arrived in the same car too."

"I agree, but you can't assume he's robbing the clerk because of what Shooter did. Even if he gets charged with everything, I want to know what he was doing."

They both looked at one another and said it in unison.

"The girl."

They watched the tape another dozen times, start to finish, taking detailed notes. Riggins summoned the forensic tech and directed her to lift more prints from both the inner and outer door handle, although she expressed doubt they'd find anything since responding deputies and emergency crews had understandably entered and exited the doorway numerous times without wearing gloves.

Rewinding the tape all the way and pressing the eject button, Riggins placed the tape into an evidence bag then made a chain of custody notation on the label. As they left the manager's office and went back over their procedure checklist, Sanchez asked, "How much longer you have all this shit to deal with?"

The crop-haired detective—shorter than her partner by almost a foot, and almost half of his two hundred pounds—smiled a wan sort of smile that still managed to crease the corners of her almond-shaped eyes.

"I'll start counting down once I get under a month," she said, turning the focus back on the case. "We've got a dead suspect who can't turn on his partner. We have a witness who fled the scene—can't blame a girl for not sticking around for that kind of party—and if we don't get her prints and she spooks, then scratch our only witness off our list."

"I'll be curious to see if Lookout talks to us once he gets out of the hospital," Sanchez said, opening the front door for Riggins. As they stepped out into the night air, they watched as a white van with a large 'Channel 5' logo on its side pulled into a parking lot on the opposite side of the street. "Here comes the circus," he said, shaking his head.

"Get with the uniforms and make sure those guys don't intrude on our scene," Riggins directed. "You can give them a general statement, but no info on the vic until we make notification."

Riggins knew their night was just beginning. The usual procedures would have to be followed, as custom. Neighborhood canvass, forensics follow-up, and eventually the surviving suspect's interview. That could wait until tomorrow though. More pressing remained the unknown female witness. *Pretty girl*, Riggins thought. *Just stopping by the store for something to drink and what does she get for her trouble? A bloodbath.* She folded her arms as she watched the camera crew set up across the street. Thinking of Chet and feeling bad at having been called to duty on their anniversary night, she felt excited about the end of her career being so close.

"Five months," she said aloud, casting a glance at the meat wagon. "Might as well be five years."

TWO HOURS LATER, as light rain fell from a slate-gray sky, the two detectives stepped away from a small home in the east part of town. They had just made notification to their victim's wife. Forensics had made quick work with the prints, running them through the state automated fingerprint system and coming back with a hit. The clerk had had an active concealed carry permit and as a result had been required to provide his fingerprints for his application. Esteban Mendez-Rodriguez, aged sixty-one. Riggins had been correct; he had been the same clerk involved in last year's case. Having to show his widow photos of her dead husband's face had been excruciating for both detectives. Never an easy part of the job, notifications were nonetheless a crucial aspect of an investigation. This one had been particularly upsetting because Mrs. Mendez-Rodriguez had smiled brightly upon opening the door, presuming the detectives to be an expected family member from out of town. A flicker of confusion had marked her face then, until her eyes moved down to their hanging detective badges. Recognition then, as she'd begun to place Riggins's face. The two women had shared many conversations during her husband's self-defense case the year before. But on this night, as Riggins had said they had news that would be very upsetting, the woman had immediately burst into tears.

Walking away from the squat home complete with burglar bars on the windows, neither detective spoke of the task they had just endured. Riggins's plan constituted waiting until morning to canvass the neighborhood and attempting to gain images from any of the surrounding traffic cameras. A description of the witness's vehicle, or even a partial plate, would be of help. The hospital reported their surviving suspect had two broken ribs and a concussion. As such, he'd likely spend a day or two before being discharged. Riggins planned to wait and interview him at sheriff's office headquarters in a formal interrogation, prior to his being booked into the county jail. It made sense to wait. At HQ Riggins's team would have full access to interview rooms, high-def digital video recorders, and other necessary tools of the trade.

Not to mention the psychological advantage of a custodial environment. Not even jail could replicate the anxiety and fear a suspect felt when made to wait in the stark confines of an interrogation room. Once jailed, a person tended to begin the process of accepting their loss of freedom, temporary or not. But prior to arrest, while wearing their own clothing and maintaining their hope of continued freedom, suspects generally agonized over the mere prospect of jail. Priorities reorganized. Riggins had seen this effect countless times over the years, even once gaining a confession from a man who had blurted his involvement in a savage murder as soon as the detective team had entered the room. After recording the man's tearful confession, Riggins had asked him what had made him announce it so quickly. The suspect had said the interrogation room itself had felt as though it had been closing in on him, and that he'd rather go to prison knowing his fate than spend another minute in that room uncertain of it.

Back at HQ, the detective team met with Lieutenant Heinke and reviewed the surveillance tape again before processing search warrants for both suspects' residences.

"You two go home and get some rest," Heinke told them after reviewing everything they had. "The patrol guys sitting on Lookout at the hospital will notify you when he gets discharged. It sounds like just an overnight for him. I'd like to be here for his interview, so let me know when you pick him up." The balding, mustached man gave both detectives weary pats on the back before sending them home to get what little sleep they could. As they each drove away from the two-story building, the clock stood at half past three in the morning. A light rain that had fallen after they'd gotten to headquarters had since stopped. The empty roads reflected an eerie glow from the line of streetlights that stood like so many sentinels guarding the pervading night.

SIX

THE FOLLOWING MORNING, a bright clear sky stretched over Springwood. In a salmon-colored house five miles from where Eddie lay in medicated sleep, Clarissa and Liam ate breakfast to the nine o'clock morning news. Another armed robbery. This time the clerk and one of the suspects lay dead. The surviving suspect remained under police guard in a local hospital after a failed getaway. Murder charges had yet to be filed but were pending. When Eddie's picture flashed on the screen, with **SUSPECT IN CUSTODY** emblazoned below his name, Clarissa's eyes went wide in shock. She'd been in mid-bite and nearly choked on a forkful of scrambled eggs. Liam, facing away from the television, saw her expression and began to turn around. Reaching for the remote, Clarissa switched the TV off and retreated to the kitchen sink, bracing herself against the metal edges as she fought back sudden tears.

"What's wrong, mommy?" Liam asked from the kitchen table.

Clarissa hung her head, feeling newfound rage flood into her. Taking in a breath, she raised her head and looked Liam in the eye. "I'm so sorry, honey, but your daddy won't be able to see you today."

Liam's face fell into a picture of disappointment. "Will he come tomorrow then?" he asked.

Clarissa fought back tears she knew would soon come. "No, honey. He won't come tomorrow. Now go to your room and play. Mommy has to make a few phone calls."

The boy dropped his head and retreated to his bedroom as instructed, and the mother sat for quite some time, silent, staring out the window and wondering how she could have been so stupid to believe yet another lie. She had always heard that the opposite of love was ambivalence, not hate. For the first time in her life she believed whoever had said that had gotten things backward.

AT A QUARTER after nine in the morning two cruisers—one marked, the other unmarked—pulled up to the main entrance of Springwood Memorial Hospital. Two uniformed deputies stepped from the marked cruiser. One of them carried a three-strapped Velcro belt, fitted with front-mounted handcuffs utilized for transporting high-risk prisoners.

Detectives Riggins and Sanchez stepped from the unmarked unit. Sanchez wore a smart gray suit, his hair slicked back to its trademarked model of perfection. Riggins, a full foot shorter than her younger partner, wore a dark blue pantsuit with black flats. Clipped to their respective beltlines sat their agency stars. On their right hips sat their exposed holstered pistols—his, a .45 Glock 21, and hers the smaller and easier-to-handle 27 model. The foursome rode the elevator to the fourth floor then swung down a wide L-shaped hallway. At the floor's nurses' station, the charge nurse handed them their prisoner's discharge paperwork and pointed them in the direction of room 438. Once there, the two uniformed deputies remained outside the door while the detectives entered. A tenet of police work went that a suspect stood a much higher likelihood of escaping in a transitory environment. Once Grassle had been transferred back to HQ for questioning, their job would not be considered complete until he'd been delivered to the county jail. The difference between the two areas was like a cardboard box versus a metal cage.

Having stepped first into the hospital room, Riggins looked to the lone hospital bed and observed their suspect, an athletic-looking man in his mid-twenties, lying awake with his head facing the window. Riggins noted one wrist and the opposing ankle were both shackled to the fixed metal bedrails. Good, the deputies on guard hadn't been lazy. She'd seen prisoners before entirely uncuffed. One story that had traveled throughout headquarters had involved an elderly man accused of bashing in his wife's skull with a hammer. The man had fought with responding deputies and had required hospitalization. Upon his discharge, the two young and well-built deputies guarding him had nearly allowed him to escape when they'd escorted him from the hospital unrestrained, having taken their eyes off him for thirty seconds. That Grassle appeared more than capable of fighting them if he so chose seemed even more reason to exercise caution.

Riggins and Sanchez stopped near the foot of the bed and exchanged nods with the seated uniforms who'd been guarding the prisoner since he'd arrived close to midnight the night before. They both appeared relieved to see them.

"Good morning, gentlemen," Riggins announced. "Your prisoner has been discharged. We're here to transport."

"It's about time," one of them said, casting a baleful look at their prisoner. "Fucker gave us a real fight earlier. Goddamn maniac."

As the two uniforms gathered their belongings, Riggins focused on Grassle. His eyes remained fixed on some unknown point outside the window. A doctor entered the room and gave Riggins a verbal account of Grassle's condition. Riggins asked him when their prisoner's last medication dose had been administered.

"All he's accepted has been Motrin. Tough kid."

"How about the concussion? Would that affect his cognitive ability?"

The doctor shrugged, seeming to understand why she'd asked the question. "Normally, yes. But his CT came back fine, and he passed all his other testing. I wouldn't have discharged him if he couldn't reason on his own or get up and walk away." He smirked. "Theoretically, of course."

Riggins thanked the doctor then summoned a wheelchair. Once it arrived, one of their accompanying deputies removed a handcuff key from his gun belt and unsecured the shackle from the bedrail, reattaching it to Eddie's other ankle. Next, the deputy unfastened the cuff from the bedrail and threaded it through a metal O-shaped ring at the front of the Velcro transport belt before securing Eddie's other wrist. Having Eddie stand (he grimaced, but to his credit, didn't make a sound), the deputy fastened the belt around his waist, feeding a lock-able plastic zip tie through a slit at the rear of the overlapping straps. This prevented the belt's wearer or anyone else without a handcuff key from unstrapping the folds. Cuffed in the front for transport pur-poses, the belt's wearer could not raise their hands more than a few inches above their waist.

With Eddie properly belted and seated in the wheelchair, Rig-gins searched his expressionless face, searching for some glimmer of regret, anger, anything she felt she could use in her upcoming inter-rogation of him. But she found nothing. The only detectable emotion from him seemed to be dejectedness as he stared out the room's window.

"Mr. Grassle, my name is Detective Riggins," she said. "I'm from the Calusa County Sheriff's Office. This is my partner, Detective San-chez. You've been charged with felony fleeing and eluding from last night and have a zero bond as of now. The doctors have discharged you from the hospital into our custody, but before we book you into the county jail we'd like to bring you back to our office to talk about some other things, okay?"

Eddie, gazing out the window until now, finally turned to face Riggins. "Do I have a choice?"

"Not for coming with us, but of course you'll have a choice in speaking with us. We'll get into all of that back at the station. Cool?"

Eddie considered what he'd just heard. Never had he been in such a position. His comparatively minor legal scrapes over the years had taught him when the police were grasping at straws and when they had him cornered. His instincts told him Detective Riggins held a better hand than she let on. True, he hadn't actually killed the store clerk, but even Eddie knew the basics of law. The fact that Detective Riggins hadn't tried to bullshit him failed to ease his nerves. His mind spun with everything that had gone on in the last twenty-four hours, and the possibilities—most of them bad—that came with what had happened. Eddie showed Riggins his manacled hands, palms out. "Ready when you are, detective. Do you mind driving, though? My hands are full."

The hint of a smile touched Riggins's lips. "Okay then." She stepped out of the room while the deputies had Eddie change from his hospital gown into a paper-like, zippered jumpsuit. With him re-secured in his belly-chain, they sat him in a wheelchair and wheeled him out of the room and down the elevator to the first floor, a pair of deputies walking ahead, Riggins and Sanchez walking behind.

As they exited a set of doors reserved for hospital employees, the mid-morning sun warmed Eddie's face. *I'm supposed to be at the park right now*, he thought as the deputies assisted him to his feet. Pain bolted through his broken ribs as the uniforms assisted him into the back seat of a cruiser. When they buckled him in and shut the door, Eddie stared into space, wondering what lay ahead for him. Jules had killed someone. Eddie had been there, had handled the gun for Christ's sake. He realized with growing anxiety that he had also touched the dead man, stepped and knelt in his blood. His clothing and shoes would already be in a police evidence room, he knew. Still, he hoped they'd understand he'd had nothing to do with the man's death. They had to. The woman with the Jeep had seen everything. And surely there must have been security cameras showing him coaxing the gun from Jules, talking him down, trying to save the clerk's life. It was all such a mess he couldn't even begin to unravel the endless possibilities. Eddie thought about all this as the caged cruiser pulled away, the two detectives he'd just met following behind. The digital clock on the cruiser's dash read ten fifteen in the morning. He should be at the park with his son right now, pushing him on a swing and listening to his shrill laughter. Instead he sat in the back of a cramped police cruiser, cuffed and shackled like an animal, and being led toward Lord knew what. He counted backward in his head, understanding this new living nightmare had barely reached its twelfth hour.

SEVEN

CALUSA COUNTY SHERIFF'S Office headquarters occupied a two story, white concrete building a mile off the interstate. The acreage, once owned and operated by slave owners, remained a bastion of the old school—until the 1970s the Confederate flag proudly flew below the American flag. A large public parking lot fronted the edifice, leading to automatic sliding doors, and beyond them the public lobby. The cruisers alternatively carrying and escorting Eddie did not use this entrance, however. Instead, they pulled around back and used a service entrance reserved for situations such as this: prisoners being shuttled in and out for interrogations without having to be paraded before the general public.

Having wheeled Eddie in a wheelchair through this back entrance, one of the transport deputies used a fob on his key ring to open the service elevator. Riggins and Sanchez stood silently beside the wheelchair. When the doors eased open, a uniformed deputy began to push Eddie inside when Riggins thanked him, saying she and Sanchez would escort the prisoner from that point. The three of them rode in silence to the second floor, the doors sliding open to an austere, white-painted hallway. The main interrogation room sat midway down this hallway and consisted of a single four-foot-long table bolted to the floor. Three chairs occupied the cramped room—a similarly bolted one against the far wall with two others opposite it. The detectives helped Eddie from the wheelchair and assisted him into the chair against the wall. Detective Sanchez removed his transport belt and asked him if he'd like something to drink. "Water," Eddie replied, and moments later Sanchez returned with a bottled water.

"We'll be back in a few minutes," Riggins told Eddie. "In the meantime, try your best to relax."

As soon as they shut the door, Eddie felt the room's immediate effect. Approximately six by ten feet in size, the room's low ceiling only added to his growing sense of claustrophobia. From the far ceiling hung a black plastic orb. They were watching him, no doubt, and their upcoming conversation with him would certainly be videotaped. He'd been through interrogations before, but never with such formality. Details from the night before flooded him. Jules. Eddie could not reason why the guy had decided to do what he'd done. It all seemed so unreal, so unfathomable to Eddie that he sat now in this room instead of standing in a park just a few miles away.

He sat alone for another twenty minutes before both detectives re-entered, taking the two seats directly across from him. Each laid a sizable folder on the table before formally introducing themselves. Detective Sanchez went first. Good-looking guy with great hair and a well-cut suit, Eddie assessed. Despite the man's professional appearance, Eddie detected a certain edge in his eyes, as if he'd grown up rough. Maybe he'd gotten into a few scrapes of his own in his younger years but had been smart enough not to get caught. Eddie had seen the same look many times, and no matter the person's sex or background he'd usually been correct in his assessment that it was caused by hard childhoods and exposure to the seedy side of society.

Detective Riggins went next. Short and attractive, with straightened, cropped hair lying smoothly across her head. She wore little makeup, possibly out of professionalism but more likely because she simply didn't need it, Eddie guessed. And expressive, almond-shaped eyes. To Eddie, she came across as more composed than Sanchez, more relaxed and comfortable in her skin. Clearly in charge, she exuded a calm reserve that achieved something Eddie hadn't encountered often with an officer of the law—with her mere presence she projected a sense that somehow things would be alright.

Before she went any further, Riggins read Eddie his Miranda warning verbatim from a card. When she finished reading, she looked Eddie in the eye. "Do you wish to continue speaking with us without an attorney present?" she asked.

Unable to decide if he should talk or not, he took a full minute to think it through. Riggins and Sanchez sat patiently, their expressions expectant yet solemn. After considering his options and then reconsidering them from every possible angle, Eddie made up his mind. If he had to go down for anything, it wouldn't be for his lack of trying.

"I don't need an attorney to talk to you guys," Eddie said, staring at his hands. He took a deep breath and looked both detectives in the eye. They seemed momentarily surprised, exchanging a quick glance before Detective Riggins began the questioning.

"I appreciate you talking to us, Eddie. May I call you that?"

Eddie nodded.

"Okay, Eddie. As I alluded to before, there is something else we'd like to talk to you about. Are you familiar with the One-Stop convenience store on Meadow Drive?"

Eddie began to answer then paused. He looked up to the black orb in the corner and swallowed. His pulse quickened and he felt his chest tighten. Sighing, he answered that he had been to the store twice yesterday.

Hearing that, both detectives exchanged another glance and jotted notes on their respective legal pads. "Explain," Riggins prompted.

Eddie recounted both his trips to the store, stressing how he had even given the clerk CPR during the second, more fateful visit.

Riggins appeared noticeably surprised. "You gave him CPR?"

"Yes, but it didn't work. I think he died as I was trying to help him."

Riggins removed from her file a color photograph of a dead man lying on a morgue table. She laid the photo on the table in front of Eddie. "His name was Esteban," she said coolly. "He was born in Cuba and rode on a crude boat made of wood and bicycle tires 90 miles through open water to get to this country. If the Coast Guard had caught his group before they landed, they would have taken them back to Cuba where they would have been imprisoned and likely killed. But he made it. For twenty years he worked three jobs so he could support his family. Last night, when I informed his wife that her husband had been killed, she told me their fortieth wedding anniversary would have been next week."

Riggins paused for effect, watching Eddie as his eyes moved between hers and the photograph. She'd considered several avenues of approach based on Eddie's initial willingness to talk. At first, she'd considered playing good cop, getting him to open up more and possibly provide added details he'd surely omitted. But her gut had told her to try a different tack. Full frontal assault. He seemed too eager to part with information. In her experience, subjects who talked so readily came from one of two camps: they were either wholly guilty, or completely innocent. Rarely did a middle ground exist. In forging ahead in a direct manner, openly confronting a guilty suspect with the evidence against them and accusing them of the crime outright, Riggins had learned they almost always changed their story in a significant manner.

But after he re-told his version a second time, she searched both her own memory and her notes and found no discrepancies at all. Moreover, her gut gave off that familiar fuzzy feeling that told her their suspect, not free to leave and knowing so, could possibly be telling the truth. On a hunch, Riggins decided to take a risk.

"The store's surveillance camera captured you stealing valuables off the clerk's body. You knelt next to him and took things from him that his wife identified were later missing. One was an heirloom his wife would very much like returned. I know she'd appreciate having it back, Eddie."

Eddie slid forward in his chair so quickly he nearly fell off the edge. "I didn't take anything from him. I was trying to help him!" He looked across to Detective Sanchez, who leaned coolly back in his chair. "I'm telling you guys the truth!"

By design, Riggins kept her expression dubious. This was despite the fact Eddie had just passed her first test. Of course, the victim's wife had reported no such theft. Her husband's wallet and jewelry—a gold chain and two expensive rings—hadn't been touched, after all.

"You said you'd been friends with Jules for years, that you'd seen him high dozens of times. It doesn't make sense that on this occasion you failed to realize this. And it doesn't make sense your friend would bring a loaded gun with him into the store without saying anything to you about it. Look at it from our view, Eddie. Not much of this is adding up."

"I just got out of prison, so I know this doesn't look good for me," he explained. "And I won't even try to explain why I decided to meet up with him. He was the reason I went away. But when I got out, I hadn't seen him in almost five years. I was in a different place. And my mind was on the next day. I was supposed to take my son to the park." He looked to the clock and swallowed hard. 11:15. "I'm supposed to be there right now."

"We all have things to look forward to," she said. "Your day at the park, and my trip to Florence. Hopefully, we both get what we want."

When the clock struck noon both detectives stood and exited the interview room. They'd been at it for nearly three hours and had asked all their questions. At his office desk Lieutenant Heinke sat in front of a monitor feed of the interview room. Having just watched most of Eddie's interview, he waved both detectives over to his office.

"Have a seat," he told the duo, rubbing his hands together and making a discarding motion. "This one's easy. He admits to being with the shooter before and during the robbery. He handled the murder weapon, and he fled the scene. If the blood on his shoe and jeans belongs to the victim—and I'd bet my pension it does—then he's a dead duck. I'm good with armed robbery and murder one, times two."

Sanchez, respecting Riggins's leading role in the case, waited for her to speak. The senior detective took a moment to form her words, and when she did speak, she gave a tight shake of her head, her expression dubious.

"I feel the legal elements are there to charge him. But if we find that witness and she corroborates his story about giving the clerk CPR, it throws a wrench in any motive he had to commit robbery."

"How so?" Heinke countered.

"Innocent actions conflict with presumed guilty ones here."

Heinke shifted his gaze to Sanchez and pointed his pen at him. "What's your take? First high-profile case. And don't tell me what you think I want to hear."

Detective Sanchez considered his options for a moment before declaring, "He was the lookout, for sure. I don't buy his story about not knowing what was going on. They're at the bar talking about hitting the place. They're getting lit, getting their nerve up. He goes into the store after his partner pops the guy. You see him taking charge. He didn't pull the trigger, but he's the leader." Sanchez gave Riggins an apologetic look and shrugged. "Just my opinion."

Detective Riggins studied Eddie's seated form on the live-stream monitor. A frown creased her brow as she started to say something, then changed her mind. "I don't agree that they both planned it. He seemed genuinely shocked all of this had happened. Again, I get the robbery and murder charges from a legal standpoint. But if you're sitting in my car minding your business and I walk inside a store and kill the clerk, what are you expected to do?"

Heinke studied the ceiling as he tapped the pen against the desk. "How does he explain jumping in the car with the shooter? If he had nothing to do with it and was really the savior he claims to be, he'd have stayed right where he was and waited for the units to get there."

"I disagree, sir. A mother catches her child with his hand in the cookie jar—what is his first reaction?"

"He eats the cookie before his mother takes it from him," Sanchez joked. He and Heinke both laughed.

"No, he pulls his hand out and denies he tried taking a cookie. Why is that?"

Heinke and Sanchez exchanged shrugs.

"This is why women make better detectives," she said. "No offense, fellas. It's because the kid is experiencing the flight portion of a stressful situation. He has two choices: admit what he did wrong or make an initial attempt to evade his mother's disapproval. Adults are no different. It isn't unreasonable to believe he realized his friend just killed someone and panicked when he heard the approaching sirens. Flight doesn't always indicate guilt."

"Now Alice, you know just as well as I do, we don't deal in guilt. Remember that minor legal factor called probable cause? I watched his entire interview and read the file you drew up. He was present at the crime scene and he possessed the murder weapon. Ballistics aren't back yet, but that'll just be icing on the cake if it comes back as a match. Give me one solid, legal reason we don't charge murder." He paused, stroking his bushy mustache as Riggins and Sanchez exchanged a silent thought. "Go ahead and work him alone," Heinke directed to her. "I'm feeling greedy. I want to give the jury dessert with their meat and potatoes." He glanced to the monitor, which showed Eddie sitting upright in his chair, his hands resting in his lap. "He looks relaxed now. He just got out of prison and knows the system. You're better at gaining confessions than I ever was, Alice. I think he knew damn well what the deal was. Turn him and we'll all sleep better tonight knowing he came clean with the whole thing."

Riggins nodded, grabbing a file marked GRASSLE and striding back into the interview room. Settling back into her chair, Riggins folded her hands atop the file and looked him straight in the eye. "Okay, Eddie, I've spoken with my boss, and we just have a few more questions for you. Where we're having a problem is with you going inside the store. I get it. You just got out of prison. I know you don't want to go back. But I need you to help me. If this was a plan that went wrong and you tried fixing it, just tell me. I know you had more involvement than what you've told us so far."

Eddie hung his head, shaking it. When he raised it again his eyes widened and seemed to implore his beliefs even more than the words he uttered. "You have to believe me. I didn't know Jules planned to do that. I had to meet my son the next day, so I wanted to go home and get some sleep. I only met Jules at the bar because I felt bad for the guy. My ex made me promise to cut him off. To be honest, I was sort of ready to end the friendship, even though I couldn't seem to actually do it. If that makes sense to you. So, Jules went to the bathroom and came back all juked up. I should have realized he was stoned; I've seen him that way a hundred times. I never did that stuff, but I've drank since I was fifteen, so I guess I'm no angel. But this stuff Jules did made him—different. It changed him. I'm sure you guys see that sort of thing all the time."

Riggins spread her hands diplomatically. "These are important questions we need answered, Eddie, so bear with me here. When did you first become aware that Jules was in fact robbing the store?"

"When I heard the shot. Wait—not right when I heard it, because I thought it was a firecracker at first. I heard the noise, and then I looked through the store window and saw Jules standing there with a gun in his hand. He had it out like this—" With his hands still chained at waist-level, Eddie turned sideways and did his best to indicate how Jules had stood. When he did that, Riggins stopped him and pressed the intercom button on the wall closest to her and asked for Sanchez to enter the room. When he appeared, Riggins asked him to unshackle Eddie's hands. Sanchez did so, taking the Velcro straps and handcuffs with him before leaving the room.

"Thanks," Eddie said, rubbing his wrists. He then stretched his arm out, pantomiming Jules holding the gun. "He had it like this. I ran inside and saw the clerk lying on the floor behind the counter. He was sort of half in and half out, you know."

"I'm not quite sure I believe you, Eddie. We have your bloody footprints leading out of the store. Forensics is going to match the victim's DNA to the blood found on your clothing. The jury is going to hear about you willingly getting into the car with a friend who'd just shot someone, and both of you fleeing the scene. Those aren't the actions of an innocent person." She paused. "Here is where you need to be honest with me, Eddie. This is serious. If you were just the lookout and got caught up, tell me now. Pretty soon, I'm going to walk out that door and it'll be too late to change your story. Do you want a jury to hear that you aren't sorry? What I think happened is you'd just gotten out of prison and needed some quick cash. Your friend volunteered to do the hold-up. But he panicked and shot the guy. You came inside to investigate, and when you did you looked to see if the clerk had any valuables. He wouldn't need them anymore. I get it. But I'm not the jury. They'll look at you as heartless if you refuse to show remorse. Now is the time to come completely clean. Why not give the victim's family some dignity in knowing the person involved admitted to it and is sorry for what he did?"

Eddie sat frozen in his seat. He felt like a trapped animal. The room seemed to close in on him even more. He searched Detective Riggins's face for any clue to how he should answer but found none. "I—I am sorry that man died. Maybe it is partly my fault. I don't think

Jules would have done that if I hadn't met up with him. Wait—that sounds bad. I'm just saying maybe he got high when he realized we weren't going to be friends anymore, then flipped out once he went into the store." Eddie put his head in his hands and muttered to himself. "I wish none of this ever happened. But it's my own fault for being here. I deserve whatever I have coming."

Riggins leaned back into her chair, searching for that final puzzle piece that would convince her one way or the other. That familiar feeling returned to her, one she hadn't felt in years, and this time she felt helpless to push it away. Briefly closing her eyes, she saw an image of her former self, then just a rookie detective, interrogating a murder suspect. How confident she'd been at first, until cracks had appeared in the case. Going to her superiors with her doubts had been a tough proposition, and only after a long talk with Chet and sleeping on it for several days had she done it. But her hunch hadn't been enough to ward off the media and politicians clamoring to find the responsible person. A child had been raped and murdered, the most abhorrent of crimes. The community had demanded justice. Images were coming back to her, troubling ones that she managed to push away out of sheer will to remain on her current task.

"I can sense you're a good guy, Eddie," she said, looking at him now. "Let the jury into this room right now. Let them see who you really are. A good guy who got caught up. You knew your friend shot and killed a man during a robbery, and then you fled the scene because you wanted to protect him, didn't you?"

Eddie felt hot tears beginning to well in the corners of his eyes. "Yes," he said through the tears. "I think I've always felt the need to protect him, even though he was two years older than me. He acted hard but inside he was really fragile."

Unable to gain a confession but content with what she had, Riggins thanked Eddie for his time, then stood to leave with Detective Sanchez. She explained that she'd be back in a few minutes to let him know when he'd be transported to the county jail. Outside the interrogation room, Riggins stood next to a seated Heinke, who was still watching the interview via the live monitoring system.

"I suppose all the elements are there," Riggins said, staring at the monitor. Even as she spoke the words, she felt conflicted. "We pop him for the robbery and the two homicide counts then."

"Manslaughter or felony murder?" Heinke asked, still eyeing Sanchez and twirling his pen between his fingers.

"Felony murder, for sure," Sanchez answered.

"Why?"

"Principal to a felony—the robbery, an enumerated crime. And not acting in any form of self-defense."

Heinke pointed to Sanchez. "I think you found yourself a full-time partner, Alice. Go ahead and get those affidavits done and have a unit deliver him to county when you're ready." A flicker in her eyes gave Heinke pause. "You okay, kid?"

Riggins took a moment of quiet reflection, then shook away the earlier feeling she'd had.

"Yeah, I'm fine. Maybe getting so close to retiring has me second-guessing everything. Can I ask just one favor though?"

Heinke offered both hands in a conciliatory gesture.

"I want to personally bring him in."

"Fair enough. But you're bringing a chase car with you."

"Okay, I'll take him now," she said, and turning to her partner she added, "Mind if I ask you to sit this one out? I want to see if he has anything else to say on the ride. I don't think he'll sing with such a handsome man sitting in front of him."

"No problem," said Sanchez as he strode toward a group of female secretaries who stood watching his approach. "Besides, I've got other things to work on back here."

RIGGINS WAVED OVER a group of uniformed deputies and gave them instructions on preparing the prisoner for transport to the county jail. Riggins explained to Eddie the new charges against him. Armed robbery and principal to two counts of first-degree murder. A shocked expression on his face, Eddie listened as the gravity of what she explained took hold in him. *Murder.* And not just that of the clerk. Of Jules too. As they hooked him back into the belly chains, Eddie's mind went through a last-second attempt to bargain his way out. *Let me go and I'll never do another wrong, I promise. I'll become a priest. I'll walk across a bed of hot coals, anything to be away from here and back at my apartment. Just give me one chance to see my boy and I'll go away forever and won't fuck anything up ever again.*

When they called for the wheelchair Eddie shook his head. As much pain as he experienced, he insisted on walking. "Suit yourself," one of the uniforms mumbled, and Riggins led the way. As they stepped into the elevator, Eddie wasn't sure what to make of the interview he'd just given. He wondered if perhaps he hadn't made a huge miscalculation in giving a statement. Detective Riggins had made it seem at first as if Eddie had been a victim himself in the whole mess. *It's what the police do,* Jules's voice inside him echoed. *They catch criminals. And what's the worst thing you can do when faced with a crime like this?* That sing-song voice, so familiar to him, repeated that same refrain inside his brain: *Don't ever talk to the police.*

The elevator doors hissed open and they led him through the rear service doors into the brilliant sunshine of the day.

The drive to the Calusa County jail took less than ten minutes. Detective Riggins drove unaccompanied in her unmarked, caged cruiser. Eddie sat on the passenger side of the back seat. Sanchez and another chase vehicle followed them. Riggins had hoped Eddie would open up even more during the short drive to jail. She'd asked to transport him alone. Exactly *why* that had been, not even she was sure of right now.

"You okay back there?" she asked, eyeing the rearview mirror.

Eddie looked out the window and caught a glimpse of a park through the trees. Not the one he had planned to take Liam to, but a park just the same. Something lurched inside his chest as he turned his gaze to the pair of eyes in the rearview mirror. "To be honest, not really," he answered. Keeping eye contact with Riggins, he asked, "Do you want to know something, detective?"

The eyes in the mirror sparkled with interest. "I'm a homicide detective. I always want to know something."

"When I was ten, my dad left me and my mom. I never saw him again. For a long time, I prayed he'd come back. For a year I would sit at the end of the driveway, listening to cars come around the bend and hoping the next one would be his. Then one day I realized he wasn't coming back. I was wasting my time waiting. I swore I would never do something like that to my own kid. But I've never even seen my own kid, and he's already five years old. I guess that makes me an even bigger piece of shit than my own dad."

The eyes in the mirror seemed to consider that. After digesting the words, Riggins said, "It sounds like you had a painful experience. I wouldn't be too hard on yourself."

Eddie sighed, watching the Calusa River pass by as they crossed over a short bridge. He wondered if this would be the last time that he would ever lay eyes on the waterway he'd grown up exploring as a kid. All those sweltering, lazy summer days, jumping from bridges into the refreshing water. Would he ever again see the way the sun sparkled against its surface, or roll his pants legs up and dip his feet into the water, shielding his eyes against the low sun? Just as quickly as it appeared, the river disappeared from view, the cruiser now moving into a more heavily wooded area. A sign announced that the county jail lay a mile ahead. In the minute it took them to reach the series of stark white concrete buildings ringed with barbed-wire fences, Eddie wondered how misfortune could appear so suddenly in a person's life. The speed at which things occurred amazed him. Like a snowball rolling downhill, picking up pieces of your life until nothing was left but remnants too small to see.

Riggins eased the cruiser up to the jail's main sally port and pressed the intercom button. After she'd announced her arrival and held her badge up to the camera, the heavy metal roll gate groaned upward. Easing the cruiser into the cavernous sally port, she parked and got out to confer with Sanchez, who'd pulled in next to her. Together, they led Eddie through the double vestibule doors into the booking area.

"These folks will take care of you," Riggins told Eddie. He met her eye and nodded his understanding.

Looking around the place, Eddie felt not much had changed since his first trip here five years before. A surreal feeling swept through him as he took it all in. How had this happened? He felt that at any minute someone would pop from behind the corner and say that all of this had been some sick joke. But as they photographed him and inventoried his property—just his wallet and the photograph of his father and grandfather that Detective Riggins handed over to them—reality sank in. No person would pop from around the corner. He wouldn't wake from a dream. After everything he'd been through, finally getting out to start over again, here he was back in the same misery he'd just left.

A hulking jail officer with a crewcut frisked him, removed his restraints then ran a metal detector over his body, head to toe. Waving over another officer standing nearby, he ushered Eddie into a room marked **STRIPS**. Having endured countless strip searches during his previous stints in prison, Eddie knew the drill. Strip naked and follow the spoken directions. Once he'd lifted his testicles then turned to bend over at the waist where he spread his cheeks and coughed, Eddie was given an orange and black striped uniform to wear before completing the rest of the booking process—photographs, fingerprints, medical evaluation, and finally classification. He'd initially be sent to the medical ward, they said, and until space was made available he'd have to sit in the open waiting area with dozens of other inmates curled up in chairs, talking on the free telephones and engaged in banal conversation with one another.

As Riggins completed her paperwork and handed the upgraded charge sheets to one of the records clerks, she exchanged nods of recognition with the woman. She recalled the same woman, whom she hadn't seen in ages, having processed her affidavits for the case. Ronald Cokley. This only succeeded in dredging up further memories, which again she pushed away.

Walking back out into the vehicle sally port and settling behind the wheel of her cruiser, Riggins waited for the large roll gate to yawn open before speeding back to headquarters. The small desk calendar next to her computer monitor had the number '159' written on today's date, Saturday, April 26th. 159 days until retirement. She'd begun this tracker first as a joke between her and another detective, until it had become something much more real in her mind. Once she'd gotten to day 182—the six-month mark—the very idea of leaving the career she'd begun at the state minimum of age nineteen had coalesced from just an abstract concept to a stark reality. She'd be gone by early October. No more death. No more weeping family members or phone calls in the middle of the night. She would be herself again. Her sentence, as they all joked, would finally be served.

Staring at the calendar and feeling herself stressed at the prospect of flipping even one more page, Riggins snatched the whole thing up and tossed it into the trash receptacle next to her desk.

BACK IN THE processing room, Eddie read the three charge sheets he'd just been given. All had been typed in bold, block letters. First: **ARMED ROBBERY / PRINCIPAL—Bond $50,000.** Then the last two sheets, even more alarming: **MURDER IN THE FIRST DEGREE—NO BOND.**

Never had he felt such a feeling of unreality, as if some theoretical door had slammed shut on him, and now he sat alone in a dark, cramped room with no way of escaping. As he finished reading the affidavits and their dry, official language detailing his alleged actions, he let them fall to the floor at his feet. He felt his world begin to spin and his mouth take on a funny metallic taste. *How did this happen?* a faraway voice screamed inside him; and before he passed out, crashing head-first onto the hard cement floor, he had a fleeting vision of a child on a swing, growing smaller and smaller in the distance until the only thing left in his consciousness was a tiny dot of light in an ever encompassing blanket of darkness.

EIGHT

THE STATE OF Florida's Twenty-First Judicial Circuit had for its criminal courthouse a large, antebellum inspired building rising three stories high, with a sprawling grassy courtyard adorned with ranks of solemn live oaks. Centering Springwood's small downtown area, the courthouse harkened more to a southern plantation than a modern edifice of law and justice. The building's white marble façade stood before yawning granite steps, which in turn led to a pair of towering solid oak doors. Two concrete columns rose on either side of the entrance like silent, century-old sentries.

To the right of the entrance stood a marble statue of a blindfolded Lady Justice. In one hand she held the obligatory scale, in the other a drawn sword. A group of attorneys gathered at the foot of the statue discussing legalese, and a young mother restrained her two young children who had attempted to climb up the statue's leg. A dark-eyed man in a tailored suit took the stairs purposefully, his movements confident and sure. He stood just shy of six feet, his thin but well-muscled physique standing testament to the countless hours he spent exerting himself in his private gym. Even his professional life had provided him with sufficient rigors to hone his mind and body into the weapon it had become. Often it demanded he keep himself in the best possible condition. On surprisingly thin legs that could squat three times his own body weight, the man reached the top of the staircase and took a moment to gaze at the statue. He felt the trace of a smile touch the edge of his lips as a thought came to him. How ironic that Lady Justice had been given a sword with which to swing blindly at her subjects. In a real-world application of law, she herself would be liable for the vast and unseen damage she would cause.

The man checked his watch—9:47 AM. His employer abhorred tardiness, which was why he'd arrived nearly a half hour before their scheduled appointment. He'd been forced to leave his pistol and favorite backup weapon—a Swiss-made carbon-bladed tactical knife—in his vehicle. An official exemption to the non-law-enforcement weapons ban could have been made on his behalf, seeing as his employer was none other than the head state attorney himself. But the business arrangement they'd entered into depended largely on discretion. Whispers would no doubt pass along the marbled courthouse hallways should it be discovered Mathias Hood himself had granted such a privilege to a civilian. Add in the fact that the man in his employ no longer existed in any state or federal databases—a virtual ghost—and those whispers could very well have turned to shouts.

The man passed uneventfully through the metal detector and collected his wallet and wristwatch from the x-ray conveyor belt. He then proceeded up the escalator to the state attorney's main office, located on the second floor. Once there, he waited patiently for several minutes until, at precisely ten fifteen, a blond-haired receptionist he recognized called his name and said Mr. Hood would now see him.

Nodding appreciatively, the man stood and approached a familiar-looking office door. He'd been here twice before, ostensibly for official court business. He'd done so again now, having called ahead with the tale of being an auditor. Straightening his tie, he knocked twice. From behind the door came a deep voice telling him to enter. He did, and after closing the heavy door behind him, stood at parade rest before the bald man seated at the desk.

"Paolo, you make me feel like a general when you stand like that. Relax and sit down."

"Just habit, sir." Paolo Bruzzi gave a slight nod of deference and chose instead to remain standing. Whatever other emotions hid behind his stoic countenance were either shielded by walled professionalism or did not exist at all. Years of secret missions in faraway locales had steeled him against distractions that did not relate to the job at hand.

"I am 'sir' to just about everyone else in this building, but most certainly not to my most valued associate. Please, Paolo, anything but that."

Paolo trained his dark eyes ahead and offered another deferential nod. "Whatever you please, Mr. Hood. You have work for me, I assume?"

Hood abandoned the papers at his desk, his features darkening. "Have you watched the news today?"

"You know I don't watch television."

"Of course," Hood said, producing the day's newspaper from his top desk drawer. He sat the paper down and indicated a front-page article. "An innocent man was murdered this past weekend," Hood stated, his features darkening even more. "Read it, and then I'll tell you what I want you to do."

Paolo picked up the paper and began reading the article.

LOCAL MAN CHARGED IN STORE SLAYING
Story by Annette Foster, Gazette staff writer

A Calusa County man was charged yesterday in connection with the robbery of a local convenience store and killing of an employee. Edward T. Grassle, 24, of Springwood, was additionally charged with the death of his alleged accomplice, Julius Sanders, 26, also of Springwood. According to Sheriff officials Grassle and Sanders entered the One-Stop convenience store on Meadow Drive just after ten o'clock Friday evening. Both men are believed to have committed a robbery before shooting and killing the store employee, Esteban Mendez-Rodriguez, of nearby Twin Rivers. During a subsequent pursuit, Sanders reportedly brandished a gun toward responding deputies, who shot and killed him. In keeping with agency policy, the deputy involved in the shooting was placed on routine paid administrative leave pending review by the state attorney's office.

Under Florida law, a person participating in a felony may be charged with murder if another person dies in relation to that felony. According to Sheriff Spokeswoman Leila Fernandez, Grassle faces murder charges due to being a principal to armed robbery and aggravated fleeing and eluding, both felonies.

Following his capture, Grassle was treated at a local hospital for injuries sustained in a vehicle crash, before being transported to the county jail. Detectives assigned to the case remained tight-lipped concerning any evidence or possible witnesses. Spokeswoman Fernandez stated her belief that the state attorney will soon move the case to the Grand Jury for formal indictment. "This case is especially troubling considering Grassle had just been released from prison several weeks ago," she said. "We have every reason to believe Mr. Grassle participated fully in this crime, and that the charges against him are justified."

Mr. Mendez-Rodriguez was a native of Cuba, arriving to the U.S. by flotilla at age sixteen. He leaves behind a wife, three grown children, and seven grandchildren. His widow said her husband was a hard-working man who loved to take his grand-children fishing and took long afternoon naps. "It all seems like a dream," Mrs. Mendez-Rodriguez told reporters as she clutched a photo of her late husband. "I do not know what will happen next. We are lost. I am lost." The deceased suspect, Julius Sand-ers, had no family of record. State records list him as having been self-employed and having several prior drug convictions. The tragedy marks the eighth reported homicide in Calusa County so far this year. In comparison, the county had six for all the previous year.

When he finished, Paolo set the paper back down and resumed his previous stance. "It would seem the situation is already handled, no?" he suggested. "One suspect dead, the other in jail charged with murder. It appears a novice could convince a jury of his guilt, from what the police already have. What further use can I be?"

Holding up one of the documents he'd been examining prior to Paolo's entrance, Hood consulted it as a man would a map to some secret treasure. "The survivor is named Edward Grassle. He would have remained a nobody to me, a mote in the vast justice system I preside over, had it not been for something I discovered this morning. Something priceless."

Paolo stood perfectly still, his silence his own response.

"Grassle has engaged in petty crimes, mostly. He did, however, just complete a five-year sentence in our fine state prison system for drug possession. Looking at his case, it appears he may have been a patsy, or simply accepted the blame for his friend. But that is unimportant. What is important is something I found during his invest this morning."

Hood handed Paolo a sheet of paper topped with state attorney letterhead. He scanned the document without any sign of understanding. "The only item of interest I see is he went through a name change at sixteen. Took back his mother's maiden name, I presume."

"Exactly," Hood said. "His mother was granted a divorce in absentia just before she passed away. She petitioned to have her son's name changed back to her maiden name as well. Call it a legacy gift."

"And?"

"And—knowing this case is sure to garner media attention due to the dead clerk having killed a robber just the year before, I took the initiative to look into the criminal history of Grassle's entire family, going as far back as state and federal records would go. Finding the truth is my specialty. And the truth I found both troubled and excited me."

Paolo's face twitched—a brief display of intrigue in a man who rarely became excited over anything.

"Grassle's father had been a low-level criminal. Only a few petty arrests in his twenties. Then I moved on to Grassle's *grandfather*. What I read shook me to my core. I stared at the page a full ten minutes, unable to believe what I'd seen. I checked state court documents and confirmed what in my heart I already knew. A divine coincidence. I felt as if God Himself had descended from heaven and gifted me Providence. Thomas Washburn—Grassle's grandfather. I gasped aloud when I read the name. The antagonist to my very lineage, Paolo."

Paolo's eyes opened as realization flooded into them. Suddenly he knew precisely what Hood had called him to his office for. His voice came deep and cold. "Your father's murderer."

Hood leaned back in his executive leather chair and steepled his fingers. "I want you to drop whatever else I have you working on. Immediately. I want your full attention on this case. I will handle Sheriff Driscoll. And Paolo—" Hood held up one finger. "I want you to notify the jail. Make sure Grassle is not..." He searched for the proper word. "Comfortable."

Hood twisted the ring around his finger as he allowed what he had just said to settle. Soon, he picked up a paper-clipped file and held it out for Paolo to take. The latter read it and, nodding his understanding, said, "I will become a detective to the detectives on the case. It is what I do best."

Hood stood and strode wordlessly to the large picture window that looked down over the sprawling courtyard below.

"Tomorrow would have been my father's eightieth birthday," he said, his deep voice reverent. "I have known no greater crime than his losing his life the way he did. No doubt he would still be alive today had that—" he drew a breath through his teeth— "had that *perversion* not occurred. Dumas said that life and fortune hang by a slender thread. I will see this man tried before the eyes of the law and be marched to the death chamber. My father will be avenged. If not by the one who committed the deed, then by one who carries his lineage. Until then, Grassle will endure the suffering his grandfather escaped."

The hint of a smile touched the corners of Paolo's mouth.

Hood moved his dark eyes across the courtyard that lay beyond the window. He stood silent for some time, the only sound in the office being the ticking clock. Paolo remained perfectly still. When Hood spoke again, it seemed as if he were standing alone and speaking to some inner version of himself instead of to Paolo.

"In my career I have seen our justice system make a mockery of the very tenets it swears to defend. The young college student gang-raped and beaten so badly she'd been left with irreversible brain damage, while her attackers snickered and sneered behind the shield of their attorneys. Do you know what would have happened had I not had the insight and fortitude to involve you? We had nothing a jury would have given us a conviction on. If we had not resorted to matters of our own choosing, not crept into the night to gather those items the law says we cannot have, or extracted information from others who would not ordinarily have given it without us changing their perspectives, then those smiling frat boys would still be living their happy lives in their happy homes. But we changed that, Paolo. *You* helped change that, and for that I am grateful." Hood approached Paolo and rested his hands atop the man's shoulders.

"The file on my desk has everything you will need to begin your work, including information on the detective team assigned to the case. I will personally supervise matters on this end."

Paolo nodded assuredly. "I will take care of everything, Mr. Hood. You have enabled me to do what keeps me alive inside. I am grateful."

Hood detected a flicker of emotion in Paolo's eyes, something he'd rarely seen before. Had some long-ago trauma truly caused the man to lust after the misery of others, or had some other thought brought the excited look? Even before hiring him as his personal investigator of sorts, Hood had heard stories of Paolo's brutal tendencies while the man had been in a CIA black-ops unit. Stories of such savagery that he had questioned his own decision to bring the man aboard. Whatever reason existed for the man's penchant for inflicting pain on others, Hood had filed it away in his mind for later exploration. In the meantime, he would enjoy the results, however they came. Donning a cool expression, Hood now offered his trusted personal investigator a placating smile and bade him goodbye.

Paolo executed an about-face and excused himself from the office. With the door closed, Hood placed a call from the burner phone he kept stored in a hidden and locked desk compartment. He'd been careful to switch the difficult-to-track anonymous cell phones several times a month, keeping them charged on a battery-operated device. Public records laws demanded his business lines fall under public scrutiny, and he would never have been foolish enough to use his personal line for such communication. Anticipating the upcoming conversation, he eased back into his chair as a familiar female voice answered on the ninth ring.

"Hello Lydia, this is Sandman," Hood said. "I'd like an appointment tonight."

A pause from the woman, then a purr as she answered, "This is short notice. But being you're one of my most valued customers, I'm sure I can accommodate you."

A contented smile creased the state attorney's normally expressionless face. "Good. Give me the same one as last time, and have her hair made up in ponytails."

What he intended to do required complete anonymity. Half of his ten thousand dollars per visit went toward its guarantee. Still, he had taken additional and painstaking methods to cloak his actions in a veil of secrecy so thick he'd enabled himself to indulge in his monthly hobby undetected for several years now. That many of the girls set out before him had been runaways, or brought into the country as virtual slaves, was no concern to him. At times, that thought alone made the experience all the better.

"And I'll use the ropes this time," he said before hanging up. "I'm in a special kind of mood today."

EDDIE DREAMED OF his former life, one he doubted he'd ever get to replicate as a free man again...

Fifteen years old and already six feet tall, looming over the casket trying his best not to cry. It wasn't any use. Tears streamed down his face in rivers. His chest hitched as his sobs came from a valley of the deepest despair he had ever known. The funeral director placed a hand on his shoulder and told him God had done His work, that now his mother no longer had to suffer. The director had witnessed similar scenes, far too many to count, and as was custom, he quietly patted Eddie on the back before returning to his stand at the end of the pew.

After the service Eddie and Jules silently watched the attendants load the casket into the hearse. Jules had allowed Eddie a bit of privacy and had not intruded on his grief. Eddie's sobs had since become more intermittent. He felt embarrassed to have become so emotional, since most of the funeral guests were either local townspeople whom he did not know well or employees of the funeral home. His only known relative—an aunt from Oregon he had never met—had made the trip. She explained that since Eddie's mother had arranged for him to live with her, they would be traveling together back to Oregon the following day. Five years of living alone with his mother had hardened Eddie around the edges, like a halved apple left on the counter. Eddie had told his aunt he didn't wish to live in Oregon, and that he had already made plans to stay with Jules's family. This had of course been a lie; Jules had no more family than Eddie. His aunt had either not cared to verify this or felt relief over the sudden freedom from her promise to her sister; she had patted Eddie on the head, telling him to call her if he ever needed anything. So now, as the hearse's rear door slammed shut, Eddie turned to the only family he had left in the world. The spiky-haired kid next to him didn't say a word. The two had become sort of psychic brothers in their three years of friendship. A pat on the back and one tight-lipped nod of the head from his pal and Eddie knew exactly what had been conveyed.

He and Jules rode in silence in the back of his aunt's car as she chain-smoked cigarettes all the way to the cemetery. This struck Eddie as somewhat ironic given the fact his mother had never smoked a single cigarette in all her life yet had died from lung cancer. When they arrived at the cemetery Eddie noticed the grave had already been dug, and as he stepped from the car, he observed two cemetery workers leaning against a nearby backhoe, also smoking. A fresh pile of exposed dirt sat next to the grave, a green tarp lying folded next to it. Eddie made eye contact with one of the workers, who dutifully stood and nudged his partner to help him cover the dirt pile with the tarp. Once they completed this, they wandered off, presumably to give the family a bit of privacy.

After the graveside service Eddie asked his aunt if she would give him a few minutes alone. She said of course, to take as much time as he needed, and she ambled down the slope to wait in the car. Jules stayed at Eddie's side, his arm draped over his shoulder, and together they said a silent prayer while looking down at the casket in the bottom of the grave.

'Hey, wanna climb up?' Jules asked after a moment of silence.

Eddie stared into the grave then back at his friend.

'No, you big lug. I meant that...' Jules looked up toward a towering oak tree that overhung the grave. 'Don't you think it's kinda cool they buried your mom next to such an awesome tree? Look at that perch.' He pointed to a naturally flattened area about fifteen feet up, where the trunk split into a series of thick branches spreading in multiple directions. Great tendrils of Spanish moss hung from the branches, obscuring the perch from angles other than from where they stood directly below it. Eddie shrugged.

'C'mon, it'll be cool,' Jules prodded. 'You can call it the Mother Tree in honor of your mom.' And just like that, Jules backed up and ran toward the tree at full speed. Planting a foot against its natural bend, he used his forward momentum to propel himself upward, grasping onto the lowest hanging branch. From there he pulled himself up far enough so that his elbows rested on the perch's natural flatness. Soon enough he was able to pull himself completely onto the ledge. Even from directly below, Eddie couldn't see him.

'What the hell are you doing?' Eddie hollered into the tree. He took a glance down the slope to where his aunt leaned against the hood of the car, smoking and gazing off into the distance.

Jules poked his head over the perch's edge and waved. 'I think this is the beginning of a beautiful friendship,' he called down in his best Humphrey Bogart impression.

Eddie thought for a moment, then smiled as recollection settled on him. 'Casablanca.'

'Yep!'

The two boys had spent the summer watching dozens of old VHS movies in Jules's foster parents' garage. They'd watched and re-watched everything from action to comedies to horror flicks, sipping stolen beer from the neighborhood market and practicing impressions of famous actors. One of Eddie's favorites had been Arnold Schwarzenegger. He'd honed it so well Jules had invariably been left in stitches every time Eddie used it.

'Get to the chaaaaaapahh,' Eddie yelled upward to Jules in his best Arnie impersonation.

'Predator. Too easy,' Jules responded. He'd propped himself up on his elbows, his face animated. 'Make me work for it.'

Eddie stole a glance back toward the bottom of the slope. His aunt had now become engaged in conversation with another woman wearing a large, flower-topped hat.

'Okay. Try this one: "You should clone yourself."'

Jules squinted in thought. 'Don't tell me, don't tell me!' He paused before his face came alive. 'I got it. So, then the other guy says, "Why is that, so I can understand your unique perspective?"'

Eddie grinned and delivered the punchline in his perfect Arnie voice. '"No, so you can go fuck yourself!"'

Jules craned his head toward the sky and shrieked laughter. 'The Sixth Day!'

'Good job!'

Eddie backed up a few steps and took his turn climbing up the tree. Before long, the two friends lay side-by-side looking down through the hanging Spanish moss to the open grave below.

'Damn, bro, I'm really sorry about your mom,' Jules said, draping an arm across Eddie's shoulders.

'Now I have nobody, and nowhere to go,' Eddie said. 'My aunt leaves for Oregon tomorrow. I lied and told her I was staying with you.'

'You can totally stay with me. Even if it's just for a few months, then we can both jump around and live wherever. We're gonna grow old together, you and me. Now we're like real brothers.' Jules removed a pocketknife from his black jeans and unfolded the blade. Without saying a word, he etched both their names into the inside of the trunk, with the words BEST BROS 4EVER underneath.

Eddie smiled, feeling morose. His head felt as though it weighed a hundred pounds. Tears threatened to return but didn't; he'd cried them all away. When he thought about it more, Jules had been right. Jules had never known his parents and Eddie had, albeit for only a portion of his youth. His mother's strength during those months following his father leaving had shown Eddie what true resolve meant. She'd been a strong woman for sure, stronger than Eddie himself. That strength and her calm, loving demeanor were two things he would miss the most. That and her baking. God, those pies!

From the road below, Eddie's aunt walked gingerly up the slope, moving between the headstones until she came to the open grave. The workers had finished their break and were just setting up to re-fill it. His aunt called out Eddie's name several times and looked in all directions, shielding her eyes from the late-morning sun. Not finding the boys, *she even stole a peek inside the grave. Unable to find them, she stood with hands on hips for a full minute as both boys lay side-by-side on the perch, cupping their hands over their mouths to stifle their giggling. They watched as she eventually ambled back down the slope and sat inside the car. A thin line of smoke soon drifted out the open car window, and music from the car stereo reached them in the breeze. Eddie rested his chin on folded hands and stared off into clouds that had begun to gather in the distance. After the workers filled the grave and left, the boys climbed down the tree and headed back toward the car. Halfway there, Jules patted his pockets and stopped. 'Aw, man, I left my knife up in the tree!' Eddie said they didn't have time to go back and get it, that his aunt had seen them and was waving them on to leave. As they slid into the backseat together, Eddie watched the grave and the tree above it diminish in the distance, until it disappeared around a hill. Fifteen years old and all alone, he thought. Except for Jules, of course. Jules, who had said the two of them would grow old together.*

Eddie didn't doubt that one bit.

NINE

COUNTY JAIL DIFFERED from state prison in one major respect: while jail inmates spent an average of a few months incarcerated, prison inmates (those convicted of felony crimes) spent anywhere from one year to a lifetime behind bars. The vast majority of county inmates were short timers, those waiting hours or days to post bail for crimes ranging from shoplifting and drunk driving to lesser felonies like car theft and burglary. Eddie had seen jail inmates get booked in then released almost immediately on their own recognizance or by loved ones paying bail of a couple hundred dollars. He had also seen the other side, where state inmates had oftentimes been serving years- or even decades-long sentences. The mood of each institution had been vastly different as well. Even the officers had had differing attitudes. While staff at the state prison had been dour and carried themselves largely like temporary residents themselves, the county jail staff had seemed much more spirited. Eddie had chalked most of that up to the fact that the jail population was, by nature, transitory. Inmates came and went on a regular basis. The longest he'd ever heard of a person remaining in the county jail had been five years, awaiting a complicated murder trial. In contrast, while in prison Eddie had once met a ninety-two-year-old convict serving a 230-year sentence for murdering his entire family. The man had arrived in prison just three years after the end of World War II.

Now, a week after being released from the hospital and booked, Eddie eased his way off his bunk and stood in line for recreation. He hadn't been outside since arriving here since his medical condition had forbade it. His ribs had already begun healing; now it only hurt when he twisted in certain ways. Having been transferred to a general population unit the day before, Eddie felt grateful for finally being able to stand from his bed and do more than watch mindless television. He stood in a line of twenty other inmates of various sizes and backgrounds in a gloomy hallway just outside their cellblock. After each man had been individually frisked (Eddie's frisk had been performed by a square-jawed officer who reminded him of the actor Dolph Lundgren), the group was led into a gated vestibule. There, they stood for five minutes in the growing heat, their bodies pressed together and the collective funk threatening to overpower Eddie's senses. He began to feel dizzy as men farted and belched, pushing up against one another, some of them grumbling about toes being stepped on and at least a few homosexual jokes. At last, an electronic buzzing sound announced the opening of the outer door, and the relieved group spilled out through a heavy metal door into the late-morning sunshine.

Under a deep blue sky, the group spread out across the square-shaped yard. Shielding his eyes from the sun, Eddie took in his surroundings. He realized he hadn't been in this particular yard before, having been housed in a more heavily populated area of the facility during his short time here five years ago. He watched as a group of black inmates quickly shed their uniform shirts and began a game of pick-up basketball on the yard's only court, a plain metal pole stuck into the center of the yard with a net-less hoop bolted onto the backboard. Another group, this one made up of white inmates, congregated at the far end of the yard. The yard itself consisted of an all-concrete surface and took up about the same space as two standard basketball courts. The yard fence itself had three sides and stood twelve feet high. Thick-gauged chicken wire had been attached to the interior of the fence's top half, which Eddie knew was to thwart inmates from climbing to the top. Not that anyone crazy enough to do so would try anyway, he figured, taking into account the Y-shaped barbed wire strung across the top of the fence. As if this barrier wasn't enough, a glistening coil of razor wire stretched out along all three sides of the Y-shaped fence top. Anyone lucky enough to even get to the top would be cut to shreds, Eddie reasoned. And that wasn't all. A free-standing guard tower stood at the far end of the yard, just feet from the fence. A fixed iron ladder extended from the ground to the tower's platform. Standing fifteen feet above the ground, the platform provided the deputy standing there a commanding view of the entire space. A small, windowed enclosure sat surrounded by a concrete catwalk, on which the deputy now stood with one boot propped against the metal railing. Eddie watched the deputy—a fat, middle-aged man with a dour expression—adjust his slung shotgun as he began counting the inmates.

Since the jail building itself took up one side of the yard, the other three directions provided Eddie a grand view through the fence. Several trees dotted the area, one standing about twenty yards beside the tower and well away from the fence line. A grassy area about fifty yards wide stretched out past the yard, giving way to yet another wire-topped fence; the jail's perimeter barrier, which stretched around the entire facility, Eddie knew. From his prior stint here, enabled by looking through housing block windows and from the various recreation yards he'd been in, to now, he felt the full power of incarceration fall over him. And if all of these physical barriers hadn't been reminder enough of being shut away, he eyed the thick, formidable woods that stood just beyond the perimeter fence in all directions.

Eddie watched as a second deputy appeared from the outside of a chained gate in the perimeter fence. *Just a kid*, Eddie thought as he watched the deputy twice drop a keyring from his pocket before fumbling with a chained gate. Skinny as a bean pole and still bearing facial acne, the young man tried several keys before managing to unlock the gate, step through it, then lock it behind him. Almost tripping over a rut in the ground (eliciting laughter from the inmates) he hurried into position beneath the guard tower. Eddie noted the glint of sunlight against the young deputy's left hand—a wedding band. *Dumb kid probably knocked up his childhood sweetheart*, Eddie thought, and at once thought of himself and Clarissa.

"You're late, dipshit!" the tower deputy hollered, casting a wither-ing glare down to his young partner. "You're supposed to be out here *before* the pukes come out. Don't they teach you newbies anything?"

The young deputy looked up sheepishly, shielding his eyes from the morning sun. The shotgun he balanced in the crook of one skinny arm made him look even smaller. "Sorry, sir. I forgot my keys and had to go back and get them."

A group of inmates who'd overheard this exchange sounded a collective "*ohhhhh,*" as kids would to one of their own who'd gotten in trouble. The tower deputy told them to "put a sock in it," reminding them to keep out of the yellow painted areas. Finished counting the inmates, he brought a chair from inside the enclosure and set it down on the catwalk. He plopped his ample rear end onto the chair, leaned it back against the enclosure and proceeded to remove his shoes and socks. When he rolled up his pant legs, exposing his fat white calves, an inmate near Eddie offered up a wolf whistle before melting into a group of other inmates. The deputy, apparently believing Eddie had been the one to whistle, shot him a baleful look.

"Do it again, asshole," he dared.

Eddie looked around for support, but the other inmates all looked away. "It wasn't me, sir," he said, offering both palms in his own defense.

"*It wasn't me, sir,*" the officer aped in a childlike tone. He stood and addressed the rest of the inmates as a whole. "Any more chick-enshit remarks from anyone else and you'll all go back inside!" Apparently satisfied with the smattering of "yes boss's," the officer sat back down and reached into his pants cargo pocket. Removing a bag of sunflower seeds, he bit off one corner and poured some into a Styrofoam cup before placing it between his arm and his potbelly. Propping his feet against the rail, his shotgun laid across his lap, the officer flipped his sunglasses down over his eyes and crammed a handful of seeds into his mouth.

Shifting his gaze back to the yard, Eddie spotted a white-haired Hispanic man in his sixties walking by himself around the yard. A three-foot-wide area had been painted yellow around the fence's inner perimeter. In various places within this yellow zone were the words **KEEP OUT** in black lettering.

"Schultz," the man suddenly said.

"Excuse me?"

"Officer Schultz," he said, pointing up to the tower. "Nasty man, he is. Most of the deputies here are okay, but this one has poison in his heart. He worked long time with—how do you say—outside workers?"

"You mean the road crews?" Eddie said.

"Yes. But he got in trouble. Boss man put him here to watch us instead. Since then, he very mean to everyone. Do not make him see you." The old man next pointed to the young deputy, who having sat in a sliver of shade beneath the tower offered up a friendly wave to Eddie and the old man. "Officer Nady. He is new, just one month. He is not like Schultz. He has good in his heart." The old man offered a crooked smile and stuck out his hand. "I am Ramon. I see you around here since you come in. You not like talking to nobody?"

Eddie shook the man's hand, surprised at the strength in its grip.

Ramon laughed. "Not bad for an old man, no?"

Eddie introduced himself and the two moved toward the back fence, out of earshot of both deputies. "I guess I just haven't been in a talking mood," Eddie said glumly. "I came in a week ago. I'm sure you heard what happened."

Ramon nodded knowingly. "Yes, I hear talk of you. You have been in here before, no?"

Eddie relayed the story of his previous trip to jail, then continued talking with Ramon for the next forty-five minutes. The conversation moved from family to women, and finally to sports. Eddie marveled at how much the two of them had in common. Ramon had played baseball as a young man in his native Puerto Rico, a fact that brought a sparkle to Eddie's eye. "My whole childhood I dreamed of playing in the majors," he said, and Ramon responded with, "It is never too late," and slapped Eddie on the back. As they spoke, Officer Nady stood to patrol the perimeter of the fence-line. He stopped near where they stood.

"Howdy, fellas," he offered with a nod. Eddie and Ramon looked to each other with raised eyebrows.

Eddie shrugged and returned the deputy's nod. "Hey there, boss. We were just talking baseball. You ever play?"

Nady's entire face lit up. "Just about every time I had a chance. But I have flat feet and can't run worth a lick. After a time, my mom pulled me out and made me learn the piano." He smiled to reveal a sizable gap between his front teeth. With his boyish face and rail-thin physique, he looked to Eddie like a kid dressed up as a policeman for Halloween.

"No shame in the piano," Eddie said. "I wish I'd learned to play something."

"Music is the sport of the soul," Ramon said, fluttering his fingers across an imaginary keyboard.

"Yeah, I suppose so," Nady said, smiling. He stood several feet from his side of the fence, with both thumbs tucked into his pockets and his shotgun slung over one shoulder. He continued chatting with Eddie and Ramon, who themselves stood just shy of the yellow painted area. Eddie wasn't accustomed to speaking with an officer so casually, but after a few minutes he began speaking more freely about cars and women and ultimately back to his greatest passion, sports. When Ramon made a joke about his wife's habit of turning on the vacuum whenever a ballgame had entered its most dramatic moment, both Eddie and Officer Nady laughed out loud. Moments later, a shout came down from the recreation tower above them.

"Time's up, ladies! Everyone inside!"

The sun had risen higher in the eastern sky and now shined brightly into Eddie's eyes. Squinting up toward the tower, he saw Officer Schultz standing at the railing, glaring down at him. The pot-bellied officer spat out several uneaten seeds, narrowly missing Eddie and landing on the ground several feet from him. A flock of birds roosting in the tree closest to the tower exploded in flight, landing in a flurry of beaks and flapping wings on the ground as they fought for the seeds. They gobbled them all before returning to their roost in the tree. Having watched this, Eddie failed to notice the other inmates lining up single file at the recreation yard door. He now stood alone at the edge of the yard, facing away from the other inmates and just inches from the yellow painted area.

"That means you too, new puke!" Schultz yelled down at Eddie. Nady motioned for Eddie to fall into line, then he conducted a count. He gave a thumbs-up to Schultz, who unlatched his radio from his belt. "All accounted for," Schultz spoke into his radio. "Twenty-one out, twenty-one coming in."

Schultz watched Eddie fall back into line, his eyes narrowing. After Eddie and the rest of the inmates had disappeared through the door, Schultz fished his keys from his pocket and unlocked the grate that covered the tower ladder and swung it open. The grate prevented any unwanted persons from climbing up the ladder and onto the cat-walk from below. With the fixed iron ladder now accessible, he slung his shotgun over one shoulder and made the fifteen-foot descent. Reaching the ground, he summoned Nady to where he stood. "That's the asshole who offed the store clerk last week. I'd be careful who you make friends with."

Nady shrugged. "I was just trying to be friendly, sir. They seem like okay guys. Dunno if it matters much what these guys are in here for, I suppose. At least that's what they taught us in—"

"Forget everything they taught you in the academy," Schultz said, disgust ringing in his voice. "And don't forget who the pukes are. Animals, every last one of them. Most of them would cut your throat first chance they had, if they knew they'd get away with it."

Nady rubbed the back of his neck, seeming not sure what to say. The two of them waited until a housing unit staff member radioed the all-clear, signaling that the recreation corridor had been emptied of all inmates, and all doors leading to the yard locked. Only then were they permitted to exit the area. They did so now through fence gates, securing each with the provided heavy padlock and chain. Having reached the exit through the outer perimeter fence, they walked toward the armory where unloading and securing of all weapons was done. As he went, Schultz looked out at the expanse of woodland surrounding the jail. He'd give anything to be back out there, instead of inside the jail proper with the collective misery that existed within its walls. Back where he'd begun his career, and after just one month of re-discovering his distaste for working side-by-side with inmates in this environment, he decided that if he were forced into this situation, he would at least find a project on which to direct his displeasure.

"Watch your blind side, new puke," he muttered to himself, spitting onto the ground and casting a scowl toward the awaiting jail interior.

TEN

Having returned from recreation, Eddie had just lain down on his thin mattress when one of the housing officers yelled his name from the barred vestibule. He slid off his bunk and reported gate-side without hesitation. He knew the officers hated repeating themselves.

"Yes, ma'am?" Eddie said to the burly female officer standing at the gate.

"You have an attorney visit," the officer said, opening the inner door to the twenty-man unit.

Eddie raised an eyebrow to several of his cellmates then stepped into the vestibule. After closing the inner gate then opening the outer one, the officer led him from his cellblock to another area of the jail consisting of a series of small meeting rooms along a hallway. The officer ushered him into one of these rooms, where a young-looking attorney in an ill-fitting suit sat flipping through a pile of paperwork.

"Please, sit down," the attorney said without looking up. The man reminded Eddie of a school librarian. As he flipped back and forth through the stack of paperwork, a confused look came over his face. Seeing this, the female officer raised her eyebrows at Eddie and lipped the words 'good luck' before closing the door.

Alone with the attorney, Eddie took a seat opposite him and waited patiently while the man continued flipping through his paperwork. He watched as the man removed a handkerchief from his coat pocket and dabbed at his nose. Eddie sat in silence for another minute until the attorney finally looked up and offered Eddie a weak smile.

"Excuse me if I don't shake hands, but I have a cold," said the attorney. "My name is Philip Passmore and I'm from the Public Defender's office. I've been assigned to represent you." He dabbed at his nose again. "As I'm sure you're aware, you have been charged with some very serious crimes, Mr. Grassle."

Eddie looked down to his folded hands atop the table. "Yes, sir."

"Do you understand what felony murder is?"

"I think so," Eddie said with a sigh. "I guess it means I can't get out on bail. Not that anyone would bail me out anyway."

A whistling sound escaped the attorney's throat as he dabbed at his nose again. "Well, it's much more than that. But yes, it does mean you are being held on no bond. That's per state statute. I can't even argue for a bond in your case." He leaned over the file of papers and lowered his voice as if he didn't wish for anyone outside the door to hear him. "Because of your murder charges, a grand jury must hear the evidence against you. If they find enough evidence to hand over an indictment—and by all indications, they will—you will be held here until your trial."

Eddie tried to swallow but felt his throat constrict. He'd known full well how serious his charges were, but the shock of his first week here had yet to completely wear off. Murder. As serious as it came. And yet, until now the information on his arrest paperwork and the ramblings of other inmates who looked upon him with pity hadn't solidified completely in his mind. Everything still seemed dream-like. He'd spent his first few days here in the infirmary, waking up to a recurring dream of the robbery and car chase. Even after having moved to normal housing, he'd walked around like a character in his own movie. At any time, he'd expected a director to yell 'cut!' and all the other inmates around him to stop what they were doing and tell him 'great scene' as they patted him on the back. But in the time it had taken the nose-dripping attorney to deliver his introduction, Eddie's mind reeled back into reality with the suddenness of a slamming door. He felt like throwing up.

"But I didn't kill anybody," Eddie professed.

"Let me explain something to you, Mr. Grassle—"

"Eddie. You can call me Eddie."

"Yes. Fine. Eddie then. Let me explain something to you. Under Florida law, you can be charged with this crime even if you did not actually pull a trigger, or stab with a knife, or strangle with your own hands. The mechanism of death does not matter to the courts. If a jury believes you engaged in another felony and *because* of that offense someone else dies, you can be charged with first degree murder. That's basically what has happened here since you've also been charged with armed robbery. The only punishment allowed by Florida law for first degree murder is life in prison without the possibility of parole. Or the death penalty if the state chooses. It doesn't appear as though you meet the aggravating circumstances for that, however."

Eddie's vision blurred to the point he had to steady himself against the table to avoid fainting. Passmore either didn't seem to notice this or care enough to comment.

"Once the grand jury returns an indictment—and again, this is assuming they do—my team and I will meet with you again. Probably in several weeks to prepare for your formal arraignment. It is during that court action that you will first be allowed to enter a plea—"

"A plea!" Eddie exclaimed, his voice sounding as if it had come from someone else. "I'm innocent. Don't the cops know that? I was just along for the ride. Jules shot that man. I don't know why he did it, but he did. If I'd known what he was going to do, I never would've gotten in the car with him." Eddie put his head in his hands, unreality causing his head to swim even further.

Passmore sniffled and dabbed at his nose again. He produced a series of papers from the file and laid them down with a here-is-something-unpleasant hand motion. If the attorney felt any amount of empathy for the desperate man across from him, his expression didn't betray it.

"This is where we have a problem, Eddie. You just served five years for possession of a controlled substance with intent to sell. Your release occurred well within the window of time that any subsequent criminal sanctions can be enhanced, should you be convicted of any other crimes. A judge will not be sympathetic to you. You won't be trusted, since it appears you were released from prison and almost immediately re-offended. I've viewed the surveillance tapes. Although it's true your accomplice shot the clerk, it appears you facilitated the crime."

"Facilitated? That sounds like I was helping him!"

"Mr. Grassle...Eddie, let's not panic. My job is to explore a worst-case scenario for you."

Eddie grasped the edge of the fixed metal table to steady himself. He felt that if he didn't hold on to something he might float away. "What do you mean 'let's not panic?' I'm the one being charged with murder here. I didn't have a clue Jules even had a gun, let alone that he was going to rob that store. I tried to help that man after he got shot—"

Passmore appeared to be finished with this aspect of the conversation. He offered up both hands, his expression insouciant. "You'll have plenty of time to give a written statement to one of the investigators from our office. I am here simply to inform you of what you can expect in the next few weeks. I want—no, I *need* you to understand the gravity of the situation here."

Eddie searched his mind for words but found nothing to express the indignation coursing through him. He felt as if he were the butt of someone's sick joke, like re-runs of the old *Candid Camera* television show his mother used to watch.

"Here is my business card," Passmore said, handing it over. "The second number is for the investigator assigned to your case. Her name is Rebecca. If you have any questions or have anything important you need to discuss before I see you again, give her a call. Until then, try to stay calm. This will be a long process."

A lump grew in the back of Eddie's throat. He struggled to articulate his next words. "Can I ask you one thing, Mr. Passmore?"

"I'll answer the best I can."

"Is there any way I can petition the judge so I can leave and come back? Even for a day? I know it sounds stupid. I—I think I'd be better about this if I got at least part of a day to handle something I missed doing the day after this happened. I've heard of inmates getting day trips with a judge's order. For funerals and other family things."

"Eddie. You are charged with very serious—"

"I know what I'm charged with!" Eddie yelled, his fists coming down so hard on the metal table it reverberated like a gong. The female officer posted outside the door peeked her head inside and asked if everything was alright.

Passmore waved her away. "Yes, we're fine. He's just upset."

The officer looked between Eddie and Passmore and offered a nod of understanding. Once the door closed again, Passmore gathered up his papers and shoved them back into his briefcase. "I'll be honest with you, Eddie. The process for trying a murder case takes at least a year, usually much longer if a defendant waives their right for a speedy trial. We can talk more about your options the next time we speak. For right now I suggest you accept being here for the long haul. I've dealt with the superintendent of this jail before, Mr. Devereux. He has final say on any inmate being granted a furlough, assuming a judge agrees to it. I can tell you that our office doesn't even forward requests for them anymore because they never get approved. So just get that out of your mind right now."

Eddie turned the business card over in his hand, noticing his own growing fingernails. "You know, I can't even use a pair of fingernail clippers in here," he said with a huff. "The officers always say to wait, that they'll look for them. Or that they're broken. Everything in here is like that." He sighed, looking into the attorney's eyes. "It's like being stuck in a nightmare you can't wake up from. Have you ever felt like that?"

Passmore stood without answering Eddie's question. "I'll be getting back with you, Mr. Grassle."

There it was. Back to formalities. Passmore knocked on the door and the female officer held it open for him. Without looking back, the attorney mumbled some half-hearted words of encouragement before he slipped out the door and was gone.

Not much of the conversation registered to Eddie as he returned to his cell. The usual sights, sounds and smells of jail passed his fog-like senses. Keys clanked; doors slammed. Men, both officer and inmate, yelled one thing or another. The collective funk of groups of human beings, some who hadn't bathed in days, hung in the air like a live thing. Something on the edge of Eddie's memory toyed with him as he lay back onto his bunk, some point he felt he should have made to the attorney but had been unable to remember.

Eddie studied the lines in the concrete block ceiling. His thoughts wandered—from his time growing up, to his friendship with Jules, to the early days with Clarissa. No matter where his mind went, it seemed to always settle on how the sky would have looked had he made it to the park that next day, how Liam would have screamed with glee as Eddie swung him higher and higher into the air. He lay this way until the officers hollered for lockdown eight hours later. He'd ignored the call for dinner, a foul-smelling stew that caused a symphony of farts from the other inmates around him. He wasn't hungry anyway and wasn't sure he ever wanted to eat again.

Now as a few of his other cellmates wrote letters or played hushed games of checkers in the dim light, Eddie slipped into a deep sleep and dreamed of him and Liam laughing and playing in the park as if nothing were amiss in the world. Everything was just as it had been meant to be. In the dream Eddie told Liam he was sorry for not being there before, that he promised to be the father he had never been. But then dream-Eddie suddenly found himself wrapped in chains, with faceless members of his past pulling at him. Moments before being dragged away, Eddie reached out and grasped Liam's hand. The boy squeezed it and told him it was okay, that he wouldn't worry because he knew his daddy loved him and would come back for him someday.

EDDIE AWOKE IN a cold sweat. His heart pounded in his chest and for a moment he thought he'd awoken back in his apartment. Once his pulse slowed and his eyes adjusted to the dim light, he realized where he was. Unsure of the time, he rolled over and began to fall back asleep when his eyes snapped open. Somehow, deep in his subconscious, he must have realized what he'd wanted to tell the attorney.

The girl.

Eddie sat bolt upright and slapped a hand to his forehead. Of course. As sleep fell away from him his mind reorganized, and he chided himself for forgetting to mention her. *What had her name been? Janey? June? Something with a 'J' for sure.* Eddie jumped down from his bunk and paced the ten-by-fifteen-foot cell as he continued to search his memory. Sure, he'd told the detectives, but they weren't on his side. They'd been the ones to put him here, after all. Clearing his mind the best he could, he closed his eyes and re-played the scene in his mind. He, standing next to the register, holding his hands out, trying to calm her. She, hands to her face, clearly terrified, telling him her name.

"Jessica!" he shouted out loud. Someone in an adjacent cell shushed him, but he felt too excited to care. Yes, Jessica. He repeated her name over and over under his breath, and his pacing intensified. Remembering the business card, he fumbled through the scattered paperwork Passmore had given him. Finding it, he scanned to the bottom name on the card: *Rebecca Conti, Public Defender Investigator.* Passmore had said to give her a call if Eddie had any useful information to share before their next meeting. Excitement rushing through him, Eddie leaped to the closed cell gate and tried to read the clock at the end of the gangway. He only made out the long hand, which indicated the quarter hour. How long had he been asleep? He couldn't be sure. But it didn't feel that late in the night, and he knew the officers wouldn't turn the telephones on until eight the next morning. He envisioned the phone call: *Hello, Ms. Conti. My name is Eddie. Eddie Grassle. Mr. Passmore spoke with me yesterday and told me to contact you in case I had information to give. There was a girl in the store that night. She saw everything. She works at a place called—what was it—yes, the Honeybee. It's a diner. If you could just find her—*

Grasping the cell bars, Eddie stood at the gate for another twenty minutes until an officer came walking down the corridor whistling an old country tune. Eddie extended his arm between the bars and waved it wildly.

"Sir, please, can you tell me what time it is?"

"What you need to know the time for, got a hot date?" He threw a cruel grin Eddie's way as he passed by. After several more steps he stopped in his tracks, his head cocking to the side. A queer look came over his face then, as if he'd just remembered something interesting.

"Hey, you're the guy who smoked the convenience store clerk last month, right?"

Eddie pressed his face closer to the cold metal bars, positioning his eye as far through the space as he could to read the clock on the control room wall. Quarter past two in the morning. Stepping back from the bars, he wondered whether it would even be worth answering the deputy's question. Deciding he had nothing to lose, he said, "Yes, I was arrested for that. I won't waste your time telling you I didn't do it. I'm sure you've heard it a thousand times before." He paused, noting the officer's expression had hardened considerably. "Look, I really need to use the phone in the morning, and I know it gets hogged by the old-timers as soon as we come off lockdown. Is there any way you guys can make sure I get a quick call? I'll only need five minutes."

From a neighboring cell came a gruff voice, thick with sleep, "Shut the fuck up, new guy! You keep me up and it's gonna be a long day for you tomorrow."

The officer grinned, tilting his head in the voice's direction. "I guess there's your answer. Sucks to be locked up, huh?" He offered a half-salute before continuing his rounds. Climbing back onto his bunk, Eddie ran the predicament over in his head until he decided on a plan of action. As soon as the unit lifted from lockdown, he would race to the telephone and stake his territory. Five minutes. That's all he would need. He knew that calls to the PD's office were free; if the investigator didn't pick up, he'd leave a detailed voice mail. He found himself wishing he'd remembered to mention the woman earlier, but as his mother used to say, 'If wishes were horses, beggars would ride.'

Eddie couldn't sleep the rest of the night. He listened to his cellmates' snoring and occasional passing of gas and began timing the footsteps of the officers as they made their twice-an-hour rounds. He declined the four AM breakfast: 'shank,' the euphemism for the chipped beef and instant potato concoction that smelled the same going in as it did out. When the lights went up and the cell gates rolled open just after eight AM, Eddie rushed to the lone wall-mounted telephone. Taking a furtive glance around, he found no one had yet to even emerge from the collection of four-man cells that formed this unit. His fingers trembling, he dialed the investigator's number. Two rings, then four, then ten, until after the twelfth ring a woman on the other end picked up and answered with a tired sounding, "Public Defender's office, Investigations."

His tongue tied itself into a knot as he struggled to find the right words. He heard ruffling of papers on the other end, then an irritated sigh. "Hello, is anyone there?"

Finally, "Yes! Is Rebecca Conti in?" He could hear his own pounding heartbeat in his ears.

"This is she. Our office doesn't open for another hour, but I suppose I can help you now. What is your name?"

A great weight seemed to lift from his chest. He propped one elbow against the wall, his lips mouthing a silent 'thank you.' "My name is—"

A voice behind him, commanding and direct, cut him off. He turned around and saw an officer standing three steps from him with hands on hips, the same officer he'd asked the time from just hours before. "Hang up the phone," he said, his voice blunt.

"But my call just went through," Eddie explained. "It's an investigator from the—"

"I don't care who it is. I said hang up the phone, or I'll do it for you."

Eddie blinked. He looked from the officer to the phone receiver, then back again. "But sir, I just need five minutes."

The officer, six-foot-five and solidly built, stepped forward in one giant stride and snatched the phone receiver from Eddie's hand. He slammed it down on the cradle so hard it made an audible chiming noise from somewhere deep inside its guts.

"Do I look like someone who actually gives a fuck what you need?" the officer said with a sneer. "Just got orders to keep you off the phones. No calls for you, not to nobody. Go pack up your shit for relocation."

Eddie looked around to various inmates who had awoken to the noise. Each of them averted their eyes when the officer stared back at them. "Where am I going?"

"To the lockdown unit. One-man cell."

"But why?"

"Order comes from the superintendent. I don't ask why, so neither should you. Pack your shit, or else I'll do it and might just happen to forget your blanket."

Eddie stared at the officer. A muscle in the man's jaw twitched, and as Eddie contemplated reaching out for the telephone—if for no other reason than out of principle—he saw the well-built officer clench his fist. Eddie decided a broken jaw or crushed eye socket would do little to help his own cause.

"Yes sir," he managed, and went off to pack his belongings. When he finished, another officer appeared at the cell gate and, together with the first, they marched Eddie down a twisting corridor toward a dungeon-like housing unit with **ISOLATION BLOCK** stenciled on the wall in stark black letters. Shown into a small six-by-nine-foot cell, Eddie regarded his new home with resignation. *What did I do to deserve this?* he wondered. The solid metal door banged closed behind him and the heavy deadbolt clanged home. Austere to the extreme, the cell consisted of a fixed concrete bunk, a stainless-steel toilet/sink combination, and a small metal writing table complete with a stool fixed to the wall. A small, thick-paned window and a lockable food trap were the only views he had out the cell, and from experience Eddie knew the trap stayed closed except for the issuance of food trays and other official matters. He placed the business card on his wall-mounted table and plopped onto his bunk. He stared so hard at the wall he imagined boring a hole through it with his eyes.

His mind returned to the old man he'd met during his time in prison, the one who'd been on the inside since just after World War II. Eddie considered what it would be like living to that age, watching the decades pass and missing out on the world that had certainly forgotten him. He'd always known a convict does his time one day at a time, but as he began counting how many days that would be for him, he quit when he got to ten thousand.

ELEVEN

LATER THAT MORNING, Detectives Riggins and Sanchez walked out of the 21st Circuit Criminal Court complex, having just attended a felony invest hearing in the Grassle case. Riggins walked ahead of her partner, who busily typed into his smartphone.

"What do you think?" she asked.

Sanchez finished his message then pocketed his phone. "I was thinking Italian or New American."

Riggins rolled her eyes. "Not your dinner date, Romeo. The whole case."

"I think it's going as expected. State attorney seems happy. Why, you still think we missed something?"

Riggins's expression didn't convey confidence. Ever since her interview with Eddie, something had been nagging her. Over the past week she and Sanchez had poured over every ounce of evidence from the case, only to pour over it again. She'd sat for hours on her front porch running the interview over in her mind. Chet had played his guitar softly at her side. Blues, to match her mood.

"Not sure if it's something we missed, necessarily," Riggins said. "It's the witness that bothers me. Where is she?"

Sanchez rubbed his chin. "Maybe she's traumatized. Think about it. You pop into a store for a soda and bag of chips and end up seeing a guy get zapped. That'd freak anyone out."

"Sanny, nothing freaks you out. You and your friends looked after a dead bum when you were a kid."

"True. But I grew up on the streets. This girl, she looked young. Not just in age, but up here." He tapped the side of his head. "She's scared."

As they reached their parked vehicles, Riggins stood with hands on hips and turned an eye toward the warming sky. "I was thinking of going back out to County and having another interview with him. Maybe jog his memory on the witness."

Sanchez frowned. "Why? An indictment is right around the corner. I know you want this one to be clean, being so close to retiring. I'd be the same way. Tie up all your loose ends so you don't lose any sleep afterwards. Anyway, L.T. would be pissed, considering he said the case is closed."

"I know. But the girl is nagging at me hard. I need to talk with her. Would have been nice to get prints of her, assuming she's in the system. How we looking with the neighborhood canvass?"

"I found two businesses that captured a Jeep leaving the scene just after the murder. No plate info. Too dark. Only one home camera from what I found. Got the Jeep, but from the wrong direction." Sanchez stepped forward and rested a hand on his partner's shoulder. "Look, I understand how much you want this to get done right. I do too. And I see how L.T. has been trying to take you out of the field since you're so close to leaving. Ever consider it?"

Riggins scoffed. "He means well, but I'm not going anywhere until the clock strikes midnight on October 2nd. I don't care if we get a case the day before—I'm working it."

A curly-haired court reporter stepped out of a nearby vehicle and arranged a wheeled equipment case. As she walked by them, Sanchez shot her a warm smile. The woman returned his smile, her eyes appraising his well-maintained body. As she walked toward the courthouse, Sanchez followed her shapely form with longing eyes.

"Do you ever quit?" Riggins asked after the woman walked out of earshot.

"What?" Sanchez asked, shrugging innocently. "I can't help it if women find me so irresistible. Besides, I'm single. Someday when I'm married and my kids are hanging from my arms, I don't want to feel like I cheated myself. My father married my mother the day after they graduated high school. She's the only woman he's ever been with. I can't imagine that."

Riggins shook her head. "Just be careful. Lotta bugs out there today."

"Thanks, ma, I'll remember to get a flyswatter," he said, removing his keys from his pocket. "Are we driving together, or separate? And I'd like the record to state that you pulled your weapon on me right now and ordered me to go with you. Just in case L.T. trips."

They both laughed.

"Thanks for backing me on this, Sanny," she said. "We'll drive separate since I need to pick up Chet's anniversary present that just came in. I got him a guitar Jimi Hendrix once played. He's gonna flip."

Sanchez nodded, impressed.

"And don't worry about L.T. I'll take the heat," she said. "What's he gonna do, make me retire?"

Sanchez gave a thumbs-up. "I'm with you all the way, boss. You backed me when I applied for detective, so I owe you. If you get written up, so do I."

Riggins nodded her agreement. "Okay, battle buddy. But can we grab some breakfast first? I'm starving like a mad dog."

AFTER A QUICK breakfast at a local greasy spoon, the detective team spun northward toward the county jail. Since admin had marked the Grassle case "closed," Riggins decided beforehand their strategy would be to be upfront and tell Eddie the truth. While they needed his help in finding the witness, they agreed it best to be straight with him concerning the possibility any help he provided could hurt his case just as much as it could help it. But Riggins hoped that Eddie saw the evidence as damning enough already, and that giving up more details wouldn't seem as big a deal to him. Whatever legal means it took to get information from him, Riggins felt willing to take.

The jail intake supervisor, a chubby man with eyes set too close together, inspected the detectives' credentials and entered their professional information into his logbook. "Legal visitation rooms are around to the right."

Riggins felt her guts churn. Heinke would be furious when he found out they had conducted an unscripted follow-up interview. After all, it had been the lieutenant himself who had proudly declared the case closed. The evidence sat inventoried in the vault back at headquarters, and Eddie's recorded statement had already been transcribed. State Attorney Hood had personally thanked the sheriff's office (or more specifically, the detectives assigned to the case) for their hard work. A formal indictment would be handed down soon, he assured them. Then the task of preparing for an undoubtedly long and arduous trial would begin. Heinke had in fact already assigned them another case. Upon initial inspection, Riggins suspected the new case was one of clear-cut gang rivalry; still, she had every intention of doing her due diligence later in the day. But the prospect of talking with Eddie again loomed largest within her. She'd tossed and turned the night before thinking about it, with Chet waking on several occasions to ask what the matter was. "Cramps," she'd said, which hadn't been too far from the truth. Her indecision on the matter had weighed on her mind to the point she'd eventually retreated to the living room couch and curled up with their Maltipoo, Gracie. After sipping a glass of red wine and playing a game on her phone, she'd finally clocked a couple hours' rest.

She'd finally decided to pull the trigger. With Sanchez's blessing, no less. A risk for sure, she would at least have to reveal to Heinke that they'd attempted to speak with Eddie, regardless if he talked or not. As good a case as any for asking forgiveness versus permission. But if Grassle agreed to talk without counsel and provided any useful information, things might not be so bad. Heinke would have a conniption in that event. Riggins also knew that she risked defense counsel arguing harassment of their client. Eddie had already been charged with a slew of felonies. Unless Riggins was investigating a new crime, going back over an established charge with an arrestee could be construed as improper policing at best. At worst, the State's case could be hampered, and both the agency's civil liability and her own could come into play.

The detectives were directed toward the jail's conference area, reserved for attorneys, investigators, and police to conduct inmate interviews. A large red sign posted on the outer vestibule gate declared that visitors must check all weapons and ammo before entering. No photography unless authorized. An officer monitoring a metal detector and conveyor belt directed them in, checking Riggins's briefcase for the lone metallic object he'd discovered—a black, digital audio recorder. He then sent them toward a room at the end of the hall marked **PRIVATE**. They waited in the sound-insulated room for fifteen minutes before Sanchez said, "He's spooked. Let's ask if he refused to see us."

"Not yet," Riggins said. "Give them another ten minutes. My cousin works here, and she says the mornings are always busy. Besides, he wants to talk. I can feel it."

Sanchez eyed his partner. Since joining homicide six months ago, he'd learned to trust her hunches. Numerous times they had encountered apparent roadblocks in cases, only for Riggins to maneuver around them in order to get the tough interview, discover missing evidence, even secure confessions from suspects who at first had seemed like brick walls.

"Okay," Sanchez said, sitting back on his fixed metal stool. "Got my date set up tonight, so I'm sitting pretty. Let's do this."

Three minutes later the door to their small conference room buzzed and Eddie Grassle popped his head inside. "You all need to talk to me?"

Riggins waved him inside. "Good morning, Mr. Grassle. Thank you for agreeing to speak with us. Please have a seat."

Eddie inspected the detectives' faces before taking a seat across from them. He eyed the digital audio recorder that sat in the center of the table, concern rising in his eyes. Riggins pressed a button and a red light displayed on the counter. Eddie remembered his lawyer's instructions about not giving any more statements to the police. But more loudly than that warning came Jules's voice in the back of his mind: *Why do you think they say, 'anything you say can and will be used against you?' If you don't talk, they can't use your silence against you. It's a fucking law, man!*

Eddie began to say that no, he wouldn't give any further statements, on advice from his attorney. Then he envisioned his public defender hurrying away as he had yesterday, confused and seeming more than a little unprepared to handle a case of this magnitude. *Why would they put a new guy on my case?* Eddie had thought. Now, as he sat with a palpable silence between him and the detective team, he looked Riggins in the eye. No, he would not talk to them without his attorney present. He'd already said too much. But as he opened his mouth to speak the words, some other compulsion came over him, something so alien and forceful he felt powerless to ignore it. In an instant he changed his mind and new words spewed from him as if spoken by someone controlling him. "Okay. I'll talk to you. I don't need my attorney."

The two detectives exchanged a quick glance. "Okay then," Riggins said. "I appreciate—we appreciate your assistance here, Mr. Grassle."

"Eddie."

"That's right. I first have to remind you that you still have the right to have your attorney present before we speak. And that anything you say to us can and will be used against you in court." Riggins repeated the remainder of Eddie's Miranda rights, which he readily waived.

"I won't sugarcoat this, Eddie," Riggins said, diving in. "You're in a world of trouble here. I understand this may seem a bit awkward, but we came out here to see if you could help us."

Eddie frowned. "Help *you* guys? I'm the one sitting in jail."

"I can understand how you must feel. The reason we came here was to see if you can tell us anything else about the girl inside the store. We know she witnessed everything."

Eddie considered for a moment. Like they'd said, anything he told them could either help or hurt his case. Jules would have screamed at him to shut his mouth and make them work for every detail. His attorney too. But Jules was dead, and his attorney wasn't the one sitting in jail facing murder charges. The ticking clock on the wall seemed amplified in the hushed room, and it could as easily have been ticking away the only chance he had to help himself. Eddie looked between the two detectives seated across from him and made his decision.

"I remembered her name."

Riggins sat up straight. "You know her name?"

"Yes. Jessica."

"No last name?"

"She never told me."

"Describe her."

Eddie did his best to pin down an accurate description of her, down to her tanned, long legs and straight black hair.

"Anything else that could help us find her?" Riggins pressed.

Eddie had been so engulfed in the drama of the situation he'd forgotten until now the very issue he'd tried so hard to raise earlier. "Yes—she said she worked at the 'Honeybee.' I've never heard of it, so it must have opened since I went to prison."

"Yes, I know where it is," Riggins said. Both detectives exchanged glances, with Sanchez scribbling a note on his legal pad.

"Well, she said she'd called into work that night to go to a party. I've never seen someone that scared before."

Beginning to jot a note of her own, Riggins dropped her pen on the metal table where it made an audible clang. When she picked it up, she noticed her fingers were trembling. "Did you relay this information to your attorney already?"

"I forgot to tell him. I was going to call the investigator this morning, the one my attorney told me to give any information to, but now the officers are saying I can't make any phone calls anymore."

"Personal, or legal?" Riggins asked.

"Neither. I guess I pissed the wrong person off."

One of the jail officers poked his head inside the door and asked if everything was going alright. Riggins told him yes, that they were finishing up.

"I just wanted to see my boy, detective," Eddie said after Riggins stopped the tape recorder and began to pack up their things.

"I can believe that," she said, extending her business card toward Eddie. "Don't hesitate to call if you can think of anything else you can add. The people here have a hard job. I'm sure whatever it was that got your calls suspended, you'll get them back in time."

Eddie huffed, but took the card anyway. Looking at it, he let out a humorless laugh. "This is only two numbers off from the one I grew up with in school," he said, palming it.

Riggins eyed him, trying to judge his character. She'd shown a knack at seeing through people, even in her early days as a detective. In fact, her nickname "Little Gypsy" had stuck until just a few years ago, when another detective had shot and killed a woman with a tattoo with the same nickname.

"And remember, if you want your attorney to be present when you talk with us, that's perfectly alright too," she added, both she and Sanchez shaking his hand.

After Eddie had been escorted back to his cell, the detectives checked out of the jail and returned to their vehicles. Sanchez paused at the driver-side door. "What do you think L.T. is going to think of this?" he asked her.

"He's not going to be happy," she said. "Neither will the State. They seem like rabid dogs on this one. We need to talk to that witness ASAP. She had a clear view from the other side of the counter. If she corroborates his story, that sort of changes things in my mind. I just need L.T.'s go-ahead. I respect him too much to blindside him any more than I already have."

Sanchez dissented. "My vote's still that the guy's guilty as hell. I think our witness will tell us exactly what we thought—Grassle was going through his clothes for valuables. I'd bet a steak dinner on it."

"We'll see about that," Riggins said, her eyes focusing on a point far into the distance. "It just doesn't feel right, Sanny. I can imagine him missing the clerk's wallet, but not the chain. If he wasn't committing robbery, there's only one conclusion I can make."

"Look, I know I'm new to the unit, but I've seen more of the streets growing up than most cops have their entire careers," Sanchez countered. "You can't fix every wrong, is what I'm saying. Maybe the guy didn't know what was going down. Maybe he wasn't trying to rob the dead guy. Shit, maybe he was trying to pin a medal on him. All that matters now is the State has control of the case and the courts will decide what happens to him. He's just one guy, Rig. One guy who made a bad decision. One thing my grandmother always told me was you make a decision and it either pats you on the back, or it haunts you forever."

Riggins climbed into her vehicle and slipped on a pair of cheap convenience-store sunglasses Chet had once teased her about ("comfortable and unbreakable, just like you," she'd responded with a grin). Turning the ignition, she looked over to her junior partner and sighed.

"Believe me, Sanny, I've got enough ghosts chasing me. I don't need any more."

TWELVE

Lieutenant Heinke rubbed his temples, unsure if he wanted to yell at his favorite detective or congratulate her.

"So, you went against my order and interviewed Grassle again. This was after the case was already closed."

Riggins sat circumspect in a chair opposite his desk. "I'm sorry, sir. I guess I exercised a bit too much discretion."

"Discretion?" Heinke asked, huffing. "I believe the word is insubordination. I feel like you're taking advantage of the fact I don't believe in sending people to Internal Affairs unless they killed Santa Claus."

Riggins nodded, tight-lipped. "I understand, sir."

"And don't think you're getting out of this either," Heinke said, pointing at Sanchez.

"No sir," the dapper young detective said, sitting up straight in his chair.

"But on the other hand, by going against my order you found the only witness in the case," Heinke added, thoughtful. "That puts me in a difficult position. I feel like a father whose kid got caught skipping school but made honor roll. I'm not quite sure what to do with you two."

Riggins raised a hand. "I'll be the first to say that it was my idea, Lieu. Sanny only went along with it because I basically put a gun to his head."

Before Sanchez could implicate himself, Riggins quickly added, "On our way here, I verified that a Jessica Rios, age twenty-three, is in fact employed at the Honeybee. The manager said Jessica called in sick the night of the robbery. DAVID and FCIC searches verified her current address. Sanny and I can swing out to her place and report back here in an hour. Just saying, sir."

Heinke alternated his gaze between the two detectives, trying to decide if it was worth the trouble to even attempt getting angry. "What's that name folks around here call me?"

Riggins raised her eyebrows. "Come again?"

"Don't bullshit me, Alice. I'm giving you permission to be honest with me."

"Old Fart," she blurted without hesitation.

"Hmmm," Heinke said, chewing his pen cap. "I thought so, although I hadn't considered fifty-four to be old. Until now. Either way, I may be an old dog, but in a fight the old dog usually gets the bone. We know all the tricks. Which is to say, I realize what you're doing here."

Riggins remained silent.

"You knew I'd be upset, but since you found the witness and discovered where she lives, you figured I'd get over it before you even left my office. Nod if I'm correct."

Riggins and Sanchez both nodded. Two kids in the principal's office.

"My therapist told me it's good to let the small stuff go, so that's what I'm choosing to do here. But in the future, I expect you both to follow my wishes to a T. Understood?"

"Yes, sir," they answered in unison.

"You know I don't have to micromanage you, although I sometimes probably should," Heinke said to Riggins. "I just know how much the state attorney wants this guy. And what Hood wants, Hood gets."

"You won't be sorry, Lieu," Riggins said, hopping up and rubbing the top of his balding head. Holding a hand over her heart, she declared, "I'll walk away from the case forever and won't breathe the name Eddie Grassle again if the witness says he tried to steal from the clerk's body."

"And what if she supports the defendant?" Heinke asked, his voice tinged with regret. But Riggins had already spun on her heel and raced out of the office, Sanchez in tow.

Alone now in his office, Heinke shook his head, his expression betraying half concern and half admiration. He glanced to a picture on his desk. His daughter, dead nearly twelve years now. He allowed his mind to drift back in time to a bittersweet memory, one that brought him both pain and pride...

When the DJ took to the mic and announced the father-daughter dance, Alice felt a rush of apprehension. All of that washed away when Heinke approached the bridal table, extending a hand toward her.

"You aren't going to stand me up, are you?" he asked with a grin.

They danced to a Natalie Cole number, Heinke whisking Riggins around the dance floor empty save for them. With Chet and the other hundred or so guests looking on, he led her with the deftness of a ballroom expert.

"I didn't know you could dance, sir," she said, pleasantly surprised.

"Don't you know it's against the laws of decency to call the man who just gave you away at your wedding 'sir?'"

She giggled, patting him on the back with her non-led hand. "I guess I'm just not used to calling my lieutenant by his first name."

"You're a rookie detective, Alice. There's a lot you're going to have to get used to."

Natalie Cole gave way to Boyz II Men. Heinke and Riggins continued to dance, him spinning and dipping her to the amusement of those watching.

"Thank you for doing this, sir—I mean Frank," she said. "I always thought my dad would be the one to walk me down the aisle. He went so suddenly I was afraid to ask you last minute."

He stopped in mid-stride, holding her with both hands at the waist. "And I always thought I'd get to dance with Penelope at her wedding. I guess God had other plans for both of them."

They shared somber smiles and continued their dance. When they finished, Heinke walked her over to where Chet sat talking and laughing with family members.

"You've got quite a bride," Heike said to him, shaking hands with the grinning young man. "I'm a lucky man to have her on the team."

Chet rose, placing a giant hand on the small of his wife's back. MC Hammer had just come on, and Chet wasn't going to miss the old skool set.

"Not half as lucky as me, sir."

Blinking the memory away, Heinke stood and closed his office door (he'd long since given up reminding Riggins to close it behind her whenever she left) and settled back into his chair. Snapping on the wall-mounted television, he surfed several channels until he came to a local news item that caught his attention. The Grassle case, with State Attorney Hood conducting a live press conference. Two of his top assistant state attorneys bookended him. As the top prosecutor spoke about the case, Heinke was reminded of a pair of dealings he had had with Hood. He had of course communicated with the man numerous times, usually via bureaucratic means. But the two occasions in which he had dealt with him one-on-one had left a decidedly sour taste in his mouth.

The first had been two years ago, during a presser over a child's murder. Heinke remembered the high-profile case well—a young boy had been abducted from his front yard while the boy's mother had been inside doing laundry. Heinke himself had helped organize the search, which had ended a week later when the boy's body had been found in a culvert. During the subsequent press conference, Heinke had felt a quiet discomfort at the level of contempt the state attorney had shown once the cameras turned off. The man's face had been a canvas of embittered outrage. All those involved had been horrified over the child's brutal slaying, for sure, but Hood had shown a fury that far surpassed what a public official would have been expected to portray. 'Someone will burn for this,' Hood had promised, sweeping to the floor several microphones that had been arranged on a nearby table. He'd gripped the edge of the podium and urged Heinke and his detective teams to track down the animal responsible at all costs. 'I will personally try the case,' Hood had declared.

And true to his word, he had done just that when a local man, Alvin Dickey, had been arrested several weeks later. Heinke, under tremendous pressure from both Hood's office and his own chain of command to make an arrest in the case, had picked the suspect up after finding only circumstantial evidence linking him to the murder. Heinke had punted the case over to Hood's office, expecting it to fall apart. But much to Heinke's surprise, and that of just about everyone else involved, the case had made its way to the jury. They deliberated long into the night, and the still-packed courtroom had collectively gasped as the foreman read the guilty verdict. **MIRACLE FOR PROSECUTION!** One headline had said. **DICKEY SENTENCED TO DEATH!** Another had read a month later at his sentencing. Afterward, a dark-eyed man Heinke had never seen before had emerged from the gallery and approached Hood. The prosecutor, fresh off his impossible victory, clasped a huge hand on the back of the man's neck and said loud enough for Heinke to overhear, 'You have done well, my friend. Justice thanks you.' An odd statement to make to an outsider, Heinke remembered thinking, since he had been privy to every investigator and aspect of the case since its inception.

His second meeting with Hood had been more casual in nature. While attending a social function for the local chamber of commerce (a responsibility his captain had delegated to him), Heinke had been sitting at the hotel bar ordering a drink when he'd witnessed a domestic scuffle between a man and wife. Having slipped away during the post-meeting gathering, he had just ordered his second Crown and Coke when the couple stumbled up next to him at the bar. Drunk and engaged in a heated argument, they'd paid him little notice, cursing each other and bumping into him several times. Just as he had been prepared to stand up to move toward the other end of the bar, the woman had knocked into his arm, his drink sloshing onto his suit jacket. Promising himself to refuse another such assignment in the future, Heinke retired to the restroom to wash his jacket. On his return he'd discovered the couple had moved their argument into a more secluded area of the hotel, through which Heinke would have to walk. It had been at this point he'd recognized the husband as one of the keynote speakers from the event, a man of great influence in the community. The man's wife, wearing an expensive red sequined dress, had been arguing loudly with her husband about another woman when she'd suddenly slapped him across the face. Not wishing to become involved since he'd been drinking, Heinke had immediately ducked behind some nearby brocade curtains.

Through a gap in the curtains, Heinke then watched as the enraged husband took hold of one of his wife's wrists and spun her around with such force, her necklace broke free and shattered onto the tiled floor. Furious, the wife slapped her husband again. In an instant, the husband pounced on the much smaller woman, his hands wrapped around her throat as the two fell to the floor. Feeling he must now intervene, Heinke had begun to step from his hidden position when a flash of movement to his right had given him pause. A looming, bald figure swept in from seemingly nowhere and bent over the couple. Heinke had recognized the figure to be none other than State Attorney Hood, who'd also been a speaker at the event. Picking the man up by his suit collar, Hood separated the still-fighting couple. Struggling to her feet, the wife had declared, 'He—he was going to kill me,' as she gasped for air. The husband had begun to protest, attempting to shake away from Hood's powerful grip, when Heinke witnessed something that not only shocked him, but had sent a shiver down his spine. Still hidden in the folds of the curtain, he'd watched with amazement as Hood picked the man up off his feet with one hand and hurled him across the floor. In one swift movement, Hood had then bent over the shaken man and raised him off his feet so that their noses nearly touched. 'Why don't you try choking someone your own size?' Hood had hissed, his face contorted with murderous fury. Just out of view in the grand ballroom, the other guests continued to converse and laugh. So far as Heinke could tell, no one else had noticed what was occurring.

Just as Heinke had decided to reveal himself and order the two men to break apart, Hood lowered the woman's husband to the ground. Brushing off the man's lapels, Hood then punched the man squarely in the midsection. As the husband bent over gasping for air, Hood looked to his left and right, and when satisfied no one had been watching, delivered a driving elbow to the man's back. The husband collapsed to the floor, groaning in pain. Smiling, Hood had then taken a deep breath and exhaled toward the ceiling as if just experiencing a post-coital release. Turning to the man's shocked wife, Hood bowed once before vanishing back into the ballroom.

And now, sitting behind his desk and watching Hood's impassioned television speech, Heinke reminded himself that, ultimately, the state attorney's office controlled all cases once charges had been made against individuals. The probability of them dropping Grassle's charge was zero, in his opinion. All that seemed left to be decided were a few minor details. And one witness, who if indeed was found, didn't seem to pose much threat to the case, no matter what she said.

Transfixed on the bald, eagle-eyed Hood on the screen, Heinke felt a growing pity for anyone not only sitting opposite the powerful man in a courtroom, but for anyone who crossed his apparent personal sense of justice outside of it.

THIRTEEN

From the Springwood Gazette, May 23, 2016
LOCAL MAN INDICTED ON MURDER CHARGES
Story by Benjamin Mixer, Gazette staff writer

A grand jury indicted a local man yesterday on murder charges stemming from a botched convenience store robbery last month. Edward Grassle, 24, has been charged with the April 25th robbery that resulted in the deaths of Esteban Mendez-Rodriguez, as well as Grassle's accused accomplice, Julius Sanders. Under Florida law, a person charged with a felony may be charged with first-degree murder if another person dies during the commission of that felony.

State Attorney Mathias Hood held a press conference yesterday following the grand jury indictment. "I'm happy to see the case reach the next phase," Hood told a gathering of reporters outside the Calusa County Judicial Building. "As already stated, I will be taking an active role in this case. During my career I have maintained a rule to lead by example, and at times that includes trying cases myself. It is times like these that make me proud to serve and protect the rights of those who are no longer here to defend themselves."

Grassle is being held without bail at the Calusa County jail awaiting trial. A spokesman from the public defender's office offered no comment when asked about Mr. Grassle's reaction to his indictment. When the closed-door proceedings began, a small crowd gathered outside the courthouse, some holding signs bearing the image of the late Mendez-Rodriguez. A man who identified himself as a nephew of the victim offered a warning to passersby: "Do you see how our court system is broken?" he implored. "This piece of scum was released from prison just three weeks before he killed my uncle. He still gets to see the sun rise every day. It's not fair."

Another senior member of the state attorney's office said the next phase of the case would be pre-trial. He warned members of the victim's family that the case could take years to wind its way through the legal system. "I've seen murder cases take five, six years to go to trial," the official said. "The sad part of cases like this is the family gets pulled through the system. They are victims also."

Eddie lay on his cell bunk, one hand behind his head and the other holding the folded newspaper article he'd just read about himself. A sympathetic officer who worked the midnight shift had opened the steel trap to his isolation cell door and plopped the section down on the opening.

"Thought you might like some reading material," the officer had said, setting Eddie's breakfast tray (two pieces of white bread with lumpy jelly, and imitation corn flakes that remained hard as rock even after soaking in milk for ten minutes) atop the newspaper. Then he'd added, "Who'd you piss off, getting stuck in here?"

Eddie hopped off his bunk and removed the food tray from the trap. Setting it aside uneaten, he'd thanked the officer and unfolded the paper, making sure to look both ways out his small window to see if a supervisor was coming. Then he'd retreated back to his bunk where he read the short article with a mixture of fascination and terror. The former because he'd never before read about himself in the newspaper. Terror because what was being said about him constituted a mandatory life sentence should he be convicted. He didn't need to be an attorney to know that.

Either by luck or a bureaucratic mix-up, the photo of his father and grandfather that had been deposited in his inmate property storage by police showed up on his trap an hour later. Eddie had witnessed other odd happenings like this during his previous stints. Occurrences such as inmates receiving fully nude men's magazines labeled with a civilian's name and address; or once, an inmate who'd called a fake bomb threat to the mayor's office, only to have the cell phone he'd used in the incident mistakenly delivered to him from the inmate property room. There had been dozens of other examples of a system often stressed to its limits. And as he hopped off his bunk and took the small envelope in his hands, removing the photo, he didn't want to complain about getting something he desperately wanted, just because it appeared under strange circumstances.

He'd almost forgotten he'd still had the picture in his shirt pocket the night he'd been arrested. As he held it up now, marveling at his own resemblance to his then boyish father, Eddie allowed himself to wonder if he would ever see his own son before he died. Just then, a tap from behind the metal cell door broke him from his thoughts. "Recreation time," came a different officer's gruff voice. A tired-looking face filled the door's small glass window. "Take it or leave it. Only chance until next week."

Eddie rolled over and faced the wall without saying a word. Since his transfer to this isolation cell, no one had told him what rules he had broken to be placed here. Likewise, no one had informed him why nearly every privilege he would normally have under his isolation status had been taken from him. With his only view outside the cell window being the bare hallway wall, he'd begun to feel increasingly claustrophobic. Every half hour an officer walked by and peered into his cell to check on his welfare. He hadn't gotten much sleep the past two nights due to the fact that one of the night shift officers had discovered an affinity for rapping a heavy brass key ring against his metal door during each check. Now, after nearly a week of broken sleep, Eddie felt too tired and deflated to even think about venturing outside.

"Well, fuck you then," the officer muttered before moving on.

Eddie heard keys jangling and the officer's footsteps leading away from his cell. Re-thinking his decision, and not wishing to be cooped up in his six-by-nine-foot cell for another four or five days, he pulled himself to his feet and moved toward his cell door. Unable to see the officer due to the bad angle, he rapped his knuckles against the steel to get his attention. "Excuse me!" he called out. "Hey, I changed my mind. I guess I could use some time out of here." He placed his ear against the cold metal and heard the footsteps stop. After a pause, the footsteps approached and soon the same pudgy face re-appeared in the window.

"Make up your mind, for Christ's sake," the officer said, folding his arms over his chest, his hands resting beneath his sweat-stained armpits. The jail's air conditioning had gone out an hour ago—the third time in as many days. "Which is it? In or out?"

"Out, please," Eddie said as he donned his orange and black striped uniform shirt and slipped into his jail-issued tennis shoes. The shoes he'd been arrested wearing still sat in a police evidence room. "Some fresh air might do me some good."

Sighing, the officer unlocked Eddie's cell door and escorted him in the direction of the recreation yard door.

"You'll be by yourself, just so you know. Segregation rules."

Arriving at the recreation yard vestibule, the officer signaled a nearby control room deputy to buzz Eddie through the first gate. A loud electric buzzer sounded, and Eddie pushed the gate open. A few seconds later another electric buzz sounded, and he pushed his way out a second door, this one solid, walking out into the bright sunshine of the day.

Fresh air flowed into his lungs for the first time in nearly a week. He felt instantly grateful for having changed his mind. Even though he'd changed housing assignments, Eddie noticed they'd placed him in the same yard as before. Not unusual, he reasoned, recalling that the Calusa jail only had a handful of functioning rec yards for their population of approximately five hundred. As he stepped across the concrete yard, he noted the same two officers from last time were on the ready. Each remained at their former positions—Schultz on the tower's concrete ledge and Nady, the rover, on foot outside the yard's chain-link fence. Eddie raised a hand to Nady, who returned it with a good-natured wave. When Eddie looked up to Schultz, he noted the man's narrowed eyes and working jaw. The overweight officer spat a chewed sunflower shell onto the pavement below before taking a seat with his shotgun across his lap.

Eddie picked up a faded basketball and began to shoot hoops. His ribs still ached a bit, but he did his best to ignore the discomfort. Ten minutes in he broke a sweat. He felt invigorated, alive. He stripped off his uniform shirt, feeling the sun soak into his bare chest and back. Exercise truly did wonders for a person's mood, he thought. Despite the dark cloud that had descended over him since his incarceration, it felt good to be outside in the elements. He'd grown up playing sports and engaging in myriad outdoor activities. The summer after he'd met Jules, the two had slept in a tent in Eddie's yard for a month straight. Exploring the area's many orange groves, swamps and rivers had been their favorite pastime. It had all been an escape of sorts after his father had left. Even now, after only a few days of being shut away inside his concrete cell for twenty-three hours a day, he'd begun to feel the pernicious effect of imprisonment. He reminded himself to accept every offer of recreation going forward, especially since they'd taken away his reading privileges.

Dribbling to the top of the free throw line, Eddie took a jump shot, the ball bouncing off the side of the rim and rolling toward the fence line. He raced to track it down before it went into the painted yellow restricted area. He scooped it up just in time, spun and took an arcing jump shot. The ball went in, the newly-installed net snapping with a clean *swish* sound.

"Nice shot!" came an enthusiastic voice behind him. At first, Eddie thought he'd been mistaken about being the only inmate in the yard. Then he looked over his shoulder and noticed Officer Nady leaning against the guard tower support beam. The sun shined hotly down from above and, from where he stood, Nady could enjoy a small sliver of shade.

"You got some skills," the young officer said, a good-natured grin riding his youthful face. "I always wanted to play sports, but my mom was afraid I would get hurt." Nady shook his head regretfully then moved out from beneath the tower so that he stood just a foot from the fence line. Eddie stood motionless for a moment, not knowing what to say. Sweat gleamed off his exposed skin. Being the only inmate in the yard, he'd nearly forgotten that he still had an audience of sorts. Now, with an apparent compliment coming directly from one of the officers, Eddie felt at a loss as to how to respond.

"Thanks," Eddie said simply. He bent and scooped up the ball, took two dribbles and laid it in off the backboard. Letting it roll away, he took a few steps toward where Nady stood, making sure to stop short of the yellow boundary. "I played every sport I could when I was a kid. Didn't make good grades, but I could play baseball and basketball with the best of them. I could dance too. All the black guys in school used to call me 'Wigger.'"

Nady let out a burst of laughter. "Not me. I got good grades but couldn't play a lick of anything. Two left feet, my momma said. She wouldn't even let me play outside or ride a bike. Still don't know how to ride one."

"What?" Eddie asked, incredulous. "You never learned how to ride a bike?"

"Nope. Isn't that something? I must be the only able-bodied adult on earth who hasn't learned. I even heard a story about a blind guy who rode one. His guide dog barked to tell him when to stop and turn."

Eddie laughed. "Just get out there sometime and give it a try. Riding a bike is just like—well, riding a bike."

"Maybe when my son gets older, I can learn so I can teach him. He just turned one the other day."

After a moment of careful consideration, Eddie switched gears. "I guess you already know they moved me into confinement. I thought I'd done something wrong but can't figure out what. No one will tell me anything."

Nady placed a hand to his chin. "Can't say as I know why, either. Supervisors move inmates around all the time. But none of them said they ordered it when I asked them the other day. Must have come from up top somewhere."

Satisfied for now, or resigned to his plight, Eddie let the subject go and for the next twenty minutes engaged in a variety of other topics with the young officer. Eddie learned that Nady had gotten this job after the factory he'd worked in folded up shop for Mexico. "Crime always pays," Nady said, invoking something Eddie himself had heard before during his previous stint in prison.

"When I went through the academy, nobody thought I'd make it," Nady continued. "Not even my mom. But I did. I did it for my little one. Wanna see a picture of him?" Not waiting for Eddie's response, Nady pulled a wallet from his back pocket and fingered through it. Removing a photo, the lanky officer (who himself didn't look a day over nineteen) grinned proudly as he held the photo up to the fence for Eddie to see.

Eddie squinted to see it but was too far away to make out any significant details. He toed up to the very edge of the yellow restricted area, careful not to step into it. He leaned in, trying his best to make out the child's face.

"I can't really see him, but I'm sure he's a real brawler," Eddie said.

"He sure is!" Nady said, pride beaming in his eyes. He glanced up toward the tower and deciding that Schultz's view was obstructed, motioned for Eddie to come nearer to the fence.

"It's okay," Nady whispered. After taking a tentative glance upward, Eddie stepped into the yellow area to a spot closer to the fence. Here, he got a good look at the child. Beaming for the camera, the toddler seemed to project nothing but joy as he sat cradled in his father's arms.

"Wow, he sure looks like he loves you," Eddie said, genuinely happy for Nady's good fortune. "What's his name?"

"Phineas. After my grandfather. He died a week before he was born."

"That's a shame. But it's cool that he's carrying on his name. I've never met anyone called that."

"That's what my wife said. She told me, 'Now, Charles, don't nobody name their little boys Phineas nowadays.' But I didn't care. It's like one of those old-timey names that makes a comeback. Like Elmer."

Eddie smiled as he focused on the child's slobbery face, his little fingers splayed out over his own face with a huge grin visible between the fingers. Part of him felt happy in seeing that picture, and yet a larger part of him felt sad. He'd just begun to thank Nady for sharing the picture when the metallic sound of a shotgun racking a round came clearly from above, accompanied by a shout. "Get back right now! Get out of the yellow!"

Eddie froze in his tracks. The hair on the back of his neck stood on end. Even Officer Nady didn't move. Looking up to see Officer Schultz pointing his shotgun directly at him, Eddie leaped backward onto the unmarked portion of the cement and held his hands up high above his head.

"Don't shoot!" Eddie implored, turning his face away out of instinct.

Schultz's voice then, measured, and deathly serious, "Nady, you back away from that fence right now, son."

Nady blinked, looking from his partner above him then back to Eddie, before shuffling backward from the fence. He cleared his throat and stuffed the photo back into his wallet. "Jeez, sir, I was only—"

"I don't care what you were doing," Schultz interrupted, keeping the shotgun trained on Eddie. "Don't you ever let me catch you cohortin' with any of these pukes again, you hear? Especially this one." Schultz slowly lowered his shotgun and, maintaining eye contact with Eddie, slung it back over his shoulder. He radioed into the housing floor that the inmate's recreation time would be cut short due to his security violation.

Nady looked up to his senior partner, holding up a hand in apology. "It was my fault. I told him to—"

"It don't matter, new guy," Schultz enunciated slowly, as if speaking to a dull child. "He's one of them. He killed someone, and if he had the chance, he'd slit your throat in your sleep."

By now, Eddie had lowered his hands and stood silently, not knowing what to do or say. This had only been the second time in his life he'd had a gun pointed directly at him, the first being the night Jules had died. He hadn't been sure what had been more chilling—looking down the barrel of Schultz's charged shotgun, or the man's eyes themselves, cold and calculating as they'd sighted their target.

Nady swallowed hard, deciding to stand up for himself. "Some of these guys are okay people, you know."

Schultz scoffed. He dug his fat fingers into his open bag of sunflower seeds and stuffed a handful into his mouth. Leaning over the top railing, he looked down at both men below—Nady on the concrete path outside the fence line and Eddie standing perfectly still, now in the center of the yard.

"Hard to feel friendly with someone who kills an innocent man," Schultz said, chewing and spitting out a shell. A grin spread across his fat face, as if daring the prisoner to challenge what he believed to be an inviolable statement. Nady began to interject but Eddie cut him off.

"It's okay, Mr. Nady. He can say whatever he wants. I don't mind."

Schultz straightened, his face turning red. "Damned right I can say what I want, you little shit. I've been doing this longer than you've been alive."

"Mr. Schultz, I wasn't trying to—"

"You refer to me as Senior Officer Schultz, you spineless puke."

Eddie blinked. He looked to Nady, whose eyes were as big as shooter marbles, then back to Schultz. "Okay. I understand, Senior Officer Schultz."

The rotund officer held a finger to his temple as if a brilliant idea had just occurred to him. "On second thought, I'd rather you refer to me as 'master.' That has a nice ring to it. 'Yes, Master Schultz.' You think you can manage that, puke?"

Eddie felt a swelling sensation rise within him. He wasn't sure if it was anger, resentment, or fear—or a combination of all three—that now made him ball his hands into fists. His teeth grinded together as he resisted the urge to respond with something that he knew he'd regret. Never in his life, not even in prison, had he been made to feel so low.

"I didn't kill that man, sir," Eddie responded, his chin held high.

"Oh no?" Schultz shot back. His mouth worked overtime now, cracking, eating, spitting out empty shells at a furious pace. "They put two murder charges on you. That much I know. I don't care if you didn't pull the trigger. You're going to hell for what you did. But before you get there, you're going to have to deal with me first. Isn't that what you want, to schmooze with all the officers?"

Officer Nady, unable to hold his tongue any longer, suddenly found the courage to speak up. "Look here, sir, there's no need for—"

"Shut up, new guy," Schultz said without looking at him. His glare remained fixed and hard on Eddie. "Get a few years under your belt before you question me."

Nady bit his lip. He looked around for help, but it was just the three of them out here. Not even any security cameras or microphones to record what happened. Nady's hand flinched toward his radio but returned obediently to his side. Better to let the grumpy old bastard get his kicks and then be done with it. Just as Nady turned to walk back beneath the tower, he heard Schultz repeat his earlier admonishment.

"Shut up, new guy!"

Nady stopped in his tracks and craned his neck up toward the tower. "I didn't say nothing else, boss."

Schultz, bent over now and tying his shoe, stopped in mid-loop, a quizzical look rising on his face. "What the hell?"

Both officers exchanged confused expressions. Not until each realized the voice—unquestionably Schultz's—had somehow come from the recreation yard, did they shift their eyes in unison to the lone figure standing still in the center of the yard.

"Was that you?" Schultz demanded of Eddie. The portly officer's eyes bulged from their sockets, fresh anger rising in them.

Eddie shrugged, a grin betraying him. He had been willing to let Schultz's previous slight against him pass, but some devilish voice within him had persuaded him to ape the man who only moments before had made him feel lower than anyone else ever had. A fair trade in his mind for any repercussions.

"You little shit!" Schultz stammered, pointing a fat, trembling finger at Eddie. Confused, Nady looked back toward Eddie, who now walked in short circles around the yard, that same devilish grin playing about his face. It took Nady another moment to realize what had happened. Howling laughter, he slapped his hands onto his thighs. "Whoa, boss, you hear that? He sounded just like you! Holy cow!" Nady raised his arms into the air then slapped them back down onto his lanky thighs in another fit of rolling laughter.

Atop the tower, Schultz hopped up and down in fury. Curses flew from his mouth as he struggled to evoke every expletive in his already limited vocabulary. "You little fucking murdering shit!" he screamed. "How did you do that? You tell me right now! You been watching me? Is that what you do the whole time you're out here?" White foam covered his quivering lips as he leaned over the railing, casting a murderous glare downward.

"Oh—Eddie, that was *funnnnnny!*" Nady wiped tears from his

eyes as he attempted to catch his breath. Just when he regained his composure, he spied Schultz's beet-red face and trembling finger and lost himself in laughter again. Eddie, not wanting to appear too disrespectful, offered a meek half-smile and simply shrugged his shoulders again.

"I'm glad you think this is so funny," Schultz said through clenched teeth. He cast a hateful glare down to his partner before turning it on Eddie. "You! Inside! Now!"

Eddie gave Nady a wink before feeling it best to do as he'd been told. He opened the heavy door leading back into the cellblock, knowing better than to utter another word. He'd surprised himself by doing what he'd already done. The words had escaped him before he'd even realized it. Maybe it had been the fresh air, or the fact he'd had a real conversation with another person for the first time since his placement into confinement—he wasn't sure. But despite everything, Eddie figured the big-bellied officer had had it coming. Assholes came in all shapes and sizes, Jules had told him long ago. He'd also said an asshole had to be cut down to size whenever possible, something Eddie realized more so now than ever before.

Once Eddie disappeared through the outer rec door, Schultz collected the rest of his gear and unlocked the protective ladder grate. As he prepared to begin his way back down the attached steel ladder, he poured the last handful of sunflower seeds from the bag onto the ground below. The same flock of birds from the nearby tree converged on the seeds in a violent flutter of wings and beaks.

"Careful where you step, Grassle," Schultz hissed beneath his breath. He shifted his slung shotgun to accommodate his girth as he began to descend the ladder. "Landmine here waiting for you."

FOURTEEN

As Eddie was stepping back inside from the rec yard, an unmarked cruiser was pulling into the parking lot outside a red-brick apartment complex in a not-too-great neighborhood of Springwood. Detective Riggins guided the Crown Victoria through the lot while Sanchez scanned for the vehicle they were seeking—an early model green Jeep Wrangler. Just an hour before, they had questioned the manager at the town Honeybee. The manager had cooperated by providing them the employment records for one of his workers, a Jessica Rios, age 23. A subsequent search of the state driver license system quickly provided them with her photo. An NCIC criminal history and DMV search found that Ms. Rios had two unpaid traffic tickets and had been recently charged with possession of a controlled substance. Oxycodone, according to the arrest affidavit. Legally prescribed by doctors, the narcotic pain pills had single-handedly taken over half of the local drug trade in recent years, even with the recurrent culling of the area's numerous pill mills.

Riggins looked at their witness's picture and shook her head. Pretty girl, with bright, intelligent eyes. Shame.

"Bingo," Sanchez said, pointing toward a shaded spot at the end of a row of cars. Riggins backed into a parking spot across the lot from where the Jeep sat so they would have a clear view of the girl's building. Apartment complexes were the bane of many law enforcement officers, and Riggins especially disliked their system of interconnect-ing parking lots and myriad open courtyards. It remained the single biggest reason car thieves and other criminals running from police chose them as their preferred bail points. The detectives climbed a flight of rotting wooden stairs and knocked on the door to unit 212. Sounds of rattling dishes and running water carried through the door. Soon enough the door opened, exposing a long-legged His-panic woman with flowing black hair. She seemed taller than her DL demographics had pegged her at.

"Yes?" the woman asked through the partially opened door. She dried her hands on a towel and eyed the badges clipped to both detectives' belts.

"Sheriff's Office, ma'am," Riggins announced. "Are you Jessica Rios?"

The woman hesitated. Once she realized the detectives likely already knew who she was, she nodded. "Yes, that's me. Is this about my case? My lawyer told me to have him present if the police tried talking to me again."

"No, ma'am, this has nothing to do with your possession charge. My name is Detective Riggins, and this is Detective Sanchez. We're from the homicide division and are investigating an attempted rob-bery that occurred April 25th at the One-Stop convenience store on Meadow Drive. A man was killed, and we have reason to believe you witnessed it. May we come in to speak with you about it?"

A young girl of about two waddled up to Jessica and wrapped one arm around her leg. Her other arm clutched a stuffed bunny that in turn held a stuffed carrot to its mouth. The woman shooed the child away and stepped further out of the doorway, leaving the door open a crack. "Look," she said, her eyes dancing with growing concern. "I can't help you guys. I don't know anything."

The detective team had worked enough cases together to have already figured out a system for questioning uncooperative wit-nesses. The two had discovered that Sanchez gained the best results when questioning female subjects. Without having to be prompted, he held up one hand in a conciliatory offering. "Look, Jessica—may I call you that?"

She nodded, brushing away strands of long black hair from her face.

"Okay, Jessica. You're only a witness in this case. I want that to be perfectly clear. And I understand your hesitation. We've seen the surveillance tape of the robbery. Anyone would have been traumatized seeing something like that."

Jessica shook her head, as if casting away some unpleasant memory. "I'd really like to help you guys, but I don't know what you're talking about."

Sanchez decided to take a risk. He handed her his business card and said, "Well, think about it and give us a call if you happen to hear anything from neighbors or friends. We thought we found the right person, but hey, we make mistakes too. If we don't find our witness, the case is still pretty solid. The surveillance tape even captured the guy taking the clerk's wallet and jewelry, so maybe we don't even need a witness's testimony."

He and Riggins had turned down the stairs when Jessica blurted, "Wait! He wasn't taking anything from him. He tried to save his life."

Both detectives turned back toward the door in time to see Jessica roll her eyes and slap herself on the forehead.

"Okay, yes, I was there. I saw everything. I wish I hadn't. I've had dreams about it every night since then, you know?"

Riggins and Sanchez looked to one another. Sanchez shrugged. "Can we come in?" he asked Jessica.

"Can you wait a minute? I want to put my daughter in her room first."

Sanchez said of course, and while they waited outside the closed door, Riggins gave her partner a tight nod of approval. "Nice job. And to think, everyone said you were just a pretty face."

Sanchez faked a hurt look, then straightened his tie as Jessica returned to the door. She ushered them inside, apologizing for the mess. She sat on a tattered armchair, leaving the detectives to sit side-by-side on the only other place to sit in the room, a flower-printed sofa. From the adjoining kitchen, several pots on the stovetop emitted a delicious aroma of cooking food.

"My ex told me I never cooked for him while we were together. Now I cook all the time. Ironic, huh?" Jessica said with a nervous laugh. There seemed to be an air of uncertainty between her and the detectives. Riggins recognized this as common apprehension—there was a definite line a witness knew they were crossing that separated anonymity and the harsh realities promised by a drama-filled court case. If her years in the agency had taught her anything, it was that this would be the moment the woman would decide if, and how far, she would cooperate. Removing her digital voice recorder from her briefcase, Riggins laid it on the coffee table and explained that since Jessica had demurred from going into the station, the recording was necessary.

"And remember, you are only a witness in this case," Riggins added. "You aren't suspected or accused of any wrongdoing."

Deciding then to immediately show their hand, Sanchez removed a printed screenshot from his briefcase and laid it on the coffee table between them. The photo bore a striking resemblance to Jessica, although due to the pixilation it was by no means definitive.

"From the surveillance camera," Sanchez said, leveling his gaze on her. "From what we saw, you had the perfect view of what happened. You say the suspect tried to help the man who was shot?"

Jessica looked between them both. She seemed conflicted on how to answer. Finally, she placed her head in her hands and said, "My best friend died from a drug overdose last year. I'd known her since fifth grade. About a week later a girl I knew asked me to try some pills, said they'd make me feel better. I was so depressed. I wanted to just shrivel up and waste away. I still took care of my daughter, but that was about it. I took the pills and they really did make me feel better. At first. Then everything started to unravel, and I found myself needing them, not just wanting them. Getting caught with those pills was the best thing that ever happened to me. I'll never touch them again." She raised her gaze from her hands and stared at both the detectives. Each of them looked back at her, silent, waiting for her to continue.

"After I saw that man get shot, I came right home and laid down in the shower for an hour. I had to get the smell of all that blood off me. It was horrible. The next day I saw it on the news and really was going to come forward, and not just because of the reward money. It was because I saw they arrested the other guy, the friend who I'd seen sitting in the car."

Riggins showed Jessica a photo pack, consisting of nine different pictures of white, clean-cut males in their early twenties. Eddie's picture was among them. "Can you pick him out for us? The guy you said gave the clerk CPR?"

Jessica took one look at the photos and picked Eddie's picture out immediately. "That's definitely him. I thought he was cute at the time. Funny how you can look back at something traumatic and still feel sexual."

Sanchez twisted his mouth a touch and nodded. "Go on, please."

"I imagined him sitting in jail after he tried to save that man's life, and I knew I couldn't live with myself if I didn't say anything. But I was scared. I thought maybe you guys would think I was with them or something." Her eyes searched the ceiling for the right words. "I think the biggest reason I didn't come forward before was out of guilt. I watched that man get shot and just stood there."

Sanchez, practicing his newly learned cool detachment, asked, "Can you describe the way he did CPR?"

Jessica shot him a quizzical look. "How else does someone give CPR? With those chest things and breathing for him. He even put his mouth on the guy's bloody lips. And the whole time I just stood there frozen like some stupid, helpless bitch."

Sanchez, his head down over his notes, looked through his brow at her. "It's common for witnesses of a violent death to have survivor's remorse. Try not to internalize it. Trust me, it'll eat at you if you do." He removed a form from his briefcase and drew up a brief description of what was about to be signed. Then he slid the form to Jessica, who in her own handwriting detailed what she'd just told them. Signing it, she slid it back to Sanchez.

"Thank you, Jessica," he said, meaning it. "I won't lie to you and tell you this will help your own case, because it probably won't. And when you come to court to testify, you'll be asked if this is a true and accurate statement. If you aren't one hundred percent positive, now is the time to say so."

She gave him the same look she'd given Riggins a few moments ago. "I think it's time you two left now. I already feel like a coward. I don't need you guys treating me like I'm stupid too."

After being shown the door, the detectives descended the staircase in silence. Behind the wheel, Sanchez whistled. "I kinda like the spunkiness in her. If it wasn't for her drug charge, I'd recommend her for the academy."

Not bothering to respond to his comment, Riggins propped her elbow against the window ledge and said, "Let's get this to L.T. right away. But stop by the drugstore first. I'm gonna pick him up a bottle of Pepto. I feel he's going to need it."

As Riggins and Sanchez pulled out of the parking lot and headed back to sheriff's office headquarters, an idling white Oldsmobile Cutlass with dark tinted windows sat at the opposite end of the parking lot. The man behind the wheel, Paolo Bruzzi, watched their vehicle disappear into the distance with a grim smile playing at his lips. He'd followed them here, using their natural assumption of invincibility against them. Hood had asked him to be the police to the police. To watch and wait for an opening. Yes, the case against Grassle appeared solid. But with a jury came unpredictability. In a case of this importance, there could be no doubt. The witness to the crime would be an important aspect to consider, for sure. And ever since that chance meeting with the brooding, bald state attorney several years before, when the two had literally bumped into each other at a charity golf outing, Paolo had begun to hone his already well-practiced skills. Of all the sensitive circumstances involved in his trade, one fundamental truth lay forever ingrained in him: the best way to manipulate another person was to find the one thing that mattered most to them. Taking that thing away did not always prove necessary, he'd found. Subtlety often worked twice as well.

Paolo pressed a button on his handheld digital voice recorder and began speaking in his usual clipped, detached diction. "May twentieth, eleven-ten hours. Rabbits have left the hole. Remained for twenty—as you were—twenty-five minutes. Subject resides in building two, apartment two-twelve. Hispanic female, early twenties." Paolo switched off the recorder and waited in his spot for another hour until the woman emerged from her apartment with a young child in tow. A little girl. Walking down to her parked Jeep, the mother buckled the child into a car seat, slipped into the driver's seat then drove out of the lot's exit. Paolo waited a moment, allowing her to gain enough distance before pulling out behind her. Ensuring he kept enough distance, he began a textbook-perfect rolling surveillance on her vehicle. Different lane, at least five lengths between his vehicle and hers. Traffic lights were to be run if necessary. He pressed the button on his recorder again and recited the woman's tag number. His contacts within the sheriff's office would get him a name and complete background soon enough. He needed to learn a bit more about her before making his approach. He followed them until they came to a squat medical office building. The woman escorted the child inside where they remained for nearly an hour. Paolo sat waiting, eating a power bar and drinking his fifth bottled water since he'd begun today's work. Twice he urinated into a plastic, half-gallon milk container he kept for situations such as this. In his experience, most despised this necessary function of the job. He relished it.

In years past he had enjoyed extorting things from female subjects such as this one, often carnal things he'd performed more out of a sense of power and control than desire. But he no longer felt interested in that. It had been years since he'd been with a woman, a fact that neither worried nor surprised him. He'd begun to experience something much stronger than lust, an emotion more primitive and innate than any he'd ever known before. The power over a person's lifeblood, the taste of their own desperation that brought crazed looks to their eyes. He had first tasted this power a dozen years ago and had had countless examples ever since. The politician who trembled with fear over the possible exposure of a scandalous affair; the journalist forced to recant a damaging story after several child pornography videos had somehow been downloaded onto his personal computer. So many instances. And all of it culminating, at one point or another, with that look in his victim's eyes once discovering they were trapped. The look of a cornered, helpless animal. Had this lust for human control been some nascent mental flower inside him, waiting years to bloom? Or a seed planted long ago during his childhood in the orphanage, when he'd endured not only brutal beatings but quiet nights when the doorknob of his room had turned, a shadowy adult figure cloaked in a floor-length robe entering, and slipping first a hand beneath his bedsheets and then a mouth? Paolo did not know, nor did he care. All he knew was that his blood moved more quickly in his veins at the mere thought of this woman's discovery of Paolo's power.

After leaving the doctor's office, the woman drove to an ice cream parlor. Paolo didn't wait to watch them finish their treats. He had what he wanted. He turned the Cutlass back into traffic and made several calls from his secured cell phone. Dialing one last number, he spoke with rising confidence to the man he'd come to admire more than any other in his life. "The rabbits are gathering their food," he said, his voice taking on an ominous tone. "They will give away their hole soon."

FIFTEEN

CLARISSA FULTON FELT sick to her stomach. She sat listening to the car radio, unsure if she should go through with the whole thing. The clock on the dash read two minutes to five in the afternoon. Her appointment was scheduled for five o'clock and had a one-hour time limit, but she knew she wouldn't need that long. Five minutes, ten, tops.

She turned the ignition back on and almost pulled out of the parking spot before she shut the car off again, making herself step out and lock the door. Roger had offered to tag along, if just to sit in the car while she conducted her business with Eddie, but she'd insisted on him staying behind. "This is my thing," she'd told him, and he'd nodded in that faraway kind of way she'd grown accustomed to. Now, as the soles of her shoes crunched over the rock-filled parking lot toward a low brick building marked **JAIL VISITATION**, she took a deep breath and steeled herself for what was to come.

The place buzzed with activity. Dressed-up women (some with babies on their hips), and an assortment of sad-looking folks who appeared to have just gotten off work, mostly. Clarissa found her place at the end of a short line, a look of concern on her face. She'd left the house without makeup and with her hair tied back in a simple pony. Roger would have thrown a fit if he'd seen her putting her face on for such a thing. For reasons she wasn't quite sure of, she'd applied some foundation, eyeliner, and lip gloss after arriving here. She'd released her hair and ran a brush through it. Part of her felt compelled to give Eddie the roughest version of herself. He didn't deserve to see her made up. But another part of her, through either egotism or just plain stubbornness, had won out. Her entire look now, down to the blue jeans and low-cut t-shirt she'd changed into after leaving the house, resembled the one on the day they'd first met. Although a faint sliver of her heart would always belong to him, a much larger part of it sat filled with resentment and anger. Since this would be the last time that he ever saw her, let him see her in her best light, she'd reasoned. Let him chew on that for the rest of his life behind bars.

When she'd made it to the head of the line, a kind-looking older woman behind the desk met her gaze. "Name of inmate?"

"Eddie Grassle."

The woman smiled, her head nodding as if her own proclivity demanded it. "Here we are, dear. Right on time. I'll just need to see identification, please." Clarissa handed over her license. She looked around the place and shuddered. How many visits had she made here during Eddie's last time in jail, when Liam had been a baby? How many times had she stood in front of the facial recognition machine, allowing the computer to analyze her features against the jumble of wanted persons out there? It had always been for love, however temporary that love had been. Like a drowning person grasping at straws. This time, as she stared the required five seconds into the camera, she felt a strange feeling pass through her. It felt like a ghost who, after haunting her for years, had finally said goodbye.

The woman typed something into her computer then directed Clarissa toward a pre-assigned visitation booth. As she turned in that direction, the woman said something that made Clarissa stop in her tracks. "It just breaks my heart seeing young loves split apart like this. You're an angel for staying by his side, miss. I hope you don't mind me saying that."

Something fluttered inside Clarissa's stomach. She nearly turned around and walked out just then. *Just walk through the door and forget the whole thing*, a voice inside her demanded. Forcing a smile, she thanked the woman and compelled her legs to carry her to the booth. She stared for several minutes at the blank monitor, checking her watch. Ten minutes past five. In another five minutes, she knew, the visit would be cancelled if he didn't show. She allowed herself to believe he wasn't coming, that he had discovered it was her and decided to just let it go. Growing more anxious by the second, she had just begun to rise when the screen flickered to life. At first, just a stark concrete wall and an empty chair could be seen. She fought the urge to pick up the phone receiver and scream into it, *come out here right now, Eddie! Come out here and talk to me and let me say what it is I need to say. You aren't getting off this easy. You owe me.*

Eddie's form filled the screen as he settled down in the chair. He picked up his end of the phone receiver and looked her straight in the eye. "I didn't think you'd come."

"Liam and I are moving," she blurted, her voice sounding far away, even to her. "With Roger. To Ohio. I didn't come here to talk about what you did. I don't care, Eddie. I just don't care anymore." She had not wanted to cry but tears welled up in her eyes and her throat grew thick before she even realized it. She watched Eddie shift nervously in his seat and lean in close to the screen, as if the extra closeness would somehow translate to her.

"Clarissa, listen to me. I know what this looks—"

"Yes, Eddie, I know perfectly well what this looks like!" she yelled into the receiver. Several nearby visitors turned to look at her. One of the visitation center workers held a finger to her lips while casting a warning glare Clarissa's way.

"What it looks like is you never changed," Clarissa said, cupping her hand around the receiver. "And you never will. I feel like an idiot for believing you. For letting you into our lives again. What was I thinking? After everything I've been through. Giving birth to Liam alone, getting up in the middle of the night with him while you were locked away for a friend who never did anything positive in his life."

Her voice had risen again, to the point that a center worker walked over to her and demanded she lower her voice or leave. Fresh tears streamed down her cheeks, turning her eyeliner into angry black streaks.

Eddie lowered his head, unable to meet her eyes. When he looked back up to her, he held one hand over his mouth while he spoke. "I wasn't there with you. I'm sorry."

"That's right. You weren't there. And now look at you. An innocent man died, Eddie. And your so-called best friend too. This isn't
some wild night out on the town. This isn't some slut you picked up
in a bar. Do you realize what they're saying about you? That you'll go
away for life? You were there when that guy got killed. Right alongside Jules. I saw the video with my own eyes. Liam was right beside
me, for God's sake. I had to cover his eyes so he wouldn't see it!"

Eddie didn't know what to say. His spirit, already downtrodden,
now lay utterly crushed. His last hope had been that, by some grace,
Clarissa would allow him a final reprieve.

"I know I don't deserve what I'm about to ask, but I'm begging
you, Clarissa, please let me see him. Bring him to me just once, even
for two minutes, and you'll never hear from me again. I won't care
what happens to me after that. I'll plead guilty just to get it over with,
I promise. Please, Clarissa, it's the only thing I have left to live for."

A new look crossed her face then, one of newfound triumph. It
was almost as if his pleas had given her emotional resurgence buoyed
by some hidden reservoir of pride.

"That is one thing I should give you," she said, a cruel smile curling her lips. "It's the right thing to do, seeing how you're about to go
away forever. But I won't. Call me selfish or a bad mother, whatever.
But then what does that make you? You don't know a single thing
about your son. That he wants to ride his bike to school since we're
too close for the bus. Or that he needs to bring an inhaler to school
every day. All you know is his name. Life isn't a video game, Eddie.
You don't get to hit the reset button every time you make a mistake."

Facing him fully, her makeup now a blotchy mess, she enunciated
clearly so that he would understand every word she spoke. "We're
leaving Saturday. I wanted to go tomorrow but the week is almost
over. There's no sense making this any harder on him."

Eddie felt as though someone had punched him in the gut. His
head fell into his hands as he stared at her, already knowing she'd
never change her mind. It took all his strength to keep himself from
throwing up. If he didn't already feel like a man trapped in a nightmare, what she said next only served as a ghoulish reminder.

"Roger wants to adopt Liam. The lawyer said all you have to do is sign the paperwork. Don't fight me on this, Eddie. If you want what's best for Liam, you'll do it."

His words floated from him. "Let me see him, Clarissa. Just once."

"No. I'll never bring him inside this vile place. I won't do that to him." A steely resolve settled over her face, as though she'd made a final decision that she would never waver from in a thousand years. "I can't control what he does when he grows up, but until then he's under my care, and I promise you, he will never set foot in this place or any other place like this. My lawyer says he can deliver the paperwork to you next week. Sign it and let us get on with our lives."

So, this was it. He looked into her eyes, searching for anything to grasp ahold of, some glimmer of hope on which to perch his already dissipating existence. All he found was cold emptiness. "This is all my fault," he muttered weakly.

Clarissa rose to her feet, wiping the back of her hand across her wet face. Just before she slammed her end of the receiver down, she leaned in close to the camera, so that her entire face filled the screen. What she said caused a chill to go down his spine.

"For once in your life, Eddie, you're completely right."

SUPERINTENDENT DEVEREUX, TOP administrator of the Calusa County Jail, looked across his desk at the pot-bellied officer standing before him and sighed. Demoting Schultz from his previous position as supervisor of an outdoor work crew several weeks before had left him conflicted. On one hand, he had had no choice. After a series of recent incidents (in one, Shultz had been discovered allowing inmates under his supervision to arrange trysts with their girlfriends while on outside work details; even more egregious, he had twice been observed falling asleep in his truck while a group of worker inmates cleaned a neighborhood park), Devereux had been forced to deal harshly with the veteran jailer—removal from his favored position to one back at the jail, and a week-long, unpaid suspension. The way Devereux had seen it, the man had been fortunate to keep his job. If not for his tenure and the fact that his brother-in-law was none other than State

Attorney Mathias Hood, Devereux would surely have recommended his termination. And as if the indignity he'd endured by having to allow Schultz to retain his employment hadn't been enough, he now resigned himself to listen to what he knew would be yet another petty complaint from the petulant yet well-connected officer.

"Tell me again why you think this inmate should have his recreation revoked permanently?" Devereux asked.

Schultz shifted in his seat. "Well, for one thing, he came out for recreation the other day and tried to make a fool out of me."

"How so?"

Schultz scratched his nose. "I'd rather not say."

Already, Devereux had ordered Eddie Grassle's placement into segregation under false pretenses. He had also revoked his telephone privileges and his ability to order commissary items, all due to an anonymous caller with information of several kickback schemes he'd taken part in earlier in his career. But despite this mysterious caller's insistence that Grassle be made to be "uncomfortable" as he'd put it, Devereux had insisted on moving with this slowly. He didn't need Grassle's lawyers or even the ACLU getting involved in such pettiness. Especially when his own illegal dealings were one or two subpoenas away from being discovered. Besides, he despised Schultz, and watching him grovel like this amused him.

"If you won't tell me what happened, I don't see the point in you sitting here."

Schultz began a stuttering recount of what had occurred in the recreation yard several days prior. When he finished, he nodded his head for emphasis and folded his arms across his ample stomach.

"I understand if you failed to see the humor in that exchange," said the superintendent. "But that's not enough for me to revoke his recreation for his entire stay here. He may be with us for years if he doesn't make a deal with the state. If you want to file a disciplinary report then do what you feel is appropriate. Maybe he misses a session or two of recreation. But what you're asking me to do, I cannot agree. He is an inmate, yes, but he still has rights."

Schultz sat steaming in his seat. Sweat began to break out on his ample brow. He'd come armed with ammunition he hoped he wouldn't have to use, but now it appeared he had no choice but to expend it. "You know who my brother-in-law is, sir?" He spoke the words carefully, watching his boss from the corner of his eye.

The superintendent had been expecting this and betrayed no emotion. "Yes, Officer Schultz, I know who he is. And if you're trying to imply since you have a political connection that I would grant your petty request, you are mistaken. I'm in charge of this facility, not you, and certainly not the state attorney. I'm a man who shoots straight, so I'll give it to you now. I don't like you. I never have. But that's just my personal opinion. I never try to let that influence how I treat my officers." He read from a personnel file he'd printed just for this occasion. "Professionally speaking, you're lazy and ineffective. Every supervisor you've had for the past five years agrees with this. You wouldn't even be working here if I'd had my say. I'll give you that, you pulled enough strings to keep your job. But that's where it ends. If you got your panties in a wad because someone finally gave you back what you've been dishing out all these years, then so be it. Now, is there anything else you'd like to discuss?"

Schultz sat up stiffly in his chair. His mouth dropped open in disbelief and for a moment he seemed completely lost for words. When the indignation finally settled in, his face flushed, and his fist came crashing down onto the padded arm of the chair. "What ever happened to officer loyalty, sir? You can't ask me to go back out there in that yard with him now. He's scheduled to have recreation today, and I can't bear to see him gloat right in front of me. It's not right."

Devereux had no intention of getting into an argument with the man. He had bigger fish to fry. "This has nothing to do with officer loyalty. It does have everything to do with having thin skin. I think yours should thicken up." He leveled his gaze at the portly officer, whose face had gone from red to an even angrier purple. "Go back out there and do your job. If he does something where I can permanently revoke his recreation, then I will do so. But not for the reasons you've given me. Are we finished here?"

Schultz started to speak, then stopped. Shaking his head, he stood and stalked toward the door. "Well then, thanks for nothing, sir," he said over his shoulder and trudged out of the room.

Devereux settled back in his seat, his mind returning to his previous rumination. The mysterious phone call from the week before had begun to become an obsession in his thoughts. After being so careful with every one of his private business deals, he now felt that his efforts had been for nothing. He lay hopelessly exposed, vulnerable. Visions of falling into disgrace had haunted his dreams ever since. His thoughts slipped into a hazy daydream as he pondered his future and what he may possibly do if the time indeed came that he would be forced to resign. He remained deep in thought an hour later when his office telephone startled him from his fugue. He looked at the caller ID and frowned. A private number, one that the jail's newly installed security software should have either blocked or decrypted.

"Devereux," he answered cautiously. "Can I help you?"

A voice, vaguely familiar. "Hello, Superintendent. Paolo Bruzzi here. Do you remember our phone conversation last week concerning a particular inmate in your facility?"

Devereux's blood chilled in his veins. He placed a notepad in front of him and scribbled a note—TRACE THIS CALL. Buzzing his secretary in, he handed her the note while holding his hand over the receiver. When she left, Devereux spoke again. "Yes, Mr. Bruzzi, I remember. How can I help you?"

Slow, measured breathing from the other end. "It seems the inmate we spoke of still enjoys an abundance of movement. It had been my belief we had an agreement that his privileges were to be severely restricted during his stay with you."

The superintendent frowned. Had it been pure coincidence that Schultz had just been in his office minutes before, asking about the same inmate? He doubted it, thinking back to the mysterious call he'd received from Mr. Bruzzi, and how he'd listened in alarm to the one word breathed like promised ruin through the phone: *Shiloh*. The code word used by Devereux and his business partners when referencing their illegal schemes. To his knowledge, only he and three other human beings knew the context of that phrase. Devereux had always prided himself on his quick-thinking mind; it had served him well over the years. An ax to be ground by an officer was one thing. High-level blackmail involving intricate security measures was something else entirely. Whatever the reason, one fact rang true in his mind: Eddie Grassle must now occupy every bit of his energy until he stood trial.

"Please get to your point, Mr. Bruzzi."

"My client feels it appropriate that Mr. Grassle be limited to his cell only. Specifically, no outdoor recreation. This is a privilege my client has expected to have already been removed. Mr. Grassle's victim can no longer enjoy this simple joy of life—watching the clouds pass above him, smelling the salt in the air—so neither shall Mr. Grassle. Is this understood?"

Devereux did not wish to push the man, yet he could not fathom explaining the blatant hypocrisy to his subordinates. Since his rise to the head administrator post at the jail, he had preached consistency, firmness, and especially fairness. Now he would be forced to go against that, and without any plausible explanation aside from a petty infraction against a staff member.

"How do you expect me to revoke something like this for years?" Devereux argued. "Any attorney fresh from law school could successfully argue a civil rights infringement—"

The voice on the other end made a shushing noise, such as a parent reprimanding a disobedient child. "You are a man of much intelligence, Mr. Devereux. I trust you will find reason enough. As for any potential lawsuits you may incur as a result of your actions laid out here, rest assured they will be met with resistance at all levels of government."

Devereux felt something flutter in his stomach. It had been years since he had experienced the kind of discomfort that gripped him now.

"Look, Mr. Bruzzi. I'm doing everything—"

"*Now*, Superintendent. You are the one in charge, so simply make it happen. It would be a shame to hear of a tragedy in Gainesville. Such poor security on college campuses these days. Your daughter is a junior there, no?"

Panic seized Devereux like a vise. His eyes moved to the framed photo on his desk—his smiling daughter engulfed in his embrace, his own eyes swimming with fatherly pride. Never before in his life had he felt a stronger desire to have his daughter with him, safe, questioning him on why he acted so concerned over her but not caring because this man could no longer harm her. In those final moments before the line went dead and he stared blankly at the ceiling, wondering how he'd fallen into this mess, one thought dominated Devereux's mind—that he would gladly resign his position on the spot, and trade in every dime he'd received from his collections of deals, for his daughter to be somehow transported into his office in the blink of an eye.

"I'll do it. But leave my family out of this."

He could almost hear the man on the other end smiling. "You have until the close of business today, Superintendent. I know you're a busy man."

The line went dead. Devereux hung up and stared at the phone. His heart pounded in his chest. His palms and forehead beaded with sweat. The fear he had first experienced quickly turned to anger. Anger toward the mysterious man who had so subtly touched the one thing that mattered most in his life; and toward Schultz, whom he suspected had just gone over his head. Anger at the rights-driven criminal justice system that prevailed in all his professional decisions, thus making his job—namely this Grassle situation—all the more difficult to manage. But mostly, he pointed his anger squarely at the one person in the world who had single-handedly placed him in this position in the first place—himself.

Devereux picked up the phone and dialed a number. The housing supervisor in that area dutifully listened to what the superintendent said, then explained that Officers Schultz and Nady had already signed out their weapons and were en route to their assigned recreation yard. Devereux ordered that a message be sent to both officers to immediately cancel Grassle's recreation, should he have been allowed outside prior to the message being delivered. He considered radioing Schultz directly but decided against it. Bad enough the man would get his way; worse was the thought of Devereux having to deliver the message to the pompous officer himself. True, he relished the idea of Schultz receiving a lesson in humility, but much more pressing was his desire to peacefully end this vexing new problem of his. During his twenty-four-year career, Devereux had learned that loose ends tended to fray if left unclipped. He typed out a memorandum on his office computer, ordering all of Grassle's privileges revoked throughout his stay in the jail, effective immediately. He would rot inside his isolation cell until he stood trial. What happened to him once he eventually shipped to state prison would be none of his concern.

His business complete, Devereux closed his office door then returned to open his top desk drawer. In the rear of the drawer, beneath a pile of innocuous official papers, sat a stainless-steel flask. Unscrewing the cap, he tilted the flask toward his lips and felt the whiskey flow like liquid heat down his throat. It had been three years since his last drink. Having placed the flask there at the conclusion of his stint with A.A. as a symbol of his own crucible, he had never felt tempted to even look at it since. But now his former willpower over his disease wavered, and he tore his eyes away from his daughter's photograph as he took another long pull, savoring the harshness in his throat and the immediate cloudiness in his head.

He looked to the clock on the wall. Eleven thirty-seven in the morning. He made a mental note to re-work all of his personal security measures as soon as he had the chance; finding out where he had erred and who had betrayed him would be a necessity as well. He decided just then to suspend all his business dealings that had even the slightest inkling of illegality.

Better safe than sorry.

SIXTEEN

MATHIAS HOOD LOOKED out the window of his second-floor office in the criminal courts complex and smiled. Things were coming together. The grand jury had indicted his current "project" with first degree murder—a formality, but one that left him relieved, nonetheless. His brother-in-law at the county jail had just telephoned him asking for a favor. Squeeze Grassle. Squeeze him good. Schultz represented everything Hood disliked about the human race. Had it not been for the sake of his own sister's pleadings, Hood would have avoided the man at all costs. But when he'd heard Schultz's breathless accounts of how Grassle had humiliated him, Hood had obliged the man's request to add his own retribution. *I want him to pay,* Schultz had said. *He shouldn't get to see the light of day.*

And Hood had indulged him, not because he needed motivation beyond his own quiet hatred for Grassle, but because in doing so he accomplished another goal, this one personal—the favor would buy him a way out of visiting his sister and brother-in-law's home for quite some time. He had grown to despise the visits increasingly as the years went by. Sometimes it wasn't just a case of killing two birds with one stone. Sometimes they collided and fell dead on their own.

The secured phone call to Paolo had taken barely a minute. Those same short, business-toned responses—*yes, sir. I'll get right on that sir. Consider it done, sir.* And Paolo had more news: the detectives assigned to the Grassle case had found the eyewitness to the convenience store killing. According to Paolo's contact within the sheriff's office, the young woman in the surveillance video had given a statement that could—in a talented defense attorney's hands—be argued as mitigation for the defendant. Hood had done his research and now glanced over the woman's information that lay in front of him. Jessica Rios, age 23. Currently on bond for illegal possession of prescription pills. No previous record except for several traffic citations and a juvenile arrest for shoplifting. She had one child, a daughter, age three. Paolo's contacts within the law enforcement community were dedicated moles, and the information they gleaned was much the same as he himself would receive from them regardless. But Hood knew law enforcement had a habit of dragging their heels when it came to full disclosure on many of their cases. It went without saying that Hood's office received up-to-the-minute updates on most evidentiary information in high-profile cases. The Grassle case qualified.

But Hood had been in the game long enough to understand cops guarded their information whenever possible. Often it boiled down to a chess match of egos. It was a well-known fact in the law enforcement community that absolute disclosure, although the law, rarely happened. Police hid things from prosecutors, and vice versa. That Hood possessed such a valuable weapon in Paolo was the ultimate ace in the hole. Unbound from the constraints of procedure and law, he had long ago discovered the immense power that unrestrained information-gathering could produce. Surely, innocent men and women had been sent to prison as a result of his own special brand of investigation. But those same people had no doubt been guilty of some undiscovered crime during their lives, he'd reasoned. And even for those few who had led proper, law-abiding lives, their fate had been a part of something much larger than themselves, larger even than Hood himself. He likened justice to Jesus's crucifixion—a sacrifice that, while tragic and unfair, had been necessary for the overall salvation of mankind.

Hood ran his fingers over the fine-boned face of Jessica's photograph. Something primal stirred within him. Perhaps tonight he would pay another visit to his secret place and take a Hispanic girl.

It had been some time since he had indulged in any other besides his favorite little redhead. Hood's lips parted slightly, his tongue wetting his lips as he imagined how he would first bind the new girl before reaching into his instrument case. Some acts she would perform willingly, because she had been taught to, lest her masters bring swift punishments once the client left. He steadfastly believed the things they did for the many men who visited that secret place, often in the dead of night and in disguise, would probably happen to them on the street anyway.

As Hood continued to trace over the woman's photograph, he thought of Paolo already fast at work on her. Hood's orders had been to find her and "encourage" her to change her testimony. She would be given a choice: recant her statement and, if necessary, lie regarding what she had seen during the robbery; or face powerful judges with the ability to strip her child custody privileges. Why ruin her own family for the sake of a criminal she didn't even know? Given his experience with such cases, Hood held high confidence in Grassle's eventual conviction anyway. And offered a choice, he would have much preferred to see Grassle dead and be done with it. But his arrest and current confinement complicated things. Jailhouse hits were things of fiction, he'd found. Too many eyes and even more mouths ready to cut deals to disclose the truth. He would have to settle for seeing Grassle rot forever in prison. The only possible hurdle he foresaw was the Rios woman's testimony.

Hood dialed a number and listened to a familiar voice answer. "Sheriff Driscoll," came the drawling, genteel voice.

"Bo Driscoll!" Hood announced, feigning enthusiasm. "How is my favorite lawman?"

A slight pause on the other end. "Mathias? Well, gosh be darned. Tell me, have you called for some of Mary-Beth's banana bread? I hate to disappoint you, but there ain't none to be had. Soon as she bakes one, I eat it!" The sheriff gave a genuine, good-natured laugh.

Hood offered polite laughter in return. He pulled another file from beneath the Rios woman's picture and opened it. "Mary-Beth is an angel departed from heaven, that's the honest truth, Bo. I believe the Lord Himself put her on earth just to bake that heavenly bread.

And normally I would call on her skills, despite what it does to my waistline. But this is business."

Hood heard a hand covering the phone, and a muffled request to be left alone in the room. When he spoke again, the sheriff's previous good-natured tone turned stiffer and more official. "I suspected as much. Tell me what it is, Mathias."

"We've worked together for a long time, Bo, and have helped each other quite a bit. Before you and Mary-Beth drive off into the sunset, I'll ask you for one final request before the two of us go our own ways. I believe there is a famous poem about diverging paths on a forest road that would fit well here."

The sheriff's voice took on a relaxing tone. "Well gosh, Mathias, you just go ahead and ask me whatever you like and consider it done. What's that term you called our working relationship?"

"Quid pro quo."

The sheriff laughed. "I'm not as schooled as you, but I understand it now."

Hood picked up the file and stared at the name he'd written across the top in bold lettering—**Detective Alice Riggins**. "The Grassle case. You are aware of it, of course."

"Put my best detective on it. She doesn't look it, but she's a ball of fire, that one. Pretty little thing too, for a black girl," the sheriff said.

"She does have a good record. And yes, a looker for sure. But if Grassle has already been charged, why is she still interviewing the suspect?"

A pause from the other end. "I'd have to check with my commander of the detective bureau. But you know how I like my people to work a case. No stone unturned."

Hood read Paolo's notes, indicating Riggins had conducted the follow-up jail interview *after* Grassle had been charged with the robbery and murder. "It would seem she is turning over stones that have already been turned. How about talking with her and telling her to move on to some other case."

Another pause, until Hood heard the sound of a closing door on the other end of the line, followed by the sheriff sitting down heavily in a chair.

"If I may ask, Mathias, if I told you I put my best detective on the case and we have the suspect in custody, why the special interest?"

Hood smiled to himself. He turned the ring on his finger, his mind drifting off to a distant memory. "When I was a child, I owned a dog that I loved more than life itself. That dog went through thick and thin with me. Even saved my life once when I fell into an old well. Ran three miles home and howled until my father followed him all the way to where I'd fallen in. One day about a year later my father woke up in a foul mood. Without saying a word, he grabbed my dog by the scruff of his neck and dragged him behind the barn and shot him. I trusted my father like a good Christian trusts the Lord, but I wanted to know why he'd done what he did. That dog was never sick a day in its life and he'd never turned on anyone, family or otherwise. What my father said to me, God rest his soul, has remained with me ever since."

Hood listened to the sheriff adjusting himself in his seat, yet the line remained otherwise silent.

"My father told me, 'Son, sometimes the line between good and evil appears slowly. Other times it appears sudden, like a remembered dream.' I never did ask my father what he'd seen in that old dog that made him realize he was going from good to bad. I trusted his judgment, and it wasn't my place to ask any further. This thing I ask you is like that."

Hood listened to the sheriff's heavy breathing and could almost hear him thinking. Finally, the sheriff let out relaxed laughter and said of course he would have Riggins spoken to. It was as simple as making one phone call. "And you'll be impressed when she testifies," said the sheriff. "So well spoken, that one."

"Yes, of course," Hood said.

The sheriff drew in a deep breath. "I'm a wood tick's eyelash from retirement, Mathias. Mary-Beth and I are looking forward to finally taking our camper out west. I'll be glad when all this business is finally behind me."

Seeming quite satisfied, Hood said goodbye and hung up. As he looked out to a small crowd of people gathered in the courtyard below, the smile that had played about his lips throughout the conversation fell into a scowl. Bringing up his father always brought him a sense of melancholy. To him it was like napping in a field of grass on a perfect day, only to be caught by a sudden rainstorm.

ON THE NORTH side of town, Paolo Bruzzi pulled his Cutlass past a weathered sign with **The Palms** etched in rotting wood letters. He backed into a parking spot two buildings down from the one his target occupied. Since he had been here earlier in the day, he felt more comfortable with the layout of the complex. If all went well his work here would proceed quickly. But women were often unpredictable, as he'd learned long ago. Women had the potential to make a plan go awry in all ways imaginable. It made them something of a wild card. It was entirely possible the Rios woman would refuse his demands. For this reason, he pulled a silver sound suppressor from his coat pocket and screwed it onto the end of his HK .45 caliber pistol. One shot to the heart and two to the head. Paolo had confirmed the child had been dropped off at the babysitter's already. But he had also learned in his many years of experience to expect the unexpected. Children by nature were also a wild card. They easily became ill, and it was entirely possible the woman had slipped out to bring her home prior to his arrival. The child appeared much too young to ever identify him. That wasn't the problem. A mother protecting her young was. If the woman started screaming, or if the child reacted badly to seeing her mother killed, then Paolo was prepared to deal with them both.

As was usually the case, though, he had not been forced to resort to violence. Twenty minutes later he exited her apartment. As he walked down the staircase, he felt light on his feet. His veins rushed with adrenaline, a drug more powerful than any other he had ever experienced, both professionally as part of his former job and personally during that dark period after he'd left the agency.

Paolo removed the digital recorder from the console and pressed the record button. "Target acquired and message delivered. She will recant her statement. Achieved full cooperation. Mission successful with no casualties." He stopped the recorder and pulled out into traffic. His boss would be pleased with the outcome of today's mission. Fifteen minutes had been all it took to convince the Rios woman that her own daughter was vastly more important than the soul of a man—a criminal who had just been released from prison, no less—whom she didn't even know.

Paolo steered the Cutlass onto the interstate, toward the place he called home. Although he had been awake nearly all night and had had nothing to eat or drink in hours, he felt in that moment like Zeus, father of the gods.

SEVENTEEN

"**W**HAT DO YOU mean 'stand down?'"

Detective Riggins planted both hands on the edge of Lieutenant Heinke's desk. She hovered so far across it the veteran supervisor could detect the vanilla nuances of her perfume.

Never a man to find himself at a loss for words, Heinke suddenly found himself searching for the right thing to say. "We've done our job. It's in the State's hands now."

Riggins frowned. "Since when does the State not want evidence that supports our decision to charge a suspect? That makes zero sense."

Heinke shrugged. "Just know this wasn't my decision."

"Whose was it then?" Riggins asked. Her face flushed, turning her light cocoa skin a deep crimson.

"From way up top," Heinke said, eyeing her. "Who gave the order doesn't matter. We've got our guy. Be happy and move on."

Undeterred, Riggins leaned even further across the desk and asked, "How far up are we talking? And why?"

Heinke threw his hands in the air. "As far up as you can go, Alice, if you insist on making me say it. And I told you, *why* isn't important. You should concentrate on a job well done. You're out of here in, what, six months?"

"Five."

"You shouldn't take this personally, Alice. We all have bosses. I realized a long time ago it isn't good to ask my own boss 'why' too often. Part of the way I made it this far is by putting my head down and doing as I was told." Heinke leaned back in his chair, his eyebrows raised.

The implication of his expression was clear enough to Riggins, but it didn't stop her from pressing him. "So you're saying the sheriff ordered me to stand down? He doesn't have a clue what actually goes on here. I have the highest conviction rate in the detective bureau. Not to toot my own horn, but hey—" She made a tooting sound as she pretended to blow into an imaginary horn.

Heinke, already feeling pulled from all sides of the case, appeared unaffected by her joke. "I don't know why he wants that information scuttled. Maybe there's some reason he feels is more important than a few words some girl with a drug charge could offer. I'm not in the position to ask questions of the man who signs my paychecks, and neither are you. Just understand that you and Sanchez are to have no other dealings with the Grassle case until it goes to trial. And I've been directed by the sheriff himself to re-assign you to desk duty until further notice."

Sanchez, who'd been standing silent behind Riggins the whole time, pursed his lips but knew better than to say anything.

Riggins straightened, smoothing out her dress shirt with her hands. Expelling a deep breath, she raised her chin proudly. "So I see where being the senior detective in the bureau gets me. Who's pulling lead now?"

"Grimes and Teliford," Heinke said with resignation.

"Grimes?" Riggins said, wide-eyed. "The same Grimes who fell asleep on surveillance and allowed a murder suspect to literally walk right by him? Who failed the sergeant's test three times in a row? And Teliford? That's like pissing in a pile of shit, sir, no offense." Her face burned even deeper, indignation flaring in her eyes.

"Granted, those two are no balls of fire. But they're all I have to work with right now. Sanchez is too green, and the secondary team is swamped with that cold case. You've done a fantastic job and should be commended for everything you've done. You're a star."

Riggins shot him a scowl. "With all due respect, sir, if I needed to be patronized, I'd head over to Internal Affairs and talk to the first person I saw."

"Alice, it isn't like that."

"I didn't work my tail off my whole career to finish it sitting behind a desk," she said, beginning to pace the room. "You've *never* bowed down to upper management before. Hell, I've seen you flat-out refuse the captain. That's what I've always loved about you— you don't let politics get in the way of what's right." She settled her gaze on him. "Is it because I personally don't believe Grassle had anything to do with the crime?"

Heinke shook his head. "That has nothing to do with it. And as far as his guilt is concerned, that's up for a jury to decide. You know that."

"But that's exactly my point," she said matter-of-factly. "Why should a case this weak even make it to a jury?"

Heinke shook his finger at her. "You're acting like Grassle was framed, Alice. He was there. He went to the scene with the shooter and he had the murder weapon in his possession."

Riggins zeroed her gaze onto him. "There's something else you aren't telling me, Lieu. I can tell, so don't lie to me."

Heinke sighed. His previous stern expression fell away and suddenly he appeared very tired. "My doctor says I need to improve my diet. Now he's got me eating kale and keen..." He searched his memory. "Keen something."

"Quinoa?" Sanchez offered from behind them.

"Yeah—what he said," Heinke said, jutting a thumb toward Sanchez. "Colon polyps. Pre-cancerous, but doc has me going in to get them removed next week. In the meantime, the sheriff needs all the notes and paperwork you two have, including the recorded statement you just got from Grassle. And we are under orders to discard that statement as being unreliable."

Riggins's brow furrowed. Why in the world would the sheriff himself request evidence from a case? Although known to be a hands-on law enforcement official, he remained first a politician, she knew. As she stared Heinke down, considering her next words, she heard the voice of her husband Chet ringing in her mind. *Can't win all the battles, boo. Gotta live to fight another day.*

"Okay, Lieu," she said, nodding to that inner voice. "I'll have everything in your office by tomorrow morning."

Heinke offered a terse smile to his favorite detective. "Make it five o'clock today."

As Superintendent Devereux delivered his order to forevermore revoke Eddie's recreation privileges, Eddie stretched out on the yard's warm concrete, feeling the comforting sunlight beat down on his face. For the better part of the past week he hadn't left the stale confines of his six-by-nine-foot cell. Once every eight hours a jail officer had opened the cell's steel food trap and lain a lukewarm tray of gelatinous substances onto it. Hungrier than he'd been in years, Eddie had eaten every bit of the bland and meager portions, using his finger to lap up the last bits of watery gravy. His recreational reading and visitation privileges had been revoked several days before, for no apparent reason. He'd asked a passing officer why, but the response he'd received had only been a shrug and upward motion of the officer's thumb. To ease the crushing boredom, Eddie had done the one thing they weren't able to take from him—exercise. For hours each day he'd resorted to performing countless push-ups, squats, and running in place. It had been the only thing to ease the madness that crouched at the edge of his mind, threatening at any moment to enter his consciousness and take from him the only free thing he had left.

Just as with his first two trips to the recreation yard, the same two officers were on duty today: Schultz again in the tower, and Nady patrolling the ground outside the yard fence. Eddie had just dozed off, his mind floating momentarily from his own predicament to a more pleasant time in his past, when Officer Schultz's excited voice startled him awake.

"Grassle, on your feet! Rec's been terminated!"

Eddie's eyes fluttered open. Lifting his head and looking in all directions, he spotted only clear skies as far as he could see. Surely his session wasn't being cancelled because of the weather. He looked up to the tower ledge where Officer Schultz sat chewing a mouthful of sunflower seeds. With one fat arm the glowering officer pointed insistently toward the rec yard door. Looking for confirmation, Eddie glanced at Officer Nady, who stood in his usual sliver of shade provided by the tower's support column. The young jailer lowered his walkie-talkie from his ear and nodded regrettably.

"Sorry, Eddie. You have to go in right away."

"But I just got out here," Eddie said, confused. Shielding his eyes from the sun, he looked up to the tower where Schultz sat spitting seed shells down into the yard below. A huge grin sat crookedly on his mouth.

"Sarge says your recreation has been yanked for good," Nady said, taking a step toward the fence. "He didn't say why, but I'll try to find out when we get back inside."

Eddie's mind began to spin. How could this be happening? Rising to his feet, he walked to the edge of the yellow restricted zone, hands on hips.

"Mr. Nady, my recreation is the only thing I have left." Eddie's breath rose high in his chest, squeezing the air from him and raising his voice a pitch. Even the sky seemed to have suddenly darkened. He took a step forward, not paying attention to the fact he now stood squarely in the yellow zone. Nady took an instinctive step forward as well, until the two stood just feet apart.

As Nady began to speak, Schultz's booming voice from above interrupted him. "Outta the yellow, inmate! Back inside now before I have them come drag you in!"

Eddie craned his neck upward. Schultz stood now and met Eddie's gaze, hatred burning his eyes. His mouth worked feverishly over a mouthful of seeds, and when he spat out a spit-soaked shell it struck Eddie on the arm and stuck there.

"Am I not speaking clear enough for you, puke?" Schultz said. "I said to get outta the yellow and move your ass inside!" A smug look settled across his face as he added, "Maybe next time you'll think twice before you lip off to the people who control your life."

The weight on Eddie's chest was like a vise. He turned toward the rec yard door, missing Officer Nady casting a disgusted look upward toward his senior partner. As his feet carried him back inside, Eddie looked toward the sky, taking in its blueness and distant clouds with all their shapes and sizes—and there in the east, a cloud shaped like two figures holding hands, one taller than the other, close enough to touch yet seeming completely out of reach at the same time.

"My boy," Eddie whispered, but neither officer heard him because now they were engaged in an argument. Hearing their voices but not truly listening, Eddie reached the door and pulled on the rusted knob. Stale, putrid air swept over him as he took a step inside. When he stopped long enough to look back over his shoulder, something in his peripheral vision caught his eye. A butterfly had flown into the open doorway, resting momentarily on the inner knob, its orange and black wings moving just so. Transfixed, Eddie reached out to touch its wing, but it fluttered back outside, dancing on the air across the yard then up and over the glistening coils of razor wire atop the fence. All Eddie could do was smile, feeling glad such a beautiful creature had never had to endure the solitude and misery that awaited him. And then a thought hit him so forcefully he flinched. It rang so clear in his mind he felt immediately at peace with his decision. He would not take another step inside. He would never again enter his cell placidly like a monster in the shadows. He would rather be killed than be forced to remain caged for another day without having seen his own lifeblood.

Before Eddie realized it, he'd backed out of the doorway and turned back toward the yard where the two officers continued to argue. Schultz saw him first. The portly officer gave a double-take at Eddie with an incredulous expression. The younger officer turned also, and as he began to shout to Eddie to head back inside, Eddie took another step away from the door, then another. Then on legs that now felt not quite his own, he was suddenly off and running directly toward the section of fence nearest the tower. As he ran, the world seemed to slow down, as if in slow motion. The breeze halted, the perplexed expressions on both officers' faces froze, and even Schultz's outstretched arm remained motionless as he pointed one stern finger back toward the yard door. Even his own heartbeat seemed to stop as adrenalin pumped from his brain and through the network of arteries in his body. As he passed the basketball hoop and entered the yellow restricted zone, he felt the intoxicating effects of that same chemical making him euphoric, raising within him a sense that the apotheosis of his entire life was now at hand. Taking a final stride, Eddie felt himself soar slowly into the air, taking minutes it seemed, until the world slammed back into real-time as he crashed high into the middle portion of the fence. Immediately he began to slip down the wire mesh, his fingertips struggling to find purchase somewhere on the impossibly small-spaced surface. The toes of his shoes dug into the bottom portion of fence not covered by the wire, but his weight was too much to hold him this way without having finger holds. Just as he felt himself pitching backward, he reached out and drove his too-long fingernails as far as he could into the mesh, for the moment keeping him from slipping back to the ground. His feet began to slip then too and deciding the biting fence strands against his bare feet were worth the gain of true foot holds, he kicked both shoes off.

To both officers watching this surreal scene unfold before them, Eddie looked like a spider, his body caught halfway up the fence, with nowhere to go but six feet below to the concrete or six feet up to the murderous coils of tightly packed razor-wire. Both officers' mouths hung open, their eyes bulging in disbelief.

Just as suddenly as Eddie's heart had stopped in his chest, the terror of the moment making it skip several beats, it began to pump again, this time pounding in triple time as the full effect of the adrenalin reached his muscles. Gasping in a breath, perhaps the last he would ever take, Eddie looked upward and began to climb.

CLARISSA FULTON STEPPED out into the bright sunshine and sighed. She held her son's hand with a firm but loving grip. Despite the warm May breeze, she shivered.

"Why are we moving, Mommy?" the boy asked as his mother walked him to their car. He swung his Spider-Man backpack onto the backseat and hoisted himself up.

"I've already told you," Clarissa said, trying her best to keep her voice happy. "Roger and I have decided Ohio will be a better place for all of us to live. Plus, Grandma and Grandpa are there. Now you'll be able to see them whenever you want." She watched Liam buckle himself in, then stood for a moment looking at the boy. Even at five years old he was a dead ringer for his father. Those same handsome eyes, deep brown and clever. The wavy mop of dark hair and that same smile that went crooked when he tried his best to get his way. Planting her hands on her hips, Clarissa started to say something else but stopped herself when Liam gave her a look that she'd never seen from him before.

"Will Daddy ever come see me?"

The question stabbed into her so sharply, she actually took a step backward. Liam had not spoken of his father since that day he'd failed to take him to the park. That morning, Clarissa had sat him down and calmly explained that she was sorry, but daddy couldn't make it today. She had told him nothing concerning his father's situation. She'd considered inventing some romantic fantasy for Liam to hold onto until the time felt right to tell him the truth, but she had chosen against it. Moving the back of her hand over his cheek, she told him, "I don't think so, honey. Daddy got into trouble and he can't leave where he is."

"If he can't leave, can you take me to see him?"

Clarissa sighed even more deeply, her head tilting to the side the way it did whenever she faced a conundrum. "No, baby, I can't do that. Daddy is in a bad place and I don't want you around that. I know it may be hard to understand now, but you will as you get older."

Liam lowered his eyes, searching the folds of the back seat until he found a plastic action figure. His fingers manipulated the limbs to create some imagined scene, but his own expression held a vacant look. "Am I a good boy, Mommy?" he asked without looking at her.

As if controlled by an invisible force, one of her hands moved to her trembling lips. Something thick grew in her throat. Instinctively, she moved in and enveloped him with her entire body, a hug so long and strong she could feel his pounding heartbeat against her chest.

"You *are* a good boy. Don't ever think it's your fault that your father isn't here." She broke the embrace and held his face in her hands. "Now, are you ready for school? We can stop and get cupcakes for your class if you want, since tomorrow is your last day."

Liam smiled but his eyes held a faraway look that betrayed any appearance of happiness. "Okay, Mommy," he said, making the action figure fly.

SOME COPS LIVED and breathed their jobs, talking shop off-duty and unable to let go of the persona that served them so well while in uniform. Others did well at keeping their work and private lives separate. Alice Riggins largely fell into the latter category, managing to keep her job from creeping into her private life for most of her career, with one exception: Ronald Cokley, her very first homicide case.

Cokley, a local divorced handyman, had seemed like the perfect scapegoat for such a shocking and rare crime in Springwood. The rape and murder of a local teen-aged girl. The photo pack from which the witness picked his image was conveniently absent the normal similar-looking characters. Riggins had questioned this but had been overruled by her captain at the time. Then there had been Cokley's connection to the family just a year before the crime. All of it culminated with an easy bow the State had been all too eager to wrap around the case, bringing an apparent end to the front-page articles once and for all.

In the days preceding Cokley's arrest, Riggins had been a mess. Heinke had tried to reason with her. *Look at the evidence. If it points to his involvement, don't worry about the rest. Sometimes our gut is wrong.* After much consideration, and even more pressure from above, she'd declared her decision: sexual battery and capital murder. Heinke had readily concurred with the charge, telling her the community could now rest, knowing someone had been held responsible for the girl's brutal murder. A picture of Riggins escorting Cokley into jail had appeared in the newspapers, the caption reading 'Calusa County's first black female detective solves grisly murder.'

Then came the news two weeks later that Cokley had hanged himself in his jail cell. In a suicide note left near his body, he'd described himself as being hopelessly despondent over the grim future that awaited him in prison. He'd signed the note simply 'Ronnie,' and expressed his condolences to the victim's family. Not for committing the crime or the girl's death; instead, he had expressed his grief over the fact that, now that he'd been indicted, the real killer would likely never be caught. Riggins had read the note, feeling the wrinkled paper in her hands, swearing she'd been able to smell Cokley's sadness emanating from the page. While the rest of the investigation team had celebrated his death, she'd felt a gnawing dread. No trial meant no opportunity for the facts to settle themselves out. She remembered Heinke drawing the eraser across Cokley's name on the white board before high fiving the other team members.

Then the gut-punch two weeks later: a drifter had been arrested for raping and killing a local mother of three. During his interrogation, the man had broken down and confessed not only to that crime, but to the rape and murder of the victim in the Cokley case. Riggins had listened to the man's confession with seizing horror. As he'd given details of the Cokley case that only police and the killer could have known, Riggins had excused herself from the interrogation room and dashed to the restroom just in time to vomit into the sink. The following days and weeks had droned by inexorably. Finally, when the true killer had sealed the case by bringing Riggins and her team to an abandoned house where he'd stashed the girl's underwear, Riggins had begun a spiraling depression so deep she'd soon lost herself. Dressing for work became a mindless chore. Her drive into headquarters each day became robotic, her senses muted by deepening feelings of guilt and self-doubt. Cokley's ghost plagued her dreams for weeks. Even Chet had failed at easing her troubled soul, something he'd always been able to do with just the deep baritone of his voice or by plucking out one of her favorite songs on his guitar. For the first time in their marriage, Alice Riggins had found herself drifting away from him—the same emotional rock that had grounded her in all other times, both good and bad.

And now, as she sat on her porch swing and felt the late-morning breeze turn warm against her bare arms and legs, Riggins forced the Cokley memory from her mind. On this, her first day off in over two weeks, she intended on doing nothing but relaxing and enjoying what was becoming one of the nicest days of the year.

Chet got up from the wicker seat beside her and put his newspaper down. "Want some lemonade? Gonna squeeze it myself."

She cast him a lecherous grin as he paused in the doorway. "I got something for you to squeeze."

Chet feigned indignation. "Why, Mrs. Riggins, you're a married woman. What would your husband think, you talkin' dirty to the hired help?"

Riggins giggled. "What if I like the hired help better than my husband?"

Chet laughed. "Okay, several squeezings coming right up." He disappeared through the screen door but returned a moment later with his wife's ringing cell phone in hand. His rugged face wore a resigned expression.

Riggins took the phone from him, adding, "I'm staying home with you today," before accepting the call. The voice on the other end was so frantic she barely recognized it as belonging to Detective Sanchez.

"Rig, it's me, Sanny. Shit, I've been trying to call you for the last twenty minutes. I got an alert from the jail about Grassle. Get down here quick."

Riggins stood up so fast the swing knocked backward and knocked a potted plant over the railing. Her heart froze a beat in her chest. "What happened?"

Static, and then a collection of raised voices on the other end of the phone before Sanchez came back on. "Just get down here. It's ugly. There's been a shooting. I'll fill you in when you get here."

Riggins pressed the END button on her phone and stuffed it into her front pocket. Her stomach sank as she ran inside, scooping up her badge and car keys from the dresser top. She strapped on her gun holster and did her best to compose herself. As she hurried through the living room, she caught sight of Chet standing at the sink, holding a lemon and a knife. His lips formed a rigid line and his eyes no longer held the luster they'd held just moments ago. She didn't tell him where she was going or why. She didn't need to.

EIGHTEEN

SCHULTZ WAS ACCUSTOMED to shooting living things. An avid hunter for much of his life, he'd shot his first wild boar at age ten. The following year he'd killed his first deer on a hunting trip in the Georgia woods. Most of his shots had come at a distance and involved a rifle; almost all had involved a moving target. But now, as he sprang to his feet, spilling his bag of seeds around him, he felt a thrill rush through him. He'd pointed his shotgun at numerous inmates before—ostensibly for real rules violations—but never had he switched the safety off and racked a live round into the chamber while doing so. The fact that *this* human being was Eddie Grassle only added to his excitement.

"Get down now, or I promise you I'll blow your fucking head off!" Schultz yelled.

Already, Eddie had managed to climb his way to the top of the fence. The speed at which he'd done so had surprised even him. If he'd clipped his fingernails as he'd wanted to recently, it would have been impossible for him to have even gotten halfway up the heavy mesh. Using one of the metal poles for leverage, Eddie pulled himself to the very top edge, but found himself hindered now by the glistening coils of razor wire.

"You get down off that fence, or I *will* shoot you dead!" Schultz yelled.

From below, Officer Nady held both hands to his face in shock and dismay. He muttered a half-decipherable order for Eddie to get down as well. But Eddie didn't hear them in his heightened state. As he forced his body through a space in the wire, becoming stuck as the heavy gauge razors began pressing into various parts of his chest and back, he looked ten yards directly ahead of him into the business end of Schultz's charged shotgun.

Still awkwardly holding his radio unit that he had been in the middle of getting out, Schultz pulled his trigger finger clear and placed it inside the guard, sighting the bead at the end of the barrel. His tongue flicked out and wetted his lips. The veteran officer and expert shot could barely believe his eyes. Grassle's upper body now lay wedged between two closely positioned coils of wire, the Y-shaped barbed protrusions blocking any chance he had of finishing his climb over the top.

The only real shot Schultz had would be one to the head. A smile crept over his lips.

From below him, Nady's frantic pleas not to shoot came to him in garbled syllables, but Schultz shut the voice out, prepared to answer for the shooting. Even in his hurried state, he knew the worst that would happen would be forced retirement at full pension, and not even the risk of civil liability. Schultz aimed the bead between Eddie's eyes and squeezed the trigger.

Just as the gun fired, a black mass emerged out of the corner of Schultz's eye, seemingly out of nowhere, and struck him in the head with enough force to knock him sideways toward the far railing. Had the mass struck him half a second later, the nine buckshot pellets would surely have blown a hole the size of a softball in Eddie's head. But whatever had hit him arrived a split second before the blast, throwing the shot a foot to the left. Eight of the large pellets missed Eddie completely, instead striking one of the metal clasps holding the coils of razor wire together. The two coils just to Eddie's right sprang back on themselves several feet as a result, like giant retracting Slinkys. The last pellet struck Eddie in the right shoulder, burying its way deep into the muscle but missing bone entirely. Eddie cried out, more in surprise from still being alive than from the pain. He'd stared directly into the muzzle, expecting to be killed and partly wanting it to happen. But now as he held himself atop the fence with one hand, he looked up toward the tower in time to see something both strangely curious and otherworldly.

Schultz was backpedaling to his right, swinging wildly with the shotgun at what seemed to be a black cloud enveloping him. Only when Schultz struck something solid with the butt did Eddie realize what had happened. Birds. Dozens of them. Descending together from the nearby tree, they'd converged on the spilled bag of sunflower seeds at Schultz's feet, a frenzy of flapping wings and claws and pecking beaks.

Swinging wildly at the screeching mass, Schultz struck his back hard against the railing, bending over backward and losing his grip on his possessions in the process. Almost in slow motion, he grabbed for the shotgun as it teetered over the railing, wrapping one hand around the still hot barrel. His fingers released their grip on reflex and the barrel flipped end-over-end, clattering along the four railings before landing on the ground below next to his fallen radio.

Eddie locked eyes with Schultz, who stood gripping the top railing and staring wide-eyed back at him. Not wasting any time, he pulled his upper body the rest of the way through the newly opened gap, catching his left pants leg on one of the razor coils that had moved back toward him due to his weight transfer. It sliced through the fabric and into his skin, causing a neat, three-inch-long gash along his thigh. Hardly feeling it due to his surging adrenalin, he pulled his trail leg over the top strand of horizontal wire, then rotated to face the other side of the fence. Now free of obstructions, including no mesh on this side, Eddie made the descent in a matter of seconds. Hopping onto the paved sidewalk, he stood upright just ten feet from Officer Nady, who stared open-mouthed and wide-eyed back at him.

"Shoot him, you idiot!" came Schultz's desperate voice from above.

More out of reflex than any obligation to obey, Nady suddenly came to life. Unslinging his shotgun and racking a round into the chamber, he thumbed the safety off, shouldered the gun and pointed it directly at Eddie's chest.

"Don't move, Eddie! I—I'll shoot you, I swear I will!" Nady yelled, his voice cracking. Instinctively, Eddie raised both hands high above his head, images of his life passing before his eyes for the second time in as many minutes.

"Don't shoot!" he pleaded, locking eyes with the young officer. He looked left and right, noting no one yet responding. Eddie spied a long, black object lying in the grass to his left. A shotgun. Several feet from it lay the smashed radio unit.

"Get on the ground now, Eddie!" Nady commanded, his voice two octaves higher than normal. The gun's barrel wavered in his trembling hands; but despite the young officer's nervousness, Eddie felt it too risky to make a run for it. He licked his lips, wondering what he should do now. He hadn't expected to make it over the fence alive. But now that he'd survived his suicidal dash over it, he didn't want to needlessly get shot by a frightened rookie officer. Life, or some semblance of it, seemed to swell within him. He felt suddenly and irrevocably reborn.

"Nady, it's me, Eddie. I'm not going to hurt anyone," he pleaded, his hands still above his head. In the tower, Schultz's frantic screams had resumed, yet from the pounding of Eddie's own pulse in his ears they seemed no more than background chatter to the drama unfolding here on the ground.

"Why are you doing this, Eddie?" Nady croaked. Tears welled in his eyes and his lower lip began to tremble. Eddie thought he looked like a kid who'd just lost his favorite dog.

"Nady, listen to me—" Eddie said, his hands extending toward the young officer now. "You're a good man, not like Schultz. I didn't do what they said I did."

Nady looked up toward Schultz before looking back to Eddie. "It doesn't matter if you did it or not, Eddie," Nady said, tears dribbling freely down his cheeks. He drew the back of one hand across his face before quickly replacing it onto the gun stock. When Eddie took a step toward him, Nady pulled the gun up into an active aim, causing him to freeze again. Eddie could almost taste his own desperation. Looking up toward the tower where Schultz was now frantically busy with the locked grate, Eddie forced his eyes away from the main cell-block, positive that when he did look that way he'd see a group of armed officers storming around the corner. He spread his arms apart and took another step forward.

"Stop right there, Eddie, or I'll shoot you, I swear I will," Nady cried.

Eddie took another step forward. Only three or four feet separated the two of them now. "I can't live with myself if I don't get a chance to make things right. Go ahead and shoot. I'd rather you do it than him." He glanced toward the tower again, where Schultz shot a murderous scowl down to him before disappearing from the railing. Moments later, a clattering sound of metal on metal came from somewhere at the rear of the tower, followed by a set of keys falling to the ground. Then Schultz's agonized roar.

Nady stood wide-eyed and helpless to stop the insanity that was happening right in front of him. Instead of grabbing the fallen shotgun, Eddie stepped over it and picked up the fallen set of keys. Standing straight, Eddie locked eyes with Nady. The young officer wept openly now, tears spilling down his youthful face. Suddenly Eddie felt very sorry for him.

"I'm going to take these keys and turn my back to you now, Mr. Nady. Then I'm going to that perimeter gate and opening it. The only way I don't do that is if you shoot me in the back."

Nady shook his head hard. "There's nothing but woods for miles out there, Eddie. You wouldn't last ten minutes."

"Maybe not," Eddie said. A certain peace settled over him then. It was as if an invisible spirit had placed an unseen hand on his shoulder and told him that, no matter what happened from that point forward, everything would somehow be okay. "I'll be back, Nady. I promise. I have business I need to tend to. Something really important. I know that sounds crazy, but this will be my only chance to do it."

Eddie backed away, slowly at first, then dared to give his back to the trembling young officer and his shotgun. If he got shot, he reasoned, he wished it would happen right away to stave off the churning suspense in his gut.

As it was, Nady didn't fire at all.

As Eddie had been stuck atop the fence, Schultz had bent over the railing and reached down in vain while he screamed to his panicked partner, "My gun! Get my gun, goddammit!" But Nady stood unable or unwilling to move. Cursing, Schultz turned and kicked at the still swarming flock of birds. As he did, he stepped on one of them, slipping on the animal's sleek wing and falling hard onto his back. Scrambling to his feet, he raced toward the locked ladder grate. Fumbling for his set of keys, he found a familiar looking brass one and stabbed it into the keyhole. No luck. "Shit!" he yelled, wildly going through the half dozen similar-looking keys until he found the right one. His fingers trembling, he jammed it home, only backward. He tried removing it, but it wouldn't budge. Wiggling and yanking on it did him no good. Out of frustration, he stood and kicked at the lock to dislodge the key. Nothing. On his second kick, the key dislodged, but the force behind it sent the entire keyring sailing through the railing and onto the ground below. A cry of rage erupted from him. Darting back to the railing facing the yard, he stared down at his partner, who still stood frozen in fear or indecision, or both. Averting his attention now back to the fence, Schultz saw something so unbelievable he would not have guessed it to be possible had the question been posed just minutes earlier. Grassle squeezed through the gap in the wire, rotated his body then scampered down the opposite side of the fence where he hopped onto the ground. Nady had by now come back to life and placed Grassle at gunpoint.

"Shoot him, for fuck's sake!" Schultz screamed down to him, but the young man was still in his own world. For an agonizing minute, Nady and Grassle stood ten feet apart in an insane game of chicken. All Schultz could do was cup his hands beside his mouth and scream as loud as he could, knowing their location at the end of the facility and the thick cellblock walls would render his voice useless.

And then, something even more unreal—Grassle walking past Nady's frozen form toward Schultz's gun, past it thankfully, and bending down to pick up Schultz's fallen keys. Then Grassle moving toward the perimeter fence, first at a walk, then a hobbling run, and all Schultz could do was watch as he gripped the railing and simmered in his silent rage.

STUMBLING ALONG THE fifty yards of open grass, Eddie arrived at the perimeter fence gate and lifted the heavy padlocked chain. His fingers trembling, he slid the first key that would fit into the lock's keyhole. Nothing. Trying the only other two keys that would fit, he found that they too would not open the lock. Looking back toward the tower, he saw Nady fumbling with something on his belt. His radio. *He's going to call for help, and then it'll all be over.*

Eddie tried the first key again, but it still didn't work. A sudden and crushing thought seized his mind just then—this set of keys didn't open the gate. There were two officers on recreation duty, of course. Maybe a security measure gave only one of them access to the gate. With the key still turned in the hole, Eddie yanked hard several times on the heavy lock, then banged it against the fence pole in frustration. Looking up, he considered scaling the twelve-foot-high fence, but coils of razor wire sat atop this one as well, and he knew he'd never get over it without getting slashed to ribbons. He looked left along the fence line but found that route would take him back toward the cellblock. Looking right, he saw the fence sweep around toward a maintenance shed, where it continued in that direction out of sight. His instincts told him it would be here, or nowhere.

Cursing his luck, he picked the lock back up and was about to try another key when he saw something unbelievable. The lock sat open, the locking arm resting loose from the heavy body. A stupid grin spread across his lips. The last key had in fact been the correct one; the lock must have been rusty and needed that last bang against the pole to fully open. Unhooking it and snaking off the chain, he flipped up the U-shaped post hinge before pushing the gate open. Looking around, he was sure someone by now would have come to the officers' aid, but he saw nobody. Nady still stood where he'd been all along, now fifty yards behind him and with his radio finally in his hands. On the tower ledge, Schultz stood gripping the railing, glaring in Eddie's direction. Despite the distance, Eddie could see the seething hate in those eyes, and he felt sure that if given another chance, the man would not hesitate to finish the job the birds had disrupted.

Closing the pedestrian gate behind him, Eddie fed the chain ends through the posts and re-fastened the lock, making sure to put it on his side this time. Standing on a narrow perimeter road, he looked left and noted what appeared to be another access gate one hundred feet away. It was unmanned for now, but they'd be coming, he knew. And soon. He limped across the road as quickly as he could manage, maneuvering his way through a watery ditch and climbing up the reverse embankment. Looking behind him and still seeing no one following, he tossed the keys into the murky water before disappearing into the thick growth of trees just beyond.

NINETEEN

SUPERINTENDENT DEVEREUX REPLACED the flask in the top desk drawer and rested his head in his hands. He switched off his radio, which he used mainly to monitor radio discipline within the facility, then turned the ringer off on his office telephone. Since the rest of his staff weren't allowed to possess their cell phones on duty, he'd refused to also, despite a loophole that allowed administrators to have them.

He needed time to think. Things were getting complicated. He racked his brain for any clue as to how his schemes had been discovered. The more he thought about it, the only plausible conclusion could be that whoever had discovered his involvement must have gained it by illegal means themselves. Even with broad investigative powers, which included warrants and subpoenas, the government had limitations. Those who operated outside the law did not. Determining where the intrusion had come from seemed to him like trying to find a pinhole leak in the Hoover Dam. Adding to Devereux's already disturbing dilemma was the fact that someone powerful out there had a personal interest in one of his prisoners. A man accustomed to reading both on and between the lines, Devereux concluded that a mob vendetta had likely occurred here. Despite his abhorrence at being forced to do so, he now understood the absolute importance of keeping this Grassle character under his strict control until he left the jail.

Just as Devereux logged back on to his computer, he heard the familiar drone of the facility escape siren. He looked to the clock on the wall and sighed. 11:43 am. Could his people not get anything right? The supervisor in charge of testing the weekly alarm had gotten the day right—Thursday—but had begun the weekly test seventeen minutes early. Ever since assuming his post as superintendent, Devereux had preached consistency. The reason for conducting the test on the same day and at the same time was simple: to prevent confusion. An amplified unit attached to the communication tower near where his office sat, the siren could be heard a mile away during the day, and two at night. His irritation mounting, Devereux reached back into his desk drawer for the flask and took another long pull. The liquid burned going down, but less so than the first mouthful had. After a full minute, the siren continued. Devereux checked the clock on his office wall, ensuring the second hand still made its sweep. His watch and computer clock both read similar times. His annoyance building, he watched the clock's second hand make another rotation—two minutes now, and still the siren wailed. Who the hell was conducting the test? Protocol clearly stated the test siren last for one minute exactly, to be followed by one loud blast from the air horn signaling it being a true test. Only in the event of a true escape should the siren continue. A fail-safe had been fitted that should the siren malfunction and not turn off during a test when intended, the master fuse could simply be taken out of the unit to silence it.

His irritation boiling over, Devereux reached for his office telephone when he saw the message button blinking, indicating a missed call. Frowning, he poked the button to turn the ringer back on. When he switched his Motorola walkie-talkie back on, the flurry of panicked transmissions coming from it froze the blood in his veins.

Alarmed, Devereux yelled into his radio mike once traffic cleared. "Superintendent Devereux to Sergeant Weeks, fifty-six my office. Now!" More voices stepping over each other on the radio. He received only broken transmissions. Something about the east recreation yard. And the perimeter fence. And of someone running on foot.

Just then his office door burst open. A breathless sergeant of the guard stood in the doorway. "Sir...I've been trying to reach you. I didn't know you were in here. You didn't answer your phone or the radio."

"What the hell is going on?" Devereux demanded, rising to his feet. Panic welled inside him and his heart began to pound in his chest. "Why is the test siren still sounding?"

Weeks, a large man with a belly that hung over his belt, drew a hand across his forehead and pointed past the superintendent, out his office window. "There's been an escape, sir. From the east yard."

Devereux turned to look out his grated office window. To his amazement, a dozen or more uniformed jail officers could be seen running across the grassy area there toward the perimeter fence line. "What do you mean an escape?"

"He went over the fence. How in three hells he did it, I don't know. Schultz got a shot off and grazed him. He's cut up pretty good, too, from the razor wire. We found a blood trail from where he went over. He won't get far though, sir, nothing but woods out there. Should I call—"

And then a realization struck Devereux like a lightning bolt. He held up a hand to quiet the stuttering sergeant. "Who just escaped from my facility?" he asked, his eyes bulging with panic.

The sergeant's face flushed. "Eddie Grassle, sir. He's the inmate who robbed—"

But the sergeant never finished his sentence. Leaping over his desk and almost slipping on a pile of papers stacked there, Superintendent Devereux pushed past the large man, knocking him into the doorframe, and ran at full speed down the hallway toward the emergency command post.

EDDIE HAD A vague sense of running east. He remembered his first visit to the yard, when he'd had to shield his eyes from the rising sun, and he knew he was loosely oriented in the same direction he'd been looking that first day. Despite the thick vegetation making it difficult to be sure of his direction, he had foremost in his mind the compulsion to keep moving. His lungs burned, his shoulder ached from the shotgun wound, and the gash on his leg throbbed terribly, but he knew he couldn't afford even a moment's rest. He had no plan for where to go. Even if he had known, he didn't have a clue how to accomplish it. It seemed amazing to him that just minutes ago he had been lying on the rec yard surface, the sun basking down on him and his mind daydreaming. That he should now be outside the jail's perimeter, running wild through the woods with no one directly behind him, seemed impossible. Cutting left toward what appeared to be an old trail, he tripped on exposed tree roots and fell flat on his face. Dirt went up his nose and into his mouth, but he made no attempt to spit it out. It tasted fresh and old at the same time, and a crazy thought coursed through his mind as he stood and resumed his lumbering run—that this may be the last time he ever tasted dirt. A crazy thought for sure, one of many that had bombarded his brain in those insane moments after jumping the fence.

Crashing through sprawling bougainvillea and thick stands of saw-grass that ripped at his exposed hands and neck, Eddie heard a sound that raised the hair on the back of his neck. A siren, loud and wailing from somewhere behind him. They'd raised the alarm. So, this was it. He felt a mixture of terror and relief—terror that they'd be sending reinforcements now, and relief that he no longer had to guess when they'd be coming for him. He knew full well this area consisted of woodland and swamps, terrain not conducive to one man evading what would likely be an army. He considered changing course, possibly circling back toward the way he'd come in order to throw them off, but he estimated he'd already gone too far to double back. He felt his best chance would be to put as much distance as he could between him and the jail. If his freedom was to be short-lived, let them endure the same elements he did, even for five minutes.

Judging from the siren's piercing wail, a sound that seemed to alert even the heavens of his flight, Eddie judged he had at best a quarter mile head start. It wasn't very far, but he knew if he had even the slightest chance to avoid immediate capture, it would have to be enough.

TWENTY

DETECTIVE RIGGINS PARKED sideways across two of the three designated handicap parking spaces at the main jail parking lot and snatched her Sheriff's Office credentials off the passenger seat. Jumping out of her unmarked cruiser, she raced toward the single-story administration building fifty yards away. Bursting through the front double doors, she met a flurry of activity: dozens of jail and patrol deputies hurried around the lobby area while a middle-aged man in a suit barked orders above the noise. Riggins immediately recognized the man as Superintendent Devereux, whom she had met numerous times. Scanning the crowd, Riggins found the face she'd sought—Detective Sanchez, who stood on tiptoes on the far side of the room, beckoning her while speaking into his cell phone. Riggins pushed through the crowd and made her way to where Sanchez stood. "I had to hear it in person. Is he dead?"

Confused, Sanchez ended his phone call and took a step backward. "Dead? Didn't you listen to your radio on the way over?"

"When you said he was gone I turned it off. I didn't want to hear the rest over the radio."

Sanchez seemed to understand what she'd assumed. "He is gone, in a way. Beat feet. Hopped a fence at recreation and somehow made it into the woods. Happened about twenty minutes ago."

Riggins frowned. "Wait a minute. Did you say he escaped? As in, he's still alive?"

"Maybe not for long, but yeah, Rig, he's still alive. The Superintendent is giving a briefing in a second, so we'll get more intel. One of the rec deputies got off a shot and wounded him. Got cut up on the wire too. Christ, Rig, he did it. The crazy fucker really did it. I can't believe—"

A loud scraping sound cut him off as a pair of jail deputies began moving a heavy row of connected chairs. Once the chairs faced the assembled group, Superintendent Devereux stood atop them and waved his arms above his head. Few in attendance seemed to notice. Placing two fingers to his lips, he gave a loud whistle that finally succeeded in quieting the crowd of excited officers.

"Alright, people, listen up!" he hollered. "As you know, we are now under escape protocol. I need everyone's undivided attention. What I *do not* need is people sticking their thumbs up their asses and playing 'How Do I Taste.' Captain Odom, what's the status on the bloodhound?"

A stern-looking man dressed in a glittering uniform nodded his head once, proclaiming, "I've got an off-duty team on the way now. Should be here in about ten mikes. Both on-duty teams are out of action. Dogs ran into a beehive during training this morning."

Devereux rolled his eyes. "That's why policy says we train with one team at a time."

Captain Odom's silence spoke for itself.

"Apparently, I need to adjust my command staff once this is over," Devereux said bitterly. "Just get me that reserve team here now. And make sure nobody tracks through those goddamn woods until the dog gets here. I don't need a bunch of goons messing up the trail."

"Yessir," Odom managed.

Devereux addressed another officer standing near him. "Addison, what's going on with the perimeter?"

"We've got a three-mile containment, with roadblocks on all roads and fifty men on the ground. Lots of woods and orange groves out there, sir, but he ain't slipping by what we have set up. My men have orders not to let a fly get through without looking up its ass first."

Devereux allowed himself a moment's respite at hearing some semblance of good news. But the worrisome look on his face betrayed the fact that deep down, his guts churned and the blood in his veins boiled. He noticed Riggins and Sanchez standing near the back of the room and acknowledged them with a brief nod before continuing his orders. "This facility is on lockdown until further notice. No inmate movement until I order it. Not for anything. All staff is to remain on post. Nobody goes home until this sonofabitch is caught. Understood?"

A murmur of assent from the crowd. "Coincidentally, we have homicide here already. Detectives Riggins and Sanchez, in the back there. I'm sure they'll be getting statements from our recreation staff. Lieutenant Fisher, you're responsible for law enforcement outside the immediate search area, so today's your day to shine. Get with PD over in Beckwith and get a status on a chopper. I want eyes in the sky, ASAP."

A faceless voice in the crowd offered a resounding "yessir!" after which a short and solidly built man ducked out of the room. That seemed to open the floodgates of activity again, as the din of police-speak rose in earnest. Detective Sanchez looked excitedly to Riggins. "What's your call, boss? We're here already. Can't we do something to help out?"

Riggins placed a hand to her head and closed her eyes. The events of the day seemed unreal to her, as if she were playing an improvised part in some surreal drama. "No, Lieu doesn't want us involved in Eddie's case anymore. I'd assume that would include his stroll through the woods."

Sanchez nodded his understanding. Just then, a grizzled looking man dressed in blue jeans, t-shirt and John Deere ball cap burst through the front door and announced that he and his dog were ready to begin their track. Devereux appeared to visibly relax as the handler and a group of officers spilled out the door to an awaiting truck. Through the room's floor-to-ceiling windows, Riggins saw a liver-colored bloodhound pulling against its rope in the truck bed. Its plaintive baying raised a sense of dread inside Riggins like none she had ever known.

"About damned time," Devereux exclaimed, hopping down from the bench. As he stormed out the door to confer with the dog handler, Fisher grabbed Devereux by the arm as he rushed past him. Amid the mixed shouting from the various people assembled, Riggins overheard Fisher murmur, "Sir, I really should be the one to lead the manhunt."

Devereux stopped and first appraised the hand on his arm before leveling his gaze onto his patrol counterpart. "First of all, Lieutenant, take your hand off me."

Grudgingly, Fisher obeyed.

"Second, this is my jail, and that prisoner belongs to me," Devereux continued. "Policy states escapees are still considered on jail grounds during fresh pursuit. Your people have the area surrounded, so unless you can prove he's breached it, this is my chase to lead. My dog teams have been the best in state two years running. They *will* lead the search in conjunction with an apprehension force made up of my officers. Just have your men sit on that perimeter and make sure he doesn't slip through. We'll push him toward you."

The lieutenant opened his mouth as if to protest then appeared to think better of it. He turned and stalked away, barking orders into his hand-held radio. Devereux followed behind him, pushing past a group of assembling jail officers who had mustered for the ensuing manhunt. Like a team of disciplined soldiers, they followed him in one stern rank out the door. For a moment, both Riggins and Sanchez stood alone in the lobby area, watching the chaotic scene unfold in the parking lot.

Sanchez let out a low whistle. "This isn't good," he said matter-of-factly.

"No, Sanny," Riggins concurred. "And I have a feeling it isn't going to end well. I just don't see him getting taken alive. There aren't any cameras or witnesses in those woods. I've seen it before." Riggins watched the dog handler unleash his bloodhound from the truck bed and hold an object beneath the animal's snout. Not until she and Sanchez followed the others outside did she recognize the object for what it was: a size 11 men's shoe.

TWENTY-ONE

FIVE HUNDRED YARDS behind Eddie, at the perimeter fence where he had keyed his way through the padlocked gate, confusion reigned. Superintendent Devereux stood in the middle of the narrow road barking commands to various officers, who either did not hear him at all or were so amped for the chase they misunderstood his words entirely. Two dozen officers in all stood ready to follow the bloodhound, having been instructed to form a wedge-shaped line beginning ten yards behind the dog and handler. Devereux's plan called for the hound to track the suspect until it cornered him, at which time the skirmish line would extend out from the ends to encircle him. Once that happened, it would just be a matter of time before one of the Patrol K9s were called in to take him down if he didn't give himself up. Heavily armed SWAT members would be held at the ready to take him into custody.

Devereux had to repeat his order several times before everyone fully understood, and since only a portion of them had been in the military, the objective had to be stripped down to its basic components. Seizing on his experience in an army infantry company, Devereux had quickly formulated a maneuver to squeeze the escapee to either the left or right quadrant of what he considered no-man's land. That area consisted of a heavily wooded area approximately three-square miles, around which had been amassed roadblocks to all roads, Patrol K-9 units, and several dozen teams of deputies arranged in a defensive perimeter. Devereux's defense was not a command bunker or fire base, as he'd been accustomed to in his army days, but rather the forty square miles of wild land beyond that inner no-man's land. Orange groves and scattered farmhouses dotted the area, and though an emergency alert had been put out for any residents who may be present, even Devereux knew it was unlikely, if not impossible, to get word to all of them. As a failsafe, he'd arranged with his patrol counterparts to search all vehicles going in and out of the area with no exceptions.

The dog handler, a part-time reserve deputy and well-respected dog expert who went simply by "Jerry," allowed his bloodhound to sniff the escapee's shoe once more. After doing so, she sniffed the ground, turning in a half circle before dutifully sitting on her hindquarters next to her handler. Panting due to the already rising midday heat, the animal's tongue hung well past her shawl, which dripped thick strands of saliva. Her eyes, mostly hidden by folds of skin, remained fixed and patient on the tree line twenty feet distant. Jerry knelt beside her now, whispered something in her ear then stood to call for quiet.

"Sheba here is the best hound I've ever had. Once she finds him, I'll call you up so you can take him how you please." Jerry drew one hand across his mouth and spat tobacco juice on the ground beside him. "She worked a trail two weeks old after a rainstorm once, and never gave up the chase. Found her man ten miles from where the trail started. Some hounds, tracking's a game. Not Sheba. I reckon she'd rather fall over dead before givin' up." He reached down to pat her on the head, and she returned his affection with two slobbery licks. "This is a hot trail, so she'll be pullin' hard. Just stay back and let her work," Jerry instructed. "Ten yards, maybe a little more to be safe. If I yell stop, everyone stops. If I say walk, everyone walks. Understood?"

An assenting chorus rose up among the assembled officers. Jerry looked to Superintendent Devereux, who in offering a single nod of his head signaled the handler to begin his chase.

"We start here from the split," the bushy handler declared, and uttering a single command, he allowed the dog a bit of slack until she hit on a spot on the ground leading down into the shallow ditch beyond the road. "Here he went!" the handler shouted, and the group of armed officers filed into the pre-arranged formation behind him. As the hound moved down the short embankment, splashing through the knee-deep water then up the other side to flat ground again, she turned in circles, sniffing excitedly. Jerry knelt a distance behind her, not wanting to intrude and allowing her plenty of slack. Men could train a hound, he knew, but they could not mimic one million years of primal instinct. Finding the scent again, the hound dug its paws into the soft earth and tugged at her leash, dragging her handler into the trees. Turning his head, Jerry grinned and waved his arm for the rest to follow.

Two officers armed with carbines balanced on their hips remained on the dirt road, their instructions to guard the split in case their subject backtracked against his own scent. On each end of the dirt road, at two hundred yards' distance, two marked cruisers sat with emergency lights flashing. Uniformed officers stood guard there also, charged with watching points north and south of the jail perimeter. This rear guard of sorts would basically block Grassle from retreating the way he'd come. The recreation yard and the gate through which he'd gone were now considered crime scenes and had been sealed off to keep their integrity.

Devereux, who had just finished a cell phone call, trotted over to where both Riggins and Sanchez had been watching the scene from the near side of the road. Riggins thought the man looked like some-one who wished very much to be elsewhere.

"Bird is on its way from Beckwith now," Devereux said to the detective duo, his voice carrying noticeable relief. "Once we have eyes in the sky, I'll breathe a little easier. You two going to interview my people now?"

"Another team is on the way to do that," Riggins said, watching the last officer disappear into the edge of the woods. As an after-thought, she added, "The subject is unarmed, correct?"

Devereux's eyes narrowed. "We can't assume that. We find shanks during shakedowns all the time. And if I didn't know any bet-ter, detective, I'd say I detect a tone of sympathy in your voice."

Riggins's face flushed. "Professional concern and sympathy are two different things, Superintendent." She leveled her gaze at him, daring him to question her ethics again, when his radio squawked with a static-filled transmission about a possible sighting in the woods. Eyes alight with hope, Devereux asked for confirmation. A brief silence, then a response: "Disregard, just a deer."

"Fantastic," Devereux offered with sarcastic cheer, but then said to the detective team that despite the disappointment he expected a quick re-capture of their prisoner. He led the way back down the road toward a different personnel gate, then ushered them through a secured rear door in the administration building. Down a short hallway to a series of offices, the group stopped at a door marked **Interview Room #1**. Riggins noted that this had been the same interview room where she had last spoken with Eddie. Detectives Teliford and Grimes, apparently having just arrived, rose from their chairs in the adjoining waiting room and exchanged nods with Riggins and Sanchez. The tension between the two pairs was palpable.

Devereux opened the interview room door to reveal a fat, dour-looking officer sitting alone at the far end of the interview table. The name **Schultz** sat emblazoned in black stitching on his uniform shirt. Riggins briefed Teliford and Grimes on the escape, watching with regret as they entered the interview room and shut the door behind them. Devereux excused himself then, stating he had urgent follow-up provisions to make.

As Riggins and Sanchez made their way toward the exit, Lieutenant Heinke entered the lobby. Taking one look at them, he rolled his eyes and beckoned her into an unoccupied conference room. Riggins followed him into the room, shooting Sanchez a wide-eyed look before closing the door behind her.

"I thought I told you to stand down on the Grassle case," he said, disappointment in his voice.

"You did, sir," she said. "I just heard about the escape and wanted to find out what happened first-hand. Grimes and Teliford are handling the staff interviews, and I haven't gotten directly involved."

"It doesn't matter," he said, hands on hips. "You do realize this entire place is a crime scene now."

"Yes, sir."

"And that the sheriff is on his way as we speak. If he sees you here, he's going to ask me why. I'm not sure I'll be able to explain it to him."

Riggins offered a bit of insight. "For what it's worth, sir, I can say Sanny and I came here to provide logistical assistance."

Heinke gave her the look of a disappointed father. "Don't split hairs with me, Alice. In case you haven't noticed, I don't have many to spare."

She pressed her lips together, nodding. "I apologize, Lieu. I was just concerned something bad had happened."

"First, your apology is not accepted. It's not enough. And second, I'd say our murder suspect escaping from jail is as bad as it can get." He sighed heavily, looking around the room as if searching for a solution other than the one he knew he had to make.

"I don't want to do this, but it's the only way to protect you. If the sheriff sees you, or hears of you being here, the only way he doesn't order an insubordination investigation is if I tell him I already issued an emergency suspension. That'll buy us some time."

Riggins gaped at him.

"Relax, Alice. It's forty-eight hours. By then, we'll have Grassle back in custody and the sheriff will forget about you. You were already on desk duty anyway."

She huffed. "I've never been suspended in my career, Lieu. I have to respectfully object to this."

He shrugged. "Duly noted, but I'm respectfully pulling rank. And don't think this is just professional. When I gave you away at your wedding, I promised to look after you, and I intend on keeping that promise. I like to think your father would thank me right now if he were here."

This last part seemed to soften her a bit. She gave him an appreciative smile before moving her eyes out the office window to the public parking lot beyond, noting that the first news van had already arrived, no doubt its crew having been tipped off by a law enforcement contact. Its antenna stretched toward the sky like that of a giant, metallic insect. Dozens of cruisers had clustered the area with emergency lights flashing and their uniformed owners standing sternly beside them. Knowing Heinke had just been briefed by Detectives Teliford and Grimes, themselves having just interviewed both recreation deputies, Riggins couldn't help but still feel amazed at how Eddie had managed to escape. With no confirmed sighting of him in the first hour, the prevailing strategy had shifted from fresh pursuit and capture to containment. Riggins, like everyone else involved, knew the issue wasn't *if* they would capture him, but *when*. According to the jail superintendent, the bloodhound team had sent back reports that the trail was still hot. A less experienced mind would have decided to flood the area with as many dogs and personnel as possible. But this tactic tended to cause confusion. One dog, especially an experienced one, was often the best option in a limited area such as this. With the perimeter having been established (the Calusa River to the north, the jail to the west, and roadblocks of all immediate roads), Devereux, in conjunction with patrol forces, seemed wholly confident the prisoner remained pinned down in that zone. Grassle would not have had time to gain access to a road, so the prospect of his escape by vehicle had been ruled out. The arrival of the helicopter had enabled aerial sweeps to be conducted, but initially these had proved largely symbolic. The heavy foliage precluded any real ability to scan by sight in daylight hours. By contrast, its nighttime thermal imaging camera turned it into a true asset in times of darkness, provided he remained contained. But sundown wouldn't be for at least eight hours, and not having Grassle captured by then was something nobody on this side of the law wished to consider.

Taking her eyes from the window scene, Riggins met Heinke's gaze. "You're right, sir. I was wrong, and I shouldn't try to deflect. I was worried something really bad had happened and I let it get to me personally. The last thing I want to do is make it seem I don't respect your decisions."

"Not my decisions, Alice. Don't forget, I have a boss too."

Riggins searched for appropriate words. She finally came up with something that impressed Heinke a great deal. "What's the first thing you taught me when I became a detective?"

He thought about it before answering, "To always trust common sense."

"That's right. Because it never lies. Well, this does not make sense. I don't know if Grassle is guilty. And you're right, it really isn't my job to determine that. But my job *is* to make sure the law is being adhered to, and to not make mistakes that can put innocent people in cages for life. I know I can never get Cokley back. I still have nightmares where he's hanging by his neck, but his eyes are open and he's asking me why I let this happen to him. It's kind of ironic that during my entire career I've never killed anyone with my firearm, but in a way, I helped kill someone with the stroke of my pen. Somehow, that feels even worse."

Heinke wrapped an arm around her shoulders and hugged her close. "Go home, Alice. We have plenty of folks here to handle this. Grassle may be able to run around in the woods for a while, but he's not going to last long. If he's smart, he'll give himself up. When we catch him, I'll call you, I promise. I'm sure some time alone with Chet will do you good anyway. Tell him I said hello, and when all this is over and you two retire on the beach somewhere, I'll have to take him up on his offer to go fishing out on the gulf."

Riggins smiled despite herself. Twenty-four years with the agency had brought her to where she stood today. Had she allowed old ghosts to interfere with the first tenet of good detective work? She didn't feel she could answer that right now. A familiar maxim came to her: When in doubt, when you feel you have lost your way, take a step back and view the facts as they lay. Then follow your gut and don't look back.

Riggins thanked Heinke, then after clearing her weapon she placed it alongside her credentials on the desk. Exiting the room, she found Sanchez talking on his cell phone as he paced near the main exit. He hung up just as Riggins approached.

"What's the verdict?" he asked.

"Any news on Eddie?" Riggins said, ignoring the question.

Sanchez opened the door for her and the two stepped out into the midday sunshine. "Still no sightings, but the bloodhound team says he's close. It's just a matter of time until they find him, or he gives himself up."

"Or until they kill him," Riggins said flatly. They passed a gaggle of reporters setting up camera equipment along the public sidewalk.

Riggins shook her head. "The vultures are already circling. They can smell blood a mile away."

Sanchez made eye contact with a pretty blond reporter standing nearby. They exchanged smiles, and twice she glanced over her shoulder toward him. He ran a hand through his hair, coming back to their conversation. "We do our thing and they do theirs, I suppose." As they reached their vehicles, he gave Riggins a double-take. "Hey, where's your badge and gun?"

"They're putting me on ice and re-assigning you to another team soon. Effective about two minutes ago. Lieu wants all our notes and interviews. Said the sheriff ordered it."

Sanchez's eyebrows raised. "Okay, now it's official. Something weird is going on for sure."

Riggins stared into the western sky where storm clouds had begun to form. "I don't know, Sanny," she said in a faraway voice. "But I do know one thing. I'm not going home to sit on my ass while everyone else does my job for me. At least not while Eddie's still out there. If I have to fly under the radar, then so be it."

Sanchez offered a wave to the pretty reporter as she glanced his way once more. "Shit, Rig, if I were you, I'd be glad to spend my last few months pulling traffic duty and helping little old ladies cross the street. Maybe working admin won't be so bad. Remember the plan—you, Chet and a condo on the beach."

Riggins popped the trunk and removed a box of file folders containing everything she'd gathered on the Grassle case. How many hours had she worked on it? How many sleepless nights on the couch cuddled up with Gracie, a pencil between her teeth and wracking her brain to make sense of everything? And Chet, for all his patience and support—how much more could she risk with him working such a physically demanding job that offered no retirement? Her job, and more importantly her pension, would be their meal-ticket out of this place. They'd each grown up here, had remained to live and work, and even appreciated the easier way of life Springwood offered. But they'd long agreed this would not be home forever, and Riggins had increasingly felt that if they didn't leave soon after she retired, they never would. Understanding how close she was to the end, to their dream of running off together to breathe the salt air and walk barefoot every morning in the sand, she felt it her duty to do everything she could to protect that dream.

Four months. After that nothing much else mattered. It would be them against the world. And what a world she felt it would be, walking next to the quiet strength Chet projected, his easy and steady love. She'd always loved her job, priding herself in concluding each case the best she could. Despite the desire to sew up as many loose ends as possible, the very idea of her coming so close to the end, only to risk their future for a virtual stranger, frightened her. She was only forty-three. She knew what would happen if she were to be fired short of the completion of her twenty-fifth year with the agency—no benefits until she turned fifty-five. Not the end of the world, but it would put their plans on hold for another decade plus.

Riggins handed the box to Sanchez then slipped into the driver's seat. She made him promise to text her with minute-by-minute updates. She'd be listening to her agency radio off and on—Heinke had either forgotten it or had not cared she didn't turn that in—but nothing could replace real-time intelligence from someone still connected to the case.

"I'm starting to agree with you that Grassle didn't have anything to do with that robbery," Sanchez called after her as she began to pull out of her parking spot.

She stopped the car and offered him a fleeting smile. "What's the first rule of being a good detective, Sanny?" she asked rhetorically, then drove away.

TWENTY-TWO

She looked like an angel lying naked atop the sheets. Moonlight spilled through the blinds and cast a faint glow against her creamy skin. Her long brown hair splayed around her head, a few strands clinging to her face and neck due to the layer of perspiration she had just earned. Her chest rose and fell as she caught her breath, her erect nipples casting short shadows across her breasts.

Eddie drew his finger lightly from her hip bone to the mounds of her breasts, until finally resting his palm across the noticeable bump in her midsection.

'Penny for your thoughts,' Clarissa said.

'I'm thinking a boy. It's got to be a boy.'

'Don't get disappointed if it's not. Little girls need daddies too.'

Eddie kissed the side of her neck then rolled onto his back. He stared at the ceiling, his mind moving through a hundred different thoughts. As cars drove by on the street outside, their headlights caused ghost-like shadows to float across the darkened bedroom ceiling. 'Yeah, but it's gonna be a boy,' he said matter-of-factly. 'I can feel it. I'll teach him to swing a bat as soon as he can walk. You just see.'

Clarissa turned onto her side and ran her fingers across his muscular torso. Biting her lip, she smacked an open hand lightly against his chest. 'I'll be right back,' she said, and bounced out of bed. Eddie watched her naked form slip into the living room, then reappear moments later.

She stood next to the bed, holding one hand behind her back. Even in the semi-darkness Eddie saw a huge grin playing across her face.

'I know I said I didn't want to find out until the baby was born, but I couldn't resist,' she said.

Eddie shot up in bed, excitement in his eyes. 'You got an ultrasound? Is it a boy?' He popped off the bed and reached out for her hidden hand, but Clarissa giggled and turned away playfully. Bringing her hand from behind her, she pressed the small black and white snapshot against her breasts.

'I haven't looked at it yet. The doctor told me he was positive. He wrote it down, but I didn't look. I wanted to wait until tomorrow morning so we could look at it together. As your birthday present. But it's technically after midnight so it's already your birthday. Do you want to see it?'

Eddie touched her chin and kissed her hard on the mouth. He placed a hand over her hand that covered the picture and felt her heart beating wildly beneath it. Switching on the bedside lamp, he kissed her again. 'Let it be a boy,' he said, and at first Clarissa refused to let go of the picture, sure that if she did it would magically turn into a girl, even if it had been a boy. She had said the sex of the baby wasn't important to her, and she'd meant it. But to Eddie, who she knew hadn't grown up with a father, she figured the difference would be huge. Sure, he'd accept having a girl; he might even prefer it in the end. But to keep the moment's excitement alive she wished on every star she'd ever seen for it to be a boy. Slowly her fingers released the photo and Eddie snapped it up, flipping it around so they could both see it together—the usual black and white field, like a radar image, with a tiny fetus form in the middle. And one handwritten word written across the top border, with an exclamation mark: Boy!

Eddie hollered, hoisting Clarissa up at the hips and carrying her around the room as she giggled and planted excited kisses on his neck. Even now at nineteen, Eddie felt the first swells of fatherly pride flow through him. A boy! He could already envision throwing a baseball to him and watching it sail over his head after the kid connected with it.

He carried her to the edge of the bed and laid her down, switching the lamp off. Clarissa wrapped her legs around his waist and looked deep into his eyes, deeper than she ever had in the two years she'd dated him. Eddie seemed manlier to her now than he'd been just a minute before.

Soundlessly, Clarissa moved her hand down to the stiffness she felt rising against her and guided it between her trembling thighs.

'You can't make me another baby right now, but you can try anyway,' she said, breathless.

As Eddie collapsed into her, she let out a low moan of pleasure and raked her nails across his broad back. For the next hour they abandoned themselves in each other, spurred by the raw, almost godlike power gained from the knowledge they'd created life. And as their movements reached another crescendo—mouths and hips and souls crashing together—Eddie imagined then that the world had aligned just right, that nothing would make him wish to be anywhere else but here with the love of his life, and with their son who lay curled in her womb like a remembered promise.

BLOODIED AND EXHAUSTED, Eddie had collapsed next to a fallen oak tree and passed out briefly, having experienced the flash of memory he hadn't thought of in months. Gasping for breath, he stared up at the spots of brilliant May sky peeking through the foliage above, wondering again if he shouldn't just give up now. He touched his shoulder, wincing in pain. The gash on his leg, although no longer bleeding freely, throbbed with each beat of his heart. He closed his eyes, forcing moist, earth-filled air into his burning lungs. He had only a vague sense of the river lying south of him. Thirst burned at his throat. Thinking about the cool river water made him wish more than anything that it lay ahead, instead of behind him. Resting now in the relative stillness of the deep woods, Eddie considered the best way to give himself up. Perhaps by allowing himself to fall asleep, and just waiting for them to catch up to him and be done with this madness. The escape siren had since stopped, but in its place had come the occasional baying of a hound. He was alone, barefooted and injured, with a hundred heavily armed men likely on his tail. Eddie considered his chances were better than not of taking a bullet from an overeager cop wanting the glory of catching an escaped prisoner, perhaps even being fearful of approaching a cornered man in thick woods.

The thought forced his eyes open. He looked down to his filthy bare feet and grimaced at the sight of them covered in fresh blisters and cuts. He stood, taking a moment to orientate himself. From his time in the recreation yard, he remembered having to shield his eyes from the sun while speaking with the rec officers. Since his rec time had always come before noon, directional law told him the tower sat east of the yard. Eddie studied the shadows cast by the many trees overhead and oriented himself due east. Taking quick but purposeful steps forward, he kept his eyes on reference points ahead of him instead of on the ground. An awkwardly bent tree here, the curve of the natural path there, he made sure to correct himself whenever possible. Going exactly straight wasn't important. Not circling back and running into his pursuers *was*.

Eddie had grown up playing and swimming in the Calusa River. Surrounded by mangroves and endless water oaks with their trademark hanging Spanish moss, the river as well as the county itself (named after an American Indian tribe that had inhabited these same lands hundreds of years before) snaked southwest from its source in the Carolina Smokies until spilling into the eastern Gulf of Mexico. As kids, Eddie and Jules had navigated long stretches of the river, traversing the entire county and beyond. River otters, myriad species of birds and fish, even alligators sunning themselves on the river's banks, had all captured the boys' attention and awe. Absent of fear as they'd jumped from bridges into the sparkling clear water, or daring each other to swim beneath passing riverboats, they'd treated the Calusa as their virtual back yard.

One summer while hiking through the woods, they had encountered a pack of vicious wild dogs. Trapped, the boys had had no choice but to make a run for the river. Crossing at a narrow bend, they'd emerged on the opposite bank dripping wet and laughing at their own near-death experience. Their laughter had abated after realizing the dogs had no intention of giving up the chase. All five of the crazed animals had leaped head-long into the water. Eddie remembered how he and Jules had finally escaped the dogs' wrath by climbing a tree and remaining there overnight. Shivering and frightened, Eddie and Jules hadn't slept a wink as they'd huddled together on a branch. As morning had broken, they'd watched as the dogs had made one last effort to climb the tree before finally giving up.

Stopping momentarily against a towering sycamore, Eddie cast a furtive glance behind him. No sign of the tracking party. Moving around the tree and sinking in mud up to his ankles, Eddie had just begun to step free from the muck when he froze in his tracks. A newer and stranger noise grew in the distance, until it seemed to surround him and caused the ground he stood on to vibrate. *What the hell?* It seemed as though the forest had somehow come alive and was preparing to open its mighty jaws to consume him.

Just then, a flash of movement from above. Looking up through the trees, Eddie saw an object that caused the hair on the back of his neck to stand on end. A helicopter. Not one of the military types he occasionally saw that ran training missions from the army airfield in nearby Hocking, and not a news chopper easily identified by their usual station logo. This one was painted dark blue and had a black sphere attached to its undercarriage. Even more chilling was the one word written on the side of the chopper's body in bold yellow letters: **POLICE**.

Like an animal discovering itself trapped, Eddie's senses sprang to full alert. Diving beneath a log, he willed himself to take a deep breath and remain calm. His breathing quickened despite his attempts, and both his vision and hearing sharpened to a razor focus. The sights and sounds and smells of his surroundings seemed magnified by ten. As his blood pounded through his veins, carrying another dose of adrenaline that even made his skin feel alive, he spoke quietly to himself. *Don't panic. Concentrate on one thing at a time.*

The helicopter changed things. Now they would be tracking him by land and air. The fact they'd already launched such a dedicated search told him his chances of escaping the immediate area had just decreased dramatically. Then again, the odds themselves told him he had *some* chance. A half hour ago he'd been walking inside the recreation yard, minding his business and enjoying the first rays of sunshine he'd seen in almost a week. Now he lay on the filthy earth, far outside the jail's walls, and at least for now no one else on earth knew precisely where he was. The thought alone felt invigorating. Watching the helicopter scream past overhead, Eddie counted to thirty before he dared move.

Kneeling, he used a finger to scrawl a stick figure in the dirt. *That's you.* Beside the figure he drew a wavy vertical line. *Okay, that's the river. It angles southwest through the county until it empties in the Gulf. Don't worry how far away it is now; just remember where it is. If you can make it there you might be able to swim your way out.* Next, he drew a large square west of the stick figure, signifying the jail. Understanding the hunt for him had likely started there, Eddie told himself that no matter what, he had to concentrate on putting as much distance from that place as quickly as possible. Roadblocks would be erected. And from the sound of it, the dog grew nearer. He'd have to deal with things as they presented themselves, he reasoned. For now, he had to force himself to continue moving. And he did so, picking himself up with a grunt and limping through the tangled brush, keeping one eye ahead and the other watchful on the sky above.

TWENTY-THREE

As Eddie ran for his life, a white Cutlass pulled into the administration parking lot of the Calusa County Jail. Paolo Bruzzi emerged from the vehicle, smoothed out his suit jacket and adjusted his sunglasses. His watch read 12:15. The escape now thirty minutes old, he'd learned from Hood that the prisoner was in all probability confined to a three-square-mile area, and had immediately made his way to the jail to assess the situation. Of obvious regret was the escape itself. His job would be to make sure it got cleaned up as quickly as possible, and to figure out how it had happened in the first place.

The lean yet well-muscled man pushed his way through the administration building's front foyer and sat calmly in a chair outside an office door marked **Superintendent**. The nervous-looking secretary smiled meekly at him and he politely gave a nod in response. After several minutes, the office doors opened, and a harried-looking Devereux stepped into the lobby. As he ushered Paolo in, his face bore the expression of a man experiencing his greatest crisis.

"You understand I have important matters to deal with," said the superintendent. He closed his office door and seated himself at his desk opposite the seat Paolo had taken. Devereux opened the top drawer of his desk and glanced at the butt of a snub-nosed .38 revolver. He'd removed it from his home safe after Paolo's first visit and placed it here, more for personal comfort than out of any real fear of ever having to use it. To quell the uneasy feeling in the pit of his stomach. Now, after an excruciating moment of silence had passed between them, Devereux tried his best to conceal his growing sense of panic. "I'll assume this visit has to do with the current situation." He glanced from his radio—which squawked with updates every few seconds—to Paolo's fingers that tapped absently against his leg.

"Let us not pretend, Mr. Devereux," Paolo suggested. "The current situation has changed considerably."

"Well—y-yes, of course," Devereux stuttered. He eyed the butt of the gun in the still-open drawer, and for one crazy moment he considered drawing it out and shooting the man dead right where he sat. Sliding the drawer closed, he took a deep breath and tried his best to remain calm. "I am embarrassed to admit he did manage to elude several of my officers," Devereux went on. "Grassle, of course. There was an incident in one of the yards he was in and—"

"I recollect he was not to be allowed outside at all," Paolo said, his voice and manner calm.

"Yes. Yes, we did discuss that. A simple miscommunication. Rest assured we have him contained. I am certain we will have him very soon." This was a lie, or least a partial one. Devereux had been in the middle of a command and control meeting when his secretary had forwarded the urgent message that Paolo had returned and was demanding to speak with him. Although no evidence suggested Grassle had yet breached the three-square-mile containment perimeter, that same land remained largely impassible by vehicle. And despite the bloodhound having tracked Grassle nearly a mile into the woods, there existed no certainty that his capture was imminent.

Paolo, who until this point had focused his attention on his own drumming fingers, leveled his gaze on the superintendent. "Mr. Devereux, I will get directly to the point. My client—"

"Pardon my interruption, Mr. Bruzzi," Devereux said, holding up his hand. "If that is even your real name. I looked you up and found nothing on you. No criminal history, no driver's license information, no property owned within the United States, no credit history. I ran your prints and plate number through the database. Nothing. You're a ghost."

A muscle in Paolo's jaw twitched. The hint of a grin fluttered at the corners of his mouth.

"And speaking of prints, you didn't leave any," Devereux continued. "I couldn't remember you wearing gloves, so I checked the surveillance footage in the waiting room to confirm you had not. I thought that very strange. I asked myself why a man who did not wear gloves would not leave even a partial print on anything he touched. That left me with one of two possibilities. Either you are not who you say you are, or you are being protected by someone in high places."

That hint of a grin now spread into an ironic smile. "I admit that I underestimated you to a degree."

The two men stared at each other. The clock on the wall ticked the seconds away. Still no word from the ground unit or helicopter crew.

"I interrupted you, Mr. Bruzzi. I don't have long, though."

His steepled fingers tapped against each other, suggesting patience in the presence of frustration. "My client is deeply troubled you allowed Grassle to escape, but instead of crying over that fact, my client has sent me here for a specific purpose. One that must be non-negotiable, I am afraid."

Devereux managed a feeble smile. "Go on."

"You will share all law enforcement intelligence on the escape and subsequent coordinated search with me. I will be made aware of all police movement in and around the area, as well as deployed forces. I understand a helicopter has arrived on scene and is involved in the search. I will be the third point of contact to all information gained, second to you and any involved ground units, of course."

The superintendent tried to swallow but his throat had nearly completely closed. When he caught his breath and finally found words, his face took on the sunken look of an utterly defeated man. "I'll do whatever I can," he said, slumping in his chair. "Do whatever you want with me, just leave Amy out of this."

Paolo's grin twisted into a grotesque sort of smile. "You will keep me apprised of the manhunt using this." He produced a slim cellular telephone and laid it on the desk between them. "You will check in with me every hour, on the half hour. Text message only. Do not call me for any reason. If I need to speak with you, I will call you.

If you do not answer, I'll assume you've reported our conversation with your superiors and a very messy scene shall have to occur in Gainesville." He checked his watch. "It is now half past twelve. Your first check will be at one thirty."

Devereux reached out to collect the older-style cell phone. He flipped it open, observed the battery to be full then closed it.

"My contact number has already been programmed; it is the only one listed. You will not contact anyone else with it. A brief update on Grassle's suspected location and any information I request is all that is needed."

"But I only have control over the initial search team and a few residual forces," Devereux explained. "The patrol division is responsible for the area outside the jail's general vicinity. Sheriff Driscoll would never have me lead the entire pursuit."

"Don't worry about the sheriff," Paolo assured him. "He will be taken care of. If anyone asks, I am a federal agent working a simultaneous investigation through the fugitive task force." He rose to his feet and turned to leave, before turning back to face him again. "Superintendent, life consists of two things, and two things only—business and pleasure. Do not mistake me for being anything but business first."

Devereux looked pleadingly into his counterpart's soulless eyes. "What place does threatening my daughter have with business? She's done nothing wrong."

"What makes you assume harming your daughter would be business, Mr. Devereux?" Paolo said, stepping out the office and leaving the superintendent open-mouthed and pale-faced where he sat.

TWENTY-FOUR

ON THE STEPS of the Calusa County Criminal Courthouse, a medley of reporters gathered before a wide podium set up for a hasty early-afternoon press conference. Along with the assembled law enforcement officials from two local agencies (the Calusa County Sheriff's Office and the neighboring Beckwith Police Department, which due to larger resources had agreed to loan their only helicopter upon request, for a fee) stood several senior members of the 21st Circuit State Attorney's Office. Of the collected group, two men commanded the most attention. Behind the podium stood Sheriff Bo Driscoll, white-haired and lean in his glittering, pressed uniform. He stood with an air of authority that both requested and demanded attention at the same time, showing how he'd earned the nickname "The Silver Fox." Despite being a holdover of the good ol' boy era, he fully understood his role in relation to public image; he believed a sheriff should look like a lawman, not a politician. Sixty-three and as fit as he'd been ten years prior, he portrayed a lean, angular example of what he expected his deputies to adhere to—equal physical and mental readiness. Despite the modernization his agency had undergone in the past decade, the sheriff insisted on personally maintaining two vestiges of the bygone era: the white Stetson that rested on his head, and the six-shot, silver-plated Smith & Wesson revolver that hung from his hip.

The other man commanding attention stood just to the sheriff's right. Dressed in a smart gray suit and red tie, Mathias Hood managed to portray an even higher level of authority than those gathered around him. He towered over everyone else assembled, his bald dome gleaming in the sunlight. He projected the image of a man who not only possessed vast professional power but relished wielding it whenever and however necessary. The anxious buzz that pervaded the crowd of reporters hushed as the sheriff cleared his throat and spoke into the microphone.

"As I am sure you are all aware, today an inmate from the county jail escaped from a secure cellblock recreation yard. His name is Edward Grassle, age 24." The sheriff indicated a poster board sitting on an easel next to him. The escapee's mugshot, as well as his current charges, were listed below his photo. "We've set a perimeter that encompasses roughly three square miles in the wooded area surrounding the jail and have a bloodhound search team on the ground as well. Despite the fact he remains at large, I want the public to know he will be captured soon."

A flurry of questions from reporters, until the sheriff pointed to a dark-haired woman in the front row.

"Is it true Grassle got past two razor-wire fences and two armed jail deputies?" she asked.

The sheriff had expected this. "Yes, that does appear to be the case. We've already launched an internal review and more details will come out when that is complete. Right now, our focus is on finding this individual as soon as possible." On cue, someone replaced the mugshot with a different poster board, this one depicting a rendering of the jail complex and its surrounding area. The sheriff used a laser pointer to show the rec yard the prisoner had escaped from and the general area he was suspected to be confined to.

"We have him contained, but individuals within two miles of this area are asked to exercise extreme caution if outdoors. There are lots of places for a man to hide out there, but rest assured he won't be able to hide for long." To emphasize this point, he touched the brim of his hat. "As my father once said, 'Ye who has faith, has contentment.'"

A reporter asked if Grassle was possibly armed.

"We have no reason to believe so," the sheriff answered. "He's wounded, barefoot and alone. Not in my best days would I want to be caught in those woods with armed men and a bloodhound chasing me." He gave a good-natured chuckle, eliciting a murmur from those assembled. For the next ten minutes the reporters took turns asking various questions related to the escape. Did the prisoner have an accomplice? Why did the recreation officers only get off one shot? Where did he think Grassle would go? The sheriff answered these questions grim-faced and self-affected. He shifted uneasily on his feet, at times removing his Stetson and wiping sweat from his brow. But this was his show. In the end it should be he who stood before the citizens of Calusa County, in both good times and bad.

When the press conference was finished, State Attorney Hood—who had been silent up to this point—ushered the sheriff around the corner of the building, away from the mulling crowd. "That must have been difficult for you, Bo," he said gravely. "We go back a way, which is why what I'm about to say is not easy."

The sheriff cast a wary eye up at the man towering over him. "I may hold elected office, but that doesn't make me a politician, Mathias. Say what it is you have to say."

Hood laughed without much humor. He placed a hand on the back of the sheriff's neck perhaps a bit too firmly for the latter's liking. The sheriff tried to shrug it away, but Hood held fast to the older and much smaller man. "You know I am a man of principle, Bo. Strong principle. The kind forged from stone. Do you understand the implications of that?"

Just then, one of the sheriff's junior staff poked his head around the corner to inquire about Driscoll's next tactical move. Annoyed, he said he was busy, then turned back to Hood. "I have business to attend to, Mathias. Skip the sermon and just give it to me straight."

Hood released his hold on the sheriff's neck and patted him on the back. "Of course. I'll give it to you in words you'll recognize. This animal who gunned down a man in cold blood needs true justice. Not the justice meted inside an air-conditioned courtroom, with endless loopholes at his side." He indicated the statue of Lady Justice next to them. "Do you know the real reason she wears a blindfold?"

Sheriff Driscoll sighed. "It's because justice is supposed to be blind."

"No. It's because she doesn't want to see everything!" Hood

raised his palms to the air like a preacher evoking God's truth. "She knows she cannot detect every crime or punish all who disobey the law. Nor should she. Do you know what would happen to our system if all crimes against the state were prosecuted? If every circumstance were brought to light and held against the fire of jurisprudence? It would fail, Bo. And without the system, society would fail, and then humanity not long after."

The sheriff let out a low whistle. "Damn it be, Mathias, if you're worried about my boys not doing their jobs right, you needn't. We'll find him alright. We'll put him back where he belongs and then you can try him however you wish."

"You've missed my point, Bo. Perhaps your boys would simply need...assistance."

The sheriff blinked. "Pardon?"

"Call it a helping hand from her." Hood indicated the statue. "She may be blindfolded, but she peeks at everything law enforcement does. *Inspects* even. Your people are held to a much higher standard than the rest of us. You must search with permission or warrants, hold with cause and proof. But ordinary citizens—"

The sheriff frowned, still not understanding what Hood meant. But then realization hit home, and he took a step backward, as if punched in the gut.

"Are you suggesting I allow a civilian to help catch him?"

"Not just any civilian. A professional hunter. One invisible to justice."

The sheriff scoffed. "How would I explain that to my people? Even if I didn't get laughed out of my hat, you do realize that any evidence gained, or arrest made, must still pass the rules of the courts."

Hood offered a throaty laugh. "Don't be naïve, Bo. You're the sheriff. Your people will do as you direct. You've stated this is your last term anyway."

"And I wish to finish it without being recalled by the governor. I value my reputation, Mathias."

Hood grinned. "I wouldn't be concerned about the governor, Bo. He has more pressing matters to worry about."

The sheriff considered this, then pointed out, "You're still not considering the courts. I can't risk a civilian, no matter how good he is, ruining this case. Men who've committed worse crimes have walked on technicalities. You of all people know that."

Hood's grin disappeared as memory washed over him. "Indeed. Which is more reason to consider my suggestion. You're also forgetting I hold great weight over every judge in the circuit. Minor technicalities can easily be forgiven. Rulings can be swayed. And if need be, certain...techniques can be levied against those who refuse to bend to our needs." As the sheriff squinted in deep thought, Hood pointed away from the courthouse in the direction of the jail a few miles distant. "He's out there now, in those woods. The community is frightened. I'm sure your boys could catch him in a day or two, at worst, but given an added player, one operating with carte blanche, I have no doubts you could catch him by sundown."

The sheriff nodded to himself after another moment of silent thought. "Grassle isn't operating legally anyway. He's an escaped felon, and regardless of how he is captured his original charges have nothing to do with whoever catches him."

"Yes."

"And if I don't deputize this civilian, and no connection exists between him and me, then vicarious liability to the sheriff's office is removed. He's acting completely on his own."

Hood's grin returned. "You would simply need to direct your people to not arrest anyone at all they find operating inside the search area. If your decree is broad and does not specify a specific person, the argument for favoritism is removed."

The sheriff inserted a toothpick into his mouth. "This civilian you suggest...you can vouch for him completely?"

"One hundred percent," Hood promised. "My man works well on his own, and I can guarantee he won't get in the way of your boys."

Always a man who valued making quick decisions, the sheriff gave a firm nod. "Okay, I'll allow it. Get with Captain Escobar for details. He'll be upset, but he wants my job so in the end I suppose he'll just have to get over it. But know this—" he shook a finger at Hood. "If your man intrudes on my people just once...if he sneezes the wrong way, I'll order his removal from the area, even if it means arresting him. Understood?"

Hood clasped his hands onto the sheriff's comparatively slender shoulders. "I knew you'd see the light, Bo."

"I'll just need his name and a description. Other than that, I don't want to know anything else about him. Less is more, in this case."

"Agreed."

Tight-lipped, the sheriff tipped his hat and disappeared back to his awaiting command staff.

Hood removed his secure-line cell phone and dialed a pre-programmed number. Seconds later, Paolo answered.

"Yes, sir."

"A change of mission. When can you be on-line for a full take-down?"

A pause from the other end of the phone, then, "It depends. I would need resources, and access I do not currently have."

"That has already been arranged. Captain Escobar is your point of contact. You will have full access to the scene."

"For how long?"

"For as long as required."

"Do you wish me to turn Grassle over to the authorities if I find him?" came Paolo's response.

Hood looked toward the gathered crowd, where the sheriff and several members of his command staff barked out orders to a team of deputies. "The woods rarely speak of what they witness. And if Grassle should somehow escape them, track him to the ends of the earth if necessary. Wherever you find him, make sure he never sets foot inside a jail again. Do you understand what I am asking of you, Paolo?"

The sound of deep, even breathing from the other end of the line.

"It will be done," Paolo said coolly.

Hood recited a series of further instructions before ending the call. He stepped back around the corner of the towering building he had grown to know better than his own home since his years as the circuit state attorney. Walking back toward the assembled group, he placed a warm smile on his lips as other members of his office and the media conferred with him. As he spoke, he glanced back at Lady Justice, her famous blindfold shielding her eyes.

It was probably best she couldn't see what was happening anyway.

TWENTY-FIVE

EDDIE FELT LIKE his heart was about to explode inside his chest. His mind, so seized by panic and a suffocating sense of dread, sent urgent messages to his muscles to stop running. Pausing, he bent at the waist and sucked for air. His lungs burned. His shoulder felt like someone had stabbed him with a hot poker and the wound on his leg screamed each time he took a step. *Go back*, a voice inside him reasoned. *You're hurt bad. If you don't give up now, they'll kill you.* And then another voice from behind, so clear and distinct he fully expected to turn around and see Jules standing there. *You gonna let them get you that easy? You busted out, and now you want to turn around and go back? At least make them earn it.*

As always, Jules was right. Tearing off a strip of his jail-issued orange and black-striped shirt, he dropped his pants to the knees, inspecting the open wound that spanned several inches across the meaty part of his left thigh. He blotted it once with the fabric, catching a glimpse of white fatty tissue inside the wound. Blood immediately filled the space as he released the pressure, and he forced his eyes away from it while he went to work. Wrapping the strip of fabric around his leg, he tied a full knot directly over the wound itself. His legs buckled momentarily as fresh pain bolted up through his testicles. He cried out once, biting his lip as he steadied himself. The brush he had been running through the last ten minutes had been thick but was so far manageable; on a hobbled leg through unfamiliar territory, he figured he'd gone no further than half a mile. The brush ahead of him appeared to be growing even thicker. And surely, they'd be surrounding him any moment. He knew that every second that passed meant an extra second they had to squeeze him into a vise.

"You wouldn't go back, Jules, would you?" Eddie spoke aloud. A light breeze came to him then, as if the trees themselves sighed their response.

"No, you wouldn't," Eddie said, answering his own question. He took a deep breath and kept moving ahead, limping into a sort of half-run and disappearing back into the thick brush. To someone watching, it may have seemed like a living thing swallowing him whole.

HE HADN'T HEARD the dog for a while. Twice he altered his direction to throw it off his trail, but he quickly realized this would be useless. He remembered the dogs he and Jules had run from as kids, and those had been mutts compared to the expert that likely tracked him now. The helicopter had made repeated passes overhead, each time forcing him to dive for cover and remain hidden until it passed.

Reaching a break in the trees, he bent with hands on knees, trying his best to ignore the pain in his leg and shoulder. A narrow clearing ran perpendicular to his direction of travel, with barely discernible wheel ruts in the long grass. From his many days in woods such as these, Eddie recognized the path as likely being an access road for local orange grove field hands. Looking south, he surmised the river lay several miles in that direction. He doubted he'd be able to make it there without being seen. Even if he did manage to make it, he figured they'd have people scouring it in anticipation of him. *But if you make it to the river, you can move northeast against its current. They'll assume you're going downriver. Upriver and away from town, the land gets thicker, woodsier. A man could lose himself in that wilderness for days. It could give you time to figure something out.*

In the opposite direction lay Springwood proper, where Liam was. But that carried the most risk, and they'd be looking for him there as well. Not to mention the hundreds if not thousands of fearful eyes that had been warned about an escaped killer on the loose.

Killer. The word alone seemed unbelievable to him to be associated with. But right or wrong, that was his new reality. His world of old seemed as distant and dead as the dimmest star in the sky.

He needed time to think. But waiting even seconds could mean his capture or his life. *Take a breath. Forget about the dog and the helicopter for a moment.* Taking the path and its long grass would be like heaven on his bare feet. And he'd be able to dive into either line of woods should the chopper appear again. But anything easier on him would be easier on them too, he reasoned. *No. Take the harder route. If they're to catch up with you, make them earn it. Sit behind bars for the rest of your life knowing you left everything on the field instead of fizzling out at the end of the game.*

Eddie limped over the path and straight into the thick brush. He forced his bleeding feet to move, dodging trees and giant clumps of ferns for several hundred yards until he stumbled onto the edge of a large orange grove. Weaving his way through the closely bunched trees, he'd gone another quarter mile when something to his right caught his interest. Cut out in a small pocket of the grove stood a small clapboard cabin, bordered on one side by a wooden rail fence. The gravel driveway sat empty of vehicles, save for a beat-up old truck on blocks. Scanning the property, Eddie didn't see anyone, and the one cabin window he observed from his position stood dark and empty.

Deciding to risk checking out the place, he'd taken a dozen steps and had cleared the near side of the cabin when a small garden came into his view. Seeing a figure standing there, he froze, his heart in his throat. Silently cursing himself for not being more careful, he told himself he should have waited to make sure no one was home. Bushes blocked part of his view, but even with his limited visibility he determined the figure to be that of a man wearing overalls and a plaid long-sleeved shirt. The man faced away from him, and when Eddie dared to take several steps backward, he noted the man still did not appear to detect his presence. *He's been busy working outside. Might not even know there's an escaped prisoner on the loose.*

But right when he was feeling impossibly stuck, he noticed something strange. Not only had the man not moved in over a minute, but Eddie realized his arms were cast outward at an unnatural angle. Daring to take a few steps forward, Eddie finally realized it was a scarecrow on a wooden pole, sewn together so realistically that it had completely fooled him. Relieved, he limped forward another ten paces to the fence, looking each direction again just to make sure no one was around. Satisfied, he slipped one leg through the fence when a flash of movement to his right caught his attention.

A horse stepped into his view from the far side of the pen. It flicked its ears, snorting in a way Eddie recognized as the animal detecting the presence of another. He figured he hadn't seen it before simply because he hadn't been looking for it. Stepping cautiously through the fence, he made eye contact with the chestnut brown mare, extending his hands in a calming gesture and making a shushing sound.

"Easy, girl, I won't hurt you," he said soothingly. He noted the chestnut mare was bareback, but that a saddle, bridle, and reins sat propped on a nearby fencepost positioned under a shaded lean-to. A coil of rope lay over another post. Taking a deep breath, Eddie took a cautious step forward. The horse, in response, neighed and flicked its ears. Eddie licked his lips, glancing up to the nearby droning helicopter. It seemed to be making a grid search from the sound of it, zigzagging over an area about a half-mile away and getting closer. In a few minutes it would be covering this area, Eddie surmised, and with the limited tree cover this grove area provided, he doubted he'd last long on foot. Deciding on a course of action, which included not to use the saddle, he took several cautious steps toward the mare. It flipped its tail but didn't move away.

"Good girl," he cooed, lifting the rope from the post, not wanting to spook the only friend he felt he may have left in the world.

TWENTY-SIX

THE BLOODHOUND, STRENGTHENED over the years by following dozens of trails, dropped her snout to the ground and began to pull. The handler, not wanting his partner to get too far ahead of him in the thick brush, drew in half the slack he'd given her since they'd started. He knew how relentless Sheba could be on a trail, how she refused to rest until she found her mark. She'd been going full-on since they'd started, and so far had ignored her master's attempts to give her a water break. The midday heat, oppressive even in the partial shade, now caused her to pant excessively. The handler observed this with a keen eye and pulled hard twice on the leash, an order for her to stop. Squatting on her massive hindquarters, the prized hound stared straight ahead into the brush, her tongue lolling from her dripping muzzle. As her master knelt beside her and compelled her to drink from his canteen, she let out a whine, as if realizing every passing second allowed her subject to gain precious distance.

"Don't worry, we'll get him," Jerry reassured her. He patted her head as a proud father might. He'd only observed intermittent fresh footprints, the left foot dragging noticeably, but they hadn't been consistent enough to track him without aid from the dog. The team leader had noticed the occasional footprints as well and nodded to himself. He then turned and relayed a series of hand signals to his men who remained positioned in a wedge formation behind him.

Each of them took a moment to adjust their slung assault rifles and take drinks from their canteens. Sweat poured from beneath their helmets and ballistic vests, the heat and humidity having risen by the minute. Their gear had been designed for the jail environment and not the early summer Florida woods. The helicopter had been making passes over the area for a half hour now, but since the spotter had been unable to detect much through the tree canopy, that meant they'd have to continue their foot pursuit.

The ground party stood once the handler urged Sheba onward. The dog took three strides before circling several times. The handler remained patient, knowing his partner well enough to know this was her way of double-checking her own work. Despite not having the capacity to fully understand emotions, dogs felt them nonetheless: love, fear, pride. The handler knew his prized hound valued the last of these greatly. Mouthing encouragement, he watched as she made another wide circle before cutting slightly off the path and tugging mightily on her leash. The handler, never doubting her, waved the team on behind him.

Twenty minutes later the party broke into a clearing and found themselves standing on a narrow access road that ran in either direction. When Sheba indicated ahead into the dense brush, the team leader realized the prisoner had made a costly error. Guessing that Grassle had decided to travel the most difficult route in hopes of shaking his pursuers, he knew he'd effectively cornered himself. Only a half mile or so of woods existed in this direction before they reached a wide road. Dozens of deputies had been positioned at interlocking intervals along its length, with it having been blocked to traffic for several miles in either direction. The jail lay behind them, and certainly Grassle could not have slipped by them without the dog detecting this. To the south lay the trap's second arm, a SWAT patrol team positioned in squad-sized elements along geographic areas of escape. Mounted on ATVs, they were to be notified via radio should the subject turn in their direction. To the north and west cut the Calusa River. If Grassle were to make it there, he could choose to cross it into the vast woodland beyond, or travel along its winding course either up- or down-river. The helicopter crew had been instructed to fly frequent passes over it to discourage

Grassle from turning that direction, and as long as the dog continued to indicate that his direction headed away from it, ground commanders felt confident this route would be his least likely to take.

This left approximately one square mile of sparse grove land. This area would be easier for many reasons, chief among them that it was clear enough for the ATV teams to join in. Now, as the search team leader radioed in their direction, a wave of relief passed through him. He and his men were on the cusp of dehydration, and the many biting bugs had begun to feast on whatever exposed skin they had. As they stalked through the thick brush, the dog and her handler weaving their way ahead, each man knew their growing misery contained a silver lining—this would all be over soon.

CAPTAIN ESCOBAR'S GUT told him the slender man Sheriff Driscoll had introduced him to would be trouble. Possessing the same innate ability to smell approaching disaster as most veteran cops did, Escobar shared a similar sentiment of many army and police field commanders—that their vast knowledge and experience went only so far as their rank. Frustrated at his boss's insistence at allowing a civilian investigator access to his search scene, he had been forced to bite his tongue. The decision was the sheriff's and the sheriff's alone to make. Granted wide discretion, sheriffs enjoyed a bygone power that hearkened to the days of frontiersmen and outlaws. And now, as he watched the olive-complexioned investigator with the eerily pockmarked face, Escobar tried to recall if he'd ever seen the man before. Ever since he'd shown up here at the mobile command center—a large tent, complete with a podium and folding chairs, hastily arranged in the parking lot of an empty shopping plaza—the man had dominated Escobar's attention. Having been told face-to-face by the sheriff that the man would have unimpeded access to the search area until further notice, Escobar felt it his duty to keep careful watch. With a chiseled look that spoke of many hours of strenuous exercise, Bruzzi held a certain bearing Escobar had seen many times during his time in the army. *Former soldier, for sure*, Escobar thought. *That, or some special ops spook who knew the sheriff personally. Why the hell else would the old bastard ever consent to this bullshit?*

Paolo, dressed in blue jeans, a crisp black polo and lightly woven jacket, stood near a group of officers who were disseminating vital information to a newly arriving pair of SWAT members. *At least the old man didn't give him a gun and a star*, he thought. This sentiment was short-lived, however, as Escobar observed what must have been the man's personal firearm holstered on his hip—an HK semi-automatic pistol—seen when he adjusted his jacket.

The last time he had witnessed anything remotely similar to this had been several years ago, when he had taken on a wounded Iraq war veteran for the day under the agency's "ride-along" program, a community outreach deal the sheriff had with numerous local charities and businesses. Meant to narrow the divide between ordinary civilians and law enforcement, it also sought to educate people on what cops actually did on a daily basis. Escobar's "rider" had been blind in one eye and wore a prosthetic leg, the result of the veteran having been struck by an IED. Riding shotgun in Escobar's unmarked cruiser, he had assisted with low risk calls for service: a noise complaint, a duck found trapped in a sewer drain, kids shoplifting candy from a corner store. Escobar had not only understood the symbolism incorporated with that day; he had appreciated it. He'd even allowed his vet "rider" to clamp handcuffs onto a suspect, a grinning homeless man well-accustomed to many such vagrancy arrests over the years.

But this was entirely different. Having searched every computer archive he could think of, Escobar knew just as much about the man in front of him now as he had before he'd met him. That is, nothing. Even his name came up blank on both the state and national criminal information centers. Having personally inspected the man's driver's license, he had searched the local DMV database for any added information, without success. The man was a ghost. That the sheriff would permit such a person, absent an extensive background check, to have full access to an active police search area seemed unconscionable to him. Adding to the already insane proposition was the fact that the man apparently worked directly for State Attorney Hood. A sitting prosecutor's investigator, however removed from official duties in the search, could only complicate things. Throw in the potential major conflict of interest and Escobar foresaw a disaster in the making, despite the sheriff's decree that neither Bruzzi nor anyone else found inside the search area be removed. Escobar wouldn't have been surprised if an old-fashioned posse would be the next step.

Figuring his best option was the wait-and-see approach, Escobar approached Paolo with feigned enthusiasm and offered his meaty hand for a shake. "Mr. Bruzzi, pleasure to have you aboard. You must be well acquainted with the sheriff. Civilians aren't usually given access to these sorts of operations. Apparently, the old man feels we need all the help we can get." He said this while forcing a smile to his lips, allowing a period of silence to permeate the air.

But Paolo did not seem phased by it. He stared back at the hulking captain with black, expressionless eyes. "I'm glad to help, captain. And rest assured, I have enough background to know when I am getting in the way." He smiled, the scarred skin on his face spreading out in genuine congeniality. "In a strictly civilian capacity, I'd feel honored to simply monitor the ongoing operation."

Escobar eyed his counterpart, feeling a strange disquiet enter him. His gaze dropped to Paolo's waistline. "Mind if I ask why you need the gun if you just intend on monitoring the search operations?"

"Now, I wouldn't feel safe if I wasn't armed, would I?" Paolo said with either feigned or genuine cheerfulness, Escobar wasn't sure which. "Not with an escaped killer out there."

An awkward silence grew between the two men, finally broken by Escobar. "Listen, Mr. Bruzzi, or whatever your name is. I know the sheriff believes he has a good reason to have civilians here. Personally, I think it's bullshit. This isn't some community program. There's an escaped prisoner out there. He's killed before and he'll surely kill again in order to get away. I've been doing this a long time, and so have all those deputies out there busting their humps looking for him."

Paolo nodded. "I can appreciate that, captain."

"Good. And I hope you can appreciate not doing anything to compromise this mission. You report anything suspicious, just like every other civilian out there is expected to."

"I understand."

"And for God's sake, keep that gun in its holster. If by some chance you spot Grassle, call the main dispatch line and give his location and direction of travel. Under no circumstances are you to attempt to take him into custody."

The ghost smiled, but little humor showed in his eyes. "All very good, captain. Now, if you could brief me on the current state of the investigation, please. As a concerned citizen, of course. Then I will no longer be an inconvenience to you."

Escobar begrudgingly complied. Just then his earpiece squawked. He held a hand to it and listened to the transmission. When it ended, he consulted a map on a nearby folding table. He waved over several special operations team members standing nearby. "The dog team says he's started bleeding again, but that doesn't mean he's down. I remember being in Fallujah when my team shot a sniper who'd had us pinned down for hours. Shot him in the head—I saw it through my binos myself. We tracked his blood trail half a mile until we finally found him leaning against a building, dead. His brains were hanging out." Escobar stood to his full height. "Do not take this individual lightly. He's cornered and desperate."

The crew-cut, gray-haired captain surveyed the group, intentionally avoiding the ghost's appraising eyes. "Hutchinson, set up your team here." Escobar pointed to a spot on the map not far from Eddie's suspected location. "The dog team should flush him right to you." Then, almost as an afterthought, he added, "Riley, I want you to cover this area here." He indicated a wooded area just a few miles from their current location. "The guy is headed toward the Parker property, from what it sounds like. Orange groves. Take your men there now and sweep into Hutchinson's right flank. I want him before he even tries to cross the highway."

Escobar released the group to fulfill his orders. He passed a hand over his face, feeling the stress of the situation but knowing it to be necessary. He must concentrate on the mission. An escaped prisoner must be caught, a community made to feel at ease.

When Escobar turned around to speak to Bruzzi, to remind him to be careful out there on his own, he discovered the man had seemingly disappeared into thin air.

TWENTY-SEVEN

SPECIAL OPS TEAM Leader Hutchinson, his face painted in black and green camouflage, led his five-man squad down the wooded path to their pre-determined staging point. He knelt at the path's edge and signaled for his team to form an ambush line just inside the tree line. From the intelligence gathered by the combined forces in the air and on the ground, he felt confident that once Grassle broke out of the most thickly wooded area, he'd be funneled in this direction. The dog still tracked him, but that sort of strategy tended to be reactive. Both Captain Escobar and Hutchinson held the opinion that capturing the escapee quickly required a more offensive-minded approach, forcing a trap closed versus waiting for it to be sprung.

As Hutchinson listened to the latest set of instructions from Captain Escobar in his radio earpiece, the chopper came to a hover overhead. He'd just begun to turn toward his team when a large form flashed out the corner of his eye. His eyes bulging in surprise, he had just registered the form as being something much larger than human when his brain commanded his muscles to move. Diving to his right to avoid being crushed by the leaping figure, the burly team leader crashed into a stand of bougainvillea. Thorns tore into his face and neck, the only area of his body not covered in protective gear. Not yet feeling the pain, he rolled hard to his left and sprang to his feet just in time to recognize the object that had nearly decapitated him.

A chestnut brown horse galloped down the path away from him, its well-muscled body glistening with sweat and its silky black tail dancing out behind it as it went. Mounted on the mare's bare back and hunched forward against her broad neck sat a rider gripping the ends of a rope. Confused at first as to why someone would be riding a horse through such thick vegetation, the orange and black striped uniform then hit him like a lightning bolt. "It's him!" he shouted, more to himself than to anyone else, and in a jumbling flurry he unslung his carbine and drew it up to eye level. But it was too late—the horse and rider had already disappeared around a natural bend in the trail.

"He's on horseback!" he hollered as the other members of his team burst from the tree line. Patting his ballistic vest, he yelled, "Where the fuck is my radio?" and touched a long, bleeding scratch on the back of his neck. He turned to the nearest team member and said, "Tell command he's headed north—no, northeast—on horseback. He's gonna be able to cover a lot more ground now, so have them spread the search area out. And shift that goddamn bird in that direction. If he gets past the highway, there's miles of wild land there for him to get lost in." After a quick tending to his wounds, Hutchinson poked through the bougainvillea bush until he found his radio suspended in a tangle of thorny branches. The antenna had been snapped clean off, rendering the radio useless.

"Where the fuck did he get a horse?" asked one of the team members.

"There's dozens of shit shacks all through this area with animals," Hutchinson huffed, ordering the team to follow him down the path at an airborne shuffle.

As they reached the bend in the trail where the horse and rider had turned, Hutchinson ordered a halt. He scanned the terrain ahead, noting that the trail opened up slightly as it continued into a less densely wooded orange grove. He knew a horse at full gallop could have covered half a mile by this point. Looking up, he spied the police helicopter making low passes above the treetops, its chopping blades from this distance sounding like machine gun fire.

Hutchinson grabbed another member's radio from him and keyed the mike. "Alpha Two to Command. I say again, Alpha Two to Command, do you read me?"

A slight pause, then a crackled response over the radio: "Go ahead, Alpha Two."

"Prepare to read coordinates." He punched a series of numbers into his hand-held GPS device. "Subject traveling at speed," he stressed. "Northeast of this point. Truck that bloodhound team to my current location. He'll ditch the horse eventually, and we'll need a good trail. Do you copy?"

Another slight pause, followed by an excited "Ten-four, we copy!" Hutchinson tossed the radio back to its owner and said what the rest of the team had already assumed. "We'll set a blocking position here. Drink water if you have it. I won't have this shitbird doubling back on us because we're thirsty. Riley, Masterson, take a partner and space out on either side of the trail. No way he could tack through swamp to get around us, so he's gonna have to stay close to the trail if he decides to double back. If he's still on the horse and doesn't stop, take the horse out. Everyone copy?"

A chorus of "yes sir!" sounded, and the team moved out as ordered. Riding a horse bareback was no small feat, even for an accomplished rider, Hutchinson knew. He allowed himself to feel a small measure of respect for his counterpart. Not only had he managed to escape from jail, but he'd lasted nearly an hour against a virtual army. Still, at some point Grassle would either get thrown from the animal or would be forced to ditch it himself. And if he did decide to double back, whether mounted or not, Hutchinson and his team would be ready for him.

ADDITIONAL TENTS AND folding tables had been hastily set up in the mobile command center. A police armored vehicle blocked the main entrance to the strip mall's parking lot and a line of marked sheriff cruisers encircled the lot perimeter. The deputies assigned to them ensured that the gawkers who had assembled over the past several minutes stayed back. Some of the onlookers exchanged whispers, while others openly speculated on the escapee's whereabouts. But most of those gathered across the street stood silently looking on, amazed at the circus unfolding before them.

Inside one of the tents a technician team struggled to set up a mobile air conditioning unit. As hot as the outside air had become, the heat inside the tent had become unbearable. *Who the hell had decided to close the tent flaps?* Escobar wondered. It would have been best to simply leave them open and let people see inside, rather than to have everyone bake the way they did now.

Escobar mopped his brow and stepped to the podium. Before him sat a collection of high-ranking members of the local law enforcement community: Sheriff Driscoll, commanders from various departments within the agency, Jail Superintendent Devereux, and Chief Prosecutor Mathias Hood. His eyes, black and cold, glared out in disgust. The bald dome of his head gleamed with sweat, but he made no attempt to wipe it away. Captain Escobar made brief eye contact with the man but for some reason found himself looking quickly away.

He began his presentation on a large dry-erase board that had been propped up on an easel. Complete with arrows and other symbols delineating friend and foe, the board resembled a battle plan as much as it did a police operation. Clearing his throat, he explained to the group the situation at hand. "Our subject has been spotted on horseback—here." He drew a red dot on the board. "The river is blocking his route north. Unfortunately, Alpha-Two team allowed him to get past them, but it means they now control his rear escape route from the west. The bloodhound team is being re-positioned to pick up the trail." Escobar used a green marker to draw a curved arrow depicting the dog team. "The bird is making constant flyovers of his suspected location as we speak. It's just a matter of time before we spot him and pour resources on top of him." Escobar locked eyes with Sheriff Driscoll, who sat silent with arms crossed over his chest. "We will catch him, sir, I can assure you of that."

As the portable AC unit buzzed to life, breathing much-needed relief to those inside the artificially lit tent, Sheriff Driscoll leaned forward in his chair. Spitting tobacco juice on the pavement, he said, "Let me get this straight. Not only did this Grassle fella escape, but he also managed to get past an entire tactical team on a *horse*?"

Escobar had no words for a response.

"And I'm not even counting the fifty deputies I have combing the area. It's been an hour now and he's still out there. Forgive me, captain, but I find your assurances a bit reeking of bullshit."

Captain Escobar looked to the other members assembled before him but found no assistance in their averted eyes. He paled slightly and his tongue wet his now dry lips. "I understand your concern, Sheriff. But you must understand the terrain involved. We should have him within the hour."

Sheriff Driscoll removed his hat and turned toward Superintendent Devereux, who up to this point had sat stone silent. "Claude, this was on your watch." The sheriff's voice sounded almost hurt. "I know the milk has been spilled, but goddammit, what kind of operation are you running out there?" He pointed toward the lowered tent flaps. "Those civilians out there are scared. They live and work in this county and it's our job to make sure they're safe. Now, I know everyone makes mistakes, and Lord knows I've made my share. But how in God's creation do we let something like this happen?" He turned to address all in attendance. "Make no mistake, I'm the one who has to take the heat on this. We're grown men and women in charge of keeping people safe. If you all can't do your jobs then tell me right now, and I'll find someone who can." He looked to each man and woman assembled. Every eye meeting his held a shade of wounded pride—except those of Hood, who barely suppressed a grin as he eyed his law enforcement counterpart.

Devereux slouched in his seat. He'd come ready to feel the sheriff's wrath and disapproval. He'd even come prepared to tender his immediate resignation if necessary. But it was something else entirely that stirred a sense of dread inside of him. Something more sinister and much closer to home than a prisoner having escaped for what would likely be an hour-long romp in the woods. "I have no excuse, Sheriff," he said flatly. "My people failed to do their jobs. And I failed to do mine."

The sheriff held up a conciliatory hand. Just as he was about to speak, a uniformed female lieutenant entered the tent and whispered something in his ear. Immediately, the sheriff rose to his feet and motioned for Escobar to be briefed as well. As the two listened, their eyes glowed with unmistakable relief. Each smiled gratefully as they pumped the other's hand.

"The chopper crew has eyes on him in an orange grove and are hovering on his position. Ground units are closing in on him now," the sheriff announced. The assembled group erupted into similar hand-shaking and smiles all around. The sheriff turned to Escobar. "This is your mission, John. I want him taken alive, if possible. Make it happen."

"Yes, sir," Escobar said, beaming. He raced out of the tent into the sunlight to get away from the cacophony of conversation that had begun inside. After an exchange of orders, he instructed two members of his command team to load with him into his unmarked cruiser. Inching past the police barricade, Escobar floored the accelerator. Soon they would be close to the area Grassle had been spotted. From there, several ATVs had been staged for their incursion into the back woods where cruisers couldn't go.

It would all be over soon.

TWENTY-EIGHT

JUST AS CAPTAIN Escobar sped away from the command post, his cell phone rang. He placed it on speaker and barked, "What is it?"

The caller was Lieutenant Fisher. "Sir, an issue has developed with the dog handler."

"Talk to me," said the captain.

"The dog tracked our guy to a farmhouse not far from here. Sal Holcomb's place. He'd just gotten home and found the gate to his corral wide open and his horse missing. He said he was positive he'd closed the gate, and that somebody must have taken his horse."

Escobar rolled his eyes. "We know all that. The chopper crew has a positive sighting two miles north of Sal's place as we speak."

"That's just it, sir. The handler says his dog is heading *south* from the farm, not north."

The captain snatched a map from one of the car's occupants and slid his finger over it. "No horse can cover that much ground, Lieutenant, unless it has wings. I don't know about you, but I haven't seen any flying horses lately. I know that dog has a solid reputation, but right now I have to go with a confirmed sighting. Tell Jerry his order stands. He is to get his dog on that truck and get dropped off near our AO. I'll need him in the area in case our guy ditches the horse and loses himself in that grove."

A brief commotion from the other end, then, "The tactical team says that Jerry insists his dog is never wrong. He wants authorization to continue south from the farmhouse, sir. He's pretty adamant."

Escobar cursed beneath his breath. Always decisive, he made his mind up quickly. "You tell Jerry that if he ever wants to work with the sheriff's office again, he is to get his dog on that truck immediately."

"Yes, sir," came the lieutenant's reply. "I'm relaying it now."

With the call ended, Escobar concentrated on the winding turns in the road. Five minutes later they reached a wooded area several miles from the jail compound and found it surrounded by dozens of police vehicles. A helicopter hovered in the near distance, tacking back and forth over an area half a mile off the roadway. The field commander of all ground operations, Escobar was familiar with every aspect of apprehending a wanted felon. Although he had done it himself countless times during his career, since making captain he had allowed his subordinates to handle the actual takedowns. But this time would be different. Opening the trunk, he slid into his ballistic vest and slung his carbine across his broad chest. All indications were that Grassle would be captured soon, and Escobar, tired of the humdrum administrative life he'd been relegated to for the past three years, wanted very much to be a part of it.

WHILE ESCOBAR SLID into his vest, the six-man, two-woman Alpha-One team moved forward on their ATVs, spreading out into a skirmish line a quarter mile from where the helicopter hovered. With its powerful rotors vibrating the ground, the chopper was easy enough to spot through the canopy. Covering ground quickly, the team scanned the area ahead of them as they rode. Keeping in constant radio contact with the chopper crew, they received a second-by-second update on the suspect's movements. As of now, the horse and Grassle could occasionally be seen through gaps in the treetops traveling at a gallop. Still clinging to the horse's neck, the prisoner had so far surprised his pursuers with his fortitude and ability to evade the dragnet built around him.

"Bird-One to Alpha-One, I have eyes on your target," came the static-filled chopper transmission. "Still on horseback, at a trot now.

It's definitely him. Two hundred yards east of your location. Be advised, dog team is approaching from the west, so watch your fields of fire. Copy?"

"Alpha-One copies," returned the team leader into his lapel mike. Keeping one hand on his ATV's handlebars, he peered through binoculars at a copse of trees ahead of their location. Briefly, he spied the head of the horse bobbing as it walked along a row of orange trees. At first he couldn't see anyone atop the animal, believing Grassle had decided to ditch and run, but then he caught sight of their man slumped over the animal's neck through either exhaustion or an attempt to keep out of view, or both.

Pointing to an area just ahead of where the horse would be traveling, the team leader gave hand signals and dispersed the other members of the team. Covered by the heavy *whump* of the chopper overhead, they moved out. At twenty yards the horse became more visible through the low-hung branches. Flanking it from downwind, one of the team members who was in better position than the others suddenly saw his chance. Realizing Grassle might reverse direction and double-back at a gallop, the team member decided his best option would be to dismount his vehicle and effect a takedown attempt on foot. Drawing his Taser, he flipped the safety off and projected the laser beam to a point the horse would have to pass through. He prepared himself to strike the horse if it bolted, and tackle Grassle from the animal if it did not. Either way, bragging rights that would last an entire career were here for the taking.

From a crouch, the deputy took five running strides from his position behind a tree. The horse had just crossed his path five yards away, and as it detected sudden movement to its right, it immediately shied. The ground here was soft and, as a result, the horse's hooves slipped in the loose soil. Leaping across the horse's back and sounding a loud shout, the deputy tackled the rider, and the two tumbled heavily to the ground. With the now rider-less horse galloping away in a panic, other team members raced in to assist the deputy on the ground. Blind with adrenalin, the deputy screamed for backup.

"Collins! Collins!" the approaching team leader yelled, pointing toward the deputy's hands.

Deputy Collins, still kneeling on the soft ground, looked down at the uniform he held. The pants and shirt had been stuffed with straw, with the sleeve and pants cuffs tied into crude knots. A burlap-clad object the size of a basketball hung from the neck.

"Congratulations, Einstein, you tackled a scarecrow," the team leader said with disgust. He grabbed the lolling head from the deputy's hands and slammed it onto the ground. It landed face side up, its button eyes and smiling mouth seeming to mock their incompetence. Despite the seriousness of the situation, the rest of the team burst out in laughter.

"I'm glad everyone thinks this is funny," the team leader said, radioing in the situation. They had lost valuable time on what had turned out to be a wild goose chase. Worse, units guarding the perimeter had been repositioned in the mistaken belief Grassle had been spotted in this area. How much ground could a man, even barefoot and injured, cover in half an hour? he wondered. Two miles at the most? But with the exposed perimeter, those two miles may as well have been twenty. As if this realization hadn't been bad enough, the team leader received news that the roving river patrol guarding against a possible crossing had been lifted as well.

Directing his team to remount their ATVs and rendezvous back at their staging point, he radioed for the helicopter to stand down. Shortly after receiving the message, the chopper crew banked the bird toward their refueling station located all the way back at their headquarters in the neighboring county. It would be another half hour before they could be airborne again, they said, considering the anticipated widened new search ahead of them.

As the last member filed past, the team leader turned toward his own vehicle, kicking first at the scarecrow's head where it struck a tree trunk and burst apart in a shower of rotten straw.

TWENTY-NINE

EDDIE HAD WORKED quickly.

Approaching the mare slowly but with confidence, he'd told himself it would allow him to rope it as long as he remained calm. *Here, girl. It's okay...I won't hurt you. See? I need you more than you know. I have a little boy I need to see and without you, I won't be able to do that. When they realize what happened, they'll lead you back here where you belong. Even cops love horses. They won't blame you for helping me.*

Two miles away, Eddie was now approaching a two-lane, paved road. Had he made it here just five minutes earlier, he'd have stumbled right into a roadblock. But his false sighting on horseback had caused the team of deputies here to be shifted a mile in that direction. Ignoring the misery that shot from his leg and shoulder, he limped across the road and into the opposing tree line. After a grueling ten-minute sprint through unmarked brush, he came to a sudden halt as he stood staring at a sight so unbelievable, he thought he was hallucinating.

Water. An ocean, it seemed. But that was impossible. The Gulf lay at least thirty miles to the west; he could not have come that far already. Then, as he bent gasping for breath, he shielded his eyes from the blazing sun and realized what he initially should have—he'd reached a wide bend in the Calusa River. Transfixed by the water's shimmering surface, Eddie fell into a trance. How long had it been since he'd stood so close to the river's shores? His mind swept backward in time, to before his five-year stint in prison, to before Clarissa and the baby, even. Life had somehow intruded on this simple pleasure he'd enjoyed throughout his childhood. Eddie marveled at the irony of how he now stood poised above this symbol of that innocent freedom he had taken for granted for all those years, thankful for its presence in a way he never had been before.

From the bank high above the river, he reached out toward the sparkling surface, still entranced by its almost mystical properties. As he planted his left foot it slipped on a patch of tightly packed dirt. Not realizing he stood so close to the edge of the embankment, he felt his foot slide downward just as he snapped out of his trance-like state. Pin wheeling his arms, he tried desperately to regain his balance; but by now it was too late, and he felt himself sliding upright down the steep embankment, surfer style. Just when he thought he'd be able to slide to the bottom upright, an exposed root snagged his lead foot and he went tumbling head over heels twice, his head striking a large rock before crashing into the water below.

For a moment he remained submerged in the waist-deep water, having exhaled the breath from his lungs during his tumble. Weightlessness and darkness. No noise existed here. All that had worked against him for the past five years—hell, for his entire life—seemed to melt away in the relative peace he floated in. And then a voice in his head, one he didn't recognize, telling him all he had to do to end this madness was to open his mouth and take a deep breath underwater. It was impossible anyway, this insanity he now attempted. Yes, he'd gotten this far, but how much further could his exhausted body take him? How much longer could he manage to evade them, having already expended his energy and used the one feint they would not fall for again? He'd last another hour, perhaps two if he were lucky. And then what? Surrender at the point of a gun, only to be shut away again in that concrete box, surely never to see the light of day again? Or would one of those guns facing him end his misery once and for all, sending him into eternal blackness or whatever awaited him on the other side of life? *Just breathe,* coaxed the voice in his head. *Open your mouth and breathe and let the water do its work. They say there is pain at first, but you've already been through pain. What is one or two more moments of it?*

As quickly as the image of floating into blackness came to him, another immediately replaced it. The image of a little boy sitting front row at Eddie's funeral, staring at the lifeless form of the father he'd never seen alive because of too many reasons, chief among them being his father simply hadn't cared enough. The boy's mother was at his side, running a comforting hand through his hair and telling him she was sorry, that it wasn't the boy's fault for what happened, that she hoped he'd grow up to be nothing like his father and to always be there for his own kids someday. Sometimes in life, giving a damn meant more than anything else, she'd say through her tears. Most of the time it was *all* that mattered.

Just as Eddie took in the first mouthful of river water, he snapped back into himself and lunged above the water's surface, coughing and spitting out the silty liquid that had already gone halfway down his windpipe. Choking, he slipped below the surface again. Instinctively, a long-learned lesson kicked in deep inside his brain, one taught to him by Jules himself during one of their many summer forays on this same river some ten years prior. During one of his stints in a juvenile detention camp, Jules had had a former Navy SEAL as one of his counselors. Part of their mandatory activities had been swimming lessons, being that half of the kids hadn't known how to swim. Utilizing the camp swimming pool, Jules and his fellow detainees had been forced to undergo a terrifying, albeit less rigid, form of SEAL drown-proofing. Blindfolded with hands bound behind their backs and their feet tied together, Jules and the rest of the kids had been shuffled off the end of a ten-meter platform into the deep end of the pool. Once underwater, Jules had explained with horror, the kids had been told they would not be helped again until they freed the simple knot tied to their hands and feet.

Jules had told the story with his usual gesticulations and wacky humor, but the lesson had become real for Eddie when Jules had convinced him to try it himself. The experience had indeed been terrifying, but he'd forced himself to remain calm while methodically removing first the knot around his wrists, then his ankles. He had broken the water's surface with not a second to spare, his lungs burning for air. Jules, whooping and cheering, had helped a coughing

Eddie to the river's edge. Eddie had never told Jules how frightened he'd been, instead opting to showcase the youthful bravado that had allowed him to keep up with his fearless (and reckless) best friend.

Now as Eddie struggled beneath the surface, he forced himself to relax. His natural buoyancy caused his body to rise to the surface, and once there he turned his head and sucked in a lungful of air. Once he'd recovered, he flipped onto his back and floated toward the middle of the river, exhausted but grateful to be alive. His senses returned, slowly at first, until his inner clock urged him to move again.

Unable to rotate his right shoulder, he kicked his feet beneath the surface, not wanting to cause any unnecessary splashing. It took him ten minutes to cross the fifty yards, when it normally would have taken him two. Reaching the opposite bank, he struggled to his knees and gathered in his surroundings. The pain in his shoulder and leg had dulled a bit, owing to the restorative quality of the cool water. Taking a moment to inspect his blistered feet, he noted numerous cuts and scrapes but realized he didn't have time to worry about it right now. That same inner clock told him they'd likely traced his movement back to the farm and had swung their search in this direction. Clambering up the embankment and spotting a grassy field approximately half a mile in width, he longed to travel over it to give his torn feet a break. But he knew he couldn't risk moving over open ground that far. If the helicopter returned before he made it back into the trees, he'd have to choose—the cold steel of handcuffs, or the hot lead of a bullet.

The part of the river he had just crossed had been at a wide bend. Looking right, Eddie realized he'd been so rushed he hadn't scouted a better place to cross. As it was now, the part of the river to his right, or upstream, snaked in from the northeast, effectively blocking his movement that way unless he crossed the river again. But he also realized that would put him back on the wrong side of the river, which would defeat the entire purpose of crossing it in the first place. Moving out to his left, or downstream, didn't seem much better. The land there fell into a sort of boggy depression. It was impossible to predict how the footing would be, but it didn't look promising. Still, it looked to be a quarter the distance that the open field presented. If he got lucky and the ground proved to be firm enough to travel across, he'd be in the opposing tree line in a minute or less. His only other option was to stay put—not really an option at all.

Halfway across the boggy ground he regretted his decision to come this way. The first few yards had been okay, but the further he went into the hundred-yard-wide muck, the deeper his feet sunk, and the more effort he had to put into pulling them back out. Each time he did so, a wet, glopping sound came from the space he'd stepped out of. He looked ahead and realized the fifty or so yards he had left would be impossible for him to continue through as quickly as he needed. At any second the helicopter would come swooshing over the surrounding treetops, its occupants grinning down at him as they radioed in his location.

With his strength rapidly diminishing and the pain in his thigh now screaming, Eddie decided his best chance to get through the marsh was not to walk through it at all. Instead, he leaned his upper body flat across the ground and began crawling. It was tedious work and the overpowering stench of the rotted ground here made him dizzy. Gagging against it, Eddie part-crawled, part-swam the rest of the way, taking him a full ten minutes and most of his remaining energy. But he made it, clawing his way up a slight embankment where he sat against a towering oak, gasping for breath and covered in thick muck from head to toe.

That's when he heard it. The *thump* of the helicopter rose over the river from the direction he'd come, soon coming into view over the marsh behind him. Hovering for a moment near his position, the copter circled the open ground for a minute. Eddie froze in his position beside the tree, unsure if he'd been spotted. His heart almost leapt out of his chest as the chopper drifted even closer, the pilot and the observer seated next to him scanning the ground he'd crawled through. They'd seen his tracks, Eddie feared. If so, men on the ground would come to investigate. *You need to get further into the trees. You can't afford to wait. Go!*

The chopper moved back and forth several more times across the marsh and open ground before moving off to search another area. Feeling tactile relief wash over him, Eddie finally allowed himself to relax to the point he felt his eyelids become heavy. He forced them open, only to feel them close again. He felt more tired than he ever had in his life. If only he could sleep for a few minutes, he'd be refreshed enough to continue on...

Don't you fall asleep, bro! Jules's voice inside him demanded. *You're almost out of the woods. Ha, get it? Seriously, my man, you can do this. Not for yourself, and definitely not for me. For your little boy. You have business to attend to, and you aren't going to get it done sitting here taking an afternoon nap. The cops fell for the horse, and now they're going to be pissed, bro.* Really *pissed.*

Eddie's eyes snapped back open. He dragged himself to his feet, shaking away the sleep he'd very nearly succumbed to, and he quickly regained his bearings. The sound of the chopper faded away, but Eddie knew it would be back. He turned into the trees and ran, swatting away branches in his path and crashing through the thick vegetation without regard to his bleeding feet. Envisioning a map in his head, he knew he was now heading southwest. The outskirts of Springwood lay several miles in that direction. Despite the gauntlet that would no doubt be waiting for him there, it's where he needed to go if he were to accomplish the impossible goal of finding his son before the law could close around him forever like the fist of an angry god.

THIRTY

STATE ATTORNEY HOOD sat at his courthouse office desk, his head buried in his large hands. The ruby-colored ring he had been twisting around his finger for the last several minutes now stood in contrast to the pale dome of his scalp. Mid-afternoon light filtering through the window reflected on the cheap stone, sending red-hued rays across the ceiling.

Several of his most trusted assistant state attorneys stood opposite him, silent as their boss finally lifted his head and stared wordlessly out the window toward the sprawling courtyard below. Only a few stragglers from the recent press conference remained, and from the look of them they were largely still speaking excitedly about the escape. Keeping his eyes on the courtyard, Hood dismissed his assistants one by one, giving them vacuous instructions on current cases. The large clock on the wall read two-fifteen. Grassle had been on the run for a little over two hours, and according to news Paolo sent him just minutes before, he still had not been apprehended. Entire search teams, including a bloodhound and a helicopter, had so far failed to find a lone escapee the sheriff himself had promised would be captured an hour ago. Amazingly, not one confirmed sighting of him had been verified since he'd first disappeared into the woods. Trying his best to contain his frustration, Hood closed his eyes against the strain that had steadily been building inside his head. A roaring headache pounded in his temples, and he had to fight the urge to call the sheriff once more and ask him what in God's name was going on out there.

Hood opened the top drawer of his desk and removed his encrypted cell phone. He pressed a button and listened to the robotic dial tone, amazed once again at how quickly life could change course. Three short hours ago he had been in the best of moods. Now, confusion, anger and yes, even fear threatened to overtake him. He had not felt true fear—for him, that of an unknown future—since standing over his father's open casket nearly fifty years ago.

The call connected and a familiar ghostly voice answered, "Yes, Mathias?"

Hood turned his eyes from the courtyard. "Give me good news, Paolo. The reports I've heard are...troubling."

A pause on the other end, then, "They believe the perimeter may have been compromised."

Hood closed his eyes, the lids fluttering as he attempted to contain his anger. Patience, a virtue he had long cultivated, finally reached its terminus. In one swoop of his powerful hand, he grasped a crystal clock that sat at the corner of his desk and hurled it against the far wall. There it shattered into a thousand glimmering pieces, so loud a security guard popped his head inside the unlocked office. Hood glared at the man, who swallowed hard and quickly disappeared back down the hall.

"Just what kind of operation is Driscoll running out there?" Hood asked, seething.

He heard Paolo inhaling deeply on the other end, as if what he was about to say would no doubt exasperate Hood further. When he finished relaying the tale of Grassle's simple ploy with the horse and scarecrow, Hood threw his head back and let out such a powerful roar the window in his office rattled in its sash. When he finally composed himself, his face wore a murderous expression so severe it could have cracked a mirror.

"He could be anywhere now."

"Not precisely. The search area seems larger than before, but the authorities are certain he is still within a relatively contained area. He will be caught. Since the perimeter has shifted, they must—"

"I understand all of that," Hood snapped. "I've worked side by side with police agencies for over forty years."

"I didn't mean to imply you lacked understanding," Paulo said, his voice reassuring. "I am simply being honest with you. The man is injured and alone and lacks any real resources. Yet he avoided capture by using the police's natural tendencies against them. It was an intelligent move. I'm impressed."

The sun had just passed below the building opposite the courthouse courtyard, washing the area in a sea of early-afternoon shadow. Fitting, considering Hood's own darkening mood. He became lost in thought for a moment, unable to decide upon two options he had been considering. Finally, he nodded to himself, a decision made.

"If Grassle is as smart as you think he is, then I can no longer trust the sheriff to contain him. How far are you willing to take this for me, Paolo?"

A brief silence passed through the line until, "It will be done, Mathias, even if I must sacrifice myself." Then, casually, as if what he'd just spoken had meant nothing to him, "What of the police?"

Hood answered the question with one of his own. "Would you truly do that for me?"

"Yes, sir."

"I've told you not to call me 'sir,' Paolo. You've always meant much more to me than just a business subordinate. I hope you know that." Hood said this in an offhand manner, spinning the ring around his finger as he stared distractedly at the collection of pictures on his office wall. But when the response came from his longtime associate, both surprise and enlightenment struck the longtime prosecutor in a subtle yet powerful manner.

"How *exactly* do you feel about me, Mathias?" Paolo's voice was gentle, sentimental. Hood had never heard him speak this way before. He could almost hear the man blushing on the other end of the phone.

"I just told you how I feel about you," Hood said, sitting up higher in his chair. He frowned, waiting for the response.

"Tell me."

So he *had* detected something in Paolo's voice. Surprised, but not wishing to betray the fact, Hood nodded to himself. A new hand dealt. A flush.

"I hold you very dear in my heart, Paolo. Not like an associate or a friend. I've—seen your eyes move over me."

There. He'd said it. A gamble for sure, considering he could have misinterpreted Paolo's words and tone. But his intuition had never failed him. It had been a calculated risk moving the conversation this way. If incorrect in his assessment, an uncomfortable business arrangement between the two would be sure to follow. Not to mention a false narrative about him being put out there for the world to potentially see, should Paolo decide to talk. But if correct, he felt his burgeoning ruse could pay untold dividends.

"Have you not moved yours over me?" came Paolo's measured reply. His voice, usually devoid of emotion, held a noticeable lilt to it now. Ever observant, Hood had heard it from his own lips numerous times during the dozens of interactions he'd had with women over the years. Never having the desire or energy to keep them for more than a time or two, he'd cultivated his persona to attract then discard. And always, that unmistakable tone of voice. Questioning. Hopeful. His carnal attraction to the female sex had been his sole desire since as long as he could remember. Queers had been an amusing conversation piece for him, the subject of locker room jokes between him and his staff, notwithstanding the current politically correct environment. Despite this, he had had no issue employing homosexuals or associating with them on a purely professional level. But the thought of their sexual practices had both disgusted and brought about an almost biblical ideation in him.

Detecting this now from Paolo of all people bordered on disbelief. Still, he felt he should have seen it before. The man's appraising eye. His stillness whenever he'd been in Hood's presence, something Hood himself had assumed to be the man's introverted personality when in fact it now appeared to have been nervousness. Hood had done his homework on the mysterious former agent, something that in hindsight should have alerted him further. Never married, no known children, no heterosexual relationships in his observable past. Hood had figured Paolo's lack of known partners to have been a by-product of the job itself. So many lonely nights spent abroad, never being able to disclose a mission or his whereabouts to others...

Hood smiled to himself, pleased that his intuition had once again served him well. The air between the two of them, even over a telephone line, grew thick with baited anticipation. It would all be up to Hood on how to proceed. His initial expression of revilement gave way to one of intrigue. He must be conciliatory, flirtatious even. If he came across as anything but, the initiative would be lost, and Paolo would likely never bring up the conversation again. He'd no doubt continue in his work for Hood, but any associated emotion—and potential sacrifice—might be lost forever.

"Yes, I have felt your eyes move over me. As mine have over you. I didn't know you felt this way too."

From the other end of the line, a pause, then the clearing of a throat. "It is not my wish to complicate things, sir."

Hood smiled. "Then do as I ask of you. When this is over, things may be different between us. Until then, we must both remain on task. Business is always first."

"Of course. Anything you ask, and it will be."

Hood reached into the top drawer of his desk. Atop the felt bottom lay a single bullet. Hood did as he'd done countless times before and picked up the round, turning it over between his fingers as he inspected the twin grooves at its base, the unmolested primer and the rust-colored, rounded bullet that sat like waiting death in its silver cartridge.

"My father carried a .45 he kept from the war. I showed it to you once," Hood said.

"I know the weapon you speak of."

"I am leaving you something. In his honor. You will find it inside a sealed manila folder, in the same place I've left you things before. Once you have eliminated Grassle, use it to make him as unrecognizable as my own father was to me resting in his casket."

A pleased sound from the other end, one of clear assent. "Is that all, Mathias?"

"Just one more thing," Hood responded. "Make him suffer first."

He ended the call and placed the phone back in the drawer. Putting a leather glove on each hand, he used a cloth to wipe the round clean of prints and had begun to place it inside the envelope when a knock came at his office door. Removing his gloves and placing them on his lap, he called for the visitor to enter. His secretary stepped in, relaying news of the ongoing manhunt she thought he'd like to see. Clicking on the wall-mounted television, Hood waited until she'd left to turn his attention to the broadcast.

Grassle still had not been found. While this information had frustrated Hood just minutes ago, now his mind lay at ease. A different approach had been taken. One that would produce a final outcome, one much more appropriate for the situation. Closing his eyes and twirling the round between his fingertips again, his mind returned to that abominable scene of his father's casket being lowered into the ground. Grassle would pay dearly for his escape, something that had at first confounded Hood, but that now pleased him very much. His lips fluttered with noiseless words. A promise to be kept no matter what. And then an image in his mind—of Grassle's riddled body, his face ruined and twisted in death—and that image was so rapturous that Hood's eyes snapped open and he found himself calmly placing his gloves back on before dropping the round inside the envelope. Dabbing a cloth into a glass of water on his desk, he used it to seal the envelope.

THIRTY-ONE

PAOLO BRUZZI CALMLY walked through the maze of police personnel and vehicles then climbed into the driver's seat of his white Cutlass. He had carefully chosen this vehicle some time ago. Nothing too new or too old, and in both a style and color that would not attract undue attention. A person asked to remember the vehicle would likely frown and respond that it looked just like any other car on the road; at a distance or in poor light its color could just as easily have been beige or tan or silver. Aside from being so ubiquitous, the color white had a more practical effect on a person—it resembled an unmarked police car on later recollection. The limousine tint provided much-needed privacy during surveillance and achieved a somewhat sinister appearance when being driven. That people tended to both avoid the vehicle and lack solid memory of it was its genius.

Not like it mattered now.

He set his 800 MHz police radio on the passenger seat and shrugged out of the plain black ballistic vest he had been issued by Captain Escobar. Paolo suspected the captain had offered both the vest and radio to more easily keep tabs on him versus having any true concern for his safety. He had read the open disdain in Escobar's eyes and understood well enough he was not wanted here. Which was understandable. Paolo knew the police game. They liked to always be in charge and detested outsiders encroaching on their turf.

Escobar clearly resented the fact that the sheriff had chosen not to ban civilians from the search area, effectively breaching the thin blue line separating the police world from the rest of society. The veteran lawman had likened his decision to wartime correspondents documenting the action. And much like a wartime general, the sheriff had tasked Escobar with arranging a call to the Florida Department of Law Enforcement for them to send additional resources. Just in case.

Paolo's new mission brought with it a new element, one that heightened his personal stakes considerably: his possible death. Having listened to Hood's description of the mission, he had immediately understood the gravity of the situation, eliminating the possibility that he would ever be arrested for Grassle's murder. He simply would not allow it. Despite his shadowed background, certain links existed between him and Hood, however faint. He of all people understood the power of local, state, and federal investigators. If they desired to know something, they would find it. But Paolo had decided his burgeoning feelings for Hood—a new type of feeling that made butterflies fly within him at the mere sound of the man's voice, or catching his approving eye—would make him like a bee, constantly buzzing and protecting its queen. Should the need arise, Paolo had reconciled his own fate, equating it with a love that would not hesitate to sting itself if necessary. The final coda to his own life would be love's ultimate sacrifice.

As the radio crackled with the voices of team members still hunting Grassle, Paolo rested his head against the headrest and closed his eyes. He concentrated on his breathing, pushing all non-essential matters from his mind. He focused only on his new task. He took immense pleasure in the knowledge that his previous watchdog role had now changed to something much more familiar to him, something more personal. Evidence tampering, surveillance, and witness intimidation were all necessary aspects of his work. And he did them well. But it tended to become mundane in the grand scheme of things. As his thoughts wandered back to Hood himself, Paolo's mind conjured the man's powerful build, his smooth alabaster head, and eyes that so rarely betrayed emotion, yet managed with just a glance to evoke hidden feelings inside Paolo he had never known before. The hint of a smile crept into the corners of Paolo's mouth as his mind dared to imagine removing Hood's suit jacket, undoing his tie then slowly unbuttoning his dress shirt. How would his chest be? Smooth, or patched with dark hair such that was present on his giant hands? And then Paolo pressing himself against that giant frame, taking in the masculine scent emitting from every pore in the man's body, as he felt a stiffness build against that of his own.

The fantasy ended as quickly as it had arrived. Paolo opened his eyes, self-discipline restored. The hint of a smile that had been there moments before was replaced by the rigid line of his mouth. *Mission first*, he reminded himself. *Do this thing Mathias has asked of you and he will be more pleased than ever. Maybe then...*

Paolo drew a notepad and pen from the glovebox. He scratched three words across the top of the paper: **Become the hunted.** Below that line he wrote, **As the hunted, what are my actions now that I have escaped?** Paolo pondered this, allowing his mind to expand from the obvious, from the expected. Inviting all options that were realistically possible, he then wrote, **A man who escapes is not necessarily avoiding something. He can just as easily be seeking something.**

This last line gave him pause. Something stirred inside him as he read the words aloud. On the next line he listed a series of biographical notes as he double-checked a fact sheet he had prepared not long after first receiving his original Grassle assignment. Satisfied his information correlated with his hunch, he began humming a classical tune he had once played on the piano as a child. When he finished scribbling an itemized list, he held the paper up to read his own flourished text:

Phone records indicate subject's only recent contact limited to two individuals—Julius Sanders (deceased), and Clarissa Fulton (mother of only child).

Employed by the Herman Manufacturing Company as a machine press operator for the two weeks preceding his most recent arrest.

Resided at 121 Schofield Lane in Springwood prior to arrest. One-bedroom apartment currently under formal eviction proceedings.

Only known living relative is five-year-old son. No known past contact.

Paolo's eyes moved over the list several times before hovering between the first and last items. His eyes narrowed. Most of his hunches began as just a glimmer deep inside his mind. A budding seed that, once watered and given sun, may not sprout for days or weeks. Others sprang forth from his mind in short order. The latter occurred now, and after a moment's thought he circled the words 'Clarissa' and 'Springwood.' Deciding if his train of thought had been caused by a distraction or by his history of well-honed detection, he placed an asterisk next to the word 'child' and moved on.

"Where do you fly, my newly freed bird?" Paulo said aloud as he turned the car's ignition. He pulled out of the command post area, pointing the Cutlass east. He passed two roadblocks guarded by equally annoyed-looking pairs of deputies, each inspecting his identification with rolling eyes before allowing him passage. Ten minutes later he arrived at his destination, a salmon-colored home with one of the house numbers hanging askew. The clock on the dash read a quarter past four. All indications pointed to the idea that Grassle had likely breached the main police perimeter, despite what authorities had admitted to the public. Miles of untamed woods and little used riverways sat to the east, Springwood and the difficulty of urban dwellings to the west. In theory, all of it was now open to the escapee. If Grassle wasn't found before nightfall, the odds of finding him before daybreak dwindled greatly.

A new perimeter had been set at a twenty mile circumference, but even Paolo knew it would take a thousand men and a dozen helicopters to properly search an area that size, resources the sheriff's office did not have even with assistance from surrounding counties and the state. Still, he understood that a person could only be in one place at a time. Furthering that idea, a wounded person with no known associates to assist him could not possibly expect to remain on the run for long. Taking that into account, as well as Grassle's demonstrated cunning, Paolo wondered if the man had things other than simple escape in mind. Thus, his decision to come here.

Giving three firm knocks on the front door, he waited and listened as typical household noises floated out from an open window. After a minute, a man of about thirty opened the door and leered at Paolo. "We already sold it," he said brusquely, not bothering to make eye contact.

He went to close the door when Paolo cleared his throat and said in an authoritative voice, "I'm not here to buy, sir."

The man opened the door fully and eyed Paolo's extended ID.

"Special Investigator Bruzzi," he said. "Is Ms. Fulton home?" Paolo delivered this with a manufactured Italian accent. He had several accents on which he could rely at a moment's notice. Italian, he found, produced a level of respect in the average American. Be it from the Mafioso reputation or other learned stereotypes, his appearance combined with the accent tended to give him desirable results.

The man made a motion with his head, as if to beckon someone from within. A moment later a pretty, dark-haired woman appeared at the man's side. As she introduced herself, her eyes flashed an equal mixture of irritation and exhaustion. "If this is about Eddie, I have no idea where he is," Clarissa said, not bothering to hide her annoyance.

Paolo pocketed his credentials and offered his right hand. "I know you must be tired of speaking with the police. I apologize on behalf of the sheriff's office for having to bother you further, but if you have a moment there are just a few things I—we, rather—would like to clear up."

Clarissa began to object then appeared to change her mind. She whispered something inaudible to the man beside her and he disappeared into the house, rolling his eyes as he went. She stepped out onto the stoop and closed the door behind her. Folding her arms across her breasts, she made no move to meet Paolo's extended hand. "You're right, I am tired of talking to you people," she said bitterly. "A detective just left here an hour ago. Don't you people talk to each other?"

Paolo studied her. Closed body language. No trouble meeting his eye. After years of interrogating subjects (many of them by the point of a blade or while strapped to a board with water pouring over their masked faces) he'd learned to tell a lie by mere sight. He felt that under certain circumstances, especially with women, he could even smell the lies. Taking a beat longer to cement his opinion, he decided on the spot the woman had no idea where the escapee was.

"I understand your frustration, ma'am. Trust that we'll inform you as soon as we find him. In the meantime, I was hoping you could give us something that could—" Paolo chose his next words carefully— "ensure nothing bad happens to Eddie before we safely catch him."

He made sure to refer to Eddie by his first name. Whether or not the Fulton woman showed it, she would be endeared by his use of it. She shared a child with the man, after all, and her dozens of documented jail visits with him over the years spoke of a deeper connection words or current attitudes could not conceal.

Clarissa's demeanor softened a bit as she extended her hand. "I'm sorry for being rude. I already have a million things going on with the move, and now this. If it wasn't enough to find out Eddie escaped, then I get a parade of detectives asking me what I know about it. I was just as surprised as anyone. Shit, I practically dropped a pot of oatmeal."

Paolo shook her hand, looking past her at the collection of boxes stacked in the living room.

"You mentioned a move? As in relocating?"

Clarissa nodded. "Yes, Ohio. We were supposed to wait until Liam finished school next week, but I just can't stay here any longer. Not after what happened today. It's just all too much. The neighbors have been walking by all day peering toward the house like we're circus freaks. 'Step right up, ladies and gentlemen, the chick with the jailbreaking ex-boyfriend!'" She laughed humorlessly. "Roger and I— that was him just now—we've been packing all week. I made him rent a U-Haul tomorrow so we can get the hell out of here as soon as Liam gets out of school. I don't care if I ever set foot in Florida again."

Paolo reached into his jacket pocket and produced a pen and notepad. He scribbled a note to himself before turning his attention back onto Clarissa. "How long have you planned this move? And when was the last time you communicated with Eddie?"

"I woke up one day a couple weeks ago and decided I just couldn't be here anymore. Roger was really good about it. Just said he wanted to be wherever I am, and since I didn't want to stay here anymore, he'd go wherever Liam and I went. He's not perfect, but he loves me. Sometimes that's all a woman needs."

Paolo nodded. "Go on, please."

"I marched right down to the jail and told Eddie he would never see Liam as long as I had anything to say about it. He begged me to let him see him, but I told him he'd lost his chance."

"Do you have any reason to believe he'd try to harm you in any way?"

Clarissa shook her head emphatically. "I slapped him once when I found another girl's lipstick on his shirt. He just touched his cheek and said he was sorry. As big and strong as he is, he'd never hurt a fly. His thing was more neglect than anything. I think the thought of him being a father started to scare him since his dad skipped out on him as a kid."

"I understand," Paolo said, his eyes clouding with memory.

"Can I ask you a favor?" she asked. "When you catch him, I'd like you to tell him something for me." Clarissa glanced over her shoulder to check that the door was still closed. "Tell him I would have taken him back if he'd shown up to get Liam that morning."

Paolo's eyes drifted from her face to the wall. A memory, one of him back at the orphanage, resurfaced. Remaining in that place for a moment, Paolo blinked and suddenly the painful image that had stolen itself into his mind disappeared. He placed a hand over his heart. "You have my word."

Clarissa smiled wanly. A loose strand of hair fell across her face and she smoothed it back, nodding to herself. "I really think that if Eddie had a second chance, he'd try to be a real dad. But it's too late for that now. That's what you call irony."

Paolo nodded. The distant flicker of a hunch that had materialized in his mind earlier seemed to blossom now like a plant fertilized and watered. Yes, it did seem possible. His own instinct, honed over years of hunting other humans, remained his greatest weapon. He had learned to trust it explicitly. Now as he stood on the stoop in the afternoon heat, Paolo felt his hunch formulate into a tangible idea like puzzle pieces coming together of their own accord. After exchanging a few pleasantries, he bade Clarissa farewell, leaving his business card and asking her to please call him immediately if she heard from the escapee—her former love and father of her only child.

But Paolo felt he was very close to knowing where Eddie Grassle was ultimately headed, even if the escapee didn't know it yet.

THIRTY-TWO

AFTER EDDIE DUCKED out of the trees and continued along the river's edge for another half mile, the land thinned until he came upon a narrow dirt road bordering a cornfield. Kneeling in a shallow ditch beside the road, he caught his breath, considering his best course of action. He was fairly sure he'd remained on a southwesterly route. That meant Springwood's outskirts lay just a couple miles past the cornfield. All he needed to do was cross the road without being seen then cut straight across the field. Providing the land there was at least partially dotted with trees or other structures that could provide him cover, he might have a chance of making it into the town proper. Even if he made it that far and managed to avoid capture—which itself would be a miracle—he had no realistic idea of how he intended on seeing Liam before they moved out of state.

First things first.

To his left, the road went straight for a hundred yards or so before turning at a 90-degree angle. To his right, it gently bent about twenty yards down as the field curved in that direction. Deciding not to waste time seeing if the road was clear around the right corner, Eddie rose and began hobbling across it. But halfway across a vehicle roared around the corner, braking hard as its driver stopped at the last second. Its brakes screeching, the vehicle came to rest just two feet from him in a cloud of dust as Eddie stood frozen in fear facing it, arms raised. He stared toward the still obscured windshield, amazed at first at not being hit, then despondent with the knowledge that if he'd waited just ten seconds to cross, the vehicle would have sped by and he'd have made it with no problem. As the dust cloud settled, Eddie expected to see one or more deputies standing beside their open doors, gun barrels pointing at him, but instead it was a Hispanic driver wearing a cowboy hat, staring back at Eddie with equal surprise. Another Hispanic-looking man sat next to him, also sporting a cowboy hat and similar shocked expression. Through the pickup's windshield and rear window, Eddie observed a dozen equally dark-skinned, sweaty men sitting cramped together in the truck bed.

Eddie stepped cautiously to the driver's side. Ranchero music floated from the truck's open windows. "*Necesita que te lleve?*" the driver asked. Eddie didn't know much Spanish but had lived around enough people who'd spoken it to piece together common phrases. He glanced at the men in the back. Each wore long-sleeved field clothing of varying styles, with most also wearing hats with neck-flaps. One of them gave Eddie a pitiful look and drew a cup of water from a yellow jug mounted on the side of the truck. He extended it toward him. "*Agua?*"

Feeling as though someone else were controlling his arm, Eddie reached out and took the cup with trembling hands. He drank the ice-cold water too fast, most of it splashing over his fingers and spilling down the front of his chest. What little of the liquid that did reach his throat felt like heaven. "Gracias," he croaked, his voice barely a whisper. He handed the cup back where the man happily refilled it. At the men's urging, Eddie drank again, this time more slowly.

"*A dónde va?*" one of the men asked when Eddie finished drinking.

"Mi casa," Eddie said, pointing past the cornfield. "Springwood."

He heard the men speak in Spanish amongst themselves until they all nodded in some sort of agreement. One of the men in the truck bed waved him near. "We take."

Eddie wasted no time. He limped toward the opened tailgate and felt a collection of arms pull him into the truck bed. Once there, several of the men *ohhhed* and *ahhhed* at his injuries, which had only then become apparent to them. One of the men dug into a toolbox and produced a bandana, which he tied around Eddie's forehead to keep the sweat pouring from his head from getting into his eyes. None of the men questioned Eddie as to why he appeared so filthy, but then again each of them had an entire day's worth of grime and sweat covering them as well. Noting his blistered and tattered bare feet, they gave him a look that said he clearly did not belong out here. But Eddie correctly surmised that most of them were undocumented seasonal pickers, and he knew from experience that they shied away from any type of law enforcement.

Sandwiched now between two of these men, Eddie rested his head on the truck bed and allowed himself a moment of respite. To keep the sun from his face, one of the workers set his own hat atop Eddie's head. As the truck rolled down the road, the wind generated from its movement flowed like a zephyr through the bed and over Eddie's sweaty face. The vehicle creaked its way around various fields for a mile before it came to a roadblock set at a highway junction. Two marked sheriff cruisers stood blocking the road, with a pair of carbine-wielding deputies standing beside them. One of them, a big country boy with the name **WADE** stitched on his uniform, directed the pickup to stop and ordered the driver to turn off the ignition. The driver obeyed and placed his hands on the wheel.

"Who are you carrying?" asked Deputy Wade, keeping one eye on the driver and another on the packed truck bed as he approached.

"*Trabajadores*," the driver explained.

With his partner standing several yards behind him providing security, Wade took a step toward the truck bed so he could inspect the faces of the men crowding it. He moved his gaze over the dozen or so dirty faces staring silently back at him, searching them for any resemblance to the BOLO mugshot he and his partner had both studied at length. Nothing to note at first glance; they were clearly all dark-complexioned Mexicans, and the driver and passenger as well. From the look of them, they'd been in the fields all day.

But as Wade turned back toward his partner, preparing to signal him that the truck was clear, he noticed an extra pair of legs sticking out between two of the sitting men that had not yet been accounted for. Curious, he stepped closer and noticed he had in fact missed one of the workers who lay on his back between his cohorts. Wearing

similar overalls and a tattered, flannel shirt, the man's face was partially obscured by a hat. Noting the man's blistered, bare feet, Wade
took a cautious step closer.

"You, laying down. Take off the hat," he ordered.

No one in the truck bed moved. The man Wade referred to could
have been asleep or dead, from the look of him.

Wade unslung his carbine and pointed it at the men. "Somebody
better wake up your *amigo*, or I will," he said, spitting onto the ground.

Wade's partner Elias took the cue and unslung his own carbine
from where he stood. "What you got, Wade?" he asked with alarm.

"I don't know." Then, to the men in the truck bed, "Tell your
amigo he has three seconds to take off that goddamn hat, or so help
me I'll run all you fuckers in for no docs, *comprende?*"

One of the men spoke up just then, in what limited English he
apparently knew. "He, accident." He pointed to a ladder that hung
attached to the side of the truck, then made a falling motion with
his hands.

"I don't give a lick if he's hurt or not. Somebody better show me
his goddamn face now or shit is gonna start getting real." Wade shouldered his rifle for emphasis, motioning at the hat with the barrel.

"*Sí, Sí,*" one of the men said, and snatched the hat from Eddic's
head. Having been in a state of semi-consciousness, Eddie immediately snapped awake, feeling sunlight splash across his mud-caked
face and sensing one of the deputies moving closer to peer into the
truck bed. Wrinkling his nose at the men's collective stench, Wade
gave Eddie a long look, studying his face for any similarities from their
suspect's mugshot. From this angle, he appeared to be the same complexion as the others. Similar clothing too. Elias had now approached,
and as they'd done countless times before, the pair silently judged
the one description factor that a person could not alter—their height.
But the man lay flat, the most difficult way to judge a person's true
height, and in the jumble of legs and arms crowding the truck bed,
the man they inspected could have easily been five-five or six-two.

Both deputies shared a glance, then retreated several steps to
get out of earshot of the men. "What are we gonna do with them?"
Elias asked.

Wade raised his eyebrows. "If we call EMS for the guy, one of us is getting stuck writing the report. It's my kid's birthday today, so it *ain't* gonna be me. Besides, I don't want to explain why we allowed an ambulance into the perimeter."

Elias countered, "But if something happens to them, it's on us. We should call it in."

"Fuck that. I say we never saw them. No paperwork, no problem."

Elias reluctantly nodded his agreement. Wade approached the driver and wagged a finger in the man's face. "I see you back out on this road today and all of you go to ICE. Got it, *ese*?"

The driver nodded his understanding and offered a parting wave. Standing and watching the dust cloud settle after their departure, neither deputy said a word for a full minute. A certain tension seemed to have settled over them.

"Fuckin' beaners," Wade said, shaking his head.

"Sarge better not find out we let them go without reporting it. I can't afford another suspension."

Both men stood silent, scanning the vast landscape around them. In the distance, the police helicopter zigzagged over an area about a mile behind their position. The midday air was hot and muggy, and as such it took several minutes for the truck's dust cloud to settle. The deputies had used the discretion given them to handle one of the countless situations individual officers ultimately faced. Life or death, or just something more ordinary. But either way, a decision nonetheless. They'd let them go and that would be that. All the better, they each thought to themselves as they scanned their surroundings. An escaped felon was out there somewhere, and in the end, all that mattered was making sure he didn't slip through the gauntlet they'd erected around him.

Placing an exclamation on the whole affair, Wade spat onto a lizard sunning itself on a nearby rock.

THIRTY-THREE

CHET RIGGINS SET his fork down on his plate and eyed his wife from across the dinner table. "I know you don't like discussing work over dinner, but tonight you're going to let me know what's going on in that beautiful mind of yours." His baritone voice came even deeper due to the three beers he'd already drunk.

Alice Riggins, lost in her own thoughts since arriving home an hour before, smiled despite her own conflicting thoughts. "Let me ask you something."

"Give it to me."

Resting her chin on her interlocked fingers, she asked, "Am I a good woman?"

Chet showed no change of expression. "Nope."

She frowned. "Explain."

"You aren't a good woman, you're a fantastic woman, with a giant heart and beautiful big eyes that can see into people's souls," he said. "You're soft and sensitive, but you don't take a bit of smack from anyone. At first, I thought you were too smart for your own good, and maybe a touch too pretty to be messing with someone like me." His eyes met hers in a way that showed he meant what he said.

Smiling, she brought a hand up to smooth one side of her cropped hair. "If you told me you were lying just now, I'd still love you for saying it."

Chet stood and beckoned her to the couch, where he lay down and made room for her to rest beside him. He drew his large, dark fingers across the exposed skin of her neck in that way that always made her shiver. "Talk to me, baby girl."

She recounted the day's events, including the fact she'd been ordered to stay away from anything concerning Eddie's escape. When she finished, she propped her chin onto her husband's broad chest and said matter-of-factly, "I've decided to work the case on my own."

He raised his eyebrows. "As in going against orders?"

"Remember when I told you Sanny and I went back to the jail to interview Eddie again? After Heinke told me not to?"

"So, you're on a first-name basis with an escaped prisoner?"

She slapped his chest. "Don't even. That interview was the test for me. I needed to go back one more time and look him in the eye, just to be sure. I guess I needed that one little push over the cliff to get me all in. I considered talking with the State about reducing the charges."

"Isn't that a conflict?"

"Sort of. But the State reduces and drops charges all the time."

"So would they do that for Eddie too?"

She bit her lip. "No way. I have the impression there's someone in the state attorney's office who has a serious hard-on for him. Not sure why, but at every formal invest and proceeding I went to they had their top dogs on the case. And there was something else too."

Chet ran his fingers through his wife's hair, knowing that when she got going it was best to shut up and let her keep up her steam.

"The state attorney himself was there every time," she said. "Hood. I've only seen him personally take on two other cases before, and those were much earlier in his career when he still had something to prove. Guys in his position are usually career politicians. But not him. During these hearings he had this certain look in his eye. So intense. He listened to every word and took his own notes. I'm telling you, there was fire in his eyes. I don't know what's going on with all of this, but one thing I'm certain of is that for some reason, he seems to want Eddie dead and buried."

This time, Chet did speak up. "You mean literally dead, like six feet under?"

Alice frowned. "I don't know. But definitely out of the way."

"But even you said Eddie was caught in the act. He even helped the other guy get away. Why shouldn't everyone want him put away?"

Riggins sat up suddenly and crossed her arms. "No, Chet, that's not what I said. I mean, yes, he was in the store, and he was in the car after it fled the scene. But here's something funny I've noticed over the years. People act as they naturally would on surveillance cameras, the kind they forget are there. We had a sexual battery case a while back where a woman claimed she'd met her alleged rapist at a bar. She claimed his advances were unwanted and that she turned him down repeatedly throughout the night. But when we watched the video, you can see her dropping her head and laughing at things he says, accepting drinks, talking openly with him. Video is unbiased, and body language goes a long way."

"I'm surprised you took the alleged rapist's side."

Riggins shook her head. "It's not that. The victim's testimony fell apart because she claimed he had been aggressively harassing her from the first moment they met, which is impeached by the video evidence. Eddie's case is the same, only in reverse. Although the evidence conflicts with his testimony, on the tape you see his mannerisms *support* it."

Chet took his wife's face in his hands and looked directly into her eyes. "You be careful with this Eddie business." He sighed, stroking the top of her head. "I have faith in you, though, so I suppose this old ox should just keep believing in you and let this thing play out the way it's supposed to."

Riggins stretched forward and gave him a long kiss on the mouth. A moment later the shrill ring of her agency-issued cell phone interrupted them. Springing to her feet, she snatched it off the counter and answered, "Sing me sweet music, Sanny."

For several minutes she talked back and forth with her partner, pacing across the living room floor like a caged tiger. After receiving answers to each of her questions, she only became more inquisitive. When she hung up, she set the phone on the countertop and sat down next to Chet on the couch. "I'm meeting up with Sanny. He says they've expanded the perimeter, which pretty much means they realize he may have slipped through after all. They've called the dogs off too, and with such a large search area the thermal imaging on the helicopter is pretty much useless. There are people all over those woods; it's impossible to keep them out." Slipping into the bedroom, she emerged shortly afterward wearing jeans, a tucked-in polo top, and sneakers. Fastening an ankle holster, she stuffed home a snub-nosed .38 revolver, usually her back-up gun but today her preferred carry. After pocketing her cell phone, she leaned over the couch to give Chet a hard kiss on the mouth.

He pulled her close and whispered something in her ear, grinning.

Before darting out the front door, Riggins glanced back and winked at him. "As soon as I get home, mister."

THIRTY-FOUR

ELEVEN MILES DISTANT, Eddie hopped down from the truck bed. This was as far as he dared travel, as another checkpoint lay ahead in the distance and he didn't dare risk another interaction with the police. Thanking the men in his broken Spanish, he shook each of their hands and insisted he'd be okay on his own. As he watched the truck disappear around a bend in the road, he understood the odds would be almost one hundred percent the men would hear word about a barefoot jail escapee matching his description. And what would the odds be that each man would remain quiet? He couldn't be sure, especially if a reward had been put up for him. His main concern had been accomplished—to put as much distance between himself and his pursuers as possible. Having no real plan after that, he decided it best to get off the road as quickly as he could so that he could formulate his next step. He'd just made it over the embankment and barely into the trees when a sheriff cruiser screamed by behind him. Not wishing to take any more chances with roads, Eddie kept to the woods for another mile until he glimpsed a roofline through the trees. He realized that he'd basically made a large westerly arc through some of the harshest terrain in the county. Not ideal, but then again, he'd had no real choice.

Soon enough he came to a fence that bordered what looked to be a small farmhouse and barn. Crouching, he considered his options. Avoiding the farm altogether would be his best option. People lived in houses. And by now, all residents in a fifty-mile radius had no doubt been apprised of his escape. He could skirt the property, keeping his direction toward Springwood. He figured he could always double-back and lose himself in the woods if necessary, but that meant doubling his travel distance, and thus doubling his chances of being seen. Besides, he still needed to find shoes of some kind. His feet were hamburger. And coming back this way negated his original intention. No, he would combine his first two options. He needed a sanctuary, some place to remain off the radar and rest. One sighting by a sharp-eyed civilian could undo in seconds what had taken him nearly three hours to achieve. He lay down beside the fence, using the tall grass as concealment. He didn't even realize he'd closed his eyes. When he opened them again the sun had begun to set. Getting to his feet took some effort, and as he rubbed his aching wounds he peered toward the house, undecided on his next move.

Eddie heard the sound of a television game show floating from the open living room window. Lights burned in several other windows in the house, and a beat-up Ford pickup sat parked in the gravel driveway. A barn sat back from the house, and from here didn't appear to be occupied. Still exhausted, with hunger and thirst gnawing at him, Eddie decided reward outweighed the risk of trying the barn. Stepping over the ranch-style fence, he crept carefully toward the wide double doors, keeping his eyes on the house the entire time. Reaching the barn, he lifted the heavy wooden beam securing the double doors and pulled one of them open enough for him to squeeze through. He did his best to close the door behind him, knowing he wouldn't be able to secure it but having little choice in the matter. With just a sliver of light slicing through the darkness within, he had to move his hands blindly over the walls until he eventually felt a light switch.

Wincing with anticipation, Eddie flipped it on. The barn came alive with light, much more than he'd expected. His pupils constricted and it took him several moments to adjust to the sudden brightness. Once his vision cleared, Eddie looked around the main bay, searching for something, anything, he felt could help him. On the wall to his left hung a variety of garden tools and a coil of rope, its ends wrapped in duct tape. With the wall to his right bare save for a few rusted farming implements and a mud-covered hose, he took several steps further into the bay to investigate. In a small alcove near the back sat a work bench covered with piles of oily rags and a disassembled chainsaw. Not sure what to even look for, Eddie felt frustrated. Turning back toward the door, he saw something that caught his eye. Lying next to a beam, hidden at first by the shadows, were a dusty pair of men's work boots. A rough guess told him they were probably a size too small. Slipping one onto his left foot, he found this to be true. Still. His feet, blistered and bloody, wouldn't be able to take much more punishment, he realized. He slipped the other one on, flexing his toes to stretch them out a bit. Tight, but they'd have to suffice.

Tying them, Eddie stood and turned toward the barn entrance, when he froze in his tracks. Staring at him in the open doorway stood a woman of about fifty, with shoulder-length curly brown hair. Wearing jeans and a long-sleeved denim shirt rolled up to her elbows, she seemed tall for a woman, nearly six feet from what Eddie guessed. Her eyes were the color of steel, and the way they stared at him told Eddie she wasn't afraid of him. The muscles in her forearms flexed as she adjusted the shotgun against her shoulder.

"Who are you and why are you on my property?" she demanded. Her voice came a pitch higher than her brusque physique suggested.

Eddie held his palms outstretched. "Please don't shoot. I'm not here to hurt anyone." He licked his lips, his eyes on the gun in her hands. He knew from this distance a shotgun filled with buckshot could punch a hole in a person the size of a grapefruit.

The woman kept the gun steady on him. "I reckon you aren't in a position to be hurtin' no one, seeing as how I'm the one with the gun."

Eddie nodded, keeping his hands up. "You have a point there. Still, I don't want any trouble."

The woman swallowed hard, her eyes moving down to the boots on Eddie's feet. "You just asked for trouble trespassing on my farm. And for stealing my daddy's boots."

Eddie looked down to his feet. "I'm sorry, ma'am. I'll take them off if you want them back. I got lost on a hike and was just looking for my way home."

She smiled a knowing and sardonic smile. "I believe that like I believe the moon is made of cheese." As if reinforcing this thought, she thumbed the gun's safety off.

Eddie silently cursed himself. All this way, and for what? To be gut-shot by some farmer's wife? A thick moment of silence passed between them. Thinking back to his many poker games with Jules and a group of their friends, Eddie remembered the feeling he'd had when trying to figure out a bluff from a winning hand. This felt no different, except instead of a pot of loose change, his very life lay in the center of the table.

His eyes moved from the gun to the partially open door. When he took an instinctive step forward, the woman gave a shake of her head, as a mother might toward a misbehaved child. "I've killed a man before. You'll be the second if you take another step."

He felt torn: to bluff with everything he had or tell the truth and live with the consequences. He opted for the latter. "What I told you wasn't true," he said. "My name is Eddie. Eddie Grassle. And I'm not lost, at least not really. I escaped from jail today. You probably heard it on the news."

The woman's expression changed as slow recognition dawned on her. "You *are* him, aren't you?"

Eddie dropped his head. This would be the end. The police would come and drag him back to his solitary cell and there he would remain until his trial in two or three or however many years it would take to stand him in front of a judge and jury, until he got shipped off to some dark, dank prison up north. The whole notion seemed so ridiculously idiotic all he could do was shake his head.

"Yes, ma'am," he said in a faraway voice. "But please believe me, I don't mean you or anyone else any harm. I'm hurt and tired and just wanted to find somewhere to rest." He shrugged, wishing with all of his being he could reverse time and make up for this, his latest mistake.

Just then, a second woman's voice, elderly by the sound of it and edged with concern, came from somewhere near the house. "Elizabeth? Who are you talking to? Is everything alright?"

The woman in the doorway paused, her eyes uncertain of what she should do or say. Keeping the muzzle pointed at Eddie, she turned her head just far enough to project her voice behind her. "It's okay, Ma. A coon got into the barn. I'm trying to talk him out so I don't have to shoot it." She faced Eddie more fully again, her hands not moving from the gun.

Feeling more desperate than ever, Eddie searched for the right thing to say. What came out sounded pathetic even to him. "Please don't call the police, ma'am. If you let me leave, I promise you won't ever see me again."

The woman uttered a nervous-sounding laugh. "So, I find an escaped killer in my barn and I'm just supposed to let him walk free?"

"You're right, I did escape," Eddie conceded, "But I never killed anyone. I had no idea my friend was going to rob that store."

The woman's tongue flicked out to wet her lips. Her eyes, deep-set and steady, never moved from Eddie's. "If I believed everything a man ever told me, I'd be a fool of a woman."

Eddie didn't know what to say, so he went with the first thing that came to him. "I wouldn't believe me either, if it means anything. But it's true."

She stared at him, her eyes moving in thought, working something over in her mind. Finally, she shook her head, dispelling a notion that seemed to have suddenly come to her. "You see, you almost did it."

"Did what?" Eddie asked.

"You almost had me convinced."

Eddie shook his head, emphatic. "No, ma'am, it's true."

"What's true?" she asked, indignation rising in her eyes. "That you didn't kill anyone, or that you didn't practice the story you just gave me?"

"Both," he said, sighing and looking toward the barn's ceiling. "If I just had five seconds with him, I'd turn myself in right after. I don't have a life anymore anyway."

Elizabeth frowned. "Five seconds with who?"

"My son," Eddie said, forlorn. "It's why I broke out. I knew I'd never get a chance to see him since his mom told me she'd never let him visit me. He's five, and it makes me feel like shit to admit I've never even laid eyes on him. I just wanted to tell him I love him and that I'm sorry to be such a shitty father."

Elizabeth pondered this for a beat, making a motion with her eyes to indicate the very barn they stood in. "I helped my daddy build this. The porch on the house too. He left it all to my mother and me three years ago when he passed. Lost a hundred pounds in his last year. Withered away to skin and bone."

A strand of iron gray hair fell out of place from atop her head and fell across her face. She made no move to fix it. "My father didn't raise a fool, Mr. Eddie. If he were alive standing right here, he'd tell me to listen to my instincts and not some man selling me a sob story. Instinct is why the dinosaurs ruled the earth for three hundred million years. They didn't have emotions. "

If Eddie had had anything in his stomach, he felt he might throw up. He looked left and right—strong-looking walls with small, multi-paned windows. Glancing behind him, he observed no rear door. His only way out appeared to be straight ahead through Elizabeth and her shotgun.

"That's right," she said, as if reading his mind. "You'll have to come through me to get out." With that, she cradled the shotgun in the crook of her right arm, keeping the muzzle pointed at Eddie's chest. From a back pocket she produced a flip-style cell phone. She opened it and pressed three numbers on the pad. Eddie took an instinctive step forward and shook his head. "No, please don't do that!"

As quickly as Elizabeth had cradled the shotgun, she shouldered it again. "Don't take another step toward me," she warned. "It's no difference to me whether they pick you up dead or alive."

In the sudden silence of the barn, Eddie could hear the phone's ringing dial tone through the earpiece. When the call connected, a professional-sounding female voice on the other end said, "911, what is your emergency?"

Keeping her gaze fixed hard on Eddie, Elizabeth gave the operator her name and address then added, "I'd like a deputy to come out here. I've got an intruder in my barn."

"Have you seen the person?" came the operator's voice.

Elizabeth hesitated. Her expression changed then, going from resolute, to reminiscent, and finally to one of such indecisiveness that she pressed her lips together in apparent frustration.

"Is anyone there?" came the operator's voice.

Elizabeth straightened then, a resigned and almost disappointed look crossing her face. "Yes, ma'am, I'm here. Hold on a second, please. I'm checking something." She pressed a button on the phone. "They'll wonder why I put the phone on mute, so you have about five seconds to tell me why I shouldn't turn you in," she said to Eddie.

Dejected, Eddie blurted, "You *should* turn me in. I want a chance more than anything, but I don't deserve it."

Her eyes narrowed in thought, and when she pressed the same button on the phone, she let out a huff of air. "I'm sorry, ma'am, but I was mistaken," she told the operator. "Turned out to be a raccoon. They get in through the loft." Something inaudible from the operator now.

"Yes, ma'am, I understand," Elizabeth said. Then, "I appreciate your concern. Okay, I'll wait for the deputy to arrive then tell him everything is okay."

When she hung up, Elizabeth pocketed the phone but kept the gun's barrel trained in Eddie's direction. "They send someone out even if you tell them it was a mistake. I guess to make sure no one was holding a knife to your throat when you called."

Eddie swallowed hard. He had no idea what to say about what had just happened.

"I'm sure of two things, sure as I'm standing here," she said. "One is my father is probably rolling in his grave right now. I'll apologize to him when I see him again. But seeing as I'm the one that has to make the decision, I know he'd tell me to do what I felt in my heart was right."

She nodded to herself, self-forgiveness at work in her eyes. "The other thing I'm sure of is if I turn you in, the son you speak of will never see his father. It isn't my job to bring a son and his father together, but it's not my job to keep them apart either."

Eddie's eyes moved past her to the small slice of sky that appeared through the partially open barn door. Twilight had arrived, the last of the day's light settling somewhere out of view in the west, and the patch of sky he could see swam in a wave of purple and red and orange.

"I just want my life back," Eddie said, more to himself than to her. It felt cathartic saying it out loud to someone, even to a stranger pointing a gun at him. "I guess that's what I was thinking when I jumped that fence. To try to do some good, even if I get killed trying.

It's weird to think I've done more in five hours to do that than I did the last five years."

Elizabeth's eyes softened a bit, but the gun barrel never wavered. "Do you know how you'll do it?"

"Do what?"

"See your son, you big goof."

"I supposed first I would—"

"I didn't mean to tell me," she interrupted. "Good Lord are you dumb. I meant you need to have a plan. Life is hard enough when you're free to do as you please."

Eddie nodded his understanding. "I may have an idea, but I can't do it until the morning."

She nodded, more to herself than to Eddie. "And know if you hurt someone, or if someone else gets hurt because of what I'm doing, I won't ever forgive myself. You may not care, but I need you to know what I would go through afterward." She gestured at the door with the shotgun barrel. "Come daybreak, I'll unlatch the door and you'll leave. You won't breathe a word about me, nor will I of you. I figure what we have between us is only God's business."

"Yes ma'am. Absolutely."

She gave a tight nod. "There's enough straw there for you to lay out on. Our only horse died last summer. Otherwise you'd be shit outta luck. She wouldn't have allowed your presence, even if I had. Guess that made her smarter than me." She paused, looking him up and down, considering something. Her shoulders relaxed a bit. "I lied. I've never killed anyone before. But if I ever see you again, I'll do just that. Is that understood?"

Eddie crossed himself. "I promise."

After switching off the light, Elizabeth backed her way out the barn door. The sound of a heavy hook closing over a latch sounded inside the barn, and suddenly Eddie was trapped inside its pitch-black confines. Standing in utter darkness, he felt his way back to the stall where he pushed together a loose bed of straw. Lying down, he fell immediately into a deep sleep, his exhaustion and pain giving way to the first real relief he'd had in nearly eight hours. The fitful nap he'd taken earlier had merely served as a precursor to the death-like slumber he slipped into now.

Outside on the house's front porch, Elizabeth sat watching the barn on a rocking chair, her shotgun across her lap. On the table beside her sat a pot of freshly brewed coffee, along with an oversized mug. A deputy would be coming soon, and when he did, she'd tell him what she needed to in order for him to go away. She understood she could be committing a grave mistake in doing so, but a quiet part of her believed her own lack of children may have contributed to her decision. Either way, she'd made up her mind, for better or for worse. If the law discovered her, she figured she'd face her punishment like a grown woman.

After a few minutes, Elizabeth's mother poked her head outside the screen door and asked about the raccoon.

"It was a big one, Ma," Elizabeth replied, pouring herself a cup of coffee. "I hope I don't regret letting him go."

As HE SAT parked in a fast-food lot, Paolo took a bite of his sandwich and listened to the police radio chatter. He'd been listening to calls for the past hour, formulating ideas about where Grassle may currently be. After a period of inactivity, a brief two-way transmission came across the channel. An otherwise innocuous report of a 911 cancellation. A farm owner on the edge of town had thought she'd had a trespasser on her property, until it had turned out to be a varmint. Paolo chewed his food slowly, paying no mind to the rest of the call as he pondered his next move. Frustrated by the lack of leads given by the police, and unsure of exactly where he should begin his own search, he shoved the remainder of his dinner back into the paper bag. Clicking on his penlight, he spread a map open across his lap. Despite the routine aspect of the service call he'd just heard, he kept to his own rule by following every lead, however mundane.

Starting from a point just east of the jail where Grassle had first traveled, Paolo slid his finger north then south to where a dirt road met a paved highway. The bloodhound had lost the trail at this point. If Paolo's theory proved correct, Grassle had also managed to cross the river and make his way closer to the outer edge of Springwood. As a matter of routine, Paolo listened for the address where the 911 trespass call had originated. The location itself seemed nondescript. But ever the hunter, he had made a habit not of just following his human prey, but of *becoming* them. Grassle's ruse with the horse had impressed him. Although rudimentary and desperate in its execution, the ploy had nonetheless fooled his police pursuers. Despite their blunder, the Calusa County Sheriff's Office remained a trained, professional force. They would be embarrassed at the fact Grassle remained at large after the prescribed time the sheriff had assured his capture. As such, what at first had appeared to Paolo to be a simple, almost mundane assignment had turned into quite the opposite.

Hunches were a funny thing. Sitting outside Grassle's apartment had been more about getting a feel for how the man thought than actually believing he'd show up there. Paolo knew that only a complete idiot would dare come anywhere near their own residence after escaping. The police would know it too. Yet it hadn't stopped them from setting up surveillance, and it hadn't stopped Paolo from surveilling the police in turn. The insight he sought had been more about feeding into Grassle's energy. It helped clear his mind and allowed him to do as he did now, re-tracing the points he'd drawn on the map. It also reinforced his hunch that Grassle, contrary to police opinion, would attempt to escape into the more populated areas of Springwood instead of the countryside. Paolo's hunch had specified an area several square miles around his ex-girlfriend's neighborhood as a possible ending point. Not to reunite with her, necessarily, but perhaps with some other aspect of her life. Human nature demanded that common sense be followed before anything else. A man with no clear motive to escape from jail must still have one. Paolo would have to discover that soon. His intuition nagged at him to the point he studied his map again, moving his eyes over it until at last he came back to the point he'd just placed. Focusing on Grassle's line of assumed travel from that point, Paolo noticed something he hadn't realized at first. Two miles of lightly wooded land and a large cemetery in that line of travel spilled into the east end of Springwood. Clarissa Fulton's neighborhood.

Paolo double-checked his map and made a snap decision. Swinging the Cutlass south, he drove to a more rural section of the county—specifically the address of the 911 call he'd just plotted. The sun had since set, day melting into dusk. Turning off the highway, he followed a dirt road for a mile until he came to a small farmhouse. Cutting his headlights well in advance, he pulled off the road and put the car into park. Having listened to the continued radio chatter, Paolo knew a deputy had just been dispatched to clear the 911 call. As he stepped from the car and began walking up the darkened road toward the house, he noted a cruiser parked ahead. Moving further back into the shadows, he watched the uniformed deputy exit the car and walk toward the front door.

The deputy had just reached the bottom of the short staircase when he introduced himself to a tall woman of about fifty sitting on the front porch. Keeping to the shadows, Paolo heard them exchange murmured conversation for a minute, followed by the deputy's good-natured laugh. Paolo watched the deputy speak something into his radio before motioning toward the barn twenty yards behind him. The deputy wanted to check the barn, probably to ease his own mind. Paolo heard the woman object, which didn't strike him as strange so much as the inflection in her voice did. Even from this distance she sounded concerned. Nervous even. His intuition gnawing at him, Paolo stepped past the cruiser and neared as closely as he dared, while keeping to the shadows. The woman's voice came clearer now, accompanied by a nervous laugh. "Really, sir, I just checked the barn myself. Just the same old junk and rotting hay."

"And that coon, of course," the deputy responded, indicating the shotgun the woman had now propped against the wall.

"Yes, the coon," the woman responded. An awkward silence, then, "Really, we'll be fine. I don't want to trouble you any further. I'm sure you have a hundred more important things to do with all this business going on."

Paolo imagined the deputy putting on a smile that said, *now ma'am, I'm going to check the barn for my own sake, so just please stand back.*

Indeed, Paolo watched as the deputy removed his flashlight from his belt and made his way across the driveway and over the short lawn, a cone of light marking his way. Once at the door, the deputy unlatched it and, positioning himself in such a manner as to not overly expose himself, threw open one of the double doors. He probed the immediate entrance with his light and, apparently feeling safe enough to do so, took a step into the barn. Seconds later, the space lit up in a wash of fluorescent lighting. Even from this angle, Paolo could see the deputy visibly relax as he switched off his flashlight, before disappearing into the barn's inner recesses.

THIRTY-FIVE

DEPUTY ERWIN "BIGFOOT" Hammer knew danger well. He could smell it. As a twenty-two-year veteran of the sheriff's office, he had proudly remained a regular patrolman his entire career. Given his nickname during the academy, he stood six-foot-five inches tall and weighed in at nearly three hundred pounds, most of it muscle. His call-sign—24 Foxtrot—held lineage to his family's hunting background. His grandfather had been born in 1924 and had been an avid fox hunter. Hammer's father had himself hunted game as well, teaching his son its finer points from an early age. Throughout his thousands of work shifts, Hammer had pulled his service pistol countless times, although he had only fired it twice outside of the firing range. Once had been to wound an alligator after it had latched onto his leg. Just after dusk, Hammer had responded to a commercial burglary call and had exited his vehicle at the rear of the building to investigate. Walking alongside a retention pond, he'd heard the reptile's guttural hiss moments before it sprang from the pond and snapped its jaws around his lower leg. Hammer still carried the scars to this day, which he vainly displayed to folks whether they asked to see them or not.

The second time he'd fired his weapon in such a manner had been to stop a fleeing murder suspect. The man had brutally slain his neighbor and had been on the verge of escaping into some woods when Hammer had fired several warning shots above the suspect's head. Despite the fact that the man had still been carrying the knife, and agency policy would have allowed him to fire on the suspect, Hammer had frightened the man into surrendering without striking him. He'd sworn on his first day of duty that he would never shoot a man in the back, no matter his crime. That day Deputy Hammer accomplished two goals: catching his suspect and retaining his own morality. That noble sensibility endeared him to others, both in and out of his professional life.

Until now, this 911 cancellation call had been about as routine as they came. Humorous even. But as he stepped further into the barn, Hammer sensed something odd in the air. Pausing as he looked through the lighted room, he began to place the odd feeling as dread. Without thinking, he pressed the retention hood on his holster forward and brought his gun up at the ready.

He cleared the first part of the barn and moved on to the back portion, which included two pairs of opposing horse stalls. Clearing the first two, he moved on to the second pair. Nothing unusual with the one on the right. Sweeping his flashlight and gun left, he saw nothing but bare concrete and a pile of moldering straw. Grinning at his own sense of foolishness, he'd just holstered up when he detected a flicker of movement from the pile. The straw itself seemed to pulse rhythmically as if it had its own heartbeat. Frowning, Hammer held the flashlight closer and leaned forward until he finally made out the source of the movement. There, mostly covered in straw and barely visible, lay the sleeping body of a man. As the man moved slightly in his slumber, turning his face toward him, Hammer immediately recalled the BOLO mugshot he'd studied at length earlier in his shift. There could be no mistake in his mind. The man lying before him was none other than the escaped prisoner, Eddie Grassle.

Reaching up to key his shoulder-mounted radio mike, Deputy Hammer had just begun his request for backup when a man's voice behind him caused the words to freeze on his lips.

"Don't make that call, deputy."

Hammer spun on his heels to face the source, his hand falling toward his holster before his mind sent the order. The barn's fluorescent lighting contrasted with the darkened doorway, so at first, he didn't see the voice's source. But a second later his eyes adjusted to the differing light and he could plainly see a man standing just inside the opening of the barn, ten yards away. His hand still resting on his gun, Hammer made an immediate subject assessment. Medium height, thin but athletic build, a pockmarked olive complexion. Two things about the man caused the hair to raise on the back of Hammer's neck. First, the grin that hinted of quiet madness. And second, the silenced pistol pointed directly at him.

From experience, Hammer knew that bad guys were generally poor shots. He also knew that with the added protection of body armor and well-practiced shooting skills, an officer held a better chance of survival if he immediately drew on an armed suspect, especially one at a distance. The ten yards between them certainly qualified. But something about this subject's appearance—how he carried himself and even the way he gripped his pistol—told Hammer that if he drew his weapon now, he would never live to see another sunrise. A line of perspiration stood out across his brow and his tongue flicked out to lick lips that had gone suddenly dry. Slowly, and with purpose as to not spook the armed subject in front of him, he chose to extend his open hands above his head.

"Sir, I am a deputy sheriff. You need to drop your weapon now," Hammer ordered.

The man gave no response.

"Now take it easy, buddy," Hammer stammered, feeling afraid for the first time since he could remember. "I don't think you heard me. I'm a deputy sheriff, acting in my lawful duty." Desperation turned his voice into something wounded, pitiful. Although he'd encountered danger countless times, he'd never been placed at gunpoint. To demonstrate his unwillingness to appear threatening, he raised his hands even higher in the air.

As soon as Hammer did this, the man took a half dozen steps forward, closing the distance between them by half. Hammer felt a sudden loosening in his bowels as he realized any chance of drawing his weapon would now be impossible to consider. As he stood sweating beneath the barn's artificial light, Hammer felt the surreal effect of his life passing before his eyes. "You don't know what you're getting yourself into, pointing that gun at me, sir," he said, his voice growing thick.

"I know precisely what I'm getting myself into," the man said, his grin widening. Paolo felt a rush of pride sweep through him, understanding that his past training and experience was paying off. He could just as easily have ignored the ordinary sounding 911 call and not bothered to follow the lead. If he had, he would not have had this opportunity to dispose of Grassle without swarms of responding deputies descending on the scene.

"In fact, you and I are on the same side, so to speak," the man said smugly. "We're looking for the same thing, after all." Using the muzzle of his pistol, he indicated the area toward the last horse stall.

As if on cue, movement from the straw pile caught both men's attention. Fresh from a deep sleep, Eddie sat up slowly, rubbing his eyes against the bright lights overhead. Straw fell from his head and upper body as he did, revealing his body from the stolen scarecrow outfit down to the stolen boots on his feet.

"I believe that man there is an escaped jail inmate," Hammer said, tilting his head in Eddie's direction. "He robbed a store, and two men were killed. You need to drop the gun now, sir and let me do my *job*."

The last word came out high-pitched and panicky. Yet despite the dire situation, Hammer dared not move for his gun.

Seeming to enjoy being in control, the armed man said, "I see you're wearing a wedding band. That tells me you have a wife who expects you to walk through the front door after your shift tonight. And few married men your age are childless."

Deputy Hammer licked his lips. His eyes shifted from Eddie— who for the most part still appeared half-asleep—back to the man. He nodded, resignation etching across his face.

"If you want to see your family again, turn around and back your way toward me," the man said.

Hammer's jaw dropped.

"You heard what I said. Do it."

Feeling he had no choice in the matter, Hammer did as commanded. Turning, he looked pathetically into Eddie's eyes for some sense of human comfort, some improbable sign that could deliver him from a situation that at any second could end his life. Finding none, he began walking backward, fear swimming in his eyes.

Eddie had by now fully awakened and instinctively rose to his feet, watching wide-eyed around the corner of the stall. Once Hammer got to within an arm's reach of his position, the man reached a hand to his duty belt and removed a pair of handcuffs. Keeping the suppressor's barrel pressed to the back of Hammer's head, he secured Hammer's right hand in one of the cuffs and brought it behind his back.

"Sit there," the man commanded, leading him toward a large wooden beam nearby.

An audible whine came from somewhere deep in Hammer's throat as he complied. The man then brought both the deputy's arms back around the beam and cuffed his other hand, immobilizing him. Ensuring first that Grassle remained where he was, the man patted both of the deputy's front pockets then felt along his gun-belt until he found what he'd been looking for—an elongated handcuff key attached to a D-ring. Double locking the cuffs, the man slipped the key into his pocket then patted down the deputy's legs. Satisfied he wasn't carrying another gun, he calmly asked, "Where is your backup key?"

Hammer stared back, wide-eyed. "I don't have one."

"I'm going to search you," the man said, squatting in front of him. "If I find one, you won't like the punishment."

Hammer licked his lips. "It's on the inside of my duty belt. In the back."

The man reached around and felt along the inside of the deputy's duty belt, discovering a two-inch Velcro pouch containing a small handcuff key. He removed it and placed it into his pants pocket as well.

"Please don't kill me," Hammer pleaded. Sweat had begun to pour down his face. "I swear I won't report you. Just leave and this never happened. If they ask who did this, I won't tell them shit. They'll let me retire on a psych discharge."

The man laughed. "You should have drawn your gun when you'd had the chance. It would have made this more fun." He looked back toward where Grassle stood at the edge of the stall before addressing

Hammer again. "Now, you be a good boy and stay right here while I finish my business."

The grin on his face morphing into a murderous scowl, the man stood and began closing the distance toward the back of the barn.

WITH NOWHERE TO go, Eddie held his hands out in front of him. "Please, n-no," he stuttered, realizing he had nowhere to go. He watched, helpless, as the man leveled the pistol at his chest. Expecting the shot to come at any moment, Eddie had just turned his head away when a sudden explosion blew a hole in the wall next to the man's head. Eddie flinched, feeling splinters of wood strike him on the face.

Ducking away instinctively, the man looked quizzically at the gun in his hand before realizing he had not been the one who'd fired. From their respective positions, Deputy Hammer and Eddie both looked confusedly at the hole in the wall. Only when the metallic racking of a shotgun sounded did all three men turn to look toward the barn's darkened opening. Elizabeth stood holding the butt of her shotgun against one shoulder, a lock of curly hair across her face. Motioning with the gun's barrel, she spoke to the man, who while dodging the shotgun blast had dropped his pistol at his feet. "I don't know who you are, mister, or why you're doing this," she said, "but the next one's going in you if you reach for that gun."

The deputy began to blurt something—some warning or instruction—which momentarily diverted Elizabeth's attention. It was all the man needed. Stepping to his right while simultaneously dropping to a knee, he reached out and snatched up his gun in one fluid motion.

"No!" Elizabeth cried, tracking the barrel to the left and pulling the trigger. Buckshot slammed into the heavy beam a foot from the man's head. Before Elizabeth could rack another round, the man took quick aim and fired three shots in quick succession. The first two rounds pierced Elizabeth's skull just above her left eyebrow, before exploding out the back of her head. A red mist clouded out behind her, forming a macabre halo against the sodium vapor light cast down from the property's lone street-style lamp. The third shot entered her throat before smashing through her spine and exiting the right side of her neck. She stood that way for several seconds, the shotgun gripped in her fingers and her eyes still wide with shock. A moment later her body pitched straight backward, half in and half out of the barn entrance, stiff as a board. As the back of her head struck the ground, it split open with an audible crack from the already gaping wounds there, blood and brain matter spilling out her head and across the dirt.

From somewhere outside the barn came a woman's bloodcurdling scream.

Still on one knee, the man turned and leveled the gun toward the deputy who sat helpless just three feet from him.

"You don't have to do this. Please, I'm—"

Two rounds bore into the top of his head, sending a fine red mist into the air above him. A quarter-sized skull fragment ricocheted against the near wall before landing near the kneeling man, spinning grotesquely before coming to a stop. The deputy's body went rigid before slumping to the right, lifeless and suspended against the damaged beam. Blood spurted out one of the holes in his head, forming a growing dark red pool on the dusty barn floor.

Standing, the man had just turned back toward the horse stalls when something crashed into him, forcing the breath from his lungs and smashing him to the floor. The gun flew from his hand and slid into the opposite stall. Stunned, he felt the first of several punches being delivered to his face and head before his brain registered the fact that Grassle had tackled him. Trained in ground fighting, the man recovered quickly, maintaining his composure as he blocked his face with both elbows. This sort of defense bought him precious seconds in which to regain his wind and formulate a plan. With the calmness of a professional fighter, he simultaneously thrust his hips upward as he grabbed Eddie's shirt, pulling him down toward him. Hooking the outside of Grassle's left leg with his right leg and pushing off with his left foot, he rolled right. This succeeded in heaving Grassle off him, causing the larger and heavier man to crash into the deputy's now lifeless body.

LEAPING HEADLONG, EDDIE had shouldered his way into the man's mid-section just as the gun had turned on him. He heard the air escape the smaller yet stronger man's lungs as the two of them flew through the air momentarily before striking the concrete floor hard. Sprawled on the ground, the wind knocked out of him, Eddie had just gotten to his knees when the man tackled him flat against the ground and straddled him. Before he could act, Eddie felt the man's hands around his neck, cutting off his carotid artery instead of his windpipe. Even in his now desperate state, Eddie realized he only had seconds until he passed out. Scratching and clawing at the vise-like hands around his throat did no good. The man had smartly lowered his hips over Eddie's, making it almost impossible to move his weight off him.

As he continued to fight, Eddie heard Jules's voice call out to him, so strident and clear it seemed as if his old friend stood right next to him. *Don't you let this bastard do this to you! Fight, you fucker!*

Eddie's eyes fluttered closed, his hands falling limp to his sides. A dry croak escaped from the last pocket of air squeezed out of his throat. His previous notion of death no longer frightened him. He felt himself letting go, slipping into a blackness that began to fold over him like an eternal, comforting blanket. He felt at peace in the idea that all would become righteous in the world if he just stepped into that darkness.

Wake up, you sonofabitch! Jules's voice screamed. *Do it for Liam if you won't do it for yourself! He needs you!*

Eddie's eyes snapped open, and he turned his head just enough to see the deputy's limp body next to him. As if controlled by an unseen force, Eddie's right arm came suddenly alive, his fingers moving across the deputy's belt and finding a cylindrical leather pouch. Unsnapping the pouch, he removed a palm-sized canister and managed to shake it twice before he extended it upward toward the man's face. Just as his eyes began to roll back in his head, Eddie slipped a finger beneath the plastic trigger guard and pressed down.

PAOLO HAD BEEN so preoccupied with finishing the choke, he'd failed to understand what Eddie had been reaching for. By the time he recognized the object held toward his face, it was too late. Releasing one of his hands from Eddie's throat, Paolo swatted the canister away, but by then a stream of aerated liquid had already struck him directly in the face. A second later, Paolo's eyes involuntarily snapped closed and began to instantly sear with an unbearable heat.

Screaming with rage and pain, Paolo rolled off Eddie and clutched at his face. He had been exposed to pepper spray several times before—twice during his special ops training, then as a result of wind blowback during crowd control procedures in Somalia. In each case he'd experienced extreme reactions but had mostly recovered after several minutes. But he'd never taken a full burst from such close proximity. Groaning against the raging fire engulfing his entire face, he did his best to follow his training by forcing himself to blink and to remain calm. Realizing his pistol lay several yards away in the furthest stall, he scrambled on all fours in that direction. His vision having doubled, he mistook the stall opening and lunged headfirst into the adjoining wall. It felt like someone had struck him over the head with a baseball bat. Flopping onto his side, he saw sparkling pinpricks within his blurred vision and almost slipped into blackness from the sudden impact. After several seconds, he recovered and found his knees again, groaning as pain pounded in his head. Clawing half-blinded along the floor, he forced his fingers to systematically search in a pattern until they eventually found the suppressor's barrel. Consumed with rage, he stood and stumbled out of the stall, the gun gripped firmly now in his shooting hand.

Having just regained his breathing, Eddie scrambled to his feet and lurched away toward the barn's opening. Tripping over the deputy's body, he came face-to-face with the dead man's gun belt. Hanging from a black metal D-ring were a set of keys sandwiched between two leather belt keepers. Struggling to free the keys, Eddie finally managed to do so, falling headlong toward the open door. He tried to step over the woman's body, but in his haste his feet became tangled in her cockeyed legs and he fell directly on top of her. As he planted his hands on the ground to stand back up, he felt a hand-sized metallic object lying on the ground next to her. Picking the object up more out of reflex than out of any real awareness of what it was, Eddie finally recognized it as an older style flip cell phone. Barely realizing he had done so, he stuffed it into his front pocket as he got to his feet. Looking back, he saw a gun rising toward him through the barn entrance. He dove out of the way just as four successive shots whizzed by him, slamming into the house's wooden frame twenty yards beyond. Darting back and forth like a cartoon character, he managed to avoid several more un-aimed shots in his general direction. Finally realizing the only way he would survive was to put immediate distance between himself and the gunman, Eddie turned down the gravel driveway, stumbling past the panic-stricken old woman on the stoop and toward the cruiser parked halfway down the drive.

A full minute after being exposed to the spray, Paolo felt the pain in his eyes intensify. He'd been forced to fire wildly due to his reduced vision; and now, feeling his way past the door opening, he burst out into the burgeoning night. Bending at the waist, he pried his eyes open with his fingers, pointing his face into the glorious breeze that offered him a bit of relief. After another minute of allowing freshly moving air to blow the worst of the spray's vapor from his eyes, Paolo could finally see without holding his eyes open. Blinking hard, he stormed past an old woman who stood weeping on the house's front stoop. The parked cruiser he'd seen on his approach was now gone.

Grassle.

Cursing his luck, Paolo made his way to where he'd parked the Cutlass just off the road. Fumbling for his keys, he finally managed to find the keyhole, then he yanked open the driver's door before diving into the seat. Still not seeing clearly but understanding he had to get away from here before backup arrived, he cranked the ignition and pulled out of the trees onto the dirt road. Two minutes later, after once running into a shallow ditch and another time nearly striking a tree, he found the main road and turned away from the direction he suspected responding deputies would come from. He hadn't heard any radio broadcast about the deputy's killing yet. Frustrated that he'd shot him, only to have Grassle escape alive, Paolo briefly wondered if he had overstepped. But as soon as the thought arrived, he silently argued it away. He'd had no choice. The deputy would have no doubt done his duty and tried his best to stop Grassle's killing.

Cops weren't assassins. And even if Paolo had succeeded in disposing of Grassle, had the deputy witnessed it he would have most assuredly testified of its illegality. As Paolo tore along the back roads, he convinced himself what had been done had been necessary. Hood would not be pleased. Still, Paolo had escaped relatively unharmed and free to engage in his pursuit. If given the opportunity to relive the scene, he would have wasted no time in killing the resourceful young man, and probably taken care of the old woman too. To borrow the sheriff's line—the proverbial spilled milk.

Five minutes later he re-entered the city proper by using side streets and seldom-used access roads. As he parked his car in the alley behind his field office, he heard the first dispatch of a deputy down. They'd be swarming the farm soon. Safely away and still enjoying his newfound status, Paolo allowed himself a bit of respite. All would be good in the end. After letting himself in, he tore off his shirt and walked straight to the bathroom. Holding his face beneath the spigot, he pried one eye open under a stream of cold water for several minutes before repeating the process with the other eye. Taking care to dab his face lightly with a towel, he sat in front of a running fan for several more minutes until the worst of the pain abated. Furious at being bested in such an ignominious fashion, he changed into a spare set of clothing he had hanging in a closet. Angrily pressing a contact icon on his cell phone, he listened as a familiar voice answered.

"It's me. I've been compromised," Paolo said flatly.

A short pause on the other end, then, "Explain 'compromised.'"

Paolo hissed, "It's complicated. I had to execute a deputy. And there's a witness, an old woman. I didn't have time to kill her too—I could barely see. Should I abort the mission?"

A pause from the other end, then a deep sigh. "Where is Grassle now?"

"Didn't you hear me? I said I had to kill a *deputy*, for God's sake. The county will be swarming with them now."

"I heard you," Hood answered. "And I'm not concerned about witnesses. They often swim in deeper waters than they should and suffer mysterious illnesses. But the deputy does complicate matters. I need you to collect yourself and find Grassle as soon as possible. I can still count on you, Paolo, can't I?"

Paolo unlocked his gun safe and removed an HK MP5 submachine gun, along with a carbon steel-bladed knife from the assorted weapons within. "Of course you can still count on me." His tone softened as his anger melted away into something tenderer, more apologetic. "I'm sorry, Mathias. I'll make it up to you."

The voice on the other end of the phone purred reassuringly. "I know, my pet. Soon we can disappear to a place where no one will know our names or faces. All in good time."

For the first time in a great while, Paolo allowed himself to believe the words he heard. Even with what he'd done back at the farmhouse, the possibility of ending this life and starting a new one, something real he'd never had before, brought a sliver of hope within him. "I will finish it. I promise you that."

"I have faith in you, Paolo," Hood answered. "Besides, the witness may even benefit us. She can attest to Grassle being on her property. It will be assumed he was involved in the deputy's killing. Low hanging fruit."

Paolo settled into a chair behind the desk. His fingers traced lightly over the gleaming metal of the MP5 that sat like blackened death on the table before him. His mind slipped briefly into a familiar daydream, one of him and Hood walking together along a quaint European city street, then waking together between crisp sheets in an exotic locale. The newness of these thoughts, long suppressed, both excited and frightened him. Like a new world order, such a future would be fraught with obstacles, he reasoned. The first of these would be doing away with Grassle, who had begun as a simple pest only to have become a larger, more personal problem. No longer considered an easy target, Grassle had elevated himself into much more of a formidable opponent. Paolo's smile, born from his daydream of him and Hood together, disappeared as a newfound tenacity grew within him. His lips pressed into a rigid line and his eyes, finally recovered, focused on the blade he'd laid before him. He would use it to cut Grassle's heart from his body. And when he did, he would hold it high above him as an offering to whatever god or gods that had so far forsaken his earthly desires.

"If I must sacrifice myself, I will await you in the afterlife," he said quietly into the phone. He closed his eyes, feeling his heart beating wildly in his chest. He had told himself he would never voice the words that rested now on his lips, but they came nonetheless, with Paolo feeling if he did not speak them now, he may never again have the chance.

"I love you, Mathias. I have since the very beginning."

The slightest hesitation from the other end. "Wait for my instructions. Any information I receive I will pass to you immediately. Now go and find me my peace."

The line went dead. Paolo stared at his phone for several moments before allowing himself to forget the lingering implication. Hood was a complicated man. He had more important things to worry about than the fluttering heartstrings of a younger, less experienced partner. And besides, Paolo had given an oath, one to selflessly assist Hood in any way he wished. It would be selfish to expect more now. Hood had once again been correct in his pragmatism. Business first.

Paolo collected his weapons and returned to his vehicle. Listening to the increasing radio traffic, he learned from responding deputies that the deputy's squad car had been stolen and Grassle had yet to be found. The only witness to the crime, an old woman, had given a description of two men on her property. Grassle had been one, but amazingly she'd mistaken Paolo for another deputy and had given a misleading description. Perhaps he would not be implicated after all.

"Come to me, little bird," Paolo said to himself, and he drove to a favorite place outside the city where he could sit and stare at the darkened sky. He needed time to think. About how Grassle's heart would feel in his hands. And about those slender threads that Dumas himself had described as hanging between fortune and life itself.

THIRTY-SIX

BY THE TIME the sun set fully below the horizon, the coordinated police search for Eddie Grassle—Calusa County's *persona non grata*—had grown to unprecedented proportions. With Sheriff Driscoll's now public concession that Grassle had likely slipped past the original perimeter, the new search area had been widened to include points as far north as Sarasota, as far southeast as Lake Okeechobee, and as far west as the Gulf of Mexico forty miles away. Driscoll's public statement had included phrasing such as "confident of his capture" and "temporary setback." This had been communicated to the media to defend the already swirling accusations of incompetence by his agency. But privately, the veteran lawman and members of his inner circle all agreed that if Grassle had somehow secured high-speed transportation, he could have slipped across the state line by now.

Still, few in the sheriff's office thought Grassle had gotten very far. The fact that he had slipped through their initial dragnet was regrettable. But statistics pulled from similar escapes in multiple jurisdictions stated most absconders remained within a twenty-mile radius within the first twenty-four hours. A vast majority of them had been re-captured in that timeframe. Other factors skewed that average, of course, such as geography, the escapee's level of experience, and any possible resources the absconder had. Since Sheriff Driscoll's late-afternoon press conference, the manpower shortage of the Calusa County Sheriff's Office had become obvious to anyone paying attention to the case. Their limited forces were simply spread too thin. Even with nearly one hundred jail and patrol deputies scouring the area—a third of them working emergency overtime shifts—the grim reality of the situation had begun to settle over the command staff like a pall.

Making matters worse, dozens of erroneous tips had begun to flood into dispatch from citizens claiming they'd seen the fugitive. Everyone wanted their fifteen minutes of fame attached to the drama, as evidenced by the first question from most tipsters invariably being, 'Will my name be in the paper?' Much handwringing had gone into whether a no-questions-asked cash reward for information leading to Grassle's capture should be offered. Publicized rewards, Escobar knew, were a double-edged sword. For every solid tip, you could expect a hundred false ones. Get lucky and you capture your man rather quickly. But direct resources toward several bad tips, and confusion can cripple your search. Deputies scattered all over the land investigating multiple red herrings did not breed success. How Grassle had been allowed to escape in the first place would be debated in time. But the initial reaction force's failure to re-capture him when he had been so well contained created an entirely new set of questions. As such, the reward idea had been scrapped in favor of flooding the media with reports of the escape, hoping one of the many tips eventually bore fruit.

Escobar had always held little respect for the jail staff's right to police the grounds adjacent to the compound, a jurisdictional no-man's-land of sorts. After much political wrangling in the early days of his tenure, Superintendent Devereux had won approval from the sheriff to oversee this area in the event of an escape. Escobar felt certain that had he coordinated the initial search, his patrol deputies and K-9s would have captured Grassle quickly. But that was moot now. And as steadfast as he'd been about the ability of his own forces, the fact remained that Grassle had slipped by not just the jail's response team, but Escobar's own tactical team as well. What should have been a rather straightforward search in favorable conditions had descended into finding the proverbial needle in a haystack.

After much discussion, Sheriff Driscoll had finally given the go-ahead to summon additional resources from surrounding agencies. A proud man, this had not been an easy decision, evidenced by the fact he'd been spotted removing his trademark Stetson and running a hand through his snow-white hair. With help from other agencies came the very real possibility that officials other than his own would capture Grassle. Despite Driscoll desperately wanting Grassle caught, everyone who knew him understood his old-school ego abhorred the idea of someone else receiving credit for it.

Captain Escobar shared this sentiment. Hunched over a map of the area, he tried his best to block out the command post's ambient noises. Voices and squawking radios, accompanied by the occasional shouts from news cameramen directing their shots from across the street, threatened to kill his concentration. He plotted a point on the map and circled it. Next to the circle he penciled the words *last known sighting*. Frowning, he moved backward from the prisoner's last known location. History indicated Grassle would likely head deeper into rural country, away from urban areas where law enforcement had many more resources. Yet his gut told him the opposite. Escobar knew urban areas were much more difficult for his forces to conduct search operations. It's true that paved roads, clearly defined perimeters and abounding resources were abundant for lawmen there, but the labyrinth of structures and the vast number of people made urban areas a disaster to conduct a search of this kind. The nightmarish experience of fighting in Fallujah's deadly streets during the Iraq invasion had taught him that.

But knowing Grassle had only one known contact in Springwood (and he'd already verified that his ex-girlfriend Clarissa had had nothing to do with him for the past five years), it was beyond the veteran captain what he could possibly be seeking there. Having just jotted a series of notes in the map's margin, his radio came suddenly alive with a transmission that caused the hairs on his neck to stand on end.

"A man shot my Lizzy! And—and a deputy has been shot also. Please send help!" An interminable pause came over the channel, during which Escobar stared wide-eyed at several nearby members of his command staff. The radio caller, clearly an elderly female and not sounding familiar with law enforcement lingo, came over again through garbled sobs. "A man in our barn...he shot them...just stole the police car. Oh God, I think they're dead! Please send help!"

A female dispatch officer's voice—clinical and well-accustomed to emergency situations—came across the channel. "Twenty-four foxtrot, are you ten-four?"

Deathly silence. The dispatcher waited several beats before trying again. When still no answer came, she methodically relayed a series of emergency codes to backup deputies. Escobar snatched up his radio and burst out of the command tent to find deputies scurrying in all directions. As a uniformed sergeant ran past him, Escobar grabbed him by the collar and barked, "Get your unit out front now! You drive!"

Within seconds, the two peeled out from the command post and followed a line of several other patrol cars, lights flashing and sirens blaring, down the main road toward the address given by dispatch. A farmhouse at the edge of town. As the sergeant floored the accelerator, Escobar's heart pounded while adrenaline flooded his system. Never in his career had he personally been in hot pursuit of an escaped jail prisoner. And never had he responded to a call of a deputy down.

Now he would respond to them both.

EDDIE FOLLOWED THE glowing lights in the west toward Springwood— and toward the only thing he felt he had left to live for.

Twice he had to turn off the car's headlights and pull off the road when sets of other cruisers neared, their blue and red lights swirling against the blackness of the night. Snaking his way along a back road with only scattered homes and several abandoned industrial buildings, he came to a sign he knew well: **SPRINGWOOD, pop. 32,189**. Now he had a reference point. The modest home he'd been raised in wasn't far from here, and as such he knew the area like the back of his hand. Needing a relatively safe place to rest and take refuge, he considered several options until an idea struck him. Cutting the headlights once again, he reversed down an embankment into some heavy brush. He'd travel on foot from here.

After a half mile of carefully skirting the road, ducking further back into the trees whenever a car drove by, he came to his destination. Staring at the rusted sign above the cemetery's entrance, a feeling of melancholy enveloped him. It had been almost ten years since he'd last been here, for his mother's funeral. He felt guilty for never visiting since then, having thought of his mother often but never bothering to make the short trip here to pay his respects. But with his own life now in question, he reasoned now may be the only chance he'd ever have to see his mother's grave again. And with it, the chance to get some desperately needed rest.

Squeezing his way through the eight-foot-high, loosely chained gate, Eddie limped up the main road past mausoleums and myriad tombstones that in the semi-darkness resembled stony fingers jutting from the ground. Trying to gain his bearings, he realized he hadn't paid much attention during his first and only trip here. The place was huge—the largest cemetery in the county—and he realized finding his mother's grave could potentially take hours. Then he thought back to the funeral, of a detail he had long forgotten. Allowing his eyes to adjust to the dark, he scanned the scattered knolls for the towering tree he and Jules had climbed that day.

Checking a dozen trees that stood above similar-looking graves, but still not finding his mother's, Eddie considered that perhaps the tree had either been removed or fallen in a storm. If so, he'd never be able to find the grave in the dark. And he couldn't wait until daylight when people would no doubt come to visit the place. Nearly giving up, he made a final pass along the back end of the property when he spied a sprawling, moss-hung oak atop a knoll. Climbing the knoll, he knelt beside the black granite grave marker set beneath the tree's massive limbs and squinted to read the inscription:

Frances Bethany Grassle
April 17, 1958
April 15, 2005
She rings Heaven's bell

Two days before her 47th birthday. Eddie had forgotten the significance. Most of the memories from those years after his father had left lay in some forgotten recess of his mind, locked away by his own pain and regret. As he traced his fingers over the inscription, he felt amazed at how difficult it was to immediately recall his mother's face. Perhaps due to the shock and stress of today, or from the grief of the memory itself. It took imagining himself back home—ten years old and playing baseball in the yard—for him to see her face again fully in his mind. Sighing, he laid down on the soft grass and watched the clouds pass over the rising half-moon.

"I miss you, Momma," he whispered to the wind. And the wind, it seemed, whispered back.

He dozed. For how long he couldn't be sure since the moon lay obscured by clouds when he opened his eyes again. He rose to his feet, knowing someone would surely spot him if he didn't at least try to do what he'd first considered. Ignoring the pain that pounded in his left leg, he backed up ten yards then ran at the tree as fast as he could, planting his good leg against the trunk while reaching up toward the lowest hanging branch. His right arm gave way almost immediately, but his left arm still retained enough strength to allow his legs to pinwheel until they found a foothold against the trunk. Shimmying his way upward, he managed to hoist his upper body across the lowest branch. Nearly falling in the process, he gained enough balance to lift himself up several more feet to the natural ledge he remembered being there.

Collapsing onto it in a heap, Eddie groaned from fresh pain that pulsed through every part of his body. But he'd made it. Looking out from his lofty position, he suddenly felt juxtaposed with the past, having shared this same spot with Jules in what seemed like a lifetime ago. Everything seemed different, yet somehow it all seemed the same. Aside from the even greater curtains of Spanish moss that now hung from the goliath's many branches, the view remained the same as before. He could plainly see his mother's grave twelve feet below, which gave him a sense of comfort. What did seem different now had to do with how he *felt*. No longer a boy, and somehow not yet the man he sought in himself, Eddie detected a strange inward disquiet that simultaneously troubled and intrigued him.

No one has been up here since she died, he thought, and for the first time since his ordeal began earlier in the day, tears burned in his eyes. Not since Jules's death had he shown this much emotion. Prison, the current charges against him, not even Clarissa telling him he'd lost both her and his son forever, had brought him to tears. But come they now did, in rivers and oceans it seemed, and he heaved his body against them, balling into a fetal position, unsure if he could be heard somehow from a mile away but not caring, because seeing his mother's grave just now confirmed once again he was alone in the world, nothing but etched granite to remind him of what he had once been.

When the worst of his sobs abated, he lay very still, wiping away the wetness from his face and resolving never to feel sorry for himself again. He was tired of feeling like shit, and he decided right then that if this crazy idea of somehow trying to find Liam didn't pan out, he would hold his head high knowing he'd spent every ounce of effort in trying. He was out of jail. That fact was amazing enough. But he also knew that could change at any moment. A swooping helicopter. An army of cops rushing him from around a hundred different corners. It could all come crashing down on him in an instant. If he could somehow get it together and formulate some semblance of a plan, anything that could remotely guide him toward that end, he felt willing to do it.

Shifting into a sitting position, he felt something hard stab him in the hip. Feeling for what had caused it, he realized the object had come from his own pocket. Confused, he slipped his hand inside and removed an older-style cell phone. Flipping it open, he saw the two-inch screen light up and the signal bar at the top waver in and out.

The dead woman's phone.

He still wasn't sure why he'd bothered to pick it up. With the man behind him and shooting, he could have gotten killed over it. But then a sense of understanding came over him as he looked off into the darkness. He realized he might very possibly never hold a cell phone again. He'd been on the run for the better part of ten hours and, as far as he knew, no one else in the world knew where he was. He felt he'd used up every trick and bit of skill he possessed. If he remained free until morning, he figured he'd be lucky. Every passing minute after that would be a miracle.

Looking at the phone's glowing screen, Eddie shook his head.

"You're crazy, you know," he said to himself, deciding right then that if he had any chance in hell to do what he intended, he wanted to tell the one person on earth who'd treated him like an actual human being how thankful he was. Doing it from a recorded jail telephone or in a crowded courtroom seemed like an insult, a waste of this final bit of privacy he felt he would ever have.

Not only do you only live once, but sometimes that one life was so shit, you just had to say 'fuck it.' Eddie dialed a phone number from memory, one he recalled being only two numbers off from the one his family had had growing up.

As soon as Riggins had heard Sanchez's voice, she'd known that it was something serious.

"Get here quick," he'd said, giving her an address. "Hammer got smoked. A female homeowner too. An old woman saw most of it and said two males were at the scene. Our guy was one of them."

She'd stuffed her .38 into her ankle holster and flown out the door, telling Chet she'd explain later. Deciding to use her personal vehicle—a sky-blue Mazda CX5—she pulled up near the farmhouse in question ten minutes later. She found pandemonium. A dozen cruisers sat at every angle imaginable, their collective blue and red lights turning the scene into a swirling purplish insanity. An ambulance also sat in their midst, its back doors open and two emergency workers standing by with hands on hips. A crime scene van sat on the lawn between the house and a barn. Yellow tape, supported by intermittent metal poles in the ground, circled the entire barn. Even more ominous were the collection of plain-clothed detectives and uniformed supervisors surveying the barn's opening, or more specifically, the body of a middle-aged woman that lay bathed in the artificial lighting provided by a portable field lamp. Parking alongside a running white unmarked cruiser, Riggins rolled her window down and stared depressingly at Detective Sanchez behind the cruiser's wheel.

"What happened?" she asked.

Leaning out his open driver's window, Sanchez cast a bleak expression and said the obvious. "*No bueno, mami.*"

Riggins looked to where a pair of detectives crouched near the woman's body. "Hammer was such a good guy. I worked with him right before I made detective. Speaking of, I see Teliford and Grimes are working it."

"Yeah. You better stay out of view. Heinke is already here and the sheriff is on his way. You don't want to be explaining why you're here, even with what happened."

She disregarded what he said with an annoyed shake of the head. "How about the stolen cruiser?"

"Nada. But check this out..." He reached through his open window and handed her his cell phone, on which was displayed an agency email to all active field members. "Hot off the presses, from the sheriff himself. He's prohibiting the removal of or arrests of any individuals inside the Grassle search area unless we can show they're actively polluting the scene. It basically deputizes every citizen."

Riggins read it, her eyebrows raising. "Interesting."

"Yeah. And some guy has been hanging around the command tent. No one can figure out who he belongs to," Sanchez said, taking his phone back. "Could be a Fed, but they almost never operate alone on a thing like this, and never without notice. Either way, he got a front row seat on all the intelligence meetings then disappeared to do his own thing. Some sort of political connection, I'm thinking."

Riggins frowned. "What's next, a mounted posse?"

"No shit," Sanchez said. "But the sheriff can hire a group of drag queens to conduct a SWAT raid if he wants. It's his show."

Riggins eyed him sideways. "Your imagination, Sanny."

"You haven't even heard the best I have to offer," he deadpanned. "One more thing—I've got a buddy in Special Ops. He's the real suspicious type, so he had forensics lift some latents from our mystery civilian. Got them from a glass the guy drank from at the command post. Just a little intel since the sheriff waived a formal background check."

"And?"

"Zip, zero. Guy's a ghost. Even his DL came back as no info. Gotta be some high-level black helicopter shit or something."

Riggins's gaze drifted back toward the barn scene, her brain just on the other side of grasping an important idea when she shook the thought away. "There's a lot lately that isn't adding up, Sanny. Like, what's going on with Eddie. I'd give a year of my pension to ask him that myself."

Just then, her cell phone rang. "Detective Riggins, Homicide," she answered. After several seconds of no response, she checked the caller ID and frowned. Pressing one finger to her other ear in order to hear better, she asked the caller to repeat themselves. When the caller did, Riggins stiffened in her seat, her face coming alive with surprise. Holding a finger up to Sanchez, she looked around furtively at the milling deputies and detectives and, like a teenager wishing to conceal an inappropriate conversation, quickly rolled her window back up.

EDDIE'S HEART SKIPPED a beat. He cleared his throat and said, "Detective, this is Eddie Grassle. I don't have much time to explain. It's—it's complicated. I have something important to tell you."

A pause on the other end. Eddie thought he heard Riggins's mouth drop open. "Go ahead."

Eddie shifted position on the tree's ledge and stifled a groan. "I was there, at the barn. There was a man, not a cop. Someone who was trying to kill me. That's when he shot the cop, and the lady too. I got away—I used the cop's pepper spray. He was already dead. I didn't know what to do, detective!"

Eddie thought he could actually hear Riggins trying to remain calm. "You're saying you saw who killed the deputy and the woman?"

"Yeah."

"Describe him."

Eddie gave as good a description as he could.

"Have you ever seen him before?"

"No," he said, then added, "He had one of those silencers on his gun, if that's important."

Riggins seized on this. "Are you sure? People don't really use those."

"I'm positive. I've shot guns before and I know the way a pistol is supposed to look. The barrel was too long and the report was only half as loud as it should have been."

"Anything else you can tell me about him?"

"It seemed like I was the reason he was there in the first place."

"How could you tell?"

"I don't know, ma'am, I just could. You know when something is, and when it isn't."

Riggins paused for a beat. "Can you give yourself up now to someone, or can you stay somewhere safe until I can arrange to come get you?"

Eddie scanned the surrounding grave markers, made ghostly by the yellow moon. "There are people around me, but they can't see me." Then, "That lady helped me, detective. She could have turned me in, but she didn't. Now she's dead. I feel it's all my fault."

Another pause on the other end. "You have to help me help you, Eddie. This has gone way further than it ever should have. A deputy is dead. An innocent civilian too. This has to stop so that no one else gets hurt."

Eddie traced his eyes across the wispy clouds. If only Jules were around to help him decide what to do...

"That's even more reason why I have to finish what I started," he said, swallowing hard. His throat burned with thirst and his body ached from head to toe, but he wouldn't allow self-pity to enter his mind. He was alive, and both the woman and deputy were dead, and there were so many differences with those two absolutes he couldn't even begin to separate them in his head.

"I'm sorry, detective, I just can't turn myself in yet. But I will. Tomorrow. And I want to thank you. For treating me like a human being."

"Eddie, listen to me—"

The phone connection dropped, leaving Eddie to stare at the blankly lit screen, a satellite icon with a line through it appearing in the upper corner. All for the best, anyway. Deciding he should disconnect the battery, he pocketed both pieces and lay down to view the little part of the night sky that was visible through the mossy limbs. The half-moon had risen higher overhead, casting the landscape in a silvery patina. Without realizing it, he closed his eyes and fell into a deep sleep, muttering both Jules's and Liam's names on his lips.

But unbeknownst to Eddie, two kids had also snuck into the cemetery to play a game of 'Dead Man Calling,' and had watched him walk along the main cemetery road while they crouched behind a crypt. They'd then watched him cut his way up the small hill and lie down beneath the massive oak, speculating about the possibility of Eddie being a ghost returning to its grave, or even maybe the escaped jail inmate, whose story by now was all over the news.

While Eddie dozed, the kids ran home to breathlessly tell their parents where they'd been and what they'd seen. Proof that, to kids, some things were just worth getting in trouble for.

DETECTIVE SANCHEZ LEANED out his cruiser's window and gaped at Riggins. "Eddie Grassle—as in *our* Eddie Grassle?"

Red stress hives began to break out on Riggins's arms. They had plagued her on and off since childhood. Her own mother had experienced them, sometimes so badly she'd been bedridden for days on end. Now, as Riggins stared dubiously at her phone's blank screen, she rubbed the welts in that same unconscious way she'd done dozens of times before.

"I thought someone was playing a joke on me."

Sanchez's expression suggested he thought the same. "What the hell did he say?"

"He said he didn't kill Hammer or the woman."

"No one ever admits to killing a cop. Where was he calling from?"

"He didn't say."

"So he breaks out of jail and just decides to call you to say hello? That makes no sense."

Riggins frowned. "He thanked me for treating him like a real person, and he said he wanted to turn himself in."

"Well shit, all he has to do is tell us where he is, and we can wrap this whole charade up in a pretty little bow."

Riggins blinked, as if coming out of a dream. "He said he had something to do first. That he'd turn himself in tomorrow after he finished whatever business he had."

Sanchez let out a sarcastic laugh. "How considerate of him. I'll bring the coffee and donuts to make his arrest more pleasurable."

Riggins lifted her gaze to the darkened sky and shook her head. "This whole thing is getting weirder by the moment, Sanny. What would be worth risking your life for if you say you're turning yourself in the next day anyway? They'll say he offed Hammer no matter what evidence may say otherwise."

"Maybe he forgot a load of laundry in the washer, or remembered that he had a hot date," Sanchez said.

They went back and forth along this line, until Riggins made a determination. "I've got to bring him in, Sanny. Personally. I'm not sure how or when, but it has to be me. Otherwise he'll be driven to the morgue instead of back to jail."

"Don't forget that one of our own is headed to the morgue because of all this," Sanchez countered.

"I know, I'm trying to process that right now," she said. "Maybe it'll hit me later. Hammer was a solid guy. He didn't deserve what happened to him. But I'm already knee deep in this and I can't sit back and watch anyone else get killed. Eddie is my responsibility. My name is on his arrest affidavits. I'm going out there to see what's up. Stay here. If they see you there with me, it'll drag you into my mess. That's the last thing I want."

Sanchez shook his head emphatically. "No ma'am. I'm not letting you do this alone. If I get fired, I can get a job back home in Miami or up in Tampa. They'd fight over someone as handsome and talented as me." He gave his trademark wink and flashed her a dimpled smile. Despite his occasional boyish arrogance and stubbornness, Sanchez had consistently shown his allegiance toward her, no matter the consequences. It was an easy trait for her to respect.

Exiting their cars together and walking up the gravel driveway, they stepped under the crime scene tape and made their way to the barn. Its interior glowed yellow from several portable lights that had just arrived on a flatbed. A crowd of uniformed officers as well as Detectives Teliford and Grimes surveyed the crime scene. Two forensic technicians busied themselves photographing and finger-printing the female civilian's body. Camera flashes came from inside the barn. As she and Sanchez approached, Riggins peered through the open door at the figure of the medical examiner crouching over Deputy Hammer's still-handcuffed corpse. Dressed in a suit and tie, and wearing blue surgical gloves, the doctor looked grossly out of place in such a scene. The two uniformed deputies guarding the barn's entrance both had tears in their eyes.

Just then, and before Riggins could duck out of sight, Lieutenant Heinke exited the barn. His face ashen and his eyes haunted, he pulled a hand over the length of his face. Over the span of the past day, Riggins felt the man had aged ten years. When he saw her, he swore under his breath as he pulled her to the side.

"What are you doing here?" he asked pointedly. "The sheriff is on his way. What am I supposed to tell him if he sees you here?"

"I don't think Grassle did this, sir," Riggins said.

The haggard-looking lieutenant rolled his eyes. "Not this again."

Sanchez stepped forward just then. Seeing him, Heinke lifted his palms and eyes to the sky in disbelief. "What is this, the Riggins and Sanchez show? You two can't just waltz into a crime scene whenever you want. As crazy as it may seem to you both, there are procedures we have to follow."

Sanchez began to speak but Riggins held out a hand to cut him off. "Grassle called me. On my agency phone. I just talked to him."

Heinke, who up to this point wore a look of exasperation, turned to her with bulging eyes. "Are you toying with me? Because if you are, it isn't the least bit funny."

Riggins removed her cell phone and punched up her call log. "Here—the call came in eight minutes ago. We talked for just under two. He said he was here, Lieu, that he saw who killed Hammer and the woman. He said a lot more, but I really didn't—"

But Heinke was already waving one of his junior supervisors over to where they stood. Taking the phone from Riggins, Heinke inspected the call log, and after conferring with the supervisor he turned back toward her, already looking years younger. "Caller ID is the same name as our female victim," he said, excited.

"He took her phone," Riggins intoned, looking down at the woman's body. Whatever thought passed through her mind just then, it made her shiver.

Heinke pointed to the barn entrance. "Do you two see that? That's what your Eddie Grassle caused, so I don't want to hear about you thinking he had nothing to do with it. I have to tell Hammer's wife and kids their husband and father isn't coming home tonight. I also have an old woman sedated at the hospital who just watched her daughter's head explode. I'm a man standing in front of a fan and someone's holding a bucket of shit."

Neither Riggins nor Sanchez dared respond at first. After several moments of painful silence, punctuated by the sight of two gurneys with bodies on them being carted toward the awaiting van, Riggins said, "There's something going on here, Lieu. I feel like someone is behind the scenes pulling strings that aren't meant to be pulled."

Heinke seemed prepared to lay into her, but his face softened at the last minute. He placed a gentle hand on her shoulder. "Let me give you some advice, Alice. If the sheriff wants you to wear a ballerina tutu for the next four months, you wear one. You can't save the world, but you already know that. You started when you were nineteen. That's unheard of now. Take advantage of the opportunity to be able to get away from all of this with half your life left."

Her lips pressing into a firm line, Riggins nodded her understanding.

"What I'm about to say is what I believe your father would tell you if he were here. Treat baggage the way it should be treated. Set it on the train and let it get carried away from you, or you'll be left hauling it around forever."

He slipped an arm over her slender shoulders and gave her a one-armed embrace. Riggins's body, rigid with the stress of the day, relaxed immediately. She turned to face him fully. "I hear you, Lieu. I really do. But I just can't shake the feeling we made a mistake in charging Grassle. A fundamental mistake, not some legal technicality. And this—" She indicated the crime scene. "This isn't him either. I know it sounds like sympathy, but there's more to it. I guess now that the end is so close, I just don't want any more blood on my hands than I already have."

Heinke pointed toward the barn. "You want to talk about blood, there's plenty of it in there. Now remember what I said. Four months. Make good and sure to keep that phone near you until further notice. Tape it to your forehead when you sleep if you have to. If he calls again, I want to know immediately. I'll take care of the warrant."

Riggins raked her fingernails across the hives that bloomed across her arms. Feeling defeated, she thanked Heinke for all that he'd done for her before walking back to her car. Knowing that a warrant for the woman's phone records (and any associated cell tower readings) would take a few hours, but that they wouldn't be able to apply it until the cell company opened for business in the morning anyway, Riggins felt enough at peace to head home for the night. Remaining in the field, especially when hampered by her admin status, seemed a waste without any real intelligence. She'd try her best to sleep. But knowing Eddie might call again would no doubt leave her tossing all night.

Fifteen minutes later she walked through her home's front door and plopped down on the couch next to her concerned-looking husband.

"I saw it on the news," he said before she could utter a word. "They didn't say the deputy's name, but I figured you knew who it was."

For all her usual hardness and stoicism, Riggins found herself emotionally exhausted. She hadn't cried due to the job in many years and thinking of Hammer and what his family would be going through at that very moment brought her to the edge of tears. But she felt as though the building snowball that had begun weeks ago now threatened to roll over her and swallow not just herself, but even her career and marriage too. Lying flat across Chet's broad chest, she rested her chin on her folded hands and said, "I know you support whatever I decide to do with this, and I love you even more for saying it. But what I want to know is—what would you do if you were in my position?"

Chet thought about it until he cleared his throat and said, "I suppose I'd look myself in the mirror and realize I'm a human being before anything else. That I'd do what would let me live with myself as a person, then figure the rest out later."

Riggins let out a long exhale and smiled wanly. It seemed as if a thousand pounds had just been lifted off her shoulders all at once, and the hurt and pain and fear of what may come seemed to slip away. A contented look settled on her face as she stared into his deep brown eyes. "Why did I know you'd say something like that?"

And then suddenly she was straddling him, kissing his mouth deeply not in a sexual manner, but out of a deeper appreciation, one that sat at the foundation of her humanity. She felt his strong hands run over her backside then up to the swell of her breasts. They kissed so hard their teeth clinked together; and for all the day's tragedies and disappointments, it didn't take her long to melt as he deftly unbuttoned her jeans and peeled them off. Without a word, he laid her back along the couch and when she tried to sit up, beginning to tell him that tonight she was going to please him, was going to do that thing she knew he loved receiving as much as she loved performing, he pushed her back down and held her firmly that way. And then, knowing sex wasn't something only undertaken in happy times and under cloudless skies, he pulled her panties down over her hips and did that thing to her he'd always known had made her troubled world just a bit better.

Damn, she loved that man.

THIRTY-SEVEN

FINGERS . . .

Eddie awoke with a start, slapping at his face from the sensation of a dozen fingers drawing over it. He sat up quickly without thinking and paid for it. Pain, which during sleep had thankfully abated, shot through his body like electricity. Groaning, he felt those fingers again and only when he grabbed at them did he realize they were not fingers at all, but hanging clumps of Spanish moss blowing in the night breeze. Settling back against the tree's ledge, he allowed himself to relax a bit, forcing away the pain as best he could. When he rolled back over to try going back to sleep, a white light formed at the edge of his vision. At first, he assumed the light had been due to the pain itself, and he tried to shake it away. But when the light began moving across his vision in a coned arc, followed in turn by another, similar arc of light behind it, Eddie quickly realized the lights he saw were in fact spotlights from a pair of approaching vehicles.

Flattening against the trunk, he watched the vehicles swing around a curve in the road below. Two police cruisers.

How the hell?

Then again, there were eyes everywhere; he couldn't possibly expect to move freely without arousing at least some suspicion. And the phone. If they'd discovered he'd taken it, they'd likely zeroed in on where the last call had come from. Thanking himself for at least having the forethought of removing the battery, he wondered how wise it had been to call Riggins at all.

Despite his concealed position, Eddie realized he was hopelessly trapped. He imagined one of the officers climbing the tree and Eddie seeing his grinning face appear above the ledge, the barrel of a gun pointed at him. *Thought you could hide from us, huh? Tell you what. We'll give you two choices—come on down and go back to jail, or you can run and we'll put some lead in your back. Your choice.*

Eddie watched the cruisers creep along the road in his direction. He prayed they continued on, perhaps just making a routine patrol. Instead, they both stopped on the road directly below Eddie's position, sweeping their spotlights around the area in his direction. Shit. For a moment, he allowed himself to believe they would move on, having found nothing of note. But then Eddie watched as each cop stepped from their respective cruiser, conferring in inaudible voices before making a radio transmission. Panicked now, Eddie watched with wide eyes as both cops removed flashlights from their belts and switched them on. Side-by-side, they then moved up the slope toward his location. Dozens of graves surrounded his mother's, but he could think of no other reason why two officers would be walking directly toward him in the middle of the night, other than to find him. When they stopped just a few feet from the tree, Eddie was finally able to hear their conversation.

"Fucking kids," said one of the deputies, exasperated. "They get spooked, and we get stuck chasing ghosts."

His partner concurred. "No shit."

Since the tree's limbs and hanging moss obscured much of his view directly downward, Eddie was left just listening to them. The sound of two pairs of feet walking over the ground around the tree came to him. He held his breath, believing they'd be able to hear the air wisp in and out of his lungs. Then an image came to his mind: One of the cops holding a finger to his lips while pointing up into the tree. The other one nodding, whispering a radio transmission for reinforcements, that they had him trapped.

"Jesus, I can't believe Hammer really bought it," said one of them. "I heard the bastard cuffed him to a pole before he capped him. Fucking execution."

"Christ."

A lighter flicking. Moments later, the sweet aroma of burning tobacco wafted up to him. Even though he didn't smoke, Eddie would've traded a finger for a single drag right then.

"Are we cancelling K-9 or what?" one of them asked the other.

"Dog's already on the way. Shame to take one out of the main search for this bullshit, though. I guarantee you there ain't no one out here."

"Oh, there's people here, alright," shot back his partner. "Except I don't think they seen much."

They both chuckled at that. One of them keyed his radio. "Bravo 44 to Comm-1. We're 10-23, do you copy?"

Eddie listened as the deputy's radio returned a staticky female's voice. "Copy, Bravo-44. Be advised, delay on K-9."

"Copy. ETA?"

More static. Then, "Fifteen mikes."

"Ten-four. We'll wait on it."

Eddie's blood froze in his veins. The dog would discover him seconds after it arrived. And climbing down the tree wasn't an option with the cops standing practically right below him. He cursed himself for coming here in the first place. He felt he should have looked out for himself better than this. *Why paint yourself into a corner when you literally had the entire countryside to hide in?*

One of the deputies said, "I gotta piss before the dog comes. You think this stiff will mind?"

The sound of a zipper being undone, then a chuckle from one of them as the sound of liquid splashing against the ground rose to Eddie. The sound continued until it changed slightly—instead of the urine striking dirt and grass, it seemed now to be striking stone.

Eddie's eyes widened in horror.

Guffaws of laughter from both deputies. Unable to resist, Eddie dared to move for the first time since they'd arrived. Rolling to his right, he ignored the roaring pain in his shoulder and leg, scooting far enough forward to peek over the ledge. Light from both cruisers' spotlights illuminated the area around and beneath the tree. And what Eddie saw in that light sent such a shock through him he jerked suddenly upward onto his knees, an involuntary sound of shock and disgust coming from his throat as he realized the cop was pissing directly onto his mother's gravestone.

"Hope you're thirsty, lady," cracked the pissing deputy. "Been saving this one up for the last hour!"

Both deputies howled with laughter. In reflex, Eddie reached outward, as if doing so could stop what was happening directly below him. As he did, his elbow inadvertently struck a small branch. Several feet long with hanging blooms of moss, it snapped free of the tree and crashed down directly onto the pissing deputy. As the branch became entangled around his head and shoulders, the deputy's laughter turned into a shriek of terror as he clawed wildly at it. Back-pedaling, he tripped over a tree root and landed hard on his back. Having been in mid-stream with his dick still exposed through the fly of his pants, warm urine sprayed upward then came showering down onto his face and chest. Gagging, he pawed wildly at his crotch until he finally managed to put himself away. Even then, he squirted an involuntary burst of piss inside his pants as he hastily clambered back to his feet.

Immediately, the other deputy drew his sidearm and pointed it up into the moss-hung tree. "Who's up there?" he demanded, his gun barrel shaking. "Get down from there, or I'll shoot!"

Swearing bitterly, his partner wiped away urine from his face and uniform shirt. Collecting himself, he followed suit and drew his own pistol.

Eddie's heart pounded so hard in his chest he felt it would explode. His eyes, wide and panicked, met those of each deputy. Yet they both hesitated, as if they either could not believe what they saw or were unsure of how to act. Then, after several seconds of such unbearable tension that Eddie felt the veins in his neck would burst, something heavy leaped from a branch next to him and scampered down the tree. A large raccoon hit the ground and lumbered away through the maze of partially lit gravestones, its bushy tail bobbing as it went. Several moments of breathless silence passed, until both deputies holstered their weapons and exchanged sighs of relief. The deputy who had pissed himself finished brushing off his uniform with disgusted swats as his partner got on his radio.

"Bravo 44 to Comm-1. As you were—we're 10-98. Cancel K-9. I say again—cancel K-9."

The dispatcher responded seconds later. "Copy, Bravo 44. Same with Eagle?"

The deputy who'd pissed himself made a horizontal cutting motion toward his neck.

"Copy," relayed his partner. "Tell the bird to stand down. There isn't anything worth searching for out here."

From his perch, Eddie tried his best to piece together what it all meant. Not knowing what would happen in the next few minutes agonized him more than if the cops had already spotted him.

"Fucking kids," said his partner, drying his hands on his pants. "I gotta head back to the station to change. This never happened, you hear?"

"What never happened?" his partner answered, shrugging. "Nothing out here anyway but coons that scare the piss out of people." Slapping his knee, he howled with fresh laughter.

His partner approached him and shook a finger in his face. "Don't you breathe a word of this to anybody," he warned. "I swear it, if anybody hears about this, Donna might have to find out about your little lady friend on the side."

Wiping tears from his eyes, his partner tisk-tisked. "Now, now, don't you start getting pissy with me." He exploded with laughter again as he made his way down the hill toward the cruisers. His partner stood in place, looking tentatively back toward the tree. He wrinkled his nose at his soaked uniform, apparently furious at having been bested by something as benign as a raccoon. Before turning back to his cruiser, he seemed to detect more movement in the tree. He had just switched his flashlight back on and trained it up into the moss-covered branches when his partner called out to him from the road below. "Let's roll! Disturbance call at the Pussy Cat. All those pussies are just waiting to get rescued!"

The deputy stood still for a moment, squinting up into the darkened tree. Shaking his head, he finally turned and walked back to his cruiser. Soon, the pair pulled away down the winding cemetery road and disappeared around a bend. The distant clang of the iron gates slamming closed floated in the night air. Only when he heard this did Eddie realize he'd been holding his breath the whole time. Gasping, he collapsed face-first onto the ledge and lay panting for several minutes. His heartbeat eventually slowed, and his eyelids closed as he allowed himself to fall back into glorious sleep. Curled there on the ledge, he dreamed of parks, and of Liam, of a life lived free without worry of the dankness of a jail cell. In another dream, the sun felt warm on his bare shoulders as he waited for Liam to leap to him from a low bridge into the river, the same river Eddie himself had frolicked in as a boy.

While he slept, a driving rain passed over the area. Spring had moved into summer. Mostly protected by the thick canopy above him, he did not stir. When he awoke eight hours later, he sat up with much effort, the sun shining through the tree's branches in shimmering ribbons. All around him, birds sang as if describing the miserable human form in their midst. To Eddie Grassle, the fact he had awoken at all seemed like a miracle itself. But even he knew miracles did not last forever. Oftentimes, they allowed for a moment of peace to exist just a few minutes longer than expected, until it disappeared and left you with what you had before. Surviving the previous day and waking alive—however pained and desperate—could only mean one thing: that the breath in his lungs and the beating of his heart must be for a reason, and that no matter what, today would be the most eventful day of his entire life.

From the Springwood Gazette, Friday May 28, 2016
JAIL INMATE ESCAPES; SUSPECTED IN DEPUTY'S KILLING
Story by Alexander Dupont, *Gazette* staff writer

A Springwood man, jailed last month for murder in connection with the robbery of a local convenience store, escaped from a secure portion of the Calusa County Jail yesterday. According to Sheriff Office officials, the brazen daytime jailbreak occurred during a scheduled recreation period, sending into motion the largest manhunt in Calusa County history. As of midnight, the escapee, Edward Grassle, 24, remained at large.

Hours after the escape, Calusa County Sheriff's Deputy Erwin Hammer was shot and killed while responding to a prowler call. The property owner, Elizabeth Downing, 56, was also killed. While detectives worked into the night, search teams scoured the area for the person or persons responsible. When asked if any connection existed between Grassle and Hammer's killer, a somber Sheriff Bo Driscoll responded, "That's certainly what it looks like right now."

According to those with knowledge of the case and speaking on condition of anonymity due to the ongoing investigation, Grassle climbed a razor-wire fence before eluding two armed deputies assigned to guard him. When pressed for details, Driscoll dismissed reporters' questions as conjecture regarding his staff's competence. "We are gathering all the facts we can right now. Our jail and patrol folks have difficult jobs. I will not second-guess them in the media."

Anonymous officials stated that during the escape, Grassle suffered gunshot and other injuries. The extent of those injuries is unknown. Most troubling for officials has been the inability of search teams to gain any insight toward Grassle's suspected location. "We're doing everything in our power to catch this individual," a visibly frustrated Driscoll said. "There's a lot of wild land out there, so it isn't easy finding someone who hunkers down. But I'm confident we'll get him soon."

Following Hammer's death, a grim-faced Driscoll made no attempt to hide his disdain for the suspected killer. "The animal who did this is a coward. A cold-blooded coward. I hope he can hear me now." When asked for a timeline on Grassle's apprehension, the normally patient sheriff lashed out at reporters. "I don't have a crystal ball, people. If I did, I'd be glad to tell you. What I do know is that I have committed every available member of this agency to his capture. I personally will not lay my head down to rest until he is found. Mark my words." Refusing to elaborate on tactics used by search teams, the sheriff concluded *his statement on an ominous note. "If you've hunted before, you know a wounded animal isn't keen on letting itself be caught."*

Records were not immediately available, but according to Jail Superintendent Claude Devereux, yesterday's escape was the first of its kind that did not result in immediate recapture. In 1995, Homer Landings, a local transient arrested for panhandling, climbed out the back window of a deputy's cruiser while it sat idling inside the jail's open sally port, but he was found within minutes.

Driscoll urged members of the community to remain on the lookout for Grassle, and asked residents to call the police hotline upon spotting the escapee. "We do not recommend the public confront this individual," the sheriff warned. "He is an extremely dangerous character."

STATE ATTORNEY HOOD finished reading the *Gazette* story and leaned thoughtfully back in his chair. He twisted the red-stoned ring around his finger, his mind unconscious of the fact. The French doors separating his home office from the flagstone pool deck lay open, and now the warm salty morning air flowed inside, filling his lungs. His appearance did not convey the angst that stirred within him. His eyes closed and the lids fluttered almost imperceptibly as he concentrated on controlling his emotions.

'Do nothing out of anger,' his father had warned him long ago. *'No matter how unsettling the situation, it is always wise to step back from it and allow your anger to pass before you act.'*

Remembering his father's words, Hood silently counted to one hundred as he regulated his breathing. He concentrated on his own senses—the smell of salt in the air, the distant drone of a boat motor on the river, the feel of the chair's leather against his bare arms. As he meditated, his mind wandered to the image of a young red-headed girl, his new favorite and the most luscious indulgence he had experienced at his "special place." As he felt himself stir beneath his bathrobe, a knowing smile creased his lips. He had not smiled in weeks, it seemed. Yet how easy it was for him to let go of frustration and anger—even amid something as upsetting as yesterday's escape—just by conjuring Pith's image.

Pith. The name given to her by her madam. During Hood's first encounter with the nubile beauty, he had taken a cup she'd drank from and later had it analyzed for fingerprints. Classified as a runaway, Natasha Lynn had a juvenile record for shoplifting and had been verified as being just sixteen years old. Her flaming red hair (Hood had purred with anticipation when discovering she was also red down there), excited him more than he would have ever imagined. That first time, she had dutifully allowed him to bind her with rope and had accepted the gag in her mouth without complaint. Having rendered the girl utterly helpless and unable to speak or cry out, Hood had proceeded to act out a violent rape fantasy, degrading her in every way imaginable. During the hour-long session, Pith had remained stoic by not closing her eyes or averting them from his even once. This had both surprised and excited Hood immensely. During that hour, Hood had done all he could do in an attempt to break her. He'd failed at every turn. Pith had fixed her deep green eyes on him until the very end, not once betraying signs of fear, shame or disgust at the vile things Hood had subjected her to. When it was over, Hood had sat naked and sweating on the edge of the bed, frustration and admiration toward her filling him. Then he'd untied her and helped her dress, kissing her gently on the forehead and whispering in her ear that she had been his favorite. That he was sorry for the things he had done and said to her. Smiling demurely, Pith had bowed her head as if to simultaneously acknowledge and render the apology unnecessary. Then she'd slipped through a darkened doorway to clean and bandage herself, the ghost of her presence lingering long after she'd left.

A month later, unable to control his wild fantasies about the girl, Hood had called on his favorite madam again. 'The redhead,' Hood had told the woman on the phone, breathless.

'Pith is not available tonight,' had come the madam's reply. Hood had promised a large premium if she were to be made immediately available. 'She does not have an appointment tonight, but Mother Nature *does. Another night, perhaps?'* Immediately, Hood insisted on making the appointment anyway, stating he would not be able to sleep without seeing her. And he had. That second visit had been absent any sexual contact whatsoever. He'd undressed her, ran his fingers over the marks he had left from the time before, feeling somehow ashamed not at what he'd done but at his own perceived inadequacies. Every one of the other girls had broken within minutes. But not her.

He'd paid for the entire night. Cradling her in his arms, he'd quickly fallen asleep, transported across the decades by the dream of himself as a boy, standing beside his father as the bullet left the killer's gun and traveled on its destined trajectory. Trapped within his dream, Hood had watched in horror as the bullet smashed into his father's chest and exited his back, that same strong back that had helped build their farmhouse and had plowed their fields. That same back that had once carried a young Mathias through five miles of woods toward home after he'd sprained an ankle on a hunt. Dreams, Hood felt, were the closest man came to God. And as Hood had writhed in the bedsheets, Pith had lain awake watching him. She'd watched his lips move silently over clenched teeth, forming the same word over and over again—*why?*

Contentedness now replaced confliction. Hood opened his eyes, moving them across the glass-like surface of the pool's water. Grassle escaping had infuriated him at first. But now that he'd been publicly suspected of two more murders, one of them a deputy sheriff, Hood realized the situation now provided him with a new opportunity. His instructions to Paolo carried real risk. Should Hood himself become implicated, his removal from his current post due to an investigation would be swift. He would certainly be subject to a criminal complaint as well. But he also realized that Grassle's subsequent death, however dubious it may be, would not likely elicit attention from FDLE, the state law enforcement agency, or the even more problematic ACLU. With the governor solidly under his control, Hood felt more confident than ever that disposing of Grassle outright would not only be safe but may even be celebrated by a public that abhorred cop killers of any kind.

Retreating into his expansive bathroom, Hood showered then dressed in one of his finest suits. He did not relish the thought of attending the upcoming press conference, scheduled for an hour from now. He'd remained awake long into the night, anxiously awaiting word of Grassle's capture. When it hadn't occurred, he'd privately celebrated the fact that Paolo's mission was for now intact.

He dialed Paolo's number. Soon, his confidant's deep, even voice answered.

"Why haven't I heard from you?" Hood asked, climbing into his Corvette's front seat. Needing to feel the power from the 500-horsepower engine soothe him, he pressed the gas pedal and relished the resulting growl.

"There has been an extreme amount of activity, as you must understand," Paolo replied.

Climbing onto the interstate, Hood observed a sheriff's cruiser parked in the median and blew by him at over ninety miles an hour. Every cop in the county recognized his vehicles, and to date none had even dared stop him for an infraction, let alone cite him. "I appreciate everything you do for me, Paolo. I hope you know how I feel about you."

Hood felt he could hear Paolo smiling through the phone. "I will do whatever you ask of me, Mathias."

"When this is over, we can take each other," Hood said, catching his own disgusted expression in the rearview mirror. "Just do what I've asked you to do. By any means necessary."

Not waiting for a reply, he ended the call. Fifteen minutes later he pulled into the courthouse parking lot. Waiting for him beside the gathering crowd of officials and reporters stood Sheriff Driscoll, his wide-brimmed Stetson in both hands.

"Good morning, Bo," said the stone-faced chief prosecutor. He hadn't expected the sheriff to be here yet.

"Not much good about it," the aging lawman replied.

Hood motioned for the two to step inside the main doors of the complex, away from the growing crowd of reporters and police. As they made their way down the wide marble hallway, Hood brusquely waved away several people who attempted to speak with him, and gravely regarded the sheriff who stood anxiously before him.

"Where are we with the search, Bo?"

Hat still in hand, the sheriff looked to the ceiling, tears welling in his eyes. "He killed one of my men, Mathias. Cuffed him to a beam and shot him in cold blood. Do you know what his wife said when I told her that?"

Hood's silence spoke his response.

"She held onto her two children, one in each arm, and said she'd known the truth when she'd seen the news and her husband hadn't returned her calls. After I told her, she knelt in front of her children and told them their daddy died so that they might grow up in a safer world. That they should be proud of him even in death and to never forget his sacrifice to this twisted world." The sheriff's eyes misted over, an urgency lighting in them that Hood had never seen before. "Then she looked me dead in the eye and demanded her husband's killer be taken alive. *Demanded* it, Mathias. Because she wants to sit in the galley as the curtain draws open in the death chamber and look him in the eye. She said she wants to be the last thing he ever sees, so that his soul never forgets. It sent chills down my spine hearing that, and I had no choice but to promise her." The sheriff shuddered, his fingers crimping the hat's brim.

Hood allowed the sheriff proper time to recover from the painful memory, then said, "I believe what is in order here is a quantified *quid pro quo.*"

The sheriff frowned.

"You scratch my back, I'll scratch yours."

"I'm not as learned as you," the sheriff said without shame. "Explain yourself."

"You make sure Grassle doesn't cross county lines. If he does, your hands are tied. My man can find him for you, and when he does, you can finally rest your head knowing you did your job for the fine citizens of the county."

"And in return?"

"Your boys won't ever need to worry about a bad shooting or using a bit more force than necessary. They have a hard enough job as it is without having to look over their shoulder. Their lives are at risk every day. What I'm suggesting is that we lean our hands on the scales of justice just enough to even them out. It's part of our jobs to do that, Bo. I think deep down you know that." Sheriff Driscoll, bent slightly by time and forty years of enforcing the law, stared into the soulless, black eyes before him. "I could never walk over the threshold of my church again if I knew I'd killed a man in cold blood. Not even one suspected of killing one of my deputies." The sheriff stood straight and raised his chin proudly. "There's a reason this star is pinned over my heart. So help me God, I will not be party to a man's murder, no matter his crime."

"Now, now, Bo," Hood said, patting the sheriff's shoulders more firmly than was necessary.

"As I said, your boys are free to do as they wish. But they will not interfere with my man in any way. Their blood will be hot now. One of their brothers was cut down, and I understand they may not feel the need to honor their master's wishes."

Without removing his hands, Hood turned his head and looked out the window at the crowd of reporters that had made their way into the courtyard. The press conference would begin soon, yet not without the two most important players present. "The cameras will turn on shortly, Bo, and when they do, I would prefer the two of us already have an arrangement."

The sheriff hesitated, staring into the black eyes that burned into his own. In the end, he nodded. He suddenly looked very tired and as if wishing to be anywhere else than where he was.

"I want him, Mathias. I want the animal who did this. If it means the devil must do it, then so be it."

A twinkle came to Hood's eye. Smoothing out the shoulders of the sheriff's shirt, he bade him farewell, watching as the old lawman pushed his way out the soaring courthouse doors.

Hood closed his eyes and allowed the voice that had lingered in the back of his mind to come fully forward into his consciousness. That voice came so clear to him he opened his eyes and looked around the deserted hallway, expecting his father's ghost to be standing beside him.

Avenge me...

His hand went to the red-stoned ring, twisting it as his eyes smoldered with hate. "It will be done, Father," he whispered aloud, before his muscular legs carried him down the hall and to the waiting crowd outside.

THIRTY-EIGHT

AS THE MORNING sun crested over the treetops, Eddie rubbed sleep from his eyes and tried to piece together exactly what had happened over the last twenty hours. His mind felt swirled in a fog of memories. Had he really escaped from jail? Was the pain that racked his body truly the result of being shot, gashed, and running barefoot through a dozen miles of woods and swamps? Then again, he did remember being in jail. And being up here in a tree overlooking a cemetery was most certainly *not* jail. Hunger like he'd never known gnawed at his stomach. Terrible thirst racked his throat. Only after he looked out over the sweeping cemetery lawn did everything begin to fall into place. Looking down upon his mother's grave, he sought answers from the source of the one pleasant memory he had left.

"What should I do, Momma?"

The simple granite marker stared back at him, its stony silence almost as loud as the chirping birds around him. He stayed that way for quite some time—an hour it seemed, when in reality it had been only minutes. Removing the two halves of the phone from his overalls pocket, he moved his fingers over the clamshell's smooth metal surface as he thought back to his conversation with Detective Riggins the night before. Why *had* he called her, other than to give her a description of the man in the barn?

For reasons he himself didn't quite understand, Eddie made his second questionable decision concerning the phone by connecting the battery and flipping open the receiver. With trembling fingers, he waited for the same lighted icons to appear before pressing redial. After a five second delay a dial tone sounded. A familiar female voice, thick with sleep, answered on the eighth ring.

"Riggins, Homicide."

What are you doing, bro? Are you asking to get caught?

"I'm—I'm sorry if I woke you, ma'am," Eddie stammered. "It's Eddie. We spoke last night..."

A hesitation from the other end, as if she were finishing the mental transition from sleep to wakefulness before the sound of her suddenly sitting upright. "Oh—wow. Eddie Grassle. I thought I'd dreamed that." Eddie heard a man's voice in the background ask if everything was okay, and Riggins assuring him that it was. "Talk to me, Eddie. Where are you?"

The sound of a vehicle's engine cresting the hill caused Eddie to sit up straight in his perch. They'd found him after all. But then the vehicle came fully into view and Eddie breathed a sigh of relief. A hearse. A line of cars followed it, snaking their way along the main cemetery road until coming to a stop fifty yards from Eddie's position. Due to a branch and large clumps of hanging moss, Eddie hadn't seen the green tent that had been erected over a nearby open grave.

"You still there, Eddie?" came Riggins's voice.

Eddie stared at the screen, wincing at the knowledge that his calling her again had likely sealed his doom. And for what? "Yes, ma'am."

"I know you're scared. But if you keep running, I can't guarantee something bad won't happen to you."

Eddie noted the words *Sandy Pines Funeral Home* written on the side of the hearse. He remembered the place, having delivered newspapers there as a kid, hurriedly passing by the somber-looking building as he'd continued his route. The hearse driver, an older black gentleman, exited and moved to open the rear door. He waited for a group of men in suits to exit their respective vehicles, and together they slid a silver casket out of the back of the hearse. Four per side, they carried the casket to a hoist that had been placed above the open grave. Several women followed. One of them wept openly, while another draped an arm across her shoulders as they walked together toward the gravesite. As he watched the mourners take their seats on a row of pre-laid chairs, Eddie wondered who had died, how old they'd been, and whether the person would be missed by the world at large. That made him wonder if *he* would be missed once he was gone.

"I'm not sure if I even care anymore, detective," he said vacantly. A beeping sound emitted from the phone just then. A quick glance showed the battery indicator at 25%.

"I know you've been through a lot, Eddie. But you have to let me help you."

"I'll turn myself in tonight," he said. "I promise. I just need to see today if I can make something good come of this whole thing. If I make it through this, you can visit me in jail and I'll tell you about it. I'll be smiling, because for once I'll feel like I did something for someone else instead of always thinking of myself."

The funeral service began; the minister started his eulogy. The small contingent of mourners sat stiffly in their chairs, a few of them dabbing at their eyes with handkerchiefs.

"What can I do to help you, Eddie?" Riggins asked, her voice low.

Eddie lifted his gaze from the gravesite toward the sky. "Nothing, really. Except maybe one thing. It probably sounds stupid, me asking the police for favors, but I don't have anyone left who will listen."

"I can't promise anything, but I can try."

He smiled, bittersweet. "If I don't make it out of this, if I get killed or something, please don't let them put me in the ground."

"Don't think like that," Riggins said, sounding concerned. "Things will work themselves out. I know the system isn't perfect, but it's the best one around."

"I think it would be nice to have my ashes scattered in the river," Eddie continued, his eyes tracing the sky. "It's where I've always been happiest. That way a part of me will wash into the Gulf, maybe all the way to New Orleans. Jules and I used to talk about going there. Just hitchhike our way and learn to play an instrument so we could play in one of those street jazz bands. They do that, you know."

"Eddie—" Riggins began. "I really don't know what to say." Then finally, with a great sigh she said, "Okay, Eddie. If anything happens,

I'll tell them. But let's not talk about that. Things will be fine as long as you tell me where and when I can pick you up."

Eddie heard her cover the other end of the phone. Muffled voices. He watched the minister continue his eulogy, one mourner (a woman dressed in black, with a matching veil) openly weeping harder than the rest.

"I'll try to call from this phone, but I'm not sure what's going to happen with me five minutes from now. If I can't use this anymore, I'll turn myself in to the first cop I can find. By midnight tonight, even if I don't finish what I need to do. I promise."

He watched the minister leave his place at the head of the grave and approach the first row of mourners, resting his hand on the shoulder of the veiled, weeping woman. Then the mourners stood and took turns placing single roses atop the gleaming silver casket before returning to their seats.

"Okay, Eddie. You do it your way. If you change your mind, call me. If you don't have access to the phone anymore, find the nearest road and walk toward town. You'll see a sheriff's cruiser sooner than you think. When you do, make sure they see you and place your hands high in the air. Do exactly what they say, understand?"

"Yes, ma'am."

"Good. I'm going to hang up. Don't forget what I said."

Once the call ended, he disconnected the battery again. He stuffed both pieces back into his pocket, cursing himself. He'd been stupid for taking it in the first place, and even more foolish for calling Riggins at all, let alone twice. For now, he knew his time would soon be up if he didn't vacate the area immediately. Mildly surprised they hadn't tracked him here yet, he looked anxiously toward the funeral, which appeared to just be ending. Mourners, giving the departed a final goodbye, filed away toward their vehicles, as did the minister once they'd all left. The hearse driver had chain-smoked cigarettes next to his vehicle during the service.

Eddie waited and watched. Several minutes passed, but the driver remained where he was. *Come on*, Eddie thought. *Get out of here already!* As if reading Eddie's mind in a way, the driver reached into his pocket and produced his ringing cell phone. Answering, he walked down the paved road, engaged in an animated conversation. Stopping about fifty feet away, he began smoking another cigarette as he continued his talk.

At the gravesite, a pair of cemetery workers arrived with a backhoe. After lowering the casket into the ground, they removed the green felt covering the dirt mound then filled in the grave. After they left, Eddie watched the hearse driver continue walking away from him on the road below. Suddenly, an idea struck him. He'd have to act fast. Flipping onto his stomach, he swung his legs out over the ledge in preparation of climbing down the tree, when he spied something shiny lodged in a far corner of the ledge. Had he not been positioned at such an angle and had the sun's morning rays not struck it just right, he might not have noticed it at all. Curious, Eddie reached out and tugged at the finger-length object. It wouldn't budge. Whatever it was, it definitely didn't appear to belong there and had apparently grown into the tree over a period of time. Only after he pulled hard at it did it break free. Turning the object over in his hand, Eddie's mind went back seven years to the last time he'd been up here on the ledge, with Jules during Eddie's mom's funeral.

"Oh wow," he whispered, staring at the rusted pocketknife in his hand. Seven years in the elements and having the growing tree form around it had almost made it invisible. Looking to his right, Eddie marveled at the faint etching barely visible in the trunk. *Eddie and Jules, best bro's 4-ever!*

Slipping the rusted knife into his pocket, Eddie lowered himself down to the branch below him. Ignoring the raging pain in his shoulder, he managed to suspend himself far enough to be able to jump safely to the ground. When he hit the grass, his left leg gave out, causing him to roll several times until he came to a stop partway down the knoll. The grass was still wet from the morning dew and, turning his head to the side, he licked the moisture from the blades of grass around him. He only managed to swallow a few drops, but even that felt like liquid gold going down his parched throat.

Getting to his knees, Eddie watched the hearse driver stop about twenty yards from his vehicle. Continuing his phone call, the man still had his back to Eddie. Eddie looked between the hearse and the driver, unsure if he should chance it. If the man chose to turn around, he'd see Eddie there in the short grass, as plain as day. Even Eddie knew he wouldn't be able to explain his presence there, and that assumed the guy wouldn't recognize him for who he really was. But if the guy *didn't* turn...

Rising to his feet, Eddie hobbled down the slope as quickly and quietly as he could toward the hearse, and hopefully toward his salvation that he prayed still sat in a classroom just a few miles from where he stood.

THIRTY-NINE

WHILE EDDIE AMBLED down the cemetery lawn toward the hearse, Detectives Teliford and Grimes pushed their way through a crowded downtown street. Their destination—the district office of the Pelican Telecommunication Service—sat in a nondescript three-story building in downtown Springwood. Just a five-minute walk from the criminal courts complex, the sidewalk along the full block it occupied bore little evidence of the ongoing manhunt that had entered its second day. Businesspeople, mothers pushing strollers, and scattered other townsfolk walked to and fro, either oblivious to the unfolding drama or uncaring of it.

Having decided to walk from the courthouse due to notoriously limited downtown parking, they'd come here seeking information on a cell phone suspected to have been used by Eddie Grassle, Calusa County's newest *persona non grata*. The detectives entered the building and then an elevator. Grimes, the younger and smaller of the two, removed a handkerchief from his pocket and blew his nose. A virus had swept through the detective bureau and claimed him several days ago. As if having the Grassle case thrown in his lap hadn't been enough. From Grimes's slender hand hung a leather briefcase containing the warrant they had procured just moments before their arrival here.

As the elevator opened on the third floor, they put on serious airs. Despite being surprised at having been given such a high-profile case at such a late stage, both shared a measure of personal satisfaction over the work they had come here to perform. It was customary for the arresting detectives to receive full recognition for a fugitive's capture, no matter the stage at which they were assigned the case. The prospect of nabbing an escaped prisoner such as Grassle would no doubt be the greatest career-builder either of them had had.

Exiting the elevator, the pair approached an open doorway marked **PTS** and stood in a lush lobby carpeted in Key West pastels. As they approached the front desk, the redheaded receptionist smiled brightly and asked how she could assist them.

"Mr. Aaron, please. He's expecting us," muttered Detective Teliford. He flipped open his agency wallet to display his credentials.

"And let him know we have our warrant," sneered Detective Grimes. He raised the briefcase so she could see it, dabbing again at his nose.

The receptionist's smile changed from friendly to one of cool politeness. She checked her computer and nodded. "Yes, he's just finishing up a conference call right now. If you'd like to have a seat, I'll let him know you're here."

The pair stood their ground, and the receptionist cleared her throat and picked up the telephone. Thirty seconds later a tall man in a well-tailored suit appeared from a closed office door marked **Theodore F. Aaron, Associate VP**. He introduced himself and ushered the detectives into his office, making sure to close the wide double doors behind him. He sat at the head of an oval conference table and passively drummed his fingers against it as both detectives settled into their chairs. The action had the effect of him demonstrating a clear ownership of his turf, with the detectives his unwanted guests.

"I was told you gentlemen have your warrant."

Detective Grimes opened his briefcase and produced a three-page document. He slid it across the table to Mr. Aaron, who took his time reading it. As he flipped back and forth between the pages, frowning over several paragraphs, the detectives exchanged dubious expressions.

"You must understand, gentlemen, we here at PTS take our customers' privacy very seriously," Mr. Aaron said gravely. "In this age of Big Brother and even bigger litigation, we can never be too careful."

A muscle in Detective Teliford's jaw twitched. He leaned forward in his chair and said, "One of our deputies was killed last night. The woman attached to this phone number is dead too. Both are lying on refrigerated slabs down at the coroner's office with their heads blown apart. In other words, sir, we really don't give a flying fuck about your customers' privacy."

Mr. Aaron nodded deferentially but made no attempt to respond to the comment. "Well then, where would you gentlemen like to begin?"

The detectives wasted no time in delivering their instructions. The court order called for all call log and text information, and more importantly, any associated GPS positions that could be gleaned from the female victim's cell phone since seven o'clock the previous evening. The writ also required any and all PTS employees with access to this information to provide it to the detectives "without delay" or be subject to arrest and a substantial fine.

"Very well," Mr. Aaron said finally, paging one of his tech assistants. Moments later, a hipster-looking young man sporting horn-rimmed glasses and a bow tie appeared at the office door.

"Ryan, these gentlemen are from the sheriff's office. They have a valid warrant. I need a cross-reference to the number listed, but that can wait. At the risk of sounding presumptuous, I will assume our visitors wish first for GPS plots. You'll note the phone number their suspect has been using." He handed the warrant to the tech, adding, "Allegedly."

Both detectives concurred with firm nods.

The tech ushered the detectives to a bank of nearby computers and explained to them in layman's speak how the company's software plotted a cell phone's positioning. He first entered the murdered woman's number into the system. Seconds later, a call and text log going back thirty days appeared on the screen. He isolated only those going back since seven PM the previous day. Moving to another screen labeled LOCATIONS, he then entered the same time frame. As he navigated through the application, a group of animated cell phone towers appeared on the screen. Each tower in turn populated onto a map of the area in grid form before the detectives' eyes. Leaning in expectantly, they watched as coordinates began listing below each tower. Atop three of the towers sat blinking red lights. It was here that the technician drew the detectives' attention.

"All these are all towers in our network, but the three with the lights received the strongest ping signals. I'll expand the map so you can see exactly where I'm speaking of."

The detectives exchanged eager grins.

"As you can see, this map covers all of Springwood and the surrounding area. The phone we're tracking has made two outgoing calls since seven last night. Since this is an older model, we can't get exact GPS coordinates from it. But through triangulation we can get close enough."

"How close?" Detective Grimes asked, his voice urgent.

"A city block, maybe two. It depends on the location. The more interference an area has the harder it is to pin down. For instance, if that phone were lying in an empty field, I could find it quickly. But in dense woods or a busy downtown area—"

"Can you see where he is now?" Teliford asked.

"That's a problem," the tech said, keying a code into the computer. "I can only get a location for any connected outgoing or incoming signals. This model phone is a relic, something you'd dig up in a time capsule from fifteen years ago. Smartphones can be narrowed down to ten square yards. This one doesn't have ingrained GPS, so it could be as large an area as a few hundred square yards, depending on the terrain."

"Do you have to call or text the phone to get a read?"

The tech shook his head. "We can ping it without the user realizing it. It's the difference between winking at someone and shouting at them."

Both detectives nodded. "But if we called or texted him, could that improve our odds? There's a lot of real estate out there for him to hide in."

"In rare instances, but it might not be worth it."

Detective Teliford paid him no mind. He dialed the victim's phone number and instructed the tech to plot the call. Moments later, the burly detective disconnected the call, his face hopeful for a possible hit.

The tech keyed another code. "I'm not trying to tell you gentlemen how to do your jobs, but if it were me and I realized the police were calling the phone I was using—"

"We'll risk it," Teliford interjected. "Just plot it on the map." He pulled his partner aside and in a low voice directed him to get Captain Escobar on the phone. Moments later, the tech printed out a color map of the area in question and plotted a triangulated location based first on the two outgoing phone calls, as well as the one Teliford had just sent to it. Both outgoing calls had originated in or around Ridgemore Cemetery, the first going out at 10:39 the night before and the second at 8:16 this morning. Now just an hour after the second call, the incoming call plotted to a point in the same location.

Both detectives shared raised eyebrows.

Teliford referenced his notes. "Tip came in last night saying two kids saw someone suspicious inside the cemetery. Uniforms cleared it, but looks like they cancelled K-9."

"Didn't the bird clear it with thermal?"

"Cancelled that too."

"So that's where he holed up all night. Fuck." Grimes called the main dispatch line to get as many units out to the cemetery as fast as they could.

Behind them, Aaron stood with arms folded. Neither detective had heard him re-enter the area. "The plot thickens," he said, his voice dripping with melodrama.

Ignoring the comment, Teliford called Captain Escobar on his direct field cell to give him an update. After several nods and "okays," Teliford hung up and addressed his partner out of earshot of their civilian hosts. "We've got units blanketing the area as soon as they can get out there. If he's on foot, we've got him." Turning to Aaron he asked, "You guys can still track him, right?"

Aaron deferred to his employee, who shrugged. "That depends. I just sent another signal to the phone, but it isn't registering anymore. Like I told you, the battery could be dead, or he could've removed it, or the phone could be sitting at the bottom of a lake. Unless he powers it up and we get another hit, we're throwing darts."

"But for sure he was at that location two minutes ago," Teliford said, pointing to the cemetery on the map for clarification.

"I'm not saying any such thing," the tech explained, his patience appearing to grow thin. "Again, the *phone* was there. Neither I nor anyone else can be sure—"

"Yeah, yeah," Teliford said, cutting the tech off. The detective team fast-walked back to the courthouse parking lot, jumped into their shared vehicle and drove excitedly toward the cemetery. It was a ten-minute drive, longer for backup units who were spread across the county conducting coordinated sweeps. Silent, each of them remained in their thoughts during the drive. Indeed, not a lot about the case made much sense to them, least of all how the escapee had managed to evade their forces for a full twenty hours thus far. At least they'd verified with great probability that Grassle was still in the area.

Hopefully, this time he wouldn't be allowed to get away.

BACK AT HQ, Captain Escobar had been addressing a squad of specialized apprehension deputies about the possibility of the FBI's involvement when a uniformed sergeant burst into the briefing room. Exchanging a few words with the man, the captain turned to the group of lower level supervisors, his eyes alive with excitement.

"We found the car!" he exclaimed, breathless. "Chopper spotted it about ten minutes ago. Stashed in some brush just off 103, about a mile from the city limits. Forensics is on it now." Just then, his cell phone rang. Detective Teliford, with even better news. The detective team had served their warrant and had just pinged the stolen cell phone to the county's largest cemetery, on the edge of town.

Rushing from his office and toward the rear employee exit door, he cast a glare back at a lieutenant making small talk with two uniformed female deputies. "What the fuck are you three lollygagging around for?" he yelled. "Get with the garage and arrange for a wrecker if it isn't already 10-51. And get me units to Ridgemore Cemetery, now!"

The three followed the captain out the door and into the bright sunlight, each tossing the contents of their coffee cups onto the grass as they ran.

FORTY

EDDIE WATCHED THE driver wander just off the roadway and prop his foot against a headstone. The man waved one arm passionately while still speaking on his cell phone. Careful to step as quietly as possible, Eddie had just reached the road when the driver turned part-way around. Eddie froze. Just a flash of movement in the man's peripheral vision and Eddie knew he'd be a dead duck.

But the man's conversation grew even more animated; at one point he pleaded for the call's recipient to 'stop being so goddamn dramatic.' Taking advantage of the driver's distraction, Eddie bent into a half-crouch the remaining way to the hearse, grabbing the rear door handle with both hands.

This is it, bro. Don't think, just do it!

Holding his breath, Eddie tugged with just enough pressure to unlatch the door. He imagined it creaking open and the driver turning around to see him standing there, a shit-eating grin on his face that said, *What, like you've never seen someone trying to sneak into the back of a hearse before?* But the door didn't creak. Opening it just wide enough for him to slip through, Eddie crawled into the back and closed it until it rested on the latch. Realizing there was no interior door handle, he pulled on the window frame until the door latch settled home. Only then did he exhale, his heart pounding in his chest.

He found himself on a wooden floorboard, complete with a series of rollers and six metal slide rails with locking devices at the front and rear. White curtains had been drawn aside on both the rear and elongated side windows. A black satin curtain sat drawn part-way across the length of the glass partition separating the front seats from the casket portion. Deciding it to be a necessary risk, Eddie drew the partition curtain mostly closed. Deciding not to press his luck, he left the rear and side curtains as they were.

For the next several minutes he lay pressed beneath the driver side's rear window, doing his best to stay out of view of anyone who should walk along that side of the vehicle. This left him fully exposed from the rear passenger window, but he couldn't do anything about that.

His shoulder and leg throbbed miserably with each beat of his heart.

Block it out, Jules's voice came to him. *It ain't shit. Remember when we squirted that beehive with water guns, and you got stung by a hundred bees and you swelled up like a balloon?*

As if Jules were right beside him, Eddie let out a hoarse whisper, "Yeah, man, I remember."

Suddenly the driver's door opened, and the driver slipped into the seat. Eddie heard the door close, the hearse's engine revving alive. The vehicle inched forward a few feet before it stopped suddenly. Through the half-open glass partition Eddie heard the man say something that caused the blood to freeze in his veins.

"What the *hell* do you think you're doing?"

Eddie almost fainted where he lay. He waited for the partition to slide fully open and the driver to stare back at him with accusing eyes.

Then another voice, this one the high-pitched tone of a woman. It took Eddie a second to realize he was listening to the driver's speakerphone conversation.

"Why you always trippin' on me like that?" came the woman's voice.

"I'm a grown-ass man, Martie," the driver said, his voice heated. He took his foot off the brake and pulled forward again. "I ain't like them other brothers you mess with, so you just watch what you say to me."

The hearse's radio came alive and Eddie heard the electronic beeping of changing stations. Finally, the driver settled on Marvin Gaye's "What's Going On." Appropriate, Eddie thought.

"I'm working," the driver continued with a huff. "I can't come over right now." The woman uttered an inaudible curse, and then a tone that signaled to Eddie that the call had disconnected.

"Damn women," the driver bemoaned as he looked out across the rows of passing tombstones. "Y'all lucky you don't have to deal with them no more." He let out a loud cackle, apparently pleased with his own joke. He pulled the hearse around a bend in the cemetery road toward the exit.

Having a clear view out the side and back windows, Eddie felt strangely comforted being back here. He thought it bitterly ironic that, should he get killed at some point during all this, he could become only one of a few people who would ever ride in the back of a hearse both alive and dead. He thought back to the last time he'd stepped inside a church, at his mother's funeral. Then as the hearse turned left out of the cemetery and headed down the two-lane road toward Springwood proper, he wished to be kneeling on a pew just then, hoping God would hear his silent prayer. He prayed that if He were to be so gracious as to let him live out the next twelve hours in freedom, Eddie would gladly repay Him with an eternity's worth of chores in Heaven when he got there.

He'd even enlist Jules to help him.

As THE HEARSE turned out the exit and headed toward the main road back into town, five sheriff cruisers roared by. Two of them branched off in opposite directions to points east and west of the cemetery, their goal to provide an initial perimeter until dispatched backup units arrived. Two others sped through the open gate, snaking their way along the main cemetery road, and stopping near the spot designated by detectives monitoring the suspect's cell phone information. The final cruiser blocked the exit, the deputy stepping from the vehicle and retrieving his carbine from the trunk. He stood guard in that position for several minutes until the *whump* of helicopter rotors approached.

A team of K-9s arrived soon after. They tracked Eddie's scent to the tree above his mother's grave. But after searching it, and combing every inch of the sprawling cemetery, the two dozen deputies dispatched there discovered he was long gone.

FORTY-ONE

THE MESSAGE HAD been clear: death in the end.

But first, a slow, grueling torture.

As he disassembled his MP5 and began the mindless task of clean-ing it, Paolo felt his pulse quicken at the thought of causing another human being pain. It had been months since his last such job—the abduction, torture, and murder of a rising star in the Florida politi-cal arena. Paolo rarely questioned Hood on the particulars of why a certain individual had been targeted, but he had on that occasion. 'Of course, you have a right to know,' Hood had answered, placing a hand on Paolo's shoulder. Even then Paolo had detected a certain warmth from the man's giant hand, almost tenderness. 'This person threat-ens to keep us from finishing what we started,' Hood had explained. 'There are many bad people in government. He is one of them.'

Not that Paolo needed any reassurance about whom he had been assigned to dispose of. On this occasion had he begun to feel the love of his life, his very soul, begin to drift away from him ever slightly. The change was subtle, like the sun blocked momentarily by a passing cloud. But he'd noticed it. Paolo had long known of Mathi-as's penchant for young girls. And so far, Paolo had managed to look the other way, chalking up the feelings that swirled within him as those of a jealous teenager, not fit to distract him so, and certainly not enough to cause him to fail in his assignment.

His last job had been gratifying for several reasons. First, the sheer rush of the abduction itself had been like a drug. So easy, ringing the doorbell and forcing his way inside. Then the rising thrill of binding the man hand to foot, naked, while the man pleaded for his life. Only after failing to gain the most prized information did Paolo allow himself the personal gratification of causing true pain. For over an hour he had systematically destroyed the man's will to live. His favorite beginning technique—placing a thin cloth over the mouth and nose as the victim lay on their back, and Paolo pouring water over it. This psychological mimicking of drowning proved so horrific few who suffered its application lasted for more than sixty seconds. Amazingly, the man had held steadfast in his resolve, persisting through a full ten minutes and repeated 'drownings' while still refusing to disclose the identity of his political informant. Paolo had then switched to the more physical aspect of the session by using snub-nosed pliers to create fractures in the metacarpal bones of the man's hands and feet. Still, the man had held firm.

Impressed, Paolo had then reached into his briefcase and extracted a series of ever-widening needles which he inserted one by one through the man's testicles. When at last the man begged for Paolo to stop, swearing to tell him whatever he wanted to know as long as he promised not to hurt his informant, only then did Paolo relent and allow him to recover. Breathless, the man had revealed the informant to be none other than his own son. This revelation, above all else, had caused Paolo the greatest pleasure. The exact moment a man sold his soul for the chance at relief from pain. Such a mortal fault, the fear of death or discomfort.

Weeping, the man had begged for Paolo to spare his son's life in exchange for his own. Paolo had then removed a clear plastic bag from his briefcase and held it tight over the man's head. Kicking the man's chair backward and sitting atop his chest, Paolo had leaned in to watch the life slowly drain from his eyes. Two minutes later, feeling the man's struggles fade to intermittent twitches, then to nothing, Paolo had stood and tilted his head toward the ceiling in exultation. Somewhere deep within he had felt the man's soul enter his own, a sublime bonding of humanity he had not felt since his days handling suspected terrorists. No other employment would have given him this release, he knew, and certainly such behavior conducted in normal civilian life would never be possible. That Hood would be the deciding voice in the unlikely event Paolo was ever caught and prosecuted was the brilliance of their irrevocable alliance.

And now Grassle.

Aside from Hood's own motives, Paolo himself now held a personal grudge. The fox had escaped him last night. Worse, he'd managed to injure Paolo's body *and* pride. Never had anything remotely similar happened to him before. Thinking back to his thirty-two prior victims, he could not remember a single significant injury to himself. None of them had ever escaped with their lives, let alone escaped at all. As he stroked the gleaming metal of the weapon before him, Paolo's hands trembled with rage. He would take extra time with Grassle when he found him. He would exult as he never had before when the thing had been completed. And when the time came for him and Hood to consummate the silent love they shared, he would remember the look in Grassle's dying eyes as he discovered that release he had never experienced before.

Control yourself, a voice inside him spoke. *Do not allow your emotions to overcome you.*

Grassle had been in his sights, literally. But Paolo had made the uncharacteristic mistake of hesitating. Just a moment had been long enough for the resourceful young man to gain an edge. In Paolo's experience, few things remained more powerful a motivator than the belief of imminent death. He'd seen it countless times, in people of all nationalities and faiths. The only wild card in those scenarios had been individuals who didn't fear death—or someone such as himself who already felt they were dead.

As Paolo polished the MP5's barrel, the police band radio he'd been listening so intently to for the past fifteen hours buzzed with a report that the dead deputy's cruiser had been located. Setting the cloth down, he took out his map and plotted several points. It could be assumed that Grassle was either on foot or had switched vehicles since ditching the cruiser. Paolo decided on the former. Consulting his notes, his mind began its usual tack—follow the facts, ignore speculation, then use his well-honed intuition to solve the riddle of what would happen next. The hunter tracking his prey. As he'd learned long ago, a hunted animal feels death stalking it. Humans, the most highly evolved animals on the planet, were no different.

Checking his map once again, Paolo traced his finger along the plotted points of Grassle's known sightings since his escape. The points zigzagged first in a northeasterly line from the jail, then changed direction southwest through miles of brush and orange groves until finally pointing toward the outskirts of Springwood proper. Along this route, Paolo noted the large cemetery where Grassle reportedly used the woman's cell phone (he'd finally checked in with Escobar's people for an intelligence update, much to the captain's frustration). The cemetery sat only three quarters of a mile from where the stolen cruiser had been found. Paolo pondered this. When he extended the line toward an imaginary point several miles further from Grassle's last known position, the tip of his finger settled on a mostly residential neighborhood. He recalled Clarissa Fulton's home being near there. Plotting her address on his map, Paolo confirmed this. Clarissa herself had told him about Eddie visiting her the day before his arrest. *Why*, had been the question. An obvious answer could be love, the ultimate mountain mover. But that fell under the category of assumption, and Paolo had learned that making assumptions was akin to following a known false path. Each step you took led you further and further away from your goal. Instead, he went back over his own notes, taking time to reconsider his original theory of what Grassle intended—that it was not his goal to run away from something, but rather toward something.

Or some*one*.

Not Clarissa. Grassle's relationship with her had been too damaged, and she currently resided with her fiancé. Grassle had no living relatives, the last of whom—an aunt from Oregon—died the year before from an embolism. Paolo had just conducted a search of Grassle's home telephone line, which had revealed only three contacts in the three weeks since it had been activated in his name—his ex Clarissa, his new employer, and Jules Sanders, now deceased.

Only one option remained—Grassle's child, a five-year-old son he had never met. Father and son had been scheduled to meet for the first time the morning following the former's arrest. Paolo felt that without any connection to the child and with the severed relationship to the mother, it was unlikely Grassle would seek the boy out. For what purpose? He could not hope for any continued relationship. Grassle himself, described as intelligent and his resourcefulness already proven, also could not expect to remain free for long. In today's environment, the average fugitive was recaptured within twenty-four hours. Any longer than that, and abundant resources and outside assistance would be needed. Grassle had neither.

Having turned off the air-conditioning to his office and opened the windows, Paolo closed his eyes and allowed his mind to free itself of outside interference. The sounds of traffic outside melted away. His breathing slowed to eight respirations a minute. He fell deeper inside himself than he had ever gone, until he seemed to transform into something else entirely. His mind worked like a movie reel, flipping past frames at speeds so fast he began to see the problem less as a series of pictures laid out before him, and more as a full-motion animation playing out in real time. As he watched in his mind's eye, he found it easier to work through the questions still surrounding the case, concentrating on the elimination of impossible scenarios then working backward tediously, patiently, until the answer found him so suddenly his eyes snapped open and he sat erect in his seat, his breathing coming fast in his growing excitement. Of course. It had to be true. The answer to Grassle's plan seemed as plain to him now as his own body seated in his chair.

Paolo returned the sub-machine gun to its case, deciding this job would best be served without it. The pistol—and more so, the knife—would be best, more personal. Unsheathing the blade, he studied the five inches of carbonized steel, imagining it slicing into flesh and crunching through bone, releasing Grassle's still-beating heart into his powerful hands. Paolo sheathed the knife and attached it to his left ankle, folding his pants leg back over it before pushing his way out the door into the dazzling sunshine of the day.

A beautiful day for death.

FORTY-TWO

"**Bad one today?**" Chet asked over the edge of his newspaper.

Closing her eyes, Riggins massaged her scalp with her fingertips. "Feels like an elephant broke loose in my head."

She could feel Chet staring at her from across the kitchen table, the usual thoughtfulness in his eyes now boring into her. She didn't need to see his expression to know he looked worried. Chet had always known how to read her. His strong, silent intuition always did a number on her conscience, and after a failed attempt to push her worries away, she opened her eyes and sighed.

"It's Eddie. I just can't seem to shake the feeling something bad is going to happen to him."

Chet raised his short, black-as-night eyebrows. "Bad—as in he might get hurt after he broke out of jail on his own? He's got to do some looking in the mirror if he wants to blame someone for the spot he's in."

She settled her half-lidded gaze onto him. "You're right, as always. But it doesn't change the fact that I share some of the blame for him even being in the position he's in."

"You didn't run out of that store with a gun in your waistband."

"True again. But we arrested him before we knew a witness could corroborate his story. I know better than anyone that folks get hooked up for being in the wrong place at the wrong time, but it doesn't always mean life or death. I'd bet you a month of cooking there's a dozen people or more sitting inside County right now that didn't have squat to do with their charge."

He regarded the ceiling, deep in thought. "A month, huh?"

"Yep. And I'd even throw in dessert," she said, distracted from her original thought long enough to smile at him.

Chet placed the paper down on the table. He took a long sip from his favorite coffee mug, the one with a giant smiley face printed on the side with the caption *Smile, God loves you!* "I was waiting for you to tell me what was wrong. I was hoping it was this Eddie deal, and not something that had to do with us."

She moved her fingers over her forehead now and shook her head. "Of course not, Chet. I just don't know what to do about all this. I'm normally good about processing things like this. As shook up as I was about Cokley dying, I knew there was nothing I could have actively done to save him. The counselor even agreed that his death meant I was able to start accepting it right away."

Chet nodded his apparent understanding. "But Eddie's different because he's alive out there. He still has a chance."

She stared hard at him, her eyes wide with realization. "Yes. He's running around in the woods with some maniac trying to kill him, for Lord knows why. We're after him too, and I can imagine some nervous rookie or an angry veteran who'd been friends with Hammer having an itchy trigger finger."

"But you're forgetting something. All he has to do is give himself up to the first cop he sees. Why all this running? Why steal a dead woman's cell phone just so he can call you and say he appreciates you treating him good, and that he didn't kill that Hammer guy? He could say all that later from jail, or even from the courtroom."

She huffed, annoyance rising within her—not at him but at the system, and fate, and everything in between. Of course Chet was right. Again. The fact his logic melded perfectly with his easy delivery made the words he spoke that much more credible. And then, as if he could also read her mind, he stood from his chair and came around to stand behind her. Placing his large fingers on her temples, he pulled her head back into his body and massaged her that way for minutes, hours it seemed, without saying a word. She purred—a vixen to her fox of a man.

When he finished, she was jelly. That coldness that had begun to creep into her spirit turned warm again. She stood, a bit wobbly, amazed at how easily he had rid her of the migraine that had threatened to shroud her in near-blinding pain. Even the hives that had begun to blossom once again across her arms were now abated. When she'd finished dressing, having arranged to meet Heinke at headquarters due to her second phone call from Eddie, Riggins paused in the kitchen doorway and asked him for a favor.

"Anything for my boo."

"If Eddie doesn't make it out of this alive, will you play me something happy on your guitar when I get home? I have a feeling I'm gonna need it."

TWENTY MINUTES LATER, Detective Riggins walked into Lieutenant Heinke's office, shut the door behind her and flopped down in a chair opposite his desk. The balding lieutenant had been holding a half-eaten fast-food breakfast sandwich in one hand while leafing through a case file when his diminutive protégé entered. Regarding Riggins above the rim of his glasses, he tossed the remainder of the sandwich onto its wrapper and wiped his fingers on a napkin. A fly buzzing nearby promptly settled onto a bit of egg poking out between the English muffin halves. If the aging lieutenant cared, he didn't bother showing it.

"We've got a hundred folks in the field looking for Grassle and they haven't even sniffed him in twenty-four hours. You get put on admin duty and he calls you twice. Maybe you can give me some lottery numbers to play," he deadpanned.

Riggins shrugged. "Sometimes you're the nail, sometimes you're the hammer."

This last word provided somber pause for them both.

"I can't believe he's dead," she said, shaking her head. "It's bad enough him getting killed, but the way it happened was just—awful."

Heinke nodded slowly. "Prints came back from last night's scene."

"And?" She scooted forward in her chair, expectant.

"Grassle's full palm print on the pepper spray canister, and right index on the depressor. No residue on Hammer or the old woman."

"He *was* telling me the truth," Riggins said, introspective.

"Seems that way," Heinke said. "And Hammer's gun was still holstered when we found him. Full magazine with one still in the pipe. Two full spare mags too."

They locked eyes, seeming to think the same thing. She said it first.

"There was definitely someone else there. Safe to say a second suspect took the murder weapon with him."

He nodded. "This Eddie Grassle may be a phone thief and a jail breaker, but he doesn't seem to be a liar."

A knock came at the office door just then. When Heinke shouted, "What is it?" a serious-looking man in a shirt and tie poked his head in.

"Internal Affairs is here to speak with you, sir." The man glanced down at Riggins before looking back to Heinke for his instructions.

"What have I always said about my office blinds being closed?" Heike asked, his face stern.

The man thought before answering. "It means you aren't to be disturbed."

"Unless what?"

The man cleared his throat. "Unless the building is on fire, sir."

Heinke sniffed the air. "Funny, I don't smell smoke. Do you, Detective Riggins?"

"No, sir," she managed, looking away to hide the grin spreading across her face.

The man muttered an apology then promptly shut the door.

"Goddamn IA," Heinke said, picking up the remnants of his breakfast sandwich and taking a bite. "We've got a dead deputy and all they care about is why my monthly report is late."

"What's the latest?" Riggins asked.

"Helicopter spotted the missing cruiser about an hour ago. A few miles from the shooting scene. Dogs got a hit, but the trail ended at the cemetery."

"Any reason to think he commandeered a different vehicle?"

"Unknown. Grimes and Teliford seem to think he's heading out of state."

Riggins shook her head. "He's staying close. And I believe him when he says he's going to turn himself in today."

Heinke took another bite of his sandwich and threw the rest down on the wrapper again. "Is that your professional opinion, or your personal one?"

She leveled her gaze at him. "Both. Does it matter?"

"Yes," he said. "He's calling you, no one else."

"And? I gave him my card. I told him to call me if he needed to talk."

"I'd imagine now would be a perfect time for him to turn himself in, then. For the sake of argument, let's take him at his word. Some whack job is trying to kill him. Mob hit, guy is mad Grassle banged his old lady, whatever. He has access to a phone, which he used to call you not once, but twice. And he's turning himself in anyway by midnight. What's he afraid of, all our cruisers turning into pumpkins?"

Riggins bit her lip and searched the ceiling for inspiration. "I don't know. I just can't get over the fact that from day one, he's been consistent with the truth. He says he had no idea his buddy was going to rob the store. I think it's safe to assume that someone complicit in a robbery wouldn't react by giving the victim CPR. He denies killing Hammer and the woman, then states he used the deputy's pepper spray on an unknown assailant. Print and eyewitness evidence support that."

Heinke frowned. "But let's not forget this—he broke out of jail. If I'm innocent, the last thing I'm going to do is escape just to turn myself back in a couple days later. It ruins my credibility."

"That's just it," Riggins said, seeming to almost grasp an idea. "I don't think he cares about his credibility."

Heinke pointed at her. "Careful. You just created an inconsistency in your own argument."

"No sir, I don't think so. When my dad was alive, he was always into war history. On TV, in books, museums, you name it. I remember him once talking about the Japanese fighting to the death on those Pacific islands, how they'd do those charges, whatever they were called."

"Banzai."

"Yes. My dad said hundreds of them would fix their bayonets and charge our machine gun nests, knowing they'd get killed."

"They were in a war, Alice. Us against them."

"No. I mean, I don't think so, sir. I wasn't into war history like my dad was, but he did teach me one thing. He said the enemy wasn't necessarily trying to win the battle."

Heinke frowned. "Now you're losing me."

"They were out of ammunition, on their last breath. Sure, they were fanatical, but they still understood there was no hope of winning. But they did have something left to prove, even if their time on earth was near its end."

Heinke raised his eyebrows in anticipation.

"An *ideal,* sir. Surrender was beneath them. They were not going to win. The only thing left was to die charging straight ahead, the way their samurai ancestors did before them. It was an honor for them to die in battle. Winning isn't just about raising a flag. Sometimes it's giving yourself up for a greater cause."

For nearly a full minute, Lieutenant Heinke sat speechless, considering what she'd said. When he spoke again, his voice had the tone of a parent who'd just learned something important from his child. "Your dad was a smart man, Alice. And I think you may be onto something. I'm an old dog, and old dogs like to lay in the sun. We're past the point of chasing balls. But you—" He jabbed a finger toward her. "You've always thought outside the box. It's what helps make you so good at what you do. Find out what you can from here. The sheriff still insists you stay on desk duty until further notice. I don't agree with it one bit, but at least your emergency suspension has been cut short."

She nodded. "I understand, sir."

As she got up to leave, Heinke said, "One more thing. The last time I spoke with your dad, he told me something I forgot until just now. I'm glad I remembered to tell you."

Riggins looked back at him, a wan look on her face.

"He said he knew he was dying, but that he wouldn't trade living another twenty years for the guarantee that you'd live even one extra day. I think you were *his* ideal."

Riggins smiled a melancholy sort of smile. "Thank you, sir," she said. This time she remembered to close the door.

LEAVING HEINKE'S OFFICE, Riggins wove her way through the lines of open workstations until she made eye contact with Detective Sanchez. He stood near the water cooler, talking to a pretty blond Riggins recognized as Captain Escobar's new secretary. Sanchez had just said something to the woman, who smiled as she twirled a lock of hair around her finger.

"Hey, Rig, I thought the principal was sending you home for bad behavior. Blinds drawn and everything," Sanchez joked. He said goodbye to the secretary and walked with Riggins toward her desk. "What'd you guys talk about?"

"Eddie calling me, mostly. And that I'm still on admin duty until further notice."

"That's some bullshit," Sanchez said, disgusted. "Someone's definitely throwing shade. Any idea who yet?"

Riggins shook her head. "But I was onto something. An idea of what Eddie might be up to. Then I lost it."

"Maybe he'll do us all a favor and walk right into the lobby downstairs."

"However it happens, he told me it'll be by midnight tonight," she said.

"Who is he, Cinderella?"

"Heinke basically said the same thing," she said, sitting and switching on her computer. She logged on to the agency's intranet site and pulled up the active call list. A quick scan resulted in no current leads in the search.

"Eddie said he needed to do something first," she said, moving back to her previous thought. "That tells me he's staying local. Obviously, something important enough to risk his life for before he turns himself in."

Sanchez shook his head. "What's up with this guy, he breaks out of jail just to run some errands? He's Signal-Twenty."

"No, Sanny, not crazy. He knows exactly what he needs to do. And I one hundred percent believe him when he says he's going to turn himself in by tonight, assuming he doesn't get caught first." She paused. "A favor?"

"Name it."

"The case info for Clarissa Fulton. I feel the answer to what Eddie is up to is there. L.T. said he had no issue with me helping out, as long as I'm not active in the field."

Sanchez nodded. "Done. Am I giving it to you or are you stealing it?"

"Definitely stealing it. Leave it on your desk and go grab some coffee."

He turned to leave but she caught him by the arm. "Thank you, Sanny. I mean it. I wouldn't trade having you as a partner for anyone else. Remember two things. First, if you always do what's right in your heart, you can live with yourself no matter how things turn out."

Sanchez smiled, forlorn. A look came to his eyes that betrayed true regret at the thought he may never work with Riggins again. Forces had been set in motion that each of them understood meant she may wrap up her limited time on the job without ever working in the field again. Each of them knew their detective assignments were a privilege, one that could be given and taken away by the sheriff without cause. With him standing and her seated, they shared a silent reflection that conveyed a measure of common respect. They'd been through a lot in their year as partners, and part of the look she gave him communicated her opinion that he was finally ready to work on his own, that she'd taught him everything she knew and that he'd be alright after she left. And his silent response offered her a depth of appreciation he would probably never be able to repay. Despite all his frat-boy jokes and dark views of the world, he was a cop through and through. And he had become a better one because of her.

He walked toward his cubicle, then logged on to his computer and printed out the case file Riggins had asked for. Before shoving the file into a manila envelope, he scribbled a message on a Post-it Note and slapped it onto the file's cover sheet. Checking to see if anyone was watching, he laid the file on his desk before disappearing into the employee break room. When he came out holding a cup of fresh coffee a minute later, the file was gone. He looked up just in time to see Riggins pushing the elevator call button, the manila envelope tucked firmly under her right arm.

"Hey, Rig!" Sanchez called out as she stepped into the elevator. "You never told me the second thing to remember."

Before the elevator door closed, Riggins shot a tight-lipped smile toward the captain's new blond secretary.

"Never shit where you sleep."

FORTY-THREE

I'M IN THE CITY.

Eddie lay motionless in the back of the hearse, listening as the driver ended his animated cell phone conversation. From his position, he had been able to see well enough through the windows, first watching only treetops zoom by, then scattered streetlamps, and finally recognizable buildings. Soon, the hearse came to a stop under a concrete awning, where the driver cut the engine before hopping out. Eddie heard a nearby door open and close, followed by silence. He waited another thirty seconds before daring to sit up far enough to peek through the window, reading the sign on the side of the building. They were back at the funeral home.

He scooted painfully to the rear door to let himself out when he remembered there was no inner door handle. Of course. Riders occupying the rear of a hearse weren't in much of a position to be opening doors. Casting aside the curtain that separated the rear compartment from the driver's seat, he slid the window all the way open and painfully squeezed through the narrow opening before plopping onto the front seat. He unlocked the passenger door, exited, and shut it behind him as quietly as he could. Wasting no time, he hobbled around the nearest corner of the building and flattened himself against the brick siding, just as a vehicle swung into the parking lot. The driver made eye contact with Eddie before he had a chance to turn around. Thinking quickly, he knelt and pretended to pick weeds in the manicured grass. Highly suspicious, he knew, but better than caving to the overwhelming urge inside himself to run.

Eddie stood and walked to the sidewalk. Thankfully, foot traffic was light in the area, just a young couple walking away from him on the opposite side of the street. With no other vehicles coming from either direction, he made his way down the sidewalk toward an intersection, doing his best to conceal his limp. Averting his eyes from an approaching car, he waited until it passed by before he crossed the street. His heart pounded in his ears. As he climbed up the opposite curb, he spied the front end of a vehicle sitting at a side street ahead of him. *A cruiser?* As if reading his mind, the vehicle pulled out and turned his direction. His blood turned cold when he spied the blue and red-colored light bar atop the vehicle.

Act normal. The only people who seem out of place are people who act out of place. If the cop makes eye contact with you, don't avoid it, and just smile.

Just as the cruiser came beside him, it stopped. But the cop must have done so to read something on his in-car computer because as Eddie passed by, he saw the deputy looking down and to his right at the screen. Moving up the block, he took the next left up a side street and recognized an old ice cream parlor he and Jules had visited numerous times as kids. A pleasant memory came to him: he and Jules sitting behind the parlor, licking their ice cream cones while they watched the creek below. Jules had dared Eddie to disrobe and jump into the stream naked. Finishing his cone, Eddie had done just that. Jules had followed, whooping and hollering as he ran down the short hill and into the cool water. That had happened in summer, and the creek had been high from the seasonal rains. The boys had frolicked in the waist-deep waters until an old woman living in a nearby house had run them off with a broom.

Taking the alley entrance that he knew would lead him behind the shop, Eddie turned left behind the businesses. The same cruiser he'd seen moments before moved toward him. Creeping along the back of the businesses from a block away, the cop had him pinned. If he turned around and went the way he'd come, Eddie felt the suspicious movement would surely give him away. But if he kept walking toward the cop, the cop would naturally make eye contact with him, if not stop him and ask what he was doing there. Feeling he had no choice in the matter, Eddie flattened himself against the building and froze. Due to the large trash dumpster next to him, he remained hidden from the cop's view. But if the cop kept coming his direction, he'd see him, and then Eddie would find it impossible to explain his presence even if he wasn't immediately recognized.

If you stop me and tell me to put my hands on the hood, I'm going to make you shoot me. Because I'm not going back. Not now. Not after everything I've done already. Please, God, just keep on going...

Eddie hoped against hope the cruiser would turn at the side street. It didn't. Instead, it continued down the alley toward where he stood. Just half a block away now. Eddie's stomach sank. This was it. After everything he'd gone through over the last twenty-four hours, just a half mile or so from where Liam sat inside his classroom, it would all end here in a filthy alley, probably by some pimple-faced deputy three weeks on the job. And how would the headlines read tomorrow? ESCAPED KILLER STRUCK DOWN BY HERO COP. Or maybe ON THE LAM NO MORE—GRASSLE CAPTURED.

Eddie made a snap decision. If his entire existence would end in the next several moments, he wanted to retain some measure of control over it. Spreading his arms wide, he stepped out from behind the dumpster, ready to release a shout, one he hoped would be loud enough for Liam to miraculously hear had he been outside just then for recess or some other outdoor activity. As he faced the cruiser, just twenty yards away now, Eddie had just begun to shout when he saw the cruiser suddenly stop, the cop turning his head toward the rear of the businesses. Eddie's mouth snapped closed and he stood perfectly still, confused as to what was happening. If the deputy faced forward, he'd see Eddie as plain as day. From his body language, he appeared to be searching for something. But what? There didn't seem to be anything back here except several employee access doors dotting the brick walls.

A moment later, as if on cue, one of the doors opened and a young woman peeked cautiously out into the alley. She wore some sort of work uniform and had her hair tied up in a bun. As she leaned out the doorway and craned her head left, Eddie realized something. She and the cop knew each other. Taking the opportunity, Eddie ducked back behind the dumpster just as the woman looked in his direction. His heart thundering in his chest, he bit into his fist to keep himself from crying out. When he heard the shop door slam shut, Eddie dared peek around the edge of the dumpster. He watched the woman open one of the cruiser's back doors and slip into the back seat, giggling as she went. The deputy stepped out and checked in both directions. Apparently satisfied no one was watching, he removed his gun belt and tossed it onto the front seat before opening the driver's side back door and joining the woman in the back seat.

Waiting for several minutes, Eddie eventually saw the cruiser begin to rock noticeably back and forth. Groaning, he stood to his feet and limped to the opposite side of the alley. Not wishing to go back the way he'd come, he decided to risk it and edged past the cruiser. Stealing a peek through the tinted rear window, he was able to make out a pair of women's bare feet suspended in the air and the deputy's naked ass pumping away from above.

Hurrying away, he came to a street lined with tattered old homes he recognized. Finding the first two houses fenced and with dogs roaming their backyards, he soon discovered a house at the end of the block with open yards and that appeared to be unoccupied. Crouching as low as he could, he made his way to the back and half-slid down a short embankment into the creek bed below. The water was much shallower than he remembered, just ankle deep. Sitting on the embankment and removing his boots, Eddie placed his aching, blistered feet into the cool water, moaning with pleasure as he did. After a glorious minute of this, he knelt and cupped both hands into the water, slurping so fast bolts of bright light flashed across his vision. Life flooded through every cell of his body, it seemed. Invigorated, he knelt and drank until he dared drink no more, fearing cramps. He splashed water onto his face and hair, washing away the worst of the grime and blood there. Deciding the too-small boots were more a benefit to him than a discomfort, he tied their laces together and draped them over his shoulder before making his way downstream.

To his knowledge, no one had seen him yet. But he knew full well that all it would take was a bit of bad luck, or someone at the edge of their yard happening to glance down at just the right time, to see him limping along the creek. And now would be the cruelest time to be discovered, since in just another hundred yards he expected to find himself at the school he prayed Liam sat in.

FORTY-FOUR

THE SHERIFF HQ building buzzed with activity both inside and out. Commanders yelled orders and deputies, both uniformed and plain-clothed, darted in every direction. Radios squawked urgent messages, and on the marked concrete pad the helicopter had just landed. Sheriff Driscoll, one hand planted atop his Stetson to keep it from flying away in the rotor wash, bent as he walked toward the awaiting chopper. Despite his fear of flying, he had expressed his desire to scout the search area firsthand. A tangible apprehension had begun to ripple its way through the chain of command. The sheriff was fully aware his decision to permit civilians in their midst had befuddled the troops, especially seeing as how the one civilian of note, Paolo Bruzzi, had seemingly vanished since the Hammer killing. Making the gesture of flying for the first time in twenty years had been one way for the sheriff to dispel the growing dissension within his own ranks, a feeling of disquiet the old lawman felt very well aware of.

Detective Sanchez watched all of this from a second-story office window. His eyes scanned the horizon and found a sea of trees in every direction. Grassle was still out there somewhere. Amazingly, a full twenty-two hours after his improbable escape, the virtual army amassed against him was no closer to finding him than they had been in the incident's early stages. Even less so, in fact. Sanchez mouthed a silent curse in Spanish then made his way to an office door marked

LT. HEINKE. He knocked before poking his head inside. "Hey, Lieu, got a sec?"

The balding lieutenant looked up over the rim of his glasses. "I'm busy, Sanchez. You have half a second."

Sanchez plopped down on a chair and ran a hand through his hair.

"I know you told me to report to Teliford and Grimes if I had any issues with my current caseload, but I'm not sure they're a good fit for me. Professionally speaking."

Heinke eyed the Latin detective suspiciously. "Detective Sanchez, if you're trying to lobby for Detective Riggins to be put back on field duty, you're barking up the wrong tree. It wasn't my decision."

"I understand, sir. I just thought—"

"It's not healthy to overthink things. My therapist told me that too."

"Yes, sir." Sanchez made sure to keep his tone respectful, despite not wanting to concede the point. "I wasn't meaning to have her brought back formally. Just to have a familiar shoulder to lean on. For my own sake until I get a bit more comfortable."

"How are your current cases looking?" Heinke asked, refusing for now to directly address the point.

Sanchez nodded. "Close to closing the Smith case already. The other two are a bit more complicated. If I had Rig to run things by, I'd probably get them done faster."

Heinke removed his glasses and wiped the lenses with the cuff of his shirtsleeve. "And you're sure Riggins didn't put you up to this?"

"No, sir. I mean, yes, I'm sure. She didn't say a thing about this, and she wouldn't. She's too proud. I could confer with her and still manage not to step on Grimes's toes. I'd say the same for Teliford, but he's got feet like a gorilla. You ever see him in sandals you'll know what I mean." Sanchez chuckled at his own joke.

Heinke, seemingly unamused, stared long and hard at his young detective. "You're not telling me something."

"Lieu," Sanchez implored, placing a hand over his heart. "I would never lie to you. I respect you too much. She has no idea I'm even in here, and—"

"Alright, alright," Heinke said, waving to cut him off. "Stop groveling and just make sure to run everything by the other two as well."

Satisfied, Sanchez thanked him and left. Seconds later, a plain-clothed detective poked his head through the office door and pointed to Heinke's muted television in the corner. "Lieutenant, press conference is on."

Heinke unmuted the television and leaned back in his chair. Several individuals he recognized bookended a podium. Captain Escobar spoke about the search radius and his belief that Grassle was still in the immediate area. Heinke also recognized a well-respected member of the apprehension team, Sergeant Wertz, who took over the microphone and said something about bloodhounds and helicopters being hampered by late-night rains. To the sergeant's right loomed a figure that caused a chill to creep up Heinke's spine—State Attorney Hood. Even through the medium of television, he seemed to be staring directly at Heinke. With black, emotionless eyes and his bald head gleaming in the fluorescent lighting, he seemed as imposing a figure as ever. Heinke couldn't help but feel sorry for anyone who ever got in the man's way.

When Sergeant Wertz finished speaking, Hood took the podium and commented on how the State would fully prosecute anyone found assisting Grassle. Additionally, he noted that Grassle was expected to soon be charged with capital murder for the deaths of Deputy Hammer and the Downing woman. His upper lip curling with unmasked disgust, Hood promised to seek the death penalty if Grassle were captured alive.

If...

FOR HIS PART, Detective Sanchez caught the conference on one of the downstairs lobby televisions. As soon as it ended, he hurried to the secured staff parking lot and pulled past the jam of cruisers and news vehicles, whose myriad antennas looked to him like so many metallic fingers reaching to the heavens. *Goddamn media hounds.*

Five minutes later he pulled into a Starbucks lot and found Detective Riggins sitting anxiously at a table inside. Between her fingers sat the note Sanchez had placed onto the Fulton file: *Meet me for coffee, normal spot?*

"I really owe you," she said, looking up from the file.

Sanchez sat opposite her and patted himself on the back. "When I was younger, the ladies called me 'The Postman.' Wanna know why?"

"I can only imagine."

"Because I always deliver," he said, beaming.

"Did you really just say that?"

"I take my reputation seriously, Rig. I can't be caught half-stepping." Then, "Hope you don't mind, but I asked Lieu if I could run my cases by you."

"Which was just an excuse for backdoor work on the Grassle case."

"Exactly."

She nodded, pursing her lips. "You're learning."

"Sometimes my awesomeness takes a while to show itself."

Despite the headache that had just conceived itself in the space behind her eyes, Riggins began poring over the file with him. Coming to a particular page of interest, she compared a notation to her own notes she'd kept and wrinkled her brow. She hadn't been sure what a clue would even look like in this sea of text, but a passage she'd scanned over in the Fulton file now seemed relevant once she compared it to one in her notes about Eddie Grassle.

"Clarissa said that Eddie had never seen his son, which is true," Riggins said thoughtfully. "But that was going to change."

"You're talking about him planning on seeing his kid that morning?" Sanchez asked.

"Yes. Look here." She showed him a passage in the file. "Clarissa visited Eddie in jail after he got booked for the robbery. She told him that he'd fucked up one time too many and that she refused to ever bring his boy to visit him in jail."

"But we knew that."

"I know, but for some reason I've been running that through my head ever since he escaped yesterday. I haven't been able to think of a single other reason he'd have to wait until tonight to turn himself in."

"He's trying to get back at his ex?"

"No. That's not Eddie's makeup. Even in his interrogation he seemed to take responsibility for what he'd done. He's never said a bad word about Clarissa."

"It's not like he can expect to ever have a relationship with the kid, then," Sanchez added. "She won't bring him to visit, and she moved out of state."

Riggins corrected him. "*Moving*, Sanny. They haven't left yet."

He read the section of notes she pointed out to him. "She said they're leaving tomorrow. Saturday."

"Yes, so the kid is still here. Eddie mentioned midnight tonight, specifically. What other reason would he have to wait until then to turn himself in?"

Sanchez looked at her like she'd just grown another head. "You think he's trying to kidnap his kid?"

"Not kidnap, Sanny. You're thinking like a cop. Try to think like a parent."

His eyes narrowed. "Hmm. I'm thinking like that, and I'm not sure I like it."

She slapped his hand. "I'm serious. Think."

He did, turning pragmatic. "I'm a dad who's never seen my kid. My baby mama is cutting me out of his life forever. I've just escaped from jail. I call the detective in my case and tell her I'm turning myself in almost at the exact time my kid is due to move out of state."

Riggins nodded. "Go on."

"I don't have any local contacts. No family. I'm not blaming anyone else for my position, and my psychological profile doesn't suggest I have any illusions of hopeful existence beyond maybe a few hours of freedom. I can only hope to accomplish a specific, limited goal."

"Remember that this is your flesh and blood."

Sanchez went quiet for a second before continuing. "I was in love with my son's mother. We were young and happy. But then I bought a five-year stretch for my friend because I knew he'd do twenty and get eaten alive. I have about twelve hours left before my deadline. A man I don't know is trying to kill me, but instead of saving myself by turning myself in, I keep risking my life by staying free. There's only one thing in my world that makes sense."

Riggins waited for him to connect the final dot on his own. Sanchez studied the ceiling, almost grasping the idea. Then, as if a lightbulb had turned on inside him, his eyes widened with a sudden realization. "Holy shit, he just wants to *meet* his son."

"Yes!" Riggins squeezed his hands tight. "I just can't figure out how he intends on doing it. He's literally running for his life, while evading us at the same time. He has no access to his kid, and even if he tried showing up at the house, Clarissa would call us before he even made it past the front door. That's not to say if the stepfather didn't shoot him first."

They sat in silence for a beat, digesting this. Finally, Riggins told Sanchez to relay their thoughts to Heinke. He did, hanging up a few minutes later.

"What did he say?" she asked.

"He said it sounded far-fetched, but to run it by Teliford and Grimes."

"It's worth a try."

Sanchez did just that, and even from listening to one side of the conversation, Riggins could tell the conversation hadn't gone well.

"Grimes said it sounded ridiculous, and to stick to my own cases," Sanchez said.

"But how the hell can Eddie expect to do it?" Riggins asked, mostly to herself. "He can't just stop by his ex's place and have a meet and greet. Besides, every cop within fifty miles is looking for him." She folded her arms across her chest. "That's the part I'm trying to figure out. I just don't know how he plans to do it."

Her face clouded over in thought, and her mind appeared to drift to darker places. Deciding it best to continue her brainstorm after her headache abated, she finished her coffee and thanked Sanchez again for the Fulton file.

"And just so you know," Sanchez said, "if anything bad happens and those IA clowns question me, I'll give them the standard answers. 'I don't know shit,' followed by, 'I still don't know shit.'"

They both stood, and Riggins patted Sanchez on the shoulder. "You don't have to lie for me, Sanny. The sheriff ordered me on admin duty, and even though Lieu is cool with me doing research, he'd be pissed if I ended up actually doing any field work on my own. But I'm committed to doing whatever I need to until this thing is over. I just want you to know that if IA ever came calling, I'd fall on my sword before I ever let anything happen to you."

They finished a few added details, Sanchez walking her to her car afterward. He leaned his elbows on the open window frame and met her eye. "I have some things to shore up with one of my cases. Keep me in the loop."

Turning the ignition, Riggins slipped her ten-dollar sunglasses on. "I'm not even sure if *I'm* in the loop."

FORTY-FIVE

AFTER LACING UP his boots, Eddie climbed the creek embankment and cut through a copse of trees until he came to a familiar-looking street. Making sure no vehicles or pedestrians were in sight, he made his way up the sidewalk. He knew the area well. Already in middle school by the time he and his mother had moved into the neighborhood, he'd nonetheless passed by Lang Elementary School dozens of times, even playing games of two-hand touch football with friends on its adjacent grass field. During her final visit with him in jail, Clarissa had mentioned Liam going to school there. When Eddie reached a sign that read **SLOW—SCHOOL CROSSING**, excitement rushed through him. He was close now.

He walked up another two blocks, thankfully encountering no one, until he stood kitty-corner to the school. Still no cars approached, and the only foot traffic he saw were a pair of older teenagers riding skateboards in the opposite direction. He had a vague sense of the time of day; he figured it must be almost noon since the sun sat almost directly overhead. Knowing from experience that meant the students had likely already eaten lunch, he wasted no time and limped across the street straight for the school's front double doors.

His plan was simple, if improbable: to bullshit them into having Liam meet him somewhere in the office area. He didn't have any other choice but to wing it. He also had no way of knowing if Liam was even in school today, but at this point that didn't matter. This would be his only chance, he figured. Clarissa had said they were moving to Ohio at the end of the week. Saturday. Knowing she'd never make a move like that on a weekday, that even if she changed her mind, she'd wait until Sunday, he banked on her and the family leaving tomorrow at the earliest. If she had decided to keep the boy home from school today, or if she'd withdrawn him early, Eddie knew his one chance would be ruined. But if she *had* sent him today...

One pitch.

Strikeout or home run.

As he prepared to press the door's call button to be let inside, he noticed something lying in an open trash can beside the door—a plastic convenience store bag. Eddie removed it and found an empty drink bottle inside. An idea formed in his head. Also seeing a soiled rag in the can, he removed that too, tying it around the top of his head. Seeing his reflection in the glass doors, he cringed. Not only was he a filthy mess, he knew his face had been plastered all over the news. He also knew that he couldn't get away with entering a school with his face totally obscured. The cover story he'd invented on the spot would just have to suffice. Taking a deep breath, he pressed the call button and waited until the door unlatched with a loud buzzing sound. Opening it, he stepped into a locked, glass vestibule.

Typing behind the front desk sat a plump, curly-haired woman in her fifties. She rose and approached the reinforced window, her smile faltering a bit once she took in Eddie's unkempt appearance. Smiling politely, she asked how she could help him.

"My name is Roger Eaton," he said, bending down to speak through the metal tray trap. "I'm here to give an inhaler to my stepson. He forgot it this morning. His name is Liam—Liam Fulton." As he straightened, he felt her eyes move over his face and bloodstained clothing. He felt like a fool standing there, imagining her turning around and picking up the phone to dial 911, having finally placed his face.

Send an officer quick! The guy you're looking for is here asking to see one of our students!

But she didn't turn toward the phone. Perhaps she'd simply taken in his filthy appearance and assumed he was part of the working class that populated this section of town. It gave him another idea.

"I've been mowing lawns all morning," he explained to her. When he saw her eyes move toward the line of dried blood down his right arm, he offered a nervous laugh. "Got into a fight with a weed-whacker. I lost." He gave her his sidelong grin, for added effect.

Whatever question had seemed to linger in the woman's eyes evaporated with his joke and open expression. She waved a hand in the air and offered a high-pitched laugh. "That's *sooo* funny! My husband is always saying our lawnmower is going to kill him someday."

Eddie laughed too, mostly out of nervousness. He watched her type into a nearby computer. Checking to see if a person by that name was on the approved contact list, and if there was an approved inhaler on file, he surmised.

Peering into the screen, she nodded, then returned to the window and asked if he wanted to simply leave the inhaler for Liam to pick up.

"He never uses it right, so we have to help him," Eddie explained. He thanked himself for remembering Clarissa mentioning Liam having asthma. Despite all this sounding weird even to him, so far it seemed to be going okay.

"No problem," she said. "All I'll need is your photo ID and I can have him come right down."

The smile on Eddie's face froze. He hadn't thought of being asked for identification. Thinking fast, he patted his pockets and feigned annoyance with himself.

"Darn it, I left my wallet in the truck. I had to park all the way down the block since I have the trailer with me. I can walk back and get it if you really need it."

He forced the smile back to his face, making sure to not become upset or annoyed with her request. In the current landscape, schools had taken an aggressive approach to student safety, so he should have expected extra security. He watched her expression falter, as if she felt conflicted over breaking one of the most ardent of school rules.

"We really do need to see ID," she said apologetically, but already Eddie could tell she was close to breaking down. He made sure to maintain friendly eye contact, keeping a genuine but tired smile on his face.

He decided to take a gamble.

"You know what? He can just take it when he gets home," he said. "He's always forgetting things, so this will just teach him a lesson. I've been working all day and have had enough of the sun already. I'm sure he won't have an attack before he gets home."

Wishing her a good day, he turned to leave when she called out for him to wait. "Aw, pickles, these laws are so cumbersome sometimes," she said through the window trap. "It's not like you're picking him up. Don't bother walking back out in that heat. I'll call him down now." She buzzed him through the inner door and into the open office area. Pointing toward a door at one end of the office that read **SCHOOL NURSE**, she offered, "If you'd like some privacy, feel free to use the nurse's office. Shelly called in sick today, otherwise I'm sure she'd tend to that herself." With a wince, she indicated the seeping wound that had bled through the shoulder of Eddie's shirt.

"Thank you," Eddie said, his heart beating wildly in his chest. He had to contain his own excitement as he made his way toward the nurse's office. Before he opened the door and stepped inside, the secretary called after him, "There are paper towels above the sink if you want to clean yourself up. Peroxide too."

Eddie offered a wave of thanks before slipping into the vacant office. As soon as he cleared the threshold and closed the door partway behind him, his legs cramped. He collapsed into a padded chair beside an examination table, the muscles in his legs seizing so badly he had to jam a fist into his mouth to stifle an agonized groan. His pulse, fast and heavy, pounded in his ears. Sweat stood out on his brow despite the relatively cold interior here. But even though he felt like he'd been hit by a train, and the likelihood his freedom could end at any second, he felt invigorated. He'd made it inside. And Liam was here.

This—is—really—happening!

Taking the secretary up on her offer, Eddie poured peroxide onto a handful of paper towels and reached beneath his shirt to dab his shoulder wound. He quickly regretted the decision. Fire raged through his arm, radiating along his back and chest. Steeling himself, he repeated the process with the gash on his leg and paid an equal price. Replacing the peroxide above the sink, he fell back into the chair, closing his eyes and mouthing a silent prayer. Seconds passed and slowly the pain receded into something manageable.

He tried to concentrate on the task at hand.

He wouldn't have much time. The secretary would tell Liam his stepfather was here with his inhaler. As soon as he walked in the room, the boy would know something was wrong. Eddie decided he would sit Liam down and tell him the truth right away. That he had meant to take him to the park that morning but had been unable, due to him going to jail. And that he'd escaped yesterday and made his way here to see him, even if for a moment, to tell him he was sorry for never being there, and that no matter what anyone said, Eddie loved him. No matter how the boy reacted, whether he ran from the room or sat quietly and listened, Eddie would have had his say. And he'd be happier than he'd ever been in his life. If Liam remained seated and listening, Eddie would tell him to return to his classroom without saying anything to the secretary. Then Eddie would walk outside and call Detective Riggins.

You can come get me now, ma'am. It's over.

He'd lay on the grass to watch the clouds float by, free ground beneath him for the last time in his life. He'd wait for them to come get him while he contemplated what might have been.

If he'd never answered the phone. Or if he'd paid better attention to the faraway look in his friend's eyes and thought of someone other than himself for once.

FORTY-SIX

From his parking spot two blocks from the school, Paolo watched through a pair of binoculars as Grassle slipped through the front entrance. Paolo had arrived thirty minutes before, convinced that this was Grassle's endgame. A gamble for sure, spending precious time conducting surveillance here, waiting and watching while whispering to himself—*crawl out of your hole and show yourself, little rabbit.*

There had been no other motive Paolo could imagine. A penultimate wager. A final showcase of humanity he had rarely witnessed in his personal or professional life. A result that, if true, spoke of the mountains human beings would climb for that one ideal that for millennia had confounded kings and paupers alike.

Love.

Watching Grassle flash at the edge of his vision as he'd viewed the school grounds through his binoculars, Paolo had actually bolted upright in his seat, excitement pulsing through him. A disciplined confirmation that it had truly been him, and now just waiting several minutes to ensure Grassle had gained entrance inside the school. The hint of a smile touched his lips. His hunch had been correct. Just as he suspected, the resourceful young man had not escaped for freedom's sake alone. Noble, if misguided. Paolo checked to make sure the police had no presence in the area. Satisfied they did not, he allowed himself a bit of self-congratulation for achieving what they had not with far superior numbers and resources: using a physical map to plot out a suspect's movements, then deducing his next move through intuition and common sense. Once again, law enforcement had been hamstrung by their antiquated investigative methods and various legal constraints. They'd been trained to work off a prescribed checklist. First, consider the obvious, then work through a convoluted progression that succeeded at times, but not at nearly the rate that Paolo enjoyed. The very nature of their trade had a built-in failure rate Paolo did not share. Tedious investigating coupled with a crippling legal bureaucracy had, over the years, reduced their effectiveness at both detecting and solving crimes. A large train did not turn easily. Even more reason for Paolo to have spurned government service for the private sector. Hood, with his almost limitless resources, had given Paolo the ability to work with such impunity that even a king's ransom would have been insufficient for him to relinquish his position. Case in point: If the police had encountered a similar situation at an occupied school, they likely would have chosen to wait and assess if an active shooter scenario was not present. Let the police founder through the dark while Paolo ended this drama once and for all. As a reward to himself, he would take his time with Grassle. A certain amount of discomfort would precede the end. This knowledge, coupled with the thought of how pleased Mathias would be once he learned Grassle was finally dead, caused his cock to stiffen.

As Paolo set the binoculars down, the beginning bars of Prokofiev's *Peter and the Wolf* rose from the vehicle's speakers. One of Paolo's favorites since childhood. The high notes of a flute, representing the bird, Sasha. The strings, Peter. Followed by menacing French horns, the wolf.

The irony was not lost on him. Except Paolo did not intend for this to end the way Prokofiev's tale had. He considered for a moment which instrument would represent him had his current role been set to orchestral music. The timpani drums, or perhaps the bass.

Holstering his silenced HK pistol, Paolo Bruzzi stepped from the vehicle and headed toward the school's entrance two blocks away, his step light. From his lips came Prokofiev's whistled notes that seemed to rise into the afternoon sky like so many birds themselves.

Paolo looked both directions and detected nothing out of the ordinary. The school sat in a quiet residential neighborhood, all the better for him to complete his work and then vacate the area undetected. The only pedestrian he passed had been a young mother pushing a baby stroller. Apparently, news of an escaped felon hadn't prevented her from taking her cooing infant for an afternoon walk. The woman hadn't made much eye contact with him, as she'd apparently been distracted by her cell phone conversation. Good. The fewer witnesses who could put his face to the crime he would soon commit, the better. More importantly, he had not seen any police nearby. One of their own had been cut down. If they discovered Paolo's involvement in the murder, his searching for Grassle would be the least of his concerns. That inner clock that had always served as a litmus for his own self-operating procedure told him he still had sufficient time to finish his task.

As he reached the school grounds, he paused to make a cell phone call. Checking in would also give him time for the trap to set even deeper.

"I have him," Paolo said when the call connected. His voice came cool and even despite his rising excitement.

"Where?" Hood asked, his voice thick with bloodlust.

"A school. He cannot escape."

A pleased murmur from the other end, before, "Report back when it is done. Find me my salvation, my pet."

Paolo, having closed his eyelids to enjoy a passing fantasy of himself and Hood in a locale far from this one, opened them. Business first. The school's entrance beckoned. Grassle would be a sitting duck now, Paolo knew, as he approached the front doors and pressed the call button. A certain softness replaced the usual hardness of his expression, making it seem less severe, human almost. But it fell away just as quickly as it appeared, replaced by an expression so sinister and cold that a crow resting on a nearby tree branch seemed to take notice and fly away, shrieking as it went.

Detective Grimes called Mr. Aaron's direct number at PTS and asked pointedly if they'd had any further success in pinging Eddie's stolen cell phone.

"Not yet," answered Mr. Aaron, his voice smug. "As my assistant suggested, it may not have been wise to call the phone directly. It seems the person you seek has disconnected the battery again."

Even over the phone, Grimes could feel Mr. Aaron grinning.

FORTY-SEVEN

Removing the makeshift do-rag from around his head, Eddie combed his fingers through his hair to make himself as presentable as possible. He sat on the edge of the chair, his heart pounding in his chest. Despite a voice inside his head instructing him to do otherwise, he couldn't keep still. *Don't be so nervous; you'll scare him. Just relax and say what you need to say. And don't forget to tell him you love him. For God's sake, don't forget that.*

As the seconds ticked by, questions bounded through his mind. How would Liam react once he realized who Eddie really was? Would he even believe Eddie was his father? And would he be frightened? If so, Eddie figured the boy had every right to be. Afraid, or even angry at his father for never being there, angry over thoughts of self-doubt laid upon his impressionable young mind, and the ever-present belief that somehow he had been the reason his father had never chosen to see him. How would Eddie respond to the boy's questions, assuming he cared enough to ask them? Something deep in his gut loosened and he suddenly felt the need to go to the bathroom very badly. His palms lay slick with sweat and his breathing shortened. The physical pain he'd endured for the past twenty-four hours seemed like a memory now. The aura of peace that had come over him after he'd decided on how to surrender himself now took a back seat to an overriding sense of anxiety. The thought of a lifetime in prison paled to the prospect that Liam would reject him, would cast aside the very idea of him as his father. Eddie whispered a silent prayer to God that if He should grant him even ten seconds with his son, to look him in his eye and tell him none of this was his fault, that it had been Eddie who had failed in his duty, he would gladly walk out the school's front doors and into the cold steel of handcuffs. He figured a release from the prison of his own conscience would easily counter any fences or bars that could ever contain his body.

Voices.

Too hushed through the partially closed nurse's door for Eddie to distinguish each word. He strained his ears, but the pounding pulse in them made it difficult to distinguish much. Had one of the voices been that of a child? Yes, he thought it had. One voice belonged to the secretary, no doubt telling the boy his stepfather was in the nurse's office with his medicine. Now the boy saying something that sounded like "but I don't need my inhaler," and the secretary responding, "Well, he came all this way already, so you may as well take it."

He heard the boy ask if he could use the drinking fountain first. Straining his ears even more, Eddie heard the metallic press bar of a fountain, then running water. *Just another thirty seconds. God, please let it happen...*

Eddie fought the urge to rise to his feet and rush into the reception area. *Wait!* Jules's voice commanded. *He doesn't know you, dummy. The secretary will know something is up and call the police when Liam tells her he doesn't know you. Wait for him to come in, then say what you need to say. After that, nothing else will matter.*

Then the sound of the front office door buzzing open, and another voice, this one male. At first, Eddie thought nothing of it. A parent picking up his child, or like himself, dropping something off. But when the man spoke again, something in the voice caused the hair on the back of Eddie's neck to stand on end. Frowning, he tried to place it. The more he concentrated, the more he convinced himself it was simply his own nerves rattling him. He didn't know many people, let alone anyone who would also be at his son's school. Shaking away a feeling of rising dread, he decided his nerves were in fact getting the better of him and he forced himself to relax. He was sure some psychological term existed for how he felt, but he couldn't remember its name. He decided *losing your shit* pretty much nailed it.

MATHIAS HOOD SETTLED back in his desk chair, looking out to the glimmering pool beyond his office's French doors. Paolo had done it. Soon, he would call back with confirmation, and Hood would wait for him here. Telling his trusted assistant what he'd wanted to hear had left a sour taste in his mouth. But promising a physical union had been necessary. The human heart could indeed move mountains. Entire empires had been both won and lost because of it; and in this case, Hood figured the enigmatic man whom he had employed for the past five years would do anything he asked. Once Hood led the man from his office to the master bedroom, painting an expression of lust on his face he knew he would have to manufacture from deep within, he would know the final trap was set. He would miss Paolo once he put a bullet into the back of his head. But what must be done must always be done.

HAVING IDENTIFIED HIMSELF as a state investigator and being buzzed in through the outer doors, Paolo entered the same vestibule Eddie had entered minutes before and held his credentials against the adjoining window. The plump secretary behind the desk nodded and buzzed him in. Now approaching the counter, Paolo took a cursory look around the office. No sign of Grassle; only a young boy of about five taking a drink at the fountain to his left. To his right, a partially open door with a sign that read **Nurse's Office.** No other adults in view, other than the secretary. When she asked him how she could help him, Paolo asked if a man matching Eddie's description had just walked in.

Predictably, the woman's eyes opened wide with concern. "Yes, it's Roger Eaton. He just went in there," she said, pointing to the nurse's office and explaining the medication situation. "Is anything wrong?"

"Not at all," Paolo said, feigning light-heartedness. "I thought that was Roger—we went to college together. I stopped by to get some information on my daughter's enrollment next year and thought I saw him walking in."

The secretary visibly relaxed. "Well, isn't that funny. I love coincidences. Do you want me to call him out here for you to say hello?"

Paolo held up a hand. "Don't bother yourself. I'll just pop my head in and say hi."

As the boy at the drinking fountain walked past him toward the nurse's office, Paolo recognized him from photos he'd researched. A sudden surge of satisfaction swept through him. So, Grassle *had* come to visit his son. How noble indeed. But in doing so, the man had unwittingly sealed his own doom. A quick appraisal of the office area told Paolo it had only two feasible exits—the front door, which he now blocked, and a doorway that presumably led to the classroom areas. Knowing this door would surely be locked, Paolo called out to Liam just as he reached the nurse's door and asked him to take a seat in the waiting area for a moment, that Paolo wanted to say hello to his stepdad first. Liam dutifully obliged. Flopping onto one of the reception chairs in an area separated from the main office area, he picked up a children's magazine and began to flip through it.

Paolo gave the secretary a wicked grin as he advanced toward the nurse's office.

Her eyes widened with concern as Paolo drew his silenced pistol and crept to the door's edge, flattening his back to the wall. Winking to the now fearful-looking secretary, he pushed the door open while pivoting into the doorway. In the same motion he raised his pistol with the ease of an experienced marksman, sweeping the muzzle across the room's interior. Behind him, the secretary let out a gasp as she held both hands to her chest. Immediately, Paolo's sight was drawn to a figure standing in the room's far corner. He'd just begun to squeeze the trigger when his brain recognized the figure as not that of a person, but of a hanging skeleton. He stepped further into the room and swept left across the vacant exam table and chair before spinning right to clear behind the door. Nothing.

He stood in silent consideration before noticing a closed closet door against the far wall. Throwing it open, he thrust the gun's muzzle forward and prepared to fire when he realized not only that Grassle was not inside, but that the space within would have been insufficient to hide even a small child. About eight inches deep, it contained nothing more than a row of shallow shelves filled with medical supplies. Stepping into the center of the room, Paolo looked upward and pressed the pistol's suppressor against one of the drop ceiling tiles. Raising it enough to see the space within, he judged it unfit to hold a grown man's weight. After re-checking every corner of the room, he re-holstered his pistol and stood with hands on hips. He was positive Grassle had not slipped out the front door prior to his own arrival, and the secretary had been adamant in her assertion he'd entered this very room just minutes ago.

As he began to walk back out of the room, Paolo heard a faint metal-on-metal clinking sound. Facing the room from the doorway, he frowned. Had he missed something? Looking toward the room's only window, he observed the closed blinds blow inward before settling back against the metal sash, causing that same clinking sound. Lunging for the window, Paolo ripped the blinds from their supports and cast them to the floor. The medium-sized window rested partway open, its screen lying on the grass several feet beyond. Inspecting the sash, Paolo found a fresh smear of blood. Thrusting the window fully open, he stuck his head out, looking wildly in every direction. To his right sat an empty playground; forward, nothing but the six-foot chain-link fence that surrounded the school's perimeter. Looking left, Paolo observed nothing noteworthy at first, until a flash of movement caught his eye. There, about twenty yards away, was the figure of a man scaling the inside of the fence. Grassle. Paolo watched with rising fury as the man who had already performed several improbable feats of evasion over the past twenty-four hours swung his legs over the top rail, rotated his weight forward, and landed awkwardly on his back on the other side. Paolo briefly locked eyes with him as Grassle first rose to his feet then began to hobble away down the sidewalk.

Roaring with anger, Paolo began to climb through the window when a voice behind him caused him to stop.

"Where did he go?" The secretary stood in the doorway, one hand pressed to her breast, the other to her mouth. She looked toward the mangled blinds on the floor, her eyes a mix of worry and fear.

"He must have heard me," Paolo snarled, deciding it best to not pursue him in this manner. Surely that would elicit unwanted attention. Best to allow the secretary to think this some elaborate game. Cursing his luck, he climbed back inside and stormed past her out of the room, explaining the situation as being an old college game the two had often played. As he reached the front doorway, the secretary asked after him in an excited voice if she should send Liam back to his classroom. Forcing calm upon himself, Paolo apologized for the blinds, explaining he would send someone out to have them repaired. Then he burst through the exit door so hard it banged against the outside wall before slamming closed behind him.

Running back to his car, he cranked the ignition and swung behind the school to the area he'd last seen Grassle. He followed the fence line until it ended, checking each side street as he went. Only a group of teenagers and a young couple walking hand-in-hand. Knowing it to be fruitless to drive aimlessly around, Paolo parked beneath the shade of a tree and pounded his fists against the steering wheel. Through years of hunting other human beings, he had honed his craft to a razor's edge. Never had a target escaped him. Grassle had done it twice in less than twenty-four hours. Consternation clouded his mind to the point he had to summon his deepest mental acuity to keep himself from slipping into panic. *Relax and breathe.* Closing his eyes to clear his mind, he counted slowly to twenty. When he opened them again, he immediately felt his pulse slow. He caressed the steering wheel, summoning an old trick by imagining an inanimate object as some living, loving thing—the naked flesh of Hood's chest, perhaps—to replace negative emotions with positive ones. He knew full well the danger of making any decision while under the weight of worry.

He placed a call to Mathias, sure of the wrath he would surely show. But his response surprised him.

"It will be okay," Hood reassured him. "We have him contained, and you have time to do your work. I have faith." Giving no further direction, Hood ended the call. Paolo sat very still for another minute before driving off in the direction he felt Grassle would most likely take. It felt foreign to search so blindly. But until more intelligence came in, it would be all he had. As he glided slowly along the many residential streets, he turned up the radio's volume and found solace in the menacing notes of French horns rising from the car's speakers.

The wolf...

FORTY-EIGHT

THE DECISION HAD been an agonizing one.

On the one hand, Eddie had reasoned that the voice may not have been that of the man from the barn. He could have misconstrued the broken pieces of conversation between the man and the secretary—"it's okay, I'll just pop my head in to say hi," and, "Liam, why don't you have a seat while the officer speaks with your stepfather." Then again, Eddie had realized something in those seconds before finally deciding to open the window and run: if he failed to listen to his gut and the man had somehow found him, he'd be dead, and there would be no second chances. Sure, leaving at just the moment he'd been about to meet Liam could very well constitute the only chance he'd ever have. Or at least a one in a million chance to try something else. But the price of being wrong, if the voice had indeed belonged to the killer from the night before, would be chances of him succeeding dropping to zero. Living to fight another day was better than not living at all, he'd figured.

The window had been the easy part. After that, Eddie had hobbled far enough to be out of pistol range then had thrown himself against the six-foot-high fence. Grabbing the top rail, he'd used his good arm and leg to pull himself upward. Reaching the top, he'd slipped momentarily before using all his strength to push his upper body up and over. His momentum had allowed the rest of his body to fall over the fence, where he crashed to the sidewalk on his back and temporarily knocked the wind out of himself. Recovering quickly, he gained his feet and looked back toward the window he'd crawled from just moments before. There, hands planted against the window sash and glaring with his black, hateful eyes, had been the killer.

Without thinking, Eddie ran. If someone recognized him, so be it. Halfway down the next block he saw a house with overgrown grass and a **For Sale** sign in the front yard. Stepping around to the side of the house, he tried the gate. Locked. Pressing his weight against it to create a gap, he noted the inner latch was not padlocked. Easing off the door, he reached over the fence until he was able to unlatch the bar. The sound of an approaching vehicle came to him just as he pushed through the gate. Closing it behind him, he'd just rested his face against it when he spied a white Cutlass rolling past through a gap in the fence. The menacing-looking driver—the man who had very nearly cornered him inside the school—checked left and right as he crept along at five miles per hour. Apparently not seeing Eddie, he rode past and out of view.

Jesus, that was him...

Half out of anxiety and half out of pure exhaustion, Eddie collapsed in the yard's high grass. He lay on his back, gasping for breath as the pain that had formerly held itself at bay returned in force. It gripped every fiber of him, causing his body to contort in a sort of spasm that made him consider, if just for a moment, giving up. It was all just so much. The best opportunity he would ever have at seeing Liam had been robbed of him. After everything he'd accomplished, so many instances of combined guile and luck and timing, he'd been reduced to a writhing fool in some stranger's yard. He'd only needed another thirty seconds. The briefest of periods, one out of millions of such periods in his lifetime. It seemed beyond cruel to have been so close. As cramps seized his legs, his arms, and the long muscles of his back, Eddie silently wished for it all to graciously end. He felt his body would no longer allow him to go on. It was useless anyway. Either the police or the madman would catch up with him at any moment. The one plan he'd been able to conjure, as improbable as it had been, had nonetheless come a hair's breadth from working.

Now he would have minutes, maybe only seconds, of freedom or life remaining.

There has to be another way, came Jules's voice inside his head. *Think! Don't just lie there feeling sorry for yourself. This isn't about you.*

"I can't go on anymore," Eddie croaked. He tried to lick his lips, but his tongue lolled uselessly from his mouth like a bloated toad. He remembered something he'd heard about people dying of thirst often losing their minds in the process. He wasn't sure if he was losing his now, or if it was already gone.

You will not *lay there and die, dipshit. Do you understand me?*

"I was so close to seeing him," Eddie moaned. The blazing sun, high in the sky and having hid for a moment behind a cloud, emerged with renewed fury. Something crawled across his face, followed by several more. He swatted at one after it stung him. Holding his hand up to inspect the dead insect, he recognized it as a fire ant. Seconds later, he felt more of them begin to swarm and sting the back of his neck. Swatting wildly at them, Eddie bolted upright as he felt several more crawl down his shirt. Reaching his hand inside to smash them, he'd been a second too late. Hot pain erupted from several more stings on his chest before he was finally able to crush the aggressive insects with the palm of his hand. It took him a full minute to swat dozens more from his chest and legs—as he realized he'd been standing in an ant pile—and successfully dance his way across the side yard to relative safety.

His skin on fire, Eddie ignored the pain as best he could and unlatched the gate. He'd just slipped through when a car whizzed by, Latin music floating from its open windows. Flattening himself against the side of the house, Eddie waited until it disappeared down the block before daring to limp toward the sidewalk again. Instinct told him to double-track from where the white Cutlass had come from. He wouldn't have the luxury of waiting to see if the route were free of vehicles or pedestrians; he'd just have to risk it. One eye on the sky, he expected at any moment for the helicopter to swoop overhead, its loudspeaker commanding him to lie on the ground. Or a pack of snarling police dogs, led by their gun-toting handlers, bursting from around the corner. But that same instinct that told him he didn't have time to worry about being seen also told him the killer from the barn wouldn't hesitate next time.

Six blocks later (having passed two kids on bicycles casting him dubious stares), Eddie came to an area he recognized well. Dunbar Avenue—one of the more active areas in Springwood. The two-lane street held a certain reverence in Eddie's mind. Host to a collection of eateries and shops, the area had become somewhat of a hangout during Eddie's high school years. He'd even lost his virginity while cruising along this very street. Ruth. A blond with pouty lips and an infectious laugh, she'd shared several classes with him despite being a grade ahead of him. Even now as he ducked behind a parked delivery truck to avoid a passing car, the memory of that night floated back to him as clearly as if it had happened yesterday. It had been a Saturday night, with Jules behind the wheel of his newly restored Mustang, Eddie and Ruth making out in the backseat. With the street packed with kids and traffic bumper-to-bumper, the three had just begun their third run of the mile-long district when Ruth had suddenly lowered her hands to Eddie's lap and unzipped his jeans. Removing his throbbing cock, she'd hiked up her skirt and scooted out of her panties in one motion. With the deftness of a gymnast, she'd straddled him before he'd had a chance to ask her what she was doing. Eddie recalled her wetness, the sensation of feeling himself slip deep inside of her. How she had ground her hips against him in such a way that had threatened to unleash an explosion that up to that point in his life had only occurred by use of his own hand. They had fucked that way despite the Mustang's windows being open and the packed summertime crowds gawking as Jules inched the car down the packed avenue. Ruth had come right after Eddie had, shuddering against his body then falling over next to him in a heap of giggles and flushed exuberance. Then she'd climbed back into her underwear and adjusted her skirt as if nothing significant had just happened. Too shocked for words, Eddie had cleaned himself up with a discarded towel he'd found on the floorboard before looking up to see Jules's grinning face in the rear-view mirror.

All of that seemed so long ago. Now, looking down each end of the avenue and finding traffic to be relatively light, Eddie knew that in another hour or two the street would start filling up with afterschool kids and young couples looking to start the weekend early. Amazingly, he hadn't spotted any police vehicles since leaving the school. Surely, they would have a much greater presence here, despite the unlikelihood of him coming to such a populous area. Out of options and with no idea of what to do next, Eddie considered walking into one of the businesses and simply giving himself up. What would be the use of continuing to run? And now that the school option had fizzled out, the likelihood of him finding Liam, let alone figuring out a way to somehow see or speak with him, seemed impossible. Looking along the row of storefront signs, imagining which one would be best to walk into and ask the first person he saw to call the police, that he was finished, Eddie spied one that sparked something in his memory. The sign sported a giant bee hovering over a pint of beer, with the words Honeybee Bar & Grill emblazoned above it.

It took him a moment to place the memory, but when it took hold, he nearly shouted the words that imprinted themselves in his mind—*the girl from the convenience store!*

Jessica.

Standing at the counter with Jules, trying to stop the girl from freaking out while the clerk lay bleeding and dying behind the counter. Her telling Eddie she had just stopped by to get something to drink, that she didn't want to die.

And that she was just a dumb waitress at the Honeybee.

Eddie shook his head at the irony. His whole nightmare had begun there with the girl. And it could just as easily end with her as well. Assuming she still worked there, of course; and if so, if she was on duty right now. He limped across the street, keeping his head low and placing a hand to the side of his face as he passed a group of teenagers. Luckily, they'd been engrossed in their conversation and hadn't given him a moment's notice.

Pulling open the Honeybee's front door, Eddie felt a luxurious wave of cold air wash over him. The heavenly aroma of cooking hamburgers and French fries instantly made his stomach cramp. As he stepped inside, still holding a hand to the side of his face, he had no idea of how his own game would possibly end. Recalling his favorite sport, he knew whatever happened in the next few moments would likely end with one of two results: an unlikely hit, or the much more likely strikeout.

FORTY-NINE

THE PLACE TEEMED with activity. Waitresses weaved their way among tables filled with couples of all ages. At the counter, several folks ate and engaged in small talk with the waitress there. Eddie stepped inside, surprised by the fact that no one was turning around to point at him accusingly while shouting to all who would hear—*look, there he is!*

Yet no one did look. The bell attached to the front door barely sounded above the din; and grateful not to have attracted undue attention, he put his head down and made his way straight to the counter, sitting on an unoccupied chair. To his right, a pair of college-aged men talked over milkshakes and burgers. To his left, down two chairs from him, sat a businessman talking on his cell phone. Placing the fingertips of both hands to his temples, Eddie kept his head low as a waitress down at the other end of the bar called out to him, asking what he wanted to drink.

"Water, please," he called out, averting his eyes. As the waitress approached him with a glass of water, Eddie dared a glance up. He recognized her immediately. She'd been pouring beer from a tap, her back to him, when he'd entered. But now, as she walked toward him, she met his eye, the two of them seeing each other fully for the first time, and in that moment before the glass slipped from her hand and shattered on the floor, her smile had been one of vague recognition.

But then something seemed to click in her mind, a memory formerly pushed away, only to be revealed like the pulling of an anchor from a muddy depth. Her feet cemented in place and her hands covered her mouth. Her eyes bulged with disbelief, and even when those around her stopped what they were doing to look at the source of the sound of broken glass, she did not move. She could have been a cardboard cutout from a horror flick.

Sarcastic applause from a nearby table.

Eddie felt his face and ears flush as he imagined every eye in the place trained in his direction. But thankfully, one of the bar backs dived into action, ushering Jessica out of the way as he swept up the glass and mopped the spilled water. Jessica's gaze remained frozen on Eddie. The shock in her eyes could just as easily have been mistaken for embarrassment, evidenced by another waitress giving Jessica a good-natured ribbing for doing something she said they all did weekly, if not daily.

Locking eyes with her, Eddie resisted the urge to bolt straight out the front door. Despite his decision to come here to turn himself in, he hadn't expected to see her this quickly, if at all. Not knowing the right thing to say to break the awkward, pained moment, he extended both palms and mouthed the words, "It's okay, I'm not going to hurt you."

The two college-aged kids to his right laughed at something one of them said.

Suddenly Jessica snapped out of her paroxysm. "What the *fuck*?" she mouthed back to him, folding her arms across her chest. She backed up against the far edge of the bar, her expression fearful but proud at the same time, as if she didn't want Eddie to know he'd gotten to her. On cue, the television behind the bar began playing a live news story detailing his escape. On the screen, State Attorney Hood spoke at a podium. His menacing black eyes glowered through the screen, so much so that Eddie believed the man could read his thoughts as their eyes seemed to lock. Sheriff Driscoll, flanked by a bevy of severe-looking law enforcement officials, took the podium next. With the television volume muted, Eddie saw his own mug shot fill the screen, with a caption emblazoned across the bottom of the screen reading: **SUSPECTED COP KILLER STILL AT LARGE. MAN-HUNT CONTINUES.**

Eddie looked from the screen to Jessica, who had just watched the same segment that he had. Her expression suggested that she clearly expected some sort of answer.

"I didn't do any of those things they said I did," he insisted, his voice low. "Except escape. Obviously." She approached his side of the bar, keeping a bit of distance while appearing to be interested (or afraid) to hear what else he had to say.

As the news story continued, bar patrons began postulating where the fugitive may be. "Canada," said someone at a nearby table. "Mexico, for sure," said another. But the common theme cast doubt that the escapee remained in the area, given that a full day had passed since the actual escape. Another voice in a back section of the place shouted an opinion that the escapee had gone to the same Caribbean island where Elvis and Michael Jackson had retired to after faking their deaths. This earned a smattering of laughter from everyone.

The businessman to Eddie's left paid his tab and slid from his seat. Jessica bade the man a good weekend and waited until her other customers were taken care of before taking a moment to apparently confirm in her own mind the course of action she would take. Nodding to herself as she looked into Eddie's eyes, she planted her hands on the bar top and leaned toward him.

"The only reason I haven't screamed yet is I don't want to make a scene," she said below the drone of surrounding conversation. "Besides, I'm not going to let someone like you waltz in here and make my manager think I'm associated with an escaped criminal."

Eddie searched for the right words. Nothing seemed appropriate given the circumstances. To an extent, he figured she had every right to be upset at his presence here. So he blurted the first thing he could think of. "I wanted to thank you for telling the police I tried helping the man from the store. The detective told me that. It means a lot."

Jessica blinked, seemingly unprepared for his statement. "Excuse me?"

"You didn't know me. You could have told them anything. My lawyer came to talk to me a couple days ago and told me—"

"You *are* crazy, aren't you?" Jessica said, sharply enough for one of the college kids to glance her way. When she shot him a 'mind your own business' look, he turned away.

"Are you telling me you broke out of jail and came in here to *thank me*?" The indignation that had so far been resigned to her face now dripped from her voice. She no longer looked scared or shocked. She looked *pissed*.

"I didn't do any of this to hurt anyone," Eddie whispered loud enough for her to hear. As he watched her eyes grow even angrier, he became increasingly sure he'd made a huge mistake in coming here.

She leaned closer to him, close enough for him to smell the peppermint on her breath. "Look—Eddie, or whatever you go by, I don't really care what you *meant* to do. I was there. I saw what happened. Sure, I believe you may not have wanted that to happen. And I understand you tried to help that man. But do you realize what kind of shitstorm you've caused for everyone else?"

Another one of the college kids down the bar glanced her way, then quickly averted his eyes once she shot a scowl at him.

"I'm sorry about any trouble I've caused," Eddie said, looking down at the bar top. "Really."

"Apology not accepted," she hissed under her breath. "Do you know that I've had someone come to my house and threaten me? Yeah. As in, telling me if I made statements on your behalf, I could lose custody of my daughter. My *daughter*, you asshole!"

This time the college kid down the bar looked back and didn't look away. He gave Eddie a once-over and frowned, but from the hard angle, he couldn't get a good look at his face. Jessica, sensing the kid might say something, told him to mind his own business. This time, he not only looked away but adjusted his chair away from them.

Eddie looked up at her, feeling even more like an asshole than ever. She was right in every way. Once again, someone else was being punished for his own bad decisions. And of all things, her kid had become involved. He thought of the man from the barn, and what Jessica had said about someone coming to her place to threaten her. Was it all a coincidence? He couldn't be sure. But as the dots continued to line up, Eddie felt sure that whoever the man had been, and why he was after him, there had to be a connection somehow.

Looking into her eyes, he suddenly understood why her blood was up. Not until yesterday had he associated such desperate emotions with his child. He'd felt that caged animal instinct to protect his own, to expose his own life to danger for the benefit of his own offspring. Why should she be any different? And a single mother at that. Adding to it all, he'd intruded on her turf, endangering and frightening her even further, and all he'd done to mitigate that was offer a meager apology and half-assed appreciation for not coming forward against him. The look in her eyes, that same wild animal expression he felt himself—new to him but just as powerful—said how dare he come here and assume she'd stayed quiet for any other reason than to protect her own family. If she reached across the bar and slapped him right then, he couldn't even object.

"I may as well turn myself in right now," he said with a sigh. "It's over for me anyway. I busted out to try doing something, but it was stupid of me to even try. People have gotten killed because of me. If I could go back to that rec yard, I'd walk inside and go right back to my cell. But I can't. All I can do now is go back to jail and try to spend the rest of my life making a difference somehow."

She scoffed at that, turning her head and asking another waitress to tend to her other customers for just a minute. When she looked back at Eddie, her expression had grown even more incredulous. "Let me get this straight. You and your buddy knock off a convenience store and your buddy kills the clerk. I get you may not have intended on the robbery even happening, but don't hang out with druggie dumbasses and you don't have to worry about shit like that. What you did has caused me a shit-ton of issues, including nightmares that have just started to go away. I'd rather get punched in the face."

Eddie nodded and lowered his eyes. "I shouldn't have come here."

"You're fucking right you shouldn't have come here," she hissed under her breath. "I'm afraid to leave my daughter out of my sight for even thirty seconds. Last week I made an appointment to get her fingerprinted at the sheriff's office. A two-year-old. Just to be safe."

Eddie started to get up. He'd caused enough trouble already. He would walk outside and call Detective Riggins and sit on the curb until the police showed up. But as he slid from his stool, Jessica leaned forward and told him to wait.

"I can't have you causing a panic. Look at you. Get yourself cleaned up in the bathroom then get the hell out of here. Do you know how many people carry guns around here? All it takes is one person to recognize you and this place is gonna turn into a shooting gallery. You have five minutes, then leave and do whatever you need to do."

Sliding from his stool, he focused momentarily on a vintage photo on the wall behind her. In it, a man and boy sat side-by-side at a diner counter, drinking milkshakes. Each wore a '30s style newsboy hat resting cockeyed atop their heads.

All Eddie could do was shake his head as he limped his way toward the bathroom.

FIFTY

THANKFULLY, THE MEN'S bathroom had a separate stall complete with sink and mirror that gave him some semblance of privacy. Finding it empty, he wasted no time in locking the swinging door behind him before painfully removing his soiled shirt and overalls. He assessed his injuries in the mirror; none of them looked good. The wounds in his shoulder and leg both gave off an ominous orange-purple hue. He groaned as he dabbed each of them with wetted paper towels. Placing a fist in his mouth, he scrubbed away dried blood and dirt from around each wound site, then shook free from the pain as best he could by placing his head beneath the cold running water. Holding his mouth beneath the stream, he quenched the worst of his thirst before forcing himself to stop before he vomited it all back up. He dried his face and hair then struggled back into his clothes. Jessica had given him five minutes. After that, he figured she probably would call the police, regardless of causing a scene here or not. No matter, Eddie felt. His time would be up soon anyway when he walked outside and shouted to passersby who he was, before sitting down on the curb and waiting for the police to show up.

As he prepared to exit the stall, the thought of him surrendering was suddenly intruded upon by a different thought altogether. He paused with his hand on the lock, an idea hitting him like a bolt of lightning. Something Jessica had said just now, about being afraid for her daughter's safety, struck him. Eddie imagined a jigsaw puzzle—the beginnings of a plan to see Liam—suddenly begin to form in his mind. Perhaps the rush of cool water over his head had cleared his mind enough to shake away all the distractions and stress he'd experienced over the past day, leaving his brain reorganized enough to formulate this grand, yet crazy, idea. And it *was* crazy. Implausible even. But it was something. And as he patted the right front pocket of his overalls, the synapses of his brain finally fit the final pieces of the puzzle into place. In a flash of inspiration, he had it. Not just an idea, but the entire plan. It came so clearly to him he slapped a hand to his forehead.

In his attempt to see Liam, he'd wasted precious time trying a direct—and as it turned out—obvious route. Indeed, going to the school had nearly gotten him killed. Whoever the man from the barn had been, he had obviously been one step ahead of Eddie. How that had happened, he had no idea. He didn't have time to try figuring it out now. But this new plan, one that would have major pitfalls of its own, conjured in Eddie some long-ago maxim he'd heard about but had never fully understood until now: Sometimes a person stared so hard at the forest they failed to see the trees.

Fumbling in the overalls pocket, Eddie removed the dead woman's cell phone. Reconnecting the battery, he powered it on and flipped it open. Anticipation rising in him, he watched as the home screen came alive in swirling blues and reds. The number eight and a percent symbol appeared in the upper corner, followed by the symbol of a battery. Okay. He'd have enough time for a short phone call. He'd like the opportunity for a longer one, but that was a luxury he simply didn't have. One may be all he'd need anyway.

Just then someone entered the bathroom and began to use the stand-alone urinal. Frustrated, Eddie waved the faceless person on, anxious for whoever it was to hurry up and leave. When the person finished, washed up and exited, Eddie breathed a sigh of relief and pressed the phone icon. The number pad appeared. With trembling fingers, he inputted the number he'd dialed so many times in the past he felt he would still remember it fifty years from now.

You'll only have a few seconds, he thought, watching the icon that read 'connecting' appear, trailed by a series of ellipses.

Please answer. Please! If I get this chance, I swear I won't ask for another. I'll go to prison for the rest of my life and will never complain about a single thing.

A dialtone. Two rings, then four, then eight. Eddie's heart began to sink. Soon, voicemail would pick up. He wouldn't have time to wait to call again later. Leaving a message wasn't an option, since the battery was about to die, and his five minutes here was about up. He needed desperately to speak voice to voice. It would be the only way his newly hatched plan—as crazy and implausible as it was—could work. All from that offhand comment Jessica had made about being fearful for her daughter's safety...

Nine rings. One more and voicemail would pick up. Then he'd be finished. A lifetime's worth of regret, thinking about how close he'd come to seeing Liam. Years, decades even, to think that if she had only answered the phone, Eddie would have had perhaps the slimmest of chances for his plan to work.

As the tenth ring began, Clarissa picked up.

ROGER PLACED THE last box into the back of the U-Haul and pulled the back roll-door closed. Flipping the latch, he connected the lock then hopped into the driver's seat. Liam already sat in the space beside him, playing with an action figure. Clarissa stood in their home's doorway, taking one last look across the bare living room floor. Out of the three of them, she had spent the most time here. She'd been the one to make the house into a home. Her hands had scrubbed baseboards and cleaned the toilets—they'd changed Liam's diapers here too, and cooked more meals than she could remember. If bittersweet described how she felt now, she wondered where the sweet possibly came from.

As she pulled the front door closed and turned the key in the lock, she felt her cell phone vibrate in her back pocket. Removing it, she read the caller ID: **Elizabeth Downing**. Curious, she searched her memory for the name but couldn't place it. Probably another telemarketer. Despite signing up for the Do Not Call list, she'd continued to be inundated on a weekly if not daily basis. But as she stared at the screen and prepared to decline the call, some unknown instinct caused her to accept it. Maybe it would do her some good to blow off some steam by livening up her standard speech. Instead of: *'I'm not interested, please take my number off your list,'* perhaps something saltier like: *'I'm being forced to move out of state and I've cried every day for a month—how can I help you?'*

Instead, she went with a simple, "Hello?"

At first, nothing. Checking to see if the call had disconnected and finding it had not, she repeated herself. Finally, a woman's voice she didn't recognize came through. "Hello, is this Clarissa Fulton?"

"Speaking."

The clearing of a throat, then, "Ms. Fulton, my name is Elizabeth Downing. I'm a civilian representative from the Calusa County Sheriff's Office calling in reference to your son, Liam."

Clarissa had been prepared to give her new *fuck you* speech but paused when she heard the words *Sheriff's Office* and *Liam.*

"What about my son?" she asked, alarmed.

Roger, watching in the side mirror, read her body language and raised both palms in the air. She waved him off, holding a free hand against her open ear so she could hear better.

"We were notified recently of your intention of removing Liam from the Florida public school system. Is this correct?" asked the woman caller.

Clarissa frowned. "His last day was today. What is this about?"

"I apologize for the late notice, ma'am, but you are on a list of parents who were inadvertently left off the automated call list. Calls were sent out yesterday notifying parents of a recent change in Florida law. All students removed from the public-school system are now required to be fingerprinted prior to enrolling in an out-of-state school system."

Clarissa's face and ears flushed red. "Excuse me?"

"Yes ma'am, that's correct," the female caller explained. "It came to our attention that you removed Liam from school with the intention of moving to—" a muffled sound, then, "Ohio. Is that correct?"

"Yes, that's right. We're leaving right now, in fact."

"*Now*, ma'am?"

"Is there an echo here?" Clarissa said, her voice sharpening. "Yes, now. Why does it matter when I decide to move my family?"

"I apologize, ma'am. You should have received our automated call yesterday, but there are a few glitches in the system. I'm afraid if Liam isn't fingerprinted before he leaves Florida, a hold will be placed on him and you'll be delayed in enrolling him in another state's public-school system until Florida officials print him."

Clarissa held the phone away from her ear and stared at it, as if doing so would help her believe what she had just heard. Telling Roger to give her a minute, she unlocked the front door and stepped back inside the barren living room. "You've got to be fucking kidding me," she said, clearly annoyed now.

"I wish I were, ma'am."

"Why can't we get him fingerprinted when we get to Ohio?"

"That would seem the obvious solution, but it's more complicated than that," the woman explained. "Unfortunately, the legislature included a provision that mandates the printing occur within the state of Florida. I imagine this has something to do with complicity laws between states. I don't see this provision staying on the books for long, but any change might take until the next session to go into effect. If that doesn't happen until after Liam is due to start school, I'm afraid the differing procedures can cause delays. It's happened before."

Clarissa rolled her eyes, mouthing a string of expletives under her breath. Tears welled in the corners of her eyes, and a lump formed in the back of her throat. With everything that had gone wrong over the past few months, she'd finally felt as though she'd put the worst behind her. Leaving would indeed be bittersweet, but the thought of a fresh start, although scary, had nonetheless buoyed her. Fresh irritation rose in her over the fact that some last-minute wrench had apparently been thrown into the mix.

"You people—you people have no idea what I've been through lately," she explained. "I took my son out of school a week early and literally just packed up my house, the house he was raised in. Now when I literally have one foot out my front door, you tell me I have to get him fingerprinted before I leave? What happens if I don't?"

A short pause. "As I said, ma'am, you may be delayed in registering him in Ohio until Florida officials make a fingerprint arrangement. I can't say I agree with the new procedure, but I'm not the one making those calls."

Clarissa stared out the open blinds at the idling U-Haul in the driveway. She could easily see Roger in the side mirror. Even though she couldn't see Liam, she knew he'd be sitting on the bench seat beside Roger, oblivious to his mother's conversation. Imagining the disappointed look on her son's face if he learned they'd be delayed in heading out, Clarissa felt the tears finally track down her cheeks. The simple act of feeling them, when she'd sworn to never cry inside these walls again, infuriated her. Just then, she made a decision. Even if it meant having to fly back to Florida with Liam in two months, or being delayed a week starting school in Ohio, then so be it. Because this was the very definition of bullshit, and she'd already eaten enough of it over the years to not stand even one more bite.

"You can take your fingerprints and shove them up your ass," Clarissa declared. Pressing **END** on the screen, she uttered a triumphant "hmmph" before locking the door behind her and climbing into the U-Haul's passenger seat.

"Let's go," she told a concerned-looking Roger, determined more than ever to start their new lives without delay.

FIFTY-ONE

Hearing the call abruptly end, Eddie stared at the phone in disbelief. On one hand, he'd been shocked to have actually spoken with Clarissa, albeit in the conjured voice of a woman. That she'd remained on the line for a full minute was astounding in itself. Indeed, Jules would have applauded the intersex voice impression. But part of Eddie's disbelief also had to do with the fact Clarissa had so abruptly ended the call, pulling the rug out from under him at the eleventh hour.

Still. Eddie *had* spoken with her, shared words with her devoid of personal acrimony. That fact alone gave him a bit of solace. If he didn't get his chance, at least he could recall during his decades behind bars that final conversation they'd shared, and how despite not knowing it had been him on the line, her voice hadn't carried the hurt and anger toward him that had been there during their previous talks.

Part of him felt bad about tricking her. Another part of him had wanted to blurt out something in his own voice, an apology, anything, so that she could hear it straight from him. Eddie. The man she'd once fallen in love with and lain beside on so many moon-filled nights, her creamy skin like alabaster in contrast to the spill of dark hair around her.

But he couldn't have done that, of course. That would have unraveled everything he'd done up to that point. Still, she'd become agitated over what the "woman" had told her, and in typical Clarissa fashion, had spoken her mind before hanging up. Eddie felt like Charlie Brown running up to kick the football, only for Lucy to pull it away at the last second. He'd underestimated Clarissa's resolve. Although it maddened him, he felt a tinge of admiration for her. As tender and romantic as she could be, she was her own woman to the very end. He found himself hoping Roger never made the same mistakes he had.

The phone's power indicator read six percent. The battery would be dead in another thirty minutes, he figured. The thought made him chuckle. *I might die before the phone does.* He considered disconnecting the battery a final time and ditching both pieces in the trash receptacle when the phone buzzed alive in his hand. Reading the caller ID, his eyes bulged in wonder. The name **CLARISSA FULTON** stood out on the blue incoming call screen. For one insane moment, Eddie looked around for a hidden camera, thinking someone was playing a cruel joke on him.

Coming to his senses, he answered in his previously improvised female voice. "Ms. Downing, Sheriff's Office."

"Yes—um, this is Clarissa Fulton calling back. I wanted to apologize. I was literally walking out of my house for the last time when you called, and it has me a bit emotional. Still, that was very rude of me saying what I did."

Eddie blinked. He wondered if he'd ever been more surprised in his life.

"It's okay, ma'am, I've had quite a few upset parents over this. It's understandable."

"I discussed it with my fiancé, and we decided it doesn't make sense to risk a delay since we're still in the area. I still think it's a ridiculous thing to have to do, but I guess that won't change anything."

Eddie checked the phone's power indicator. Five percent, in red now.

"It's alright," he said, reading the phone's clock. Two-thirty. He quickly calculated his approximate distance to the only realistic place he could make this thing happen. "We have several appointments coming up, but we can get you in at three-thirty. Can you make it to sheriff's headquarters then?"

Static on the line. Panicked, Eddie prayed the call wouldn't drop. Finally, Clarissa came back on and said three-thirty would be fine, that they'd stop to get ice cream on their way.

He hung up, his hands shaking. In his excitement, he stuffed the phone back into his pocket and exited the stall. Adrenaline rushed through his veins.

Okay, don't fuck this up, bro. You haven't accomplished shit yet, so don't get cocky.

Before leaving the bathroom, he hesitated. He removed the phone from his pocket and thumbed out a text message to Detective Riggins:

It shouldn't be long, detective. Maybe an hour. I'll find another way to let you know where to pick me up.

No need to separate the battery, he thought. The power indicator stood at four percent—it'd be dead soon anyway. Pushing his way out the bathroom door, he headed back toward the main door, keeping his head lowered and a hand to the side of his face as if he were experiencing a headache. In his mind, the plan was coming together. He'd need to beat her to the headquarters building so that she didn't walk inside and discover his lie too soon. Since he'd been there recently, he could still recall the layout of the land surrounding the building. Lots of wooded area near the parking lot to stay hidden in until she showed. They'd be in a truck or van of some kind; he knew her and was certain she'd move more personal effects with her than a regular car or van could hold. If he were fortunate enough to make it there undetected, and even more fortunate to have her show up as she'd promised, then he'd have a chance. Even if all he had was five seconds to approach her and Liam as they walked up to the building, he would take it. At this point, it was either that or nothing.

As he reached the counter, Eddie heard the bell to the front door ding. Glancing up, he caught sight of a figure clad in all black—with a matching ball cap and backpack—enter the restaurant. Not until the figure fully stepped inside did Eddie recognize it as being a sheriff deputy. Having little choice, Eddie plopped down onto the same stool he'd occupied before, holding his hands beside his face and pretending to study the menu. Naked terror seized him. Unsure if the deputy had seen him, a wild image of a dozen cops outside, ringing the street with guns drawn, came to him. Perhaps Jessica had changed her mind, or some other customer who'd noticed him had called in a tip. Why else had the cop entered just as Eddie had prepared to leave?

But when he glanced up and saw the equally shocked expression on Jessica's face, he knew it hadn't been her. Someone else then. His instincts made him consider bolting out the door, pushing his way past the deputy and racing outside. Anything would be better than being trapped in here for Lord knew how long, while Clarissa made her way to the headquarters building. If only he'd left thirty seconds earlier. The timing horrible, he struggled to understand how much worse his luck could have been.

When the deputy took the stool directly to his left, Eddie quickly realized his luck *had* gotten worse. Panic froze him in his seat. He needed to leave, but he feared moving an inch would place a spotlight onto him, maybe even sound some alarm or create a neon sign pointing directly at him.

For her part, Jessica planted her hands atop the bar top and addressed the deputy, her voice a pitch higher than it had been before.

"Cold beer for you, sir?" she joked.

Using a handful of napkins to mop sweat from his brow, the deputy laughed. "Don't tempt me." He balled the napkins and set them on the counter. "Water for now. It's a goddamn sauna out there." Then, in a hushed voice intended for just Jessica to hear, "Between you and me, you didn't see me in here. I broke away from my search team and am not technically supposed to be in this sector. Screw that, though. I need a break." The deputy unfolded a copy of Eddie's mugshot and slid it across the bar to her. "Any chance you've seen this guy since yesterday?"

"Who is he?" Jessica asked, feigning ignorance.

The deputy gave her a quizzical look. "Haven't you seen the news?"

"I'm too busy to watch TV."

The deputy tapped a finger onto the photo. "He escaped from jail yesterday. Killed three people, including a cop."

Jessica stole a nervous glance at Eddie, who kept his hands planted beside his face. So far, the deputy hadn't as much as glanced beside him.

"You think you'll catch him soon?" she asked.

"Who knows," the deputy answered, draining the glass of ice water Jessica placed in front of him. "He could be in Mexico by sundown for all I know."

Eddie listened to this while stealing a peek beside him in between his splayed fingers. When the deputy suddenly moved his hand down toward his gun, Eddie felt his heart stop in his chest. He waited for the sound of an unholstering pistol followed by the cold steel of a barrel being pressed against his head. He'd have a split-second choice between running for it and feeling hot lead pump into his back or accepting his fate of handcuffs and then the clank of a cell door being closed behind him.

But instead of unholstering his pistol, the deputy instead reached into the cargo pocket of his tactical pants and extracted a plastic bag. He tore off a corner of the bag with his teeth and poured something into his meaty palm. Bringing his hand to his mouth, he began crunching on whatever he'd thrown into it. "I'm from the jail," he added. "Volunteered to help in the manhunt."

Jessica nodded. "Aha. Well, good luck catching him."

When the deputy asked Jessica for a Styrofoam cup, Eddie frowned. Something seemed strange about his voice. Or familiar.

"Thanks," the deputy said, lowering his voice conspiratorially. "I got a hundred dollar bet with the boys that I'd be the one to catch the puke."

If Eddie hadn't been so frozen with terror, he might have made the connection a bit sooner. The deputy brought the Styrofoam cup to his lips and spat something into it. Like the end of a mystery, where all the dots connected and the last puzzle piece fell into place, he suddenly realized what had seemed so familiar about the deputy. Peeking sidelong through his splayed fingers, he saw a single chewed sunflower seed clinging to the cup's lip.

At the same time, Jessica leaned across the bar top and said to Deputy Schultz, "Now that I think of it, maybe I have seen the guy you're looking for."

FIFTY-TWO

Paolo listened to his police scanner with newfound intensity. His dark eyes narrowed into slits and a muscle twitched in his jaw. He had parked in a busy shopping center parking lot, preferring to cut the engine and sit in the rising heat instead of running the air conditioning. His stomach growled, and he'd felt the first pangs of thirst come on hours ago.

But Grassle's current experience would no doubt be much worse. All the better to become Paolo's prey.

Perspiration soaking through his shirt, he watched random shoppers pass by. "Where are you, rabbit?" he whispered to himself. As if in concert with that thought, his hand slipped inside his jacket, his fingers tracing over the grip of his HK pistol that sat like silent death in his shoulder holster.

Looking at his ringing cell phone, Detective Grimes saw the PTS tech's name on his caller ID and answered it expectantly.

"You wanted me to notify you in case we got another hit?" the tech asked rhetorically. "Well, we got one."

Grimes dabbed at his dripping nose with a handkerchief and sat forward in his chair. He and Teliford had stopped by the mobile command center for a briefing when the call had come in.

"What do you have?"

"A call went out from the phone a few minutes ago. Followed by a return call from the same number."

"Who was the call to?"

Typing sounds on the other end. "Traced it to a Clarissa Fulton. Both the outgoing and incoming call seem to have occurred in the same place. Forty-fifth and Dunbar."

"That's downtown Springwood," Grimes said, amazed. "So...he *is* still close." He put the call on hold and relayed the information to Captain Escobar. After a quick conference with him, Grimes came back on the line.

"Captain wants us to keep calling to see if he picks up. Maybe he'll agree to give himself up. Track my number for his location." He hung up and exchanged grins with Teliford. They each knew without saying a word how big of a mistake Grassle had made in still insisting on using the phone. How could he possibly expect them not to be tracking him? Finally, a solid lead on his current location. The possibility of someone other than Grassle using the dead woman's stolen phone to call his ex-girlfriend lay outside the realm of common sense. It was definitely him. All it would take would be a slight shifting of the tactical teams half a mile from their current blocking positions to move in on him, and to take down the pariah that had caused a career's worth of problems for them all in the past thirty hours alone.

PAOLO READ AN incoming text message from Hood. He reported that the sheriff had given the full go ahead for his forces to move in on Grassle at any cost. Civilian casualties would just have to be accepted. More pressing by far was the matter of Paolo first finding Grassle and disposing of him before the police closed in. The prospect of failure was one he did not even wish to consider.

Any advantage he himself had enjoyed up to this point—his untethered requirement from following law and troublesome procedure—would soon evaporate. As for the dead deputy and woman from the night before, that was something not even Mathias could make go away. If the police succeeded in connecting him to the crime, there could only be one escape for him. Having once been captured and tortured by Middle Eastern enemy operatives (he'd narrowly escaped at the last minute), Paolo had decided to never again be subjected to imprisonment of any kind. Afterward, and borrowing a tactic used by some allied pilots flying missions over Japanese-held territory during the second world war, Paolo had decided to retain an 'insurance' round everywhere he traveled. Like those pilots, Paolo understood how easy it was to expend all your ammunition during the heat of battle. Counting rounds to save one for oneself could not be a trusted solution when the penalty for miscounting could be capture by an enemy who held zero regard for human suffering. In the pilots' case, tales of gruesome torture, beheadings, and wonton inhumanity from their enemy had made some decide to never be taken alive. For Paolo, his own decision lay predicated on his refusal to live the rest of his days caged like an animal. Should his numerous crimes ever become uncovered, he may be sentenced to a thousand years behind bars, he knew.

There was Mathias, as well. The emotional torture of forever being separated from him would far surpass any physical hardship he would ever endure. It had seemed fitting that, if necessary, he'd chosen as his insurance the single bullet Mathias had given him to use on Grassle.

The police radio channel he listened to teemed with the expected activity of a massive manhunt. From what Paolo determined, Grassle was suspected of being in a nearby six-square-block area. Paolo having missed two opportunities to kill him hadn't been for naught, he reasoned. Although succeeding in escaping from both the barn and the school, Grassle had made one glaring mistake: taking and using the dead woman's cell phone. Even the average teenager understood the basics of network cell phone tracking.

His phone buzzed with another message, this one from his predetermined sheriff contact. At least that resource remained intact. Police intelligence had just plotted Grassle in an area around Dunbar Avenue, downtown.

With the sting of his most recent failure still fresh on his mind, Paolo watched as a pair of sheriff cruisers flashed by him. A radio transmission confirmed the perimeter had indeed shifted. The heavy chopping of the helicopter's rotor beat down from somewhere overhead. With such a concentrated police presence converging, it would be difficult to move about as he preferred. Paolo's instinct told him that all vehicular traffic in the area would soon be limited, including that of deputies, to reduce congestion. Feeling it his best option, Paolo decided to travel on foot from here on in. With his radio earpiece in place, he stepped from the Cutlass and headed toward the shifted search area. The fox lay somewhere inside that zone. Like a pursuing hound on a hot trail, Paolo felt confidence swell inside him. The delicate thread between victory and defeat felt both terrifying and exhilarating. As he carefully made his way up an alleyway toward the small downtown area, he felt a wave of calm wash over him. He imagined the peace those pilots must have felt knowing that no matter what, they would never face capture from a merciless enemy.

It was funny how the fear of death disappeared once you accepted it with open arms.

EDDIE STARED DUMBLY at Jessica. His stomach sank as he watched her lean close toward Schultz and whisper something to him.

So, she's giving me up. After all that, and after convincing Clarissa to bring Liam to me.

Not that he could be upset with her. It had been too much to expect anything else. He'd rolled the dice and come up with craps.

The pot-bellied deputy raised his eyebrows as Jessica continued to whisper to him. Eddie strained his ears but couldn't make out what she was saying. But he did detect her faintest glance in his direction, more of a micro expression that had taken just a fraction of a second to convey. Eddie remembered something about that from one of his high school psychology classes, one of the few lectures he'd actually paid attention to. A non-verbal cue that communicated a person's true intent, despite what they'd conveyed verbally. What exactly her glance had meant, he didn't know. But as the seconds ticked by, he gained the sense that Jessica had hinted at one of two things: *Sorry, I'm giving you up.* Or, *I'm distracting him. Hurry and get out while you can.*

Eddie made a snap decision and rose from his chair. Schultz kept his head straight ahead as he listened intently to what Jessica was saying. It would be now or never, Eddie thought. Either Schultz spun around on him now with his gun drawn, a sly smile on his face, or Eddie would walk past him and out the door. He figured there wasn't any sense debating the outcome. He'd come this far already. To screw up everything he'd already done out of fear would have made his ordeal up to this point completely pointless.

As he walked behind Schultz's hunched-over form, Eddie noticed a small outer pouch on the man's tactical backpack hanging partway open. Inside the pouch sat a ring of keys with a Ford emblem on the fob, and other cop gear. Making another snap-second decision, Eddie performed a deed so gutsy he managed to impress even himself.

Holy shit, bro, what are you doing? Jules's voice screamed inside his head. Too late to undo what he'd just done, Eddie lowered his head and limped straight out the front door.

FIFTY-THREE

Captain Escobar, ever the pragmatist, had wasted no time disseminating his orders. First, communicate with his field units and direct them to encircle the perimeter. Grassle could not be allowed to escape again. Second, ensure the appropriate supervisors on the ground had the necessary resources to spring the trap set against their newfound nemesis. And lastly, provide a backup plan in case the unthinkable happened— that somehow Grassle, in all his resourcefulness and guile, somehow slipped through the dragnet placed against him. That backup plan, one concocted by himself, included a provision specifying that, should Grassle somehow evade the takedown unit, an emergency request would be sent to all local and state law enforcement agencies requesting their full assistance. Pride was indeed one of the deadly sins, and in this case, it would have to take a backseat to results.

Detective Grimes had returned to the PTS building on Lieutenant Heinke's orders. The prevailing thought held that a detective was better prepared to give up-to-the-minute briefs on Grassle's movements, instead of relying on civilians to do so. Ryan, the tech from earlier, reported no new activity since the outgoing and incoming calls to Grassle's ex-girlfriend. Grimes had been directed to place a call to the phone every minute, in the hopes of catching Grassle slipping once more. The escapee had already been foolish twice, after all. If he were to connect the battery and power the phone again, they'd almost certainly have another location. With the encirclement around him tightening, he stood almost no chance of repeating what he'd managed to do with the horse.

For his part, Detective Teliford had immediately attempted to contact Clarissa as soon as they received the intelligence, but her phone had gone straight to voicemail, and deputies responding to her home reported it absent of all signs of habitation. Frustrated at not being able to reach her by phone, Teliford tried no fewer than another dozen times. Voicemail each time.

Now at a desk in the PTS office, Detective Grimes polished off a bag of peanut butter crackers he'd bought from the employee snack machine. Watching the blinking icon on the computer screen, he directed a question to the bored-looking tech seated next to him.

"Can you tell exactly where he is based on the pings? I need to relay this to our units on the ground."

"As mentioned, it narrows it down to one or two city blocks," the tech explained, trying to remain patient. He shot a look to Mr. Aaron, who stood back from the computer terminal, alternating between inspecting his own fingernails and yawning.

"Cell towers are quite ubiquitous these days," said the tech. "It's difficult for someone to avoid being located once their device is connected to a network. There's even talk of setting up towers in Yellowstone."

Detective Grimes leaned toward the computer screen and squinted. A blue location icon, representing the last known ping from the phone, sat in the middle of downtown Springwood. "That area has a lot of businesses in it," he said. "It would help if we knew exactly how many blocks to search."

From behind them, Aaron sighed, his eyelids fluttering as if he were about to explain an elementary school problem. "Once again, detective, this is the best we can do with what we're working with. If the device in question was GPS-enabled, we could tell you which way his dick leaned."

Grimes nodded, apparently satisfied. As a matter of routine, he sent a text to the dead woman's phone, this time outright requesting Grassle turn himself in immediately. It was worth a try.

"Okay then," Grimes said. "We'll have our apprehension team set up in a more general area. He'll be traveling alone, so that narrows it down. Maybe he—" Grimes paused, double-taking at the computer screen. "Wait—it looks like he's moving!"

Both he and the tech crowded toward the screen and watched the blinking icon begin drifting. Aaron, seeing this, approached the desk as the tech keyed in a code into the computer.

"Hold on," said the tech.

They all waited, until Aaron, seemingly interested now, tapped the screen with one manicured fingernail. "He must have re-connected the battery. I can tell he's moving east since we're getting a new ping from a different tower."

Grimes called Captain Escobar and reported his findings. "Are you sure?" the gray-haired commander asked, his voice coming in staticky over the line.

"I'm looking at it live, sir," Grimes responded, indignant. "He got us last time, but now we've got technology on our side. He can't do anything about a satellite in space."

"Okay," answered the captain, hanging up and ordering the perimeter to shift a half mile to the east. They'd set an ambush there and let him walk right into them.

Grimes sat back in his chair, confident in the manhunt's outcome for the first time. The grandest spotlight of all was now cast upon both his and Teliford's entire reputations. He also knew that the fact that they had been tasked with coordinating the technical side of the search meant if they failed, the spotlight that shined so brightly upon them could instead become a lighted exit out of the homicide division forever.

PAOLO COULD ALMOST taste his prey.

Nearly walking into a group of teens appearing from around the corner, he ducked out of sight behind a business. Waiting for them to pass, he checked his text messages, sent by order from the sheriff's criminal intelligence squad and relayed by Hood: **SUBJ. EAST FROM PREV. LOC. DUNBAR/MAIN.**

Paolo made a quick calculation then darted up the alley to the street parallel to where Grassle had been pinged just minutes before. He turned east up the street and stood looking in a storefront, acting as inconspicuous as possible. The weekend would be in full swing shortly, and already increased foot traffic appeared in this busy part of downtown. Souvenir shops, several eateries, and a hardware store stood on the opposite side of the street. So far, no sign of Grassle. The last hard location on the phone had been six minutes ago, in or around the area of the Honeybee Bar & Grill that sat a block up the street from Paolo's location.

Paolo relaxed his mind to allow himself to once again step into the shoes of the one he hunted. Using an alleyway, he moved east. If Grassle felt brave enough to travel along the busier Dunbar a block away, Paolo would be able to keep pace with him. If he turned south, he would walk directly into him. He'd just come from the west and would unlikely double back along his route with the increasing police presence there. If he turned north, that only fed into an even heavier populace, making that route unlikely as well. Taking a moment to collect himself, Paolo tapped a short text message to Hood.

Will be offline. He is mine.

Turning off and pocketing his phone, Paolo continued up the alleyway. He felt confident that even with the police soon entering the chase, it would take them some time to regroup before they made their move. If he were to have even twenty minutes with which to work unimpeded, it would likely be enough.

Thunder rumbled in the distance. Rain clouds swept in from the Gulf forty miles away. The air became heavy and the foliage all around opened to the coming deluge, seeming to portend the stormy end that was sure to come.

Detective Grimes, Mr. Aaron, and Ryan the PTS tech all leaned toward the monitor expectantly. The tech had taken another reading of the subject's cell phone, triangulating its current position based on an outgoing text from just several minutes prior. To Detective Riggins. The information wasn't in exact real time, the tech explained, but the delay shouldn't be more than thirty seconds or so. Surely not enough time for Grassle to escape the extensive trap being placed around him, no matter what strange event may occur. After moving several blocks from the busy Dunbar Avenue, he appeared to be heading east, on foot probably. Grimes knew the area well—he had been assigned to that area just off downtown during much of his time as a patrol deputy. He relayed this information via a secure special operations radio channel. Watching the blinking icon on the computer screen pulse with an urgency that matched his own racing heartbeat, Grimes tapped a nervous beat on the desktop.

It wouldn't be long now.

CAPTAIN ESCOBAR STOOD beside his unmarked cruiser with a pair of binoculars pressed to his eyes. He scanned the area ahead of their current position, the approach of downtown Springwood. Escobar had already given the order to block off the area, hoping to trap Grassle in a two-pronged pincer movement he'd instructed his forces to execute. Receiving confirmation on Grassle's position, he gave the order for the helicopter to move in. Once they had a visual on him, regardless of whether he ditched inside a structure or other hiding place, they'd be able to close in on him. Moments later, the sound of thumping rotor blades cutting through the thickening afternoon air approached from the north, until the helicopter arrived at a hover some two hundred feet over their position.

The two SWAT teams crouching to Escobar's left waited patiently for his direction to move out. Once given the word, their orders were to move in a linear pattern down this first street of scattered businesses and run-down structures, clearing them one at a time. Thankfully, this area was a few blocks off Dunbar, and thus would be easier to clear. It being mid-afternoon on a Friday, there would have been quite a bit of foot traffic to clear back where they'd first captured Grassle's phone signal. The decision on whether to evacuate downtown of all civilians had been debated. In the end, Escobar had decided it best not to cause a general panic. Plus, it would allow them to keep an element of surprise. All that would remain would be to squeeze Grassle between the pincers.

With a hand signal, Escobar ordered the teams to move out. He had decided against using K-9s for the simple reason he feared the dogs would once again be led down a false path. One failure could be overcome in time; two would seriously erode the sheriff's confidence in the entire program, Escobar's pride and joy. Besides, the sheriff's orders had been clear: take Grassle alive. K-9s could be invaluable resources; but should Grassle become engaged by one and attempt to harm it, Escobar knew his deputies would not hesitate in using deadly force to protect it. Having to explain to the sheriff why Grassle had been killed over a dog—albeit beloved animals that were considered deputies themselves—was not something he wished to do.

Shaking the thought from his mind, Escobar stared hard into his binoculars and followed the team's progress. The outer perimeter of fifty fully armed deputies and special operations personnel stood by patiently. In the distance, thunder rolled closer. The smell of approaching rain came strong to him. The helicopter would have to be grounded soon, but he doubted it would even be needed. If things went the way he thought they would, Escobar had every intention of watching Grassle being handcuffed and driven off to jail before the heavens inevitably opened above them.

FIFTY-FOUR

DETECTIVE ALICE RIGGINS dialed the phone number to the Orlando office of the Florida Department of Law Enforcement, biting her lip as she listened to the ringtone. An operator answered, and after attempting to argue that most office personnel had already left for the day, she finally connected Riggins to the person she sought. A distinctive voice picked up the transferred line, a comforting male baritone she hadn't heard in over a year.

"Agent Linden."

"Bert, it's Alice. Alice Riggins. I need your help."

A pause from the other end, then, "I don't know if I should be worried or offended. Since when do old academy classmates and rookie partners refer to themselves with last names?"

"Who are *you* calling old?" Riggins shot back with a dry laugh.

Agent Linden chuckled, his voice lowering even further. "Just because you were the baby of the academy doesn't mean you never age. If my math is correct, you're in the over-forty club yourself."

Riggins smiled, despite herself. It had been an epically long day, and in all her stress she had almost forgotten what it felt like to relax a bit. Bert had always had that effect on her, even as far back as the academy when the towering, good-natured Georgia native had been assigned to sit next to her during classroom instruction.

The two made brief small talk before the conversation turned crisp and business-like.

"Is this about your manhunt down there?" he asked.

"Yes and no."

"Give me the yes part first. And why didn't you call me on my personal cell?"

Riggins shifted uneasily in the driver's seat, having parked in an area several blocks from the Grassle search perimeter. Sanchez had kept her abreast of the proceedings, texting her updates. As she considered her answer to Bert's question, she eyed storm clouds forming on the horizon. They seemed to mirror her own swirling emotions.

"Long story, but the sheriff put me on desk duty. I must have ruffled the wrong person's feathers. The timing is just too weird."

"Ruffled feathers?" he asked. "But you closed it."

"I know. But I went back and found the only known witness to the robbery. Her statement could lend support to Grassle's defense."

"And someone attached to the case doesn't want that information known."

"That's what it seems like."

"But you didn't say why you didn't call me on my cell."

"I've been ordered to have no more direct dealings with Grassle. If they find out I'm still digging into aspects of the case, I don't want your name to come up in case they pull my phone records."

"Which explains why you had them transfer the call to me, since the transferred numbers don't show up. Okay, this must be serious then. Go on."

Once again, she considered the ramifications of him getting involved. Small county politics notwithstanding, she knew Bert could still get wrapped up in something messy that could potentially place a stain in his personnel file. It was the last thing she wanted to happen. And yet she recalled the conversation they'd had when Bert had left the sheriff's office for a job with the state law enforcement arm. *You call me if you need anything, Alice. I don't care if it's large or small, day or night.*

Thinking back to what Chet had said about doing what she felt was right in her heart, and his past comments reminding her that it was okay to ask the people you cared about for help, she sighed and said, "There's something strange going on down here, Bert. Now that I think about it, there's been strangeness going on for a long time. You know the deal. Mostly rural county, good ol' boy network. Politics takes a back seat to secret handshakes and backroom deals. Shit, it was front page news when I became detective. The first woman of color in the agency's history to ever make it."

"I remember your office party. We got you a cake shaped like handcuffs."

Riggins laughed at the memory. "And it had a key made of chocolate."

"After I left for FDLE, I got a chance to work with some really great cops," Bert said. "But to this day, I've never known a better cop than you, Alice. Just tell me what's really going on."

Riggins sighed and repeated the entire story from the beginning. She included a few investigation details not given to the media. She finished by telling Bert she believed Grassle should never have been arrested in connection with the convenience store robbery.

A paternal sigh from the other end. "Now, this is where the tough love comes in," Bert said pointedly. "You've been on the job almost twenty-five years. You've arrested a few innocent people in that time, just like all of us. It happens. It isn't your job to try them, remember."

"I know—the lieutenant and Chet both reminded me of that too. But there was such enormous pressure from within the agency to charge him that it seemed unnatural. Forced. Much more than normal on a case like this. You've seen the evidence. Open and shut, right?"

"You would think so."

"We've both done this for a long time, Bert. How many times have we seen someone walk because a charge wouldn't stick?"

"Hundreds. That's part of our business."

"Correct. And how many times have we charged someone believing—not legally, but morally—they had nothing to do with the crime?"

Another pause from the other end. While Riggins waited for a response, she turned a knob on her hand-held police radio, changing to the channel used by the main apprehension team.

"I wasn't a philosophy major, Alice. What are you getting at?"

"Well, it's happened to me twice. Twice I've felt sure that I was charging someone with a crime I knew in my heart they should not have been charged with."

"I probably did that twice last week."

"But both times the suspects were charged with murder, Bert. *Murder*. Not domestic battery or possession, where they could bond out of jail in a few hours. Do you know what happened to the guy in my first case?"

"I remember."

"The only real evidence we had were footprint impressions we took from the murder scene. Too muddled to get a proper sole pattern, but the same size as our suspect's. Size ten and a half. Do you know how many people have size ten and a half shoes?"

Linden gave a short, humorless laugh. "That's my size—point taken. But hindsight is twenty-twenty. Innocent people have also been known to confess to crimes they *didn't* commit. You know that."

"No, Bert, you don't understand." Riggins looked up at the slanting gray mass extending down from the fast approaching clouds. "There's someone else involved this time. I feel it's someone outside the agency itself. Even the sheriff seems to be controlled by whoever it is. The fact that he ordered me to stand down from anything else having to do with Grassle—there's no valid reason for it. And he let a civilian work on the Grassle search. Those two decisions have to be connected. What's one of the first things they taught us in the academy?"

"Not to accept a coincidence as fact."

"Yep. Plus, I've heard from people around headquarters that the civilian used to be some sort of Fed spook, and that he's somehow connected to the state attorney."

She could almost hear Linden thinking through the phone connection. "That's about as big of a conflict of interest as you can get, risking getting personally involved in a case you're prosecuting."

"Tell me about it. But that's just it. Nothing is on the record. It's all backdoor stuff. Things like that have been going on around here for longer than I've been around. Smaller-sized sheriff's office, overshadowed by Orlando, Tampa, and Miami. You remember the stories of all those gangsters back in the day dumping bodies in the swamps, when not even us cops asked questions. I haven't seen it quite that bad, but there's always been a large rug associated with this place."

"And a bigger broom."

"Yes. But this time it feels different. And definitely personal."

"So you called me because you don't want to make too much noise rooting around."

"Yes. Or ruffle any more feathers."

A pause between them, then in unison: "Bunches of hunches." They shared a short laugh, recalling the term Linden had coined several years ago for resourcing his vast number of connections.

"But I refuse to get you officially swallowed up in this. If at any time—"

Riggins's radio squawked a message, the apprehension team asking for an update on Grassle's location. Nervousness creeping into her more than ever, Riggins asked Linden to put feelers out for anything improper associated with Hood. The fact he'd long been suspected of nefarious dealings—his office formally investigated by state and federal officials, in fact—spoke of an even greater urgency to dig deep while using a soft shovel.

When a second radio message suddenly came through her radio, this one more excited, Riggins sat up straight in her seat. When it ended, she got back on the phone with Linden, her voice urgent.

"The apprehension team has Eddie cornered. They're tracking the phone he's using."

Almost as an afterthought, Riggins looked at her phone's screen. No missed calls on the upper indicator bar, but an unread text icon showed. Swiping down so the text information would appear, she noted no name attached to it, but the number seemed familiar. It hit her the second she read the message:

It shouldn't be long, detective. Maybe an hour. I'll find another way to let you know where to pick me up.

"Eddie!" she uttered, mostly to herself. Checking the time stamp, she realized the message had come in about ten minutes ago. She must have missed it somehow during the rush of activity.

"We're moving in on him, Bert. I have to go!"

"But I thought you're on desk duty," Linden replied.

But Riggins didn't have time to answer. Ending the call, she jumped out of the car and made her way down the street toward a row of parked police cruisers barricading an intersection. Glancing left and right of her position, she saw the intersections in those directions blocked also. Considering Eddie had been successfully tracked to this specific area, and the massive amount of manpower brought to bear against him, Riggins couldn't imagine a single way he could slip by them this time. Even though the helicopter had just been grounded due to the coming storm, she felt it was just a matter of time before Eddie's luck ran out. She knew her administrative assignment still allowed her to make physical arrests, but the sheriff's mandate overrode everything else. Her wings had effectively been clipped. Still, she figured she'd do everything in her power to make his capture go as smoothly—and safely—as possible. Not so much as a favor to Eddie, but to herself.

When a hand rested on Riggins's shoulder, she spun around, her heart in her throat. Detective Sanchez stood smiling at her.

"No civilians in the area, ma'am," he said, only half-jokingly. He guided her to the sidewalk away from the line of officers bent over their vehicles, their weapons trained on the street beyond. "What are you doing here?" he asked. "If L.T. sees you, he'll have you for dinner and me for dessert." Sanchez ran a hand through his hair as he looked nervously in all directions.

"I can't just sit by and listen to what's going on," Riggins said, ignoring her partner's warning. "I'm more and more convinced that somebody is out to get Eddie. If I can bring him in myself, I will."

Sanchez moved his eyes along the line of officers nearby. "Um, newsflash. The entire sheriff's office is out to get him."

"That's not what I meant," she said. "I mean someone with a personal stake in his case. I've got an idea I just bounced off an old friend. It's like Connect the Dots. You can sort of see it before you start drawing lines."

Just then, movement from several of the officers as they stood from their bent firing positions and headed off down the street at a full run.

"What's happening?" Riggins asked, her face flushing. She watched Sanchez put his radio to his ear, his eyes widening. Riggins held her own radio close but had trouble making out anything intelligible over the shouting officers.

"I think they got him," Sanchez said, clipping his radio back onto his belt. "A couple blocks down. Stay here. I'll go down and call you with an update." He turned in the same direction the other officers had just run, then Riggins reached out and grabbed his arm.

"Sanny, if they do have him in custody, ask Lieu if you can do the transport back to the county, or wherever they take him first. For me?"

Sanchez nodded, then ran off down the street.

FIFTY-FIVE

WITH HIS FACE driven into the asphalt, Deputy Schultz screamed in fury at the three SWAT members on top of him. "Get the fuck off me, you imbeciles!"

The tactical team members kneeling across his back and legs looked to each other and shrugged. Five other members stood nearby, one of them propping a shotgun on his hip. The beanbag round he'd just fired had struck Schultz's right buttock, sending him to the ground in a fit of agony. In the ensuing tussle with backup officers, his black BDU pants had inadvertently been pushed down to expose an ugly red welt on his ample ass.

"Get off me, you fucking idiots!" Schultz screamed, struggling against the weight of the men atop him. "I'm with the goddamn search team! You got the wrong person!"

By now the other squad of SWAT members, having heard of the reported takedown, had converged on the scene. A crowd of perimeter deputies, acting on their own and against orders not to move from their positions, also moved in. Each of them lifted their goggles and looked from Schultz to one another with mixed expressions of humor and wonder. Still cuffed, Deputy Schultz managed to rub the spot on his backside where he'd just been hit with the less-than-lethal, but no less painful, beanbag projectile.

It soon became obvious to everyone what had happened. Having operated on his own and without notifying his chain-of-command, Schultz had been spotted and challenged by the first SWAT team as he walked between two buildings. The sheriff markings on his tactical vest having been obscured by his backpack, he had apparently been mistaken for a civilian. Ordered to stop and lie on the ground by the SWAT members, he'd instead reached into a back flap of his backpack and removed a vibrating cell phone. Turning it over quizzically in his hand, and with the SWAT members believing the phone to be a weapon, he'd been shot with the bean bag. Now, as confusion gave way to the reality of the situation, it became clear that the cell phone the intel team had been tracking, the one assumed to be on their suspect Eddie Grassle, had somehow found its way into the fat jail deputy's backpack.

The jail veteran rolled onto his side and cast a baleful look to the crowd of deputies around him. "Get me out of these things, for fuck's sake!" he screamed.

Thunder boomed from directly above, and the first sprinkles of rain began to fall from the ever-darkening sky.

"And you, you fucking ape—" Schultz said, eying the burly deputy holding the shotgun, "I'll have your goddamn job if it's the last thing I do!" The deputy he referred to, Otis Cribbs, was one of only two black SWAT team members in the agency. He'd been on the job nine years, SWAT for three, and had never before fired a beanbag round at a human being. Deputy Cribbs looked from the grinning faces of his fellow SWAT members down to Schultz's writhing, fat form and shrugged. "Sorry, man. Thought you were a different asshole I knew."

The other SWAT members and gathered deputies roared with laughter. Schultz swept a murderous scowl among them all. "Take these things off me now, you cocksuckers! He's getting away!"

The moment's levity quickly ended with the team's realization of their mistake's impact. It soon became apparent that elements of the perimeter guard were not in place as they should have been. As one of the members uncuffed Schultz and had him attended to by a paramedic (his right buttock had already taken on an ugly purple bruise that extended halfway down his leg), Captain Escobar arrived. Rain beginning to slash at them, the furious captain stood his prized

SWAT team in a single line and promised that if Grassle escaped the area, Escobar would personally see to it that each of them be removed from the team by day's end.

Spread out along five linear city blocks, groups of three-man mini teams backtracked the way they'd come until they hit the beginning of the business district. Most civilians had been evacuated, Escobar feeling he had no choice in declaring the suspect perhaps being in their midst. It took much longer this way, but they'd been left with few options. When they'd completed the initial search, Escobar retired the team to the edge of an open field to assess the situation. Pacing back and forth and already soaked by the now-pouring rain, he considered his next move. They hadn't as much as caught Grassle's scent. He'd managed to disappear again. Worse, the tight perimeter he'd ordered had collapsed during the false takedown scene, creating a gap that had lasted for several minutes. Not long, but plenty of time for Grassle to have slipped through. Not wanting to send the radio transmission, but knowing he must, Escobar changed radio frequencies and keyed the mike secured to his vest. "Eagle two to Eagle one. Suspect is still Signal-6. I say again, suspect is Signal-6."

ESCOBAR'S RADIO TRANSMISSION reached Sheriff Driscoll, who stood beneath the command center tent a mile away. When he signed off, he adjusted the Stetson atop his head then folded his arms across his chest. He stared off into the pouring rain, a toothpick working its way from one side of his mouth to the other. When one of his lieutenants approached him with questions of what he wanted to do next, the old sheriff held one hand up to deliver a silent message. *Not now*, it meant. *I'm thinking.*

MOMENTS AFTER SCHULTZ'S takedown, Riggins's cell phone rang. She held a protective hand over it to protect it from the intensifying rain.

"You won't believe this," Sanchez blurted, sounding out of breath.

"Talk to me, Sanny." Riggins paced the vacated street, feeling as though her heart would pound through her chest.

"You know the phone Grassle was using? Well, I guess the IT folks were able to pinpoint it after all. Captain is pretty upset about what happened."

Riggins's hands trembled so badly she could barely hold on to her phone. She recalled the sheriff's mandate that Grassle be taken alive at all reasonable costs. "Did they shoot him?"

"Um—not exactly. They hit one of our guys with a beanbag. Grassle's gone. It'd be easier for me to tell you in person."

Riggins began to respond when a flash of movement half a block to her left distracted her. Her head snapped in that direction just in time to catch the fleeting image of a youngish-looking man limp across the street. Even from this distance, and through the falling rain, she recognized enough details of the man to cause her to call out to him.

"Eddie?"

The man skidded to a stop, looked in her direction, then disappeared into an adjoining alley. That settled it for her. She'd just taken a step in that direction when more movement caused her to stop dead in her tracks. There, from the same place she'd seen Eddie emerge between a garbage dumpster and a white cinderblock building, came the dark figure of a man brandishing a gun. Believing him to be part of the tactical team, Riggins began to call out to the figure when an odd feeling caused the words to freeze on her lips. Something about the man's clothing seemed off. Clad in blue jeans and a light jacket, the man looked nothing like a tactical team member. Not even the undercovers dressed that way. In the seconds it took her brain to process the information, Riggins watched the man disappear down the same alley Eddie had slipped into moments before. That odd feeling struck her again, and finally she recognized it to be her inner sense of danger. It normally went off earlier in a situation; she realized the unusual confusion and stress of the moment had thrown her off. She'd been taught early on in her career to listen to that sense, to respect it, because if you didn't and had not prepared yourself for the worst, it would be too late when you finally came face-to-face with its source.

Keeping her eyes on the alleyway, she bent and drew her personal .38 revolver from her ankle holster. Her feet moved quickly and quietly over the pavement, which already sent tendrils of vapor into the air as the first wave of rain continued to fall first in sporadic spatters, then finally in a solid sheet. Reaching the point she had seen Eddie and his pursuer disappear, she flattened herself against the side of the building and counted to ten. A quick glance behind her, then a double-take when she thought she'd detected movement from where she'd come. Was her mind playing tricks on her? Had the man with the gun perhaps doubled-back on her position? Deciding to continue ahead, she moved tactically down the alley, taking her time to clear darkened doorways and obstructions as she went. Rain fell freely now in great gray sheets. Not the typical early summer shower that had rejuvenating qualities, but one that brought with it a more ominous and funereal quality. Like rain during an execution.

As she reached the end of the block, she peered from behind the service pole she was crouching behind and examined both sides of the street. No movement. She had only been behind the armed man by about thirty seconds, and due in large part to the now torrential downpour, she reasoned anybody choosing to remain in such weather was either a complete idiot, or had a very good reason to do so.

Gun at her side, Riggins crossed the street and slipped into the next alley, sure Eddie and whoever stalked him had gone in that direction. Unknown to her, a figure hiding in a sunken doorway some twenty yards behind her watched with narrowed eyes before taking care to follow as silently as possible.

FIFTY-SIX

SLIPPING THE PHONE into Schultz's backpack before exiting the Honeybee had taken every bit of nerve Eddie possessed.

It had also been one of those spontaneous acts a person performs in their lives which cause them to look back with both fondness and amazement. Providing of course a person lived long enough to reflect upon it.

Pushing his way out the front door, Eddie had elected to travel west along Dunbar, doubling back the way he'd come. Because of a shadow. Schultz's shadow, to be exact. In exiting the restroom and heading toward the front door, Eddie had remembered seeing the fat man's shadow approach the restaurant's entrance from that direction. Of course, Eddie hadn't known it to be Schultz at the time. But it *had* been him. And in deciding which way to initially walk as he pushed his way outside, Eddie had quickly postulated that Schultz would continue his search east, the direction he'd been walking when he'd entered the Bee.

Eddie had planned to ditch the phone no matter what. That he'd had the opportunity to do so in Schultz's backpack had been a display of epic kismet, and a final *fuck you* to his tormentor. Now keeping his head low to avoid eye contact with anyone, Eddie traveled west along the block until he came to an intersection. He waited for several cars to pass then crossed the street, continuing in the same direction. He assumed they were still tracking the phone, and if so, felt it might buy him a few minutes. If they weren't, and he turned blindly back into the enveloping trap around him, he'd lose his last chance.

It was a gamble he felt he had to take.

He had backtracked two more blocks along Dunbar when he saw a pair of sheriff cruisers approach. He darted left down a side street and waited with his heart in his throat to see if they turned in his direction. Grateful when they did not, he turned south at a fast limp, understanding from his vast knowledge of the area that the sheriff's headquarters building sat about two miles in that direction. Edging a wooded preserve that everyone in the county older than ten years old knew would never be developed, the county-owned property served as not just offices for the sheriff's office, but as the communication center for the entire county. Eddie figured if he could manage to avoid detection long enough to make it there, he might have one chance in a thousand to pull off his plan.

As he zigzagged his way through adjoining alleyways and side streets, Eddie felt the rejuvenating quality of the driving rain that soaked him to the bone. Aside from refreshing him, the rain also kept people from walking the streets. The few cars that passed by him did so with drivers concentrating on the road instead of the man limping his way down the sidewalk. Pausing to catch his breath behind an old wooden fence, Eddie gathered his thoughts. According to his inner clock, he'd called Clarissa about twenty minutes ago. With his created character having arranged to meet her at the headquarters building at three-thirty, that left about forty minutes, probably less since he'd need to ensure he got there before she did. Clarissa had been many things. But late had never been one of them.

WITH THE RAIN slashing at him sideways, Eddie stumbled out of the alley and faced an open field made muddy by the torrential rain. About fifty yards into the field stood a ten-story building still in mid-construction, a chain-link fence surrounding the entire property. Not much else inhabited the soggy ground for almost a hundred yards in every other direction. The building's unfinished walls enabled Eddie to look straight through from one side to the other. Temporary wooden railings had been erected along each of the unfinished floors, and enclosed stairwells rose in each of the building's four corners. Eddie looked left and right. Nothing but that same open, sloppy ground. Looking behind him, he considered going back the way he'd come, but a sense of foreboding told him he wouldn't last another minute if he did that. That left the building.

Slogging his way across the muddy field, and twice nearly spilling headlong into giant puddles, Eddie reached the fence and collapsed against it. A moment later his leg and back muscles began to spasm, causing his face to twist in agony.

"I don't know if I can make it," Eddie yelled toward the sky, wishing—needing—for Jules to help guide him. Just then, a flash of movement to his left caused him to turn his head in that direction. A man had just emerged from the same alley Eddie had just hobbled from moments before. Only faintly recognizable through the undulating sheets of rain, the man looked left then right before settling his gaze on Eddie fifty yards ahead. Even from this distance, Eddie saw the man's lips curl into a severe sort of smile as the man raised one finger, wagging it back and forth in a mocking *no-no-no* gesture. In the man's other hand hung a black pistol with a suppressor attached to the barrel.

Something threatened to turn loose in Eddie's guts. As if controlled by some invisible force, he rolled onto his side then struggled to his knees. A panic he had never known before seized him as he realized that the man from the barn, the same one who had butchered the woman and the deputy too, had somehow found him again; and whoever he was and for whatever reason he wanted Eddie dead, he wouldn't stop until he finished the job.

Groaning against the pain that shot through his entire body, Eddie rose to his feet and began clambering along the fence line, desperately looking for a way through it.

RAINDROPS DRIPPING FROM his head and face, Paolo watched jovially as Eddie moved down the fence line, banging and pulling desperately at each section as he went. No need to rush. The man had nowhere to run this time. No last-second reprieve would save him. A measure of comfort he had not felt in some time soothed him, just as the meditative quality of the driving rain did now. Learning from his police radio that the police had once again tripped in their frenzied search for the increasingly resourceful escapee, Paolo felt a level of comfort he had not yet enjoyed throughout this mission. Not only would he succeed, thus earning Mathias's favor, but the absence of police would enable him to take his time with Grassle. Feeling an almost baptismal resurgence flow through him, Paolo took slow and deliberate steps toward his prey.

FIND A WAY IN! Eddie's mind screamed. Frantic, he shook the fence along its length, desperately seeking an opening. Reaching its nearest corner, he flung himself around it, only to see another fifty-yard length of fence-line along the structure's rear. Looking left, he considered crossing over the open ground to a row of garage-type businesses several hundred feet away. But he would be a sitting duck. And the ground there was a quagmire, filled with mud and puddles that would hamper his already slowed progress. Glancing over his shoulder and seeing the man following in leisurely, measured steps, Eddie stumbled over his own feet and crashed to the muddy ground. Mud and rainwater splashed across his face and into his mouth. Spitting it out, he struggled to his feet and continued along the fence, desperate for a way in. Halfway down the fence's length, he came to a chained gate he hadn't seen at first. Crying out in relief, he pushed at it but could only create about an eight-inch gap. The man continued toward him in that almost playful gait, a sinister smile now on his lips. Throwing the full weight of his body between the gate sections, Eddie created a few more inches of space, enabling him to squeeze an arm and leg through. His head wouldn't fit. Looking up, he noticed the man had cut the distance between them by half. Just twenty yards away now.

Soon he'd be in easy pistol range. Knife range, not long after. Crying out, Eddie forced his head and upper body through the gap, scraping both sides of his face and feeling one of his ribs crack in the process. Falling headlong to the muddy ground within, he wobbled to his feet and locked eyes with the man, who had stopped a few yards from the gate. The man's eyebrows raised, and he brought his hands together in mock applause. A certain level of respect seemed to glimmer in his dark eyes, combined with something else Eddie recognized—horrifically—as excitement.

The man loved this.

Desperate, Eddie extended his palms toward the man, standing twenty yards away.

"Why are you doing this?" Eddie cried. His voice came cracked and weak and was barely audible over the driving rain. As if choosing to answer with action instead of words, the man holstered his silenced pistol and unsheathed a long-bladed knife from beneath his jacket. After inspecting the blade's edge, he executed an authentic-seeming bow toward Eddie before moving toward the gate. Thirty pounds lighter than Eddie, he would have no trouble slipping through. One arm now. Then a leg, followed by his head. Eddie's eyes bulged as he backpedaled, nearly slipping on a discarded piece of cardboard in the process. Searching for a way into the building, he spotted a nearby staircase. Clawing his way through the yellow caution tape cordoning off the open entrance, he looked up into the darkened stairwell. He would essentially be trapping himself by going upward. But he had little choice. The man was almost through the gate and would be on him in a matter of seconds if he didn't make a decision.

Steeling himself for an end he knew would come in some manner soon, Eddie began to climb the staircase.

Reaching the second-floor landing, Eddie bent with hands on knees to catch his breath. The stairwell opened straight onto the unfinished concrete floor, the doors not having been installed yet. Counting to five, he began toward the next flight of stairs when he discovered his legs would not move. Cramps had turned them into dead logs. Picking his left leg up with his hands, he moved it forward one step, then did the same with the other leg. He repeated this process again but soon realized how hopeless this would be. Choosing to face his doom standing rather than on his knees or back, he propped himself against the wall and prepared to watch his pursuer advance up the staircase. When he didn't see him after several seconds, he began to wonder if the man had for some reason changed his mind. But this notion was quickly dispelled when he heard shouting from below. Moving through the open doorway to the wooden barrier, he looked down and saw a curious sight. The man, who moments before had been chasing him, stood just outside the stairwell's entrance, both hands held high in the air. The knife he'd been carrying lay on the muddy ground beside him. Frowning, Eddie scanned left and right, noting nothing out of the ordinary. Rain continued to slash down in ever-increasing intensity. Looking back toward the fence, he was astonished to see a light-complexioned black woman standing just outside the gate. She held the man at gunpoint and was shouting orders for him to step away from where he'd placed his knife down. Since the woman wore blue jeans and a plain, dark t-shirt, Eddie didn't make the connection at first. But when he heard her bark another command, this one louder and rising above the roaring storm, recognition hit him like a ton of bricks.

Detective Riggins.

An involuntary, excited shout escaped Eddie's throat. Simultaneously, he detected movement behind Riggins—a balding man in a suit—who had worked his way across the muddy ground to where she stood. When the man approached her side, he said something to her before pointing his own gun at the gunman. Recognition clicked in Eddie's brain again—he remembered the man as being Riggins's boss, Lieutenant Heinke, who had been present during his initial booking process the month before.

They've got him! Eddie thought, a surge of excitement bolting through him as his brain struggled to reconcile the difference between death and capture.

FIFTY-SEVEN

"**W**HAT DO WE have here?" Heinke asked Riggins, keeping his sidearm leveled at the jacketed man.

"I don't know," Riggins answered, keeping the muzzle of her own weapon trained on the man. Moments ago, as he'd been steps away from entering the stairwell Eddie had just disappeared into, he had obeyed her command to slowly place his knife on the ground and raise his hands in the air.

"What are you doing here, Lieu?" she asked as an afterthought.

"I saw you back near the takedown scene and followed you. I figured if you were going to insist on working this case, I couldn't just sit by without backing you up."

An awkward moment passed between them. Rain soaked them both, and while the man kept his hands in the air, Riggins gave Heinke the quick rundown.

"I saw Grassle. This guy followed him here. I'm not sure, but he could be that civilian the sheriff allowed into the search."

Heinke cursed. "I'll take it from here."

Instructing the man to take several steps to his left then lie on the ground, Heinke reinforced this by waving the muzzle of his pistol in that direction. The man began to obey, but then with the suddenness of a cat, he dove into a roll while drawing a pistol from beneath his jacket.

Heinke fired on instinct. The round ricocheted off a strand of fencing, throwing it off target and slamming into the building's concrete siding a foot above the man's head. Riggins fired also, her own round coming so close behind Heinke's that the two reports sounded like syncopated thunderclaps. Her shot would have hit its mark had the kneeling man not tumbled out of the way just as she pulled the trigger. Instead, her round smashed into the concrete six inches to the man's left.

As he came out of his roll, the man rose to one knee while extending his pistol at eye-level. He squeezed off two quick shots, the suppressed muzzle giving off a suppressed *pffft* sound barely audible above the driving rain. The first round struck Heinke square in the chest, continuing through his body until it blew a walnut-sized hole out his back. Having abandoned the use of his tactical vest since moving from his regular patrol position fifteen years prior, he'd declared that if his time were to come in the field, it would at least happen with him being comfortable. Grunting at the effect of the bullet punching through him, he collapsed in a heap.

The second round struck a fence support pole, shattering in a shower of sparks. Diving out of the way, Riggins narrowly avoided a subsequent four-shot volley aimed squarely at her. Landing in a puddle, she rolled back to cover Heinke's body with her own. Taking no time to align her sights, she thrust her revolver in the shooter's direction and fired it dry. Thumbing the cylinder release, she popped the cylinder open and dumped the empty cartridges onto the ground in front of her. Instinctively reaching for her belt line, she realized her mistake—no speed loaders. The plastic bullet holders were easy enough to hold over the revolver's open cylinder and quickly load, but in her haste to leave the house she'd forgotten them. She owned a personal .40 caliber Glock other than her issued weapon but had eschewed it for her trusty revolver. Now she regretted that decision since the Glock held 10 in the mag and one in the pipe.

Thinking quickly, she reached over Heinke's stilled form and pried the Glock from his hand, casting aside her now-useless revolver. Sweeping the barrel over the area where she'd last seen the man, she detected nothing but muddy ground and the opening of an empty staircase. Cursing herself for not having taken aimed shots, Riggins switched into lifesaving mode. Pressing two fingers against Heinke's carotid neck artery, she felt nothing. Repositioning her fingers, she tried again. A faint pulse. "Stay with me, Lieu!" she pleaded, looking into his glazed eyes. Turning her ear to his face, she heard a raspy wheeze. This confused her since she did not see his chest rise or fall. Holding her ear even closer, she listened for the sound again. When it came, she realized it wasn't coming from his mouth or nose, but from the single bullet wound through his lung. A sucking chest wound. Propping herself on her elbows to look directly into his ashen face, where his glasses sat askew, Riggins felt she stared into the eyes of a dying man. Heinke's mouth hung half-open, blood trailing from it and down his cheek to blend with the groundwater in a macabre, pink pool. Pushing his suit jacket aside and ripping open his button-down shirt, Riggins found the entry wound—a neat, dime-sized hole two inches in from his right nipple. Another inch to the right and the bullet would have struck his heart, she estimated. Dead before he hit the ground. Alive for now, Heinke struggled to breathe, each exhale causing aerated blood to bubble from the wound. Tearing off a strip of his shirt, Riggins balled it up and covered the wound, placing as much pressure over it with one hand as she could, while at the same time doing her best to not expose too much of herself to the gunman.

Mere seconds after Riggins covered the wound, Heike took a wheezing breath in through his mouth, his chest noticeably rising.

"Keep your eyes open, Lieu!" she pleaded, keeping the pressure down on his chest. With her free hand, she felt for her radio but realized she'd lost it in her tumble. Removing her cell phone from her pocket, she thumbed the home button. Shielding it the best she could against the driving rain, she pressed the phone icon and had just selected the contact 'Sanny' when the signal dropped. Cursing rain and fate alike, she smeared the water-soaked device against her already soaked shirt in a failed attempt to dry it off. It wasn't any good. The rain fell so hard that without any cover she was sure it would short out completely. Not like anyone would be able to hear her over the roar of the storm anyway. Patting Heinke's belt line, she found his radio missing as well. Spying it several yards away in a muddy puddle, she chose not to risk moving out of cover to try retrieving it. She would do neither of them any good if she herself got hit. Lying behind her gravely injured lieutenant and out of contact with anyone else at all, much less anyone in the sheriff's office, Alice Riggins thought of Chet and of how he had no idea of her predicament. He would be at home washing dishes or making an afternoon snack, waiting to hear from her about how things were going. He might even have decided to pick up his guitar and strum a few chords to ease the tension he no doubt had, knowing she'd gone out on her own to help bring Grassle in alive.

Lying there in the mud, pressing desperately down on Heinke's wound, Riggins also thought of how fast and unexpectedly death could find you. It was amazing to her that the life you'd lived without worry or concern on so many occasions could end in an instant, and that nothing you had ever experienced could compare to holding dearest the ones you loved the most.

DURING THE EXCHANGE of gunfire, Eddie had yelled in vain for Riggins to watch out. His voice drowned by the shots and pounding storm, he'd been resigned to helplessly watch the action unfold a story below him. At one point, he'd considered throwing himself over the wooden railing and jumping the twelve or so feet to the ground, knowing he wouldn't have time to help by going back down the flight of stairs. But as quickly as he'd considered this, he'd seen the man spring to his feet and duck into the safety of the stairwell.

Shit! He's only a floor below me!

Having no choice, Eddie had clambered up the next two floors, painfully banging his shins and knees on the stairs as he went. Pausing now on the fourth-floor landing, he dared a glance back down the staircase, sure he'd find the assailant's grinning face but seeing only the darkened stairs for now, and hearing the sound of someone mounting them purposefully, one by one. Willing his broken body up the last six flights, his lungs on fire, Eddie collapsed in exhaustion on the tenth floor. The end of the line. Scattered construction equipment and supplies lay across the expansive concrete floor, but nothing seemed large enough to hide behind or appropriate enough to use in his own defense. He pulled himself along the temporary wooden railing, stopping halfway between the staircase he'd just exited and another one that sat on the opposite side of the building. His position offered no true defense, but at least now he would have the opportunity to face his fate head on—the trapped rabbit watching the snake slither its way toward it.

FIFTY-EIGHT

SELDOM HAD CAPTAIN Escobar allowed his temper to get the better of him. His vast patience and acceptance of the inevitable mistakes prone to even the most experienced officers only added to his legend within the agency. Having risen through the ranks without currying politics or embracing nepotism, he had earned the moniker "Mount Escobar" several years before. A born leader, he had been promoted to head patrol operations (and thus served as the sheriff's second-in-command) for no other reason than that he had simply been the best candidate for the job. He refused to discipline any of his deputies for anything he himself had ever gotten away with during his own career, regardless of the infraction. That, combined with the fact that he never shied from toiling in the trenches alongside his troops, helped buoy an undying respect for him among anyone he led.

But now, as he paced in front of his circumspect SWAT members, their eyes averted from him, Captain Escobar felt his patience finally snap. In a mind-bending mix of curses and shouts that could be heard above the roar of the thunderstorm, he dressed each member down one by one. When he finished, he stood perfectly still in front of them, rain dripping from his face. He'd dodged bullets in Iraq while under worse conditions, so merely becoming soaked with rain was nothing to him. Besides, it helped him think. None of the

SWAT members dared to utter a word as they listened to their commander speak.

"It happens," Escobar said, almost to himself. Then, "Taglia, get me intel on the perimeter."

"Yes, sir!" called a nearby officer, making several radio transmissions. With the necessary logistics completed, Captain Escobar rallied his team and formulated a new perimeter that unfortunately doubled the previous one. But all was not lost. For Grassle to have slipped past them meant he had to still be in the immediate area. No man in his condition could have traveled that distance on foot in enough time to escape this new cordon. Especially with all vehicular traffic to and from the area eliminated. Escobar still had every confidence his team would find Grassle as long as they maintained a systematic search. Discipline would be critical. As they cleared the area structure by structure, he figured the only other possibility for Grassle having slipped past the new perimeter would have been for him to literally have flown away.

Considering this preposterous idea, his gaze lifted toward a construction site half a mile away. The ten-story building sat only partly completed and lay surrounded by what appeared to be open ground. Despite the site lying just beyond the newly formed perimeter, something stirred within him. During his career, he had learned to listen to that stirring, his sixth sense. It had saved him countless hours of unnecessary police work, and on several occasions, it had saved his life. With most other areas around them already cleared, there simply weren't many places for Grassle to have hidden. Escobar knew he would need every man he had available in the search; a wild goose chase could derail their chances of finding him by nightfall, an edict demanded of by the sheriff. Yet that stirring remained. Making a snap decision, the grizzled veteran hailed one of his sergeants and directed him to take a team to clear the building site. The young sergeant sounded an enthusiastic assent before selecting a five-man team from the ranks of dripping wet SWAT members.

Rain slashed at Eddie's face. Wind whipped at him, aided by the open ground around the building site, causing him to rock unsteadily against the wooden railing. The end had finally come. There was no place else for him to run, nowhere to go. Above the wind and rain, he heard faint whistling, a familiar classical piece he couldn't quite remember the name of, then he watched with widened eyes as the man appeared at the top of the staircase. As if playing some school-yard game, the assassin raised one hand and waved a little hello with his fingers before brandishing the large knife Eddie had seen earlier. He started toward Eddie, taking methodical, purposeful steps. An image came to Eddie's mind—of he and Liam at the park. He stood behind the boy as he pushed him on a swing. Laughter, lilting and high-pitched, coming from his son. A sweet breeze blowing. Eddie laughing as Liam squealed with joy. Eddie felt fatherly pride swell within him. In his mind, the sky was so blue it seemed as though someone had painted it.

But as quickly as the image had come, it disappeared as the man cut the distance in half. Eddie felt himself slipping downward onto his backside, arms extending outward, his fingers splayed open in a universal sign of pleading. He'd wanted to die on his feet, like a man. But his legs had given out beneath him and now he was look-ing up at his would-be killer, disbelief swimming through him. He couldn't fathom his life would end here and now. It seemed fake, this thing that was happening. But it wasn't. It was real. He was here, the man was here, and no one could stop what would happen. After everything he'd been through, all the bullshit and time he'd wasted on possibilities that hadn't added up to a single fucking thing, he'd reached the end of the line. That he'd literally come twenty minutes and a mile away from completing the only thing left in his life he cared about, seemed almost funny.

As the man took the last few steps and stood directly over him, his knife held now in both hands, a certain peace washed over Eddie. A calmness he had never felt. The dying process started in your mind, he discovered. From there it traveled along your nerve endings until a strange sensation reached even your fingertips, your toes, the end of your very being. Awareness heightened. Smells you'd never smelled before came to you, memories long and distant reappearing suddenly, like the light from a dusty lightbulb in a seldom-used basement. After coming so far and enduring so much, he felt amazed that this was how it would end. Alone and sitting in the hull of an unfinished building. There would be no dramatic speeches, no loved ones crowded around him to usher him into the void. It was no way to die. But then again, he figured his life had really been no way to live.

FIFTY-NINE

EDDIE WATCHED AS the man's lips peeled back, exposing teeth so white that Eddie was reminded for one insane moment of his childhood, when he'd placed a pair of plastic vampire teeth into his mouth on Halloween. As quickly as that thought came, Eddie's conscious mind snapped back to one so clear and limpid that its truth seemed already fact: *I'm going to die.*

Something strange happened to him as he watched the man grip the knife high over his own head, bringing it down hard toward Eddie's chest. He sensed himself leaving his own body, floating to a point several feet above his would-be killer. Peace, at last. The end of his cramped, dank jail cell; the sneering jail guards peering into the tiny window in his steel door; the half-rotten food; the tease that was recreation, freedom lying just beyond the fences. A hundred images flashed by his eyes. A thousand. One of his favorites, of inner tubing on the river with Jules while they drank stolen beers from the local liquor store, joking and laughing and speaking of girls they'd never fucked but wished they had. That freedom which for nineteen years had come so cheaply, taken for granted like the air and the wind and the sky above him. Not even the five-year stretch he'd done for Jules had diminished his assumption that life and youth were both his God-given right. He had been *alive.* Free and breathing. What force existed that could possibly take that away? The culmination of a lifetime of experiences, all twenty-four years and eight months of it to this point, had only now taught him the true value of mortality. And attached to him, the son whom he'd never known and never would. How close he'd been to seeing him. Even if for a moment. The goddamned shame of it all was that, with a simple and innocuous decision, his life and that of his only flesh and blood would forever be altered for the worse.

Hello, son. I'm your dad. Remember that I love you, even though I can't ever be with you.

A QUARTER MILE away, the team that Captain Escobar had sent to clear the construction site slogged their way toward it, hampered by the still-driving rain. Their boots sunk into the muck at every step, doubling the five-minute trip. The squad's team leader looked toward the looming structure and imagined that in the unlikely event their suspect had holed himself inside of it, it would be impossible for him to get away this time.

RIGGINS PRESSED DOWN on Heinke's chest, praying aloud for him to just hang on, damn it, she wasn't ready to bury another father. Keeping Heinke's Glock trained on the building, she considered once again going for his radio that lay five feet away in a growing puddle of water. *No one knows I'm here*, she thought again. Recalling her training, she knew the danger of being isolated in a life-threatening situation without dispatch or backup knowing your location. It was a worst-case scenario pounded into every police recruit. But she knew exposing herself to fire wouldn't just risk her own life, but Heinke's as well. He was badly injured, dying even, but for now retained a pulse and was breathing on his own. If only the damn rain would lessen, she may be able to detect movement from inside the structure that would help her decide her next move. She told herself that if no one came in the next few minutes, she'd have to risk exposing herself, or even risk shorting out her phone if she tried to make an emergency call. But no matter what, she wasn't leaving him.

"Stay alive, please," she whispered to her barely breathing lieutenant, keeping as much pressure on his wound as she could.

TIME CAUGHT UP with itself.

In an instant, Eddie felt himself sucked back into his body. As if commanded from an unknown source, his left hand shot upward, his palm extended toward his attacker. As the man drove the knife downward, Eddie's hand slid into the carbonized blade more than it was stabbed by it. At first, he felt no pain, just a curious pressure, one his mind still had not processed as the pointed steel slid through the metatarsal bones between his second and third fingers. It severed a vein and a cluster of nerves before exiting with the remaining four inches of steel stopped mere inches from his chest. As his brain finally configured this new trauma, electricity seemed to course through his entire body. His hand went instantly numb as warm, coppery blood spurted from the wound and splashed across his face. He pressed upward more out of instinct than any real sense of survival. His right arm lay helplessly at his side, the strength in it gone. Above him, the man still gripped the knife with both hands, his upper body suspended in mid-air as he drove downward with his body weight. The knife point touched Eddie's chest at one point, piercing through his shirt and into the skin there. Eddie's eyes shot wide as he detected this. If he lessened his upward pressure even a bit, he knew the remaining blade would crunch through his breastplate and punch through his heart. Screaming for his very life, he exerted as much force as he could, succeeding in raising the blade— and the killer behind it—several inches.

The killer looked down at Eddie's outstretched arm as if some magic trick had just been executed. For one almost comical moment, both he and Eddie looked calmly into each other's eyes, allowing several beats to pass in near total stillness until the man re-gripped the knife handle and forced his chiseled one hundred and eighty pounds downward with everything he had.

Somewhere far away, Eddie heard a cry rise above the roaring downpour. It wasn't until he saw the knife move back toward his chest that he realized the cry had been his own.

"No, I won't let you kill me!" Eddie heard himself scream above the booming thunder. "I have to see my son!"

The man adjusted his feet as he continued pressing his weight downward. "Just let go," he said, looking calmly into Eddie's eyes. "It will make your passage easier."

And then, like the light from a firefly sparking on a summer's dusk, an image lit in Eddie's mind, of something he had forgotten about since waking that morning in the tree above his mother's grave.

As if moved by some alien will, his right arm came suddenly alive, his hand fumbling into the overalls' right pocket. His fingers grasped a rigid, cylindrical object—Jules's pocketknife. Removing it, Eddie brought it to his mouth, moving his lips along its length until he found the notch in the blade top. Biting down, he pulled the knife handle away from him with all his might. Nothing. After years of exposure to the elements, it had rusted shut. He pulled again, but still nothing. Trying yet again, this time biting down with his incisor, he yanked and emitted a gurgled scream. A blinding pain exploded in his mouth as his tooth came loose in its socket. Blood poured back into his throat, gagging him. Turning his head to spit out a mouthful of blood, Eddie heard a *clink* as his tooth struck the concrete floor next to him, spinning to a stop in a bloody pool. But looking back to the knife in his hand, he was surprised to see that the rusted blade now lay open. Without hesitating, he swung the knife upward in a looping arc. The three-inch blade sunk into something soft, and it wasn't until Eddie blinked away rain and blood from his eyes that he realized the blade had plunged into the side of the man's neck.

Nothing happened at first, and Eddie thought perhaps he'd mis-judged his aim. His right arm gave way again and fell to his side, the temporary adrenalin that had enabled it to move, now spent. But as his vision cleared, Eddie realized the knife handle jutted from the side of the man's neck like some macabre appendage. As if realizing this just now also, the man's eyes widened in shock and surprise, his lips moving but making no sound. Releasing his downward pressure, he brought one hand upward and found the knife handle in his neck. With the calmness of a surgeon, he slid it free. A jet of bright red blood immediately shot from the wound, splattering across the already wet concrete floor. The man fingered the inch-wide wound in his neck, a curious look spreading across his face. A second later, in concert with his beating heart, another jet of blood jettisoned from the wound.

An overpowering coppery stench struck Eddie, like a wheelbarrow full of pennies being dumped next to him. He'd smelled this before—the convenience store. Sickened by the smell and with what he'd just done, he turned his head and vomited what little fluid remained in his cramped stomach.

Turning back to face the killer above him, Eddie saw his face contort in a mix of fury and confusion. With a final effort he leaned onto his knife blade with all his weight, trying desperately to drive it down into Eddie's chest. But with each beat of his heart and every spurt of blood from his wound, the force behind his weight waned. Eddie shifted his body to the right, pushing up with his knees. This motion had the effect of shifting the man's center of gravity to his own right, toward the wooden barrier. Eddie kicked out with both feet. An instant later, he felt the knife blade slide free from his hand. Pain swept up the back of his arm and along the middle of his back like an electric current. He screamed, but the blood from his dislodged tooth turned it into a garbled croak. His eyes rolled back in his head and he nearly passed out from the pain. The result of his kicking, however, caused the man to slide along the slippery floor and crash through the temporary wooden railing. One moment he had been kneeling over Eddie, ready to kill him. The next, he clawed fruitlessly at the shattered railing before disappearing over the open edge.

"Oh God!" Eddie screamed, finding his knees and crawling to the shattered barrier. Looking over the edge, he expected to see the man's broken body lying ten stories below. To his surprise, the man had not fallen after all. Instead, he grasped the floor's rough edge, his body dangling with nowhere to go but either back up onto the floor or one hundred feet to the ground below. Looking into his would-be killer's eyes, Eddie expected to see panic. Instead, he stared into two emotionless discs whose life force faded with each passing second.

"Let me help you!" Eddie yelled to him, reaching down with his ruined left hand and grasping desperately at the man's arms. Feeling himself slipping over the edge, Eddie spread his legs wide to gain leverage, then grasped the man's jacket sleeves in an attempt to pull him back up onto the floor. But Eddie had no real leverage, the rain and blood-spattered floor beneath him countering any strength he'd been able to summon. Thick globs of blood from his gashed hand ran down onto the man's own hands, causing Eddie's grip on him to slip. He felt he would lose him at any moment.

"You tried to kill me!" Eddie yelled—both a question and a rebuke in one utterance. What life remained in the man's eyes cast a defiant and fearless glare back up at him. The wind up here caused his body to twist precariously as he continued to somehow hang by his fingertips; but as blood continued to pump from the side of his neck, he either made no attempt to help himself upward or didn't care to.

Then his lips moved, speaking in a voice that sent chills down Eddie's spine. "You have...no idea...what this is about, do you?"

Eddie clutched at those hands in a final attempt to pull him up over the edge, but his own legs slipped out from under him and he felt himself being dragged slowly over the edge by the counterweight.

"Why is this happening to me?" Eddie cried, tears coursing down his face and mixing with the stinging raindrops.

And then, low and guttural, a dying groan came from the man's throat. "Behind...Hood's father," he croaked, his eyes rolling back in his head, "Your truth..."

Keeping himself suspended by one hand, the man released the other from the ledge and reached into his pants pocket. Removing a single bullet, he placed it between his teeth. He then reached into his jacket and un-holstered his pistol. Instead of pointing it toward Eddie, he depressed a button beside the grip and allowed the still-loaded magazine to fall to the ground. Turning the pistol sideways and placing the rear sight against the ledge, he then rammed his hand forward. This action succeeded in locking the pistol's slide to the rear and ejecting the already chambered round. A one-handed combat re-load. Eddie himself had practiced the move once while shooting guns with Jules. As the ejected round tumbled to the ground, the killer angled the pistol's open chamber toward his mouth—toward the single round between his teeth.

Eddie reached down in one final attempt to pull up on the man's arms, but the combined blood and rain caused the hanging man to finally lose his one-handed grip. Eddie felt the man's arms slip through his grasp, and then he was watching him plummet ten stories with frightening speed. As the man fell, his black eyes never left Eddie's. No fear or regret resided in them, and it was clear to Eddie that there had never been a soul inside those eyes, at least not one that contained any goodness. The man's body struck a series of iron reinforcement rods extending up from an unfinished building wing directly below. His body, traveling at over sixty miles per hour by the time it struck, became impaled by three of them—one each through his chest and stomach, and one through his left leg—and came to rest just inches from the concrete slab from which the rods extended, all four feet of them.

Ten stories up, the top half of Eddie's body hung dangerously over the slippery ledge. Looking down, he realized he too would slip over the edge if he did not act now. His left hand, numb and still pouring blood, retained just enough strength for him to slide his upper body backward across the floor. His right arm still dangled uselessly at his side; the day-old gunshot wound finally succeeding in turning it to rubber. He lay on his back, spitting blood and gasping for breath. His lungs burned and his body convulsed as it teetered once again on the edge of shock. He blinked away the large rain droplets that continued to slash sideways at him. The storm's last gasp passed, wind howling and a final boom of thunder crashing overhead. Twice he felt himself slip into unconsciousness, each time willing his eyes open as he refused to go under.

Get up! Get up now, you fucker! They're still after you!

Eddie coughed up a thick glob of blood that landed inches from a figure seated next to him. Jules. Somehow, he'd materialized into that familiar image—spiked hair, his favorite Metallica t-shirt beneath his faded leather jacket, and of course that sideways grin. Jules's image faltered a bit, like that from an old film reel. For a moment, Eddie thought he was already dead and had met Jules in the afterlife. But Jules shook his head as if reading Eddie's mind.

You aren't dead, but you will be soon if you don't get out of here, Jules's specter said. Then, silently, he extended a bony finger toward an area of ground about two hundred yards away. Eddie looked that way and observed five black-clad SWAT members slogging their way through the mud toward the building. Jules's eyes held an expression Eddie had never seen before in life, or wherever he currently resided. Solemn. Urgent.

If they find you, they will either kill you or take you back to jail. You need to go. Now!

"I know," Eddie croaked. He rolled onto his stomach and planted both hands against the concrete. The gash in his left hand opened into a grotesque pink grin as he exerted pressure downward. Somehow, he made it onto one knee without passing out, then the other. Then both feet. He wavered and imagined himself falling over the open ledge to where the assassin lay impaled below, but Eddie's head cleared and his body remained upright. He coughed up another glob of blood, wincing at the stabbing pain in his rib as he did. When he looked back over his shoulder to say something to Jules, he paused. The entire floor in that area was bare. Jules was gone.

"Goodbye, bro," Eddie croaked. Somehow, he knew he would never see Jules's image or hear his voice again. His time had come to pass fully into the next world. Eddie understood with stinging clarity that if he were to survive long enough to escape this place, let alone figure out how to finish this thing he'd started, he'd have to do it completely on his own.

Tearing off a strip of fabric from his shirt, he wound it tightly around his hand, groaning as he did. The bleeding slowed momentarily before it began soaking through the fabric. Knowing he couldn't survive long with this amount of blood loss, he scanned the cluttered floor for an object he could use for a tourniquet. He'd been taught how during the First Responder course he'd taken for his high school lifeguard class. Settling on a six-inch piece of wood from the shattered railing, he removed the strip of fabric from his hand and used it to tie a half knot around his wrist. He placed the piece of wood on top of the half knot he'd just secured then tied another half knot on top of the stick. Next, he wound the stick several times until the fabric constricted around his arm so tightly the bleeding stopped completely. All circulation to his hand ceased as well, but he couldn't be concerned with that now. If he bled out here, nothing else would matter. Using his teeth to hold the stick still, he wrapped the remainder of the fabric around his arm, knotting it atop the original half knot. This succeeded in holding the tension on the stick.

There. Now get the hell out of here.

As he limped toward the nearest stairwell and began hobbling down the stairs, Eddie prayed he had enough time to make it down before they got here, and if so, that he had enough time to find his final salvation before all hell descended upon him.

SIXTY

THE FIVE-MAN SEARCH team tramped across the muddy ground, the building site just one hundred yards away. Each member carried an M4 assault rifle slung across their chest and a Glock handgun on a leg-mounted tactical holster. Led by one of Captain Escobar's most capable special ops sergeants, the team had been given orders to shoot to wound, if necessary, to take Grassle into custody. The sheriff remained adamant that he be captured alive. The team members knew firing to wound was not only unsafe but stood contrary to the sheriff's own policy. Dangerous consequences, both legal and practical, could result.

Now, as the team members crouched in a semi-circle fifty yards from the half-completed edifice in front of them, one of them pointed to a nearby trio of fresh footprints. Following them to a fence encircling the site, they unslung their carbines. The team leader called in an update to Captain Escobar, who remained half a mile away and coordinated other aspects of the search.

"We're looking for one man, not three," the captain responded back. "But go ahead and clear it anyway. Advise when complete."

The rain that had deluged the area for the past half hour had since subsided to a fine sprinkle. The team leader scanned the building's fence line and detected no movement. The open floors allowed a sightline through most of the structure, although the far half of the building's first floor lay out of sight due to construction material having been erected there. Not wanting to break up his team but feeling he had no choice, the team leader ordered three members to sweep around and cover the rear side of the building while he and the other member followed the footprints. Once they'd cleared the perimeter, the plan would be to clear one floor at a time via one stairwell, then finally clear the other stairwell on the opposite side of the building.

As the trio moved right around the fence line, the sergeant and his partner began following the footprints. Ten yards down he noted something alarming—a fresh smear of blood on a fence post. Pointing to it, he radioed for the other three members to double back to their position; he waited until the second team arrived before continuing. Escobar was sending backup, but it would take them up to five minutes to redirect ATVs around the sloppy ground. In the meantime, they were to do as ordered and clear the building. If Grassle was indeed here, he could look forward to having both kneecaps shot through before being hauled away to his fate.

EDDIE STUMBLED DOWN the stairs as fast as his broken body could carry him. His collection of wounds and his overall exhaustion had drained nearly every ounce of strength in his body. But he knew he only had fifteen minutes to get to the headquarters building, twenty tops. If he failed to make it there, he'd be left with an entire lifetime of wondering 'what if.'

Once on the ground floor, his legs suddenly gave way and he collapsed hard onto both knees. Catching his breath, he stood and began to step out the open stairwell exit when the sound of approaching voices froze him in his tracks. Official sounding, with crackling radio transmissions audible over the final drops of rain from the departing storm. If they entered the fence line and began searching the building, he'd be finished. There was no way he could risk exposing himself now, yet remaining in place meant he lost precious time, something he could not afford. Just when he considered making a run for it anyway, knowing that time itself could never be rewound, and that he'd rather be captured making a physical effort than to lose his opportunity hiding scared inside some stairwell, he heard an excited voice, this one higher in pitch from the previous ones he'd heard. It took a second for Eddie to register the voice as belonging to Detective Riggins. Relief washed over him as he realized she was alive.

"Start rescue, Heinke's hit!" Eddie heard her scream. Her voice seemed to be coming from around the building's corner, just outside the fence line. Flattening himself against the stairwell's inner wall, Eddie caught a flash of movement as three black-clad figures rushed around the fence corner in the direction of Riggins's voice. Eddie dared a peek around the doorway and saw the figures meet with two others, all of them kneeling around Riggins's and Heinke's sprawled bodies. From the activity, Eddie judged the man to still be alive.

Please live, he thought. *Too many people are getting hurt because of me.* Seconds later, the wail of sirens approached in the distance. Eddie made his move. Under cover of the sirens, he slid out the doorway and followed the building left until he felt safe exposing himself momentarily. Blocked partly by the building itself, he threw himself onto the fence. Grasping the top rail, he felt the sickening sensation of his hand wound opening wide as he hoisted himself upward and over the top. Landing on the other side in a heap, he blacked out momentarily from pain and shock. When he came to, he struggled to his feet and limped as fast as he could over fifty yards of open ground toward the series of unoccupied garage businesses he'd seen earlier. He collapsed beside one of them, taking thirty seconds to catch his breath before forcing himself back to his feet and moving south in the direction of the headquarters building.

THE PARAMEDIC CREW had been forced to park some distance away and slog through the mud to get to them. As they worked on Heinke, Riggins peered anxiously over their shoulders for any sign of life from the balding lieutenant. After several moments, one of the medics declared he appeared stable enough for ground transport to a nearby trauma unit. Suddenly, the tactical team sergeant stepped forward and placed a hand on Riggins's shoulder, turning her around to face him. "What are *you* doing here? I'm sure the captain would like to know why you're tramping all over our search area."

"Your search area?" Riggins said, indignant. She pointed to where the medics carried Heinke toward the waiting ambulance. "Do you see that, you asshole? That's my lieutenant. He got shot having my back. Which is something you'll probably never understand. Go ahead and call Escobar. And while you're at it, tell him that Grassle was here."

The sergeant's eyes went wide. "You saw him?"

"Yes. I followed him here. Someone else too. I think it was the civilian Sheriff Driscoll allowed into the search area. He's the one who shot Heinke, and he tried to shoot me too."

The sergeant made a radio transmission then shook a finger at her. "I have half a mind to arrest you right now for impeding an official investigation, detective."

"Official investigation?" Riggins retorted, raising her palms to the sky. "There's nothing official about any of this. Did any of you stop to ask yourselves why any of this is happening the way it is?"

Cursing, the sergeant glanced at the paramedics loading Heinke into the ambulance. He took Riggins by the arm and led her away from the gaggle of emergency workers and crowd of responding deputies. "You really saw Grassle here?"

"Yes."

"Okay. Shit. Let me think. Give me a direction of travel."

Riggins looked toward the building then scanned the entire perimeter. She shook her head. "I honestly don't know. I was getting shot at, for Christ's sake. And it was pouring rain."

The sergeant removed his hand from her arm and nodded to himself. "Of course. I'm sorry." He made another radio transmission, followed by receipt of a verbal report from the tactical team that the entire building had been cleared. "Fuck, he must have slipped by us," the sergeant said. "We've got K-9 deploying as soon as they can get here. The storm is passing so we'll get the bird back up soon. For now, I need you to vacate the area, detective. If Captain Escobar sees you here, you're toast. He'll ask me why I haven't placed you in custody, and then I'll be toast too. I don't like toast, detective. Got it?"

"Yes, I got it," she said, frustrated. She walked to the ambulance and peered expectantly into the open back door. "Is he going to make it?" she pleaded with one of the medics. Without looking at her, he said he couldn't be sure, adding if they didn't get him to a trauma center soon his outlook could grow even more bleak.

Feeling guilty at having to abandon the scene in this fashion, Riggins backtracked the way she'd come until she found her car. Slipping into the driver's seat, she called Detective Sanchez on her cell. As soon as she heard his concerned voice, she broke into tears. "It's my fault," she managed after composing herself. "He must have sensed I was in danger and he got shot looking out for me. He could *die*, Sanny. If that happens, I don't think I'll ever be able to forgive myself." Through her guilt, another part of her felt angry for shedding tears in the first place. She felt she didn't deserve them, that her position here was her fault. She'd dealt with personal tragedies before, but those had had no impact on anyone else. Heinke seemed even more like a father to her now than he ever had. And she couldn't help but understand that he wouldn't be fighting for his life if she had simply done as he had ordered. As a testament to his razor-sharp intuition, he must have somehow predicted she would continue working the case, admin duty or not. He had disregarded his own safety and ignored the other demands of his job. For her. The scariest aspect of him clinging to life wasn't just her own guilt over his possible death. She worried about Chet, and how it would affect him seeing her rise each day to plod through the hours, languid and emotionally distant, their early retirement effectively going to waste over her inability to ever forgive herself. Unlike Heinke dying outright, she would be left to die a little bit at a time. It wasn't fair to Chet, and she hated a part of herself for putting them in this position.

Hanging up with Sanchez, Riggins drove toward the hospital where Heinke had been rushed. She prayed he made it long enough for her to see him, and to tell him how sorry she was. She told herself that no matter what happened, the only way to begin fixing the mess she'd helped cause was to end this Grassle business once and for all.

SIXTY-ONE

CAPTAIN ESCOBAR SNATCHED a chair and threw it out of the command post tent where it struck a parked cruiser. An audible crunch could be heard by the dozens of deputies and various supervisors gathered. In the momentary fight of chair versus cruiser, the first round had gone to the chair.

"Holy...mother...of fuck!" the barrel-chested captain roared as he slammed both hands down on a nearby folding table. The frozen-faced SWAT members who had just returned from their mission at the construction site stood at rigid attention. None of the men dared wipe their faces clean after Escobar had just screamed at each of them nose-to-nose.

"I'm going to say something now, and I don't want anybody to so much as fart until I'm done," Escobar said, his anger continuing to boil. He began pacing the interior of the tent with arms folded and a scowl on his reddened face. "Just so I'm clear on this, we've had him surrounded three times, and each time he's magically slipped by trained, fully equipped deputies. He's wounded and tired. He didn't eat a steak dinner last night then go to sleep in a nice warm bed like you all did. He's had no true resources we know of to assist him, whereas ours are almost unlimited, including a fucking helicopter and a team of K-9s. Does anyone here see a problem with any of this?"

The sergeant in charge of the building site search held a hand in the air. "Sir, there was a lot of area to search."

Captain Escobar approached the sergeant and leaned in close to him. "Have you heard of such a thing as a rhetorical question, sergeant?"

The sergeant swallowed hard. "Yes, sir."

"I don't care if a herd of raging elephants trampled over you, or if fairies with glitter on their wings distracted you." Escobar stepped back and addressed all deputies present as a whole. "I expect results, ladies and gentlemen, not the same lame dick excuses I've heard a million times. He's *one man*, for Christ's sake!"

Escobar's cell phone rang. He turned his back momentarily to take the call then hung up after a short, inaudible conversation. "The sheriff is fifty-sixing our location as we speak. I suggest all of you prepare for a serious ass-reaming. If I don't get lube, neither do any of you." He passed a hand over his face. "Robarts, where are those pics I asked for?" He directed this to a bespectacled lieutenant standing just outside the tent.

"They're on the way, sir."

"And someone get me an update on Heinke. We had a unit go to his house and drive his wife to the hospital. After God, I want to be the first person to get updates on his status."

Just then, a female forensics tech entered the tent, brandishing a digital camera. Escobar snatched the camera from her and thumbed through a series of pictures he'd ordered taken from the construction site crime scene. When he finished looking at them, he turned the camera off and walked out of the tent. Ensuring he stood out of ear-shot from the rest of the group, he called the sheriff back.

"Tell me you caught him," a tired voice on the other end said.

"We didn't, sir," Escobar said flatly. "There's something I need to show you when you get here. In private."

Escobar disconnected the call without waiting for a reply. His face turned ashen gray and his mouth drew a firm line. He looked toward the clearing sky, and for the first time in his career he wondered if perhaps he wasn't the right man for this job.

Soon AFTER, A white, unmarked SUV with dark tinted windows pulled into the lot just outside the command tent. Sheriff Driscoll stepped from the vehicle, gripping his trademark Stetson in one hand. Above them, the newly deployed helicopter hovered, on the heels of the passing storm. This added asset seemed to do little to ease the look of concern on the sheriff's face.

"They say good news never waits," the sheriff deadpanned to his trusted captain.

"I'm not sure what kind of news this is," Escobar said, taking the sheriff aside. He began thumbing through a series of still camera shots taken of Paolo, impaled on the rods and clearly dead. "These were taken about twenty minutes ago at a construction site not far from here."

The sheriff leaned in, his eyes narrowing with each subsequent photo. "This isn't Grassle," he said matter-of-factly.

"No, sir, it isn't. It appears to be the civilian you had help with the search."

You, and not *we*.

Several of the shots had been taken full body, the apparent purpose being to include the surroundings for reference. But several had been taken up close, focusing on the puncture wounds themselves, and of the man's blood-smeared face.

"This won't go over well," the sheriff said with a grimace.

"No, especially since we found something on him that, well—that complicates things a bit."

Escobar thumbed through a few more shots until he came to several depicting an HK .45 pistol lying next to the man's impaled corpse.

"And?" questioned the sheriff. "We knew he carried a gun."

"Not ones with illegal suppressors, or ones without serial numbers."

The sheriff sighed heavily. "Do we think he had something to do with Hammer or Heinke?"

Escobar knew his answer could propel the two of them, and the entire sheriff's office, into disarray. But he hadn't gotten where he was by sugar-coating a difficult situation with anything but the truth.

"I had my people check it out, and right now it appears likely."

"How many people know about this?"

"Enough," Escobar said. "Once I found out, I gave the order to shut down any further official comments from dispatch. But my supervisor on the ground said our folks were taking cell phone pictures of the guy when he got there."

The sheriff looked toward the sky. "Good God."

"That's not all. I just got a call from Hood. He demanded to know what was going on at the construction site. I guess news travels fast. I told him it wasn't his place to intrude in our investigation—"

The sheriff placed a hand across Escobar's chest. "Let me handle Hood. Did he specifically ask about his investigator, this Bruzzi character?"

"Yes."

"Okay." The sheriff looked hard into Escobar's eyes. "He doesn't hear a word about this. Not until Grassle is captured. Understood?"

"Sheriff, with all due respect, may I ask what's going on here? I feel it's time you leveled with me about what this guy was even doing here in the first place. The troops are losing confidence."

Sheriff Driscoll sighed again. Any other time, a subordinate questioning him, even such a trusted second-in-command as Escobar, would have sent him into a fury. But this entire incident had consumed so much of his mental capacity that he felt he had no more anger to offer. He felt like a man teetering on the edge of a cliff. What at first had seemed like a manageable exercise in political back-dealing had now spiraled out of control. Now that Hood's investigator lay impaled and very much dead not far from where Driscoll now stood, it would only be a matter of time before the media hounds took the information and ran with it. It was bitter irony for Calusa County's longest-running sheriff that a lifetime's worth of protecting the community at large might very well end with a giant, ignominious thud.

Then, as if a switch had been flipped inside of him, the old sheriff forced a meek smile to his lips as he placed a hand on Escobar's shoulder. "You've been an excellent leader, John. I couldn't think of a better man to replace me once this business is finished."

SIXTY-TWO

EDDIE RAN FOR his life, and for the life he wished he'd had all along.

Through back alleys, side streets and riverbanks he'd taken for granted for as long as he could remember, he ran with everything he had left. No longer did he concern himself with watching for cruisers or curious persons looking out windows. Only time mattered now. He felt his life was like a nearly empty hourglass, with only two options left: either his sand would run out, and thus would any chance he had at succeeding with what he'd begun; or by some grace from whatever being was watching over him, the hourglass would turn over, giving him a new start.

He'd take another fifteen minutes of freedom.

Once, he came to an intersection and watched a cruiser blast past him, its lights flashing. The deputy behind the wheel didn't even turn in his direction.

Another quarter mile, maybe a bit further. Moving into a wooded area, he limped his way west for another five minutes until he came to a fence. Exhausted, he knelt and looked at a parking lot fronting a two-story building. Just a handful of sheriff cruisers and a collection of civilian vehicles, all sedans, or smaller SUVs. Nothing he felt could constitute a vehicle large enough to transport the three of them and their belongings. So, here it was. He'd either missed them, or they hadn't arrived yet. Two sides to a coin. With each passing second,

Eddie pictured that coin flipping end-over-end in the air, inexorable in its flight of chance; until suddenly from down the street, a U-Haul truck appeared around the corner and eased into the lot. From his position, Eddie determined the driver to be a man. Not much else since the afternoon sun created glare on the windshield. But in shifting his position several feet, Eddie was able to reduce the glare enough to make out a woman with dark-colored hair sitting in the passenger seat. And between her and the male driver, observable just above the truck's dashboard, was very clearly the top of a child's head.

He'd made it.

DETECTIVE RIGGINS FLOORED her Mazda's accelerator, whipping the zippy four-cylinder toward Springwood Regional Hospital. She'd made this same easy commute dozens, if not hundreds, of times over the years. But now time seemed to have frozen. Once she made the exit and pulled into the hospital parking lot, her heart sank. No fewer than ten cruisers were already on scene, with several deputies huddled around each other in an open embrace. The gray, dripping sky seemed a direct reflection of the scene below it.

She parked and approached the group at a near run, not wanting to hear what she feared most.

"How is he?" she asked the group of deputies, breathless.

A female deputy in the group broke from the group and took her aside. "I'm sorry, detective, but we have orders from Escobar to notify him if you showed up here."

Riggins pulled her arm away from the woman's grasp and stood akimbo. "Why is everyone up Escobar's ass? Go ahead and notify him. I'm off duty—a civilian visiting a friend in a public hospital. Now answer my question—how is he?"

The deputy looked back to the others in her group before offering Riggins a solemn gaze. "He arrived critical, but as of now he's alive. He's still in the—"

Riggins didn't wait for the rest. She ran into the ER entrance and approached the receptionist.

"Lieutenant Heinke, please," she said to the older woman behind the desk.

"I'm sorry, ma'am, but you can't see him now," the woman explained without much emotion. "Family only."

Riggins planted her hands on the counter and leaned toward the woman. "He gave me away at my wedding, if that's family enough for you. Besides, I'm the reason he's in this position. I need to see him before—before anything happens to him."

The receptionist began to object but relented when Riggins bore a gaze into the woman that said *I'm not going anywhere until you let me in to see him.* "Okay. But you'll have to stand back and let the doctors work. I'll tell them you're an essential family friend."

The woman reached into a drawer, wrote out a visitor name tag for Riggins, then stood. "Follow me, ma'am. But just know they're bringing him into surgery soon. Not even the Pope can see him then."

She ushered Riggins into the trauma room where a team of doctors and nurses worked in a coordinated effort on Heinke's unconscious form. He'd been intubated, and a host of other wires and tubing snaked from him in all directions. One of the doctors noticed Riggins's concerned look and waved her near. "Are you his wife?"

Riggins put a hand to her mouth, touched by the sentiment. "No, I work with him. His wife is on the way now."

The doctor stepped aside and motioned for the other doctors and nurses in the area to do the same. Riggins took one of Heinke's hands in both of hers and said a silent prayer over his unconscious form. Then she bent and kissed him on the forehead. "You better make it," she whispered into his ear. "Because if you don't, Ferguson will take your office, and you can't stand that bastard."

Just then, the trauma door opened and a woman in her fifties was ushered in by a pair of uniformed deputies. Clutching her purse to her chest, she wore the expression of a woman waiting for news she did not wish to hear. Riggins recognized her immediately.

"Oh Daphne," she said, embracing her. "I'm so sorry. He had been trying to protect me when he got shot."

Daphne cupped Riggins's face in her hands. "Don't blame yourself, honey. If it's God's will for him to live, he will," she said.

Downcast, Riggins nodded. "If you need anything at all, just call me direct." Handing Daphne one of her business cards, Riggins retreated into the parking lot, choosing to give her father-like lieutenant some privacy with his wife.

Detective Sanchez had just pulled up. "How is he?" he asked.

"Critical. They're taking him to surgery soon. His wife just got here, thank God."

"Jesus, Rig. This isn't good."

"No, Sanny. Not good at all."

Sanchez's radio buzzed with an alert. Having missed the transmission, he radioed for the last caller to repeat it. Each of them listened, wide-eyed, to the dispatcher's repeated call.

"I'll ride with you," Riggins said excitedly, racing around to the passenger side of Sanchez's unmarked cruiser. Not bothering to fasten her seat belt, she reached over to activate the car's front-mounted emergency lights and siren. It was normally a ten-minute drive from the hospital to sheriff's headquarters.

Riggins told Sanchez to make it in five.

SIXTY-THREE

Clarissa looked out the U-Haul's passenger window and watched the rain drip from the side mirror. The sky had cleared moments before their arrival here at sheriff's headquarters. The clock on the dash read three twenty-seven. Three minutes early. She felt disdain at the thought of spending even a second longer than was necessary inside the place. For everything the building represented, she felt she may lose her patience if she were made to wait inside. Out here would be better, where she had some level of control over her environment.

She had sworn to Roger she would never return to Florida once they left, and she'd meant it. Too much pain and history remained here. Still, tears had stung the corners of her eyes and a lump had formed in her throat the moment she'd crawled onto the U-Haul's bench seat next to Liam. She'd lived in Florida her entire life; except for a trip to Ohio to visit her parents when Liam was a toddler, she'd never been out of the state save for a high school band tournament in Georgia. The decision to pull up her roots had seemed hasty at the time, but now she wouldn't have backed out even if given the opportunity. Ever since this latest business with Eddie, she had grown increasingly restless. Just the thought of driving over the state line seemed like a salvation of sorts. Like discarding a spoiling bag of trash. She had told Roger she wanted to drive straight through to Georgia before they stopped for the night. Rest, she said, wouldn't come to her until they'd left Florida behind forever.

"You want me to come with?" Roger asked, placing the U-Haul in park. Clarissa began to tell him no, that she didn't want to inconvenience him also, but then changed her mind.

"Do you mind?"

Smiling wanly, he turned the ignition off and climbed out. Clarissa took Liam by the hand. "Come on, baby," she told the boy, "This shouldn't take too long."

STATE ATTORNEY HOOD stepped from his Mercedes, leaving the driver's door open as he approached Sheriff Driscoll and Captain Escobar. He had come here from his office to the mobile command tent to discover any new developments in the case. Paolo had not returned his last two messages, and concern had begun to etch itself across the glowering prosecutor's face.

"Give me an update," he growled. An order, not a request.

Escobar stepped forward. "Mr. Hood, if I may—"

The sheriff gave his captain a dissenting look before deciding to end the charade he'd created once and for all.

"Mathias, this thing is going on far longer than it should have. I never should have allowed what I did. One of my deputies is dead, for God's sake. For that I'll have to answer to my Creator. It's high time I stop letting you get your way."

Hood nodded, as if finally deciding something he'd considered for some time. "Sometimes the best way may not seem to be the right way. Bo, you mustn't think this has been personal. This will all be over soon. And when it is, you can retire with Mary-Beth and take your RV out west the way you've always wanted to. I won't ask anything more of you, as long as Mr. Bruzzi is allowed to transport Grassle to jail. Call it a final favor between old friends."

Recalling the gruesome photos of the construction site crime scene, it was Sheriff Driscoll's turn to issue a rejoinder of his own. "Your man can wipe Grassle's goddamned ass if he wants to."

CLARISSA OPENED THE passenger door and helped Liam down from the U-Haul's cab. She took him by the hand and began walking quickly toward the building's tinted front doors, not bothering to wait for Roger to catch up. Distracted and angry for being forced here, she fully intended on giving whomever she spoke with inside a piece of her mind. As she strode through the lobby doors, Roger hurried to catch up. Annoyed, Clarissa approached the raised lobby desk, the female deputy behind it asking how she could help her.

"I have an appointment to get my son fingerprinted," Clarissa said. Roger arrived at her side, himself annoyed at having been left behind. Either unaware of this or not caring, Clarissa asked him to take Liam to the nearby waiting area. As he did so, Clarissa stated her name to the deputy and explained the phone call she'd received.

The deputy frowned. "You said someone called you to get your son fingerprinted *here*?"

Clarissa placed both hands on the desk and leaned forward, clenching her teeth. "That's what I said. A woman who works here. Something about needing to fingerprint my son before we enroll him in school out of state."

The deputy glanced over to where Liam sat, his legs dangling from the chair on which he sat. He watched a cartoon that played on the waiting room television.

"Who did you say called you?" the deputy said, her eyes narrowing. "Because juveniles don't get fingerprinted here anymore. And that's news to me about the school thing you mentioned."

Confused, Clarissa repeated the woman's name who'd called her, even checking the caller ID on her phone. "I'm telling you, this woman said I had to get my son fingerprinted," she insisted. "She said to be here at three-thirty. Unless there's another headquarters building."

The deputy explained there was not. She clacked several keys on her computer. "You said the woman's name was Elizabeth *Downing*?"

"Yes."

"Well, there's no one who works for the sheriff's office by that name. There *are* three techs who do our juvenile printing, but like I said, they don't do them here. That's done at the courthouse. Maybe you heard it wrong?"

Clarissa's nostrils flared, her ears and cheeks turning red. "Let me tell you something, ma'am," she said, seething. "To hell with all of you cops. I know what I heard, so don't sit there and try to make me feel stupid." From behind her, Roger perked up. Sensing that from him, Clarissa turned and held a hand up to keep him away. She could handle this. "You can't even keep criminals locked up, for Christ's sake," she said. "We're leaving. How about that? If I have to come back, it'll be once you people get your heads out of your asses and figure out what the hell is going on."

The deputy sat up straight in her chair, her expression changing from one of shock to indignation. "I'm going to have to ask you to leave, ma'am. I won't take being talked to like that."

Roger stood, having heard this last exchange, and began walking toward Clarissa and Liam, where he took the boy by the hand.

With her chin raised defiantly, Clarissa turned on her heels and tugged Liam away from Roger's grasp a tad rougher than she'd intended. Roger looked back to the frowning deputy and shrugged.

"I'm sorry about that," he said. "She's been through a lot. Today especially." Then he turned to follow her out the door, but she was already ten yards ahead of him, Liam half a step behind her and struggling to keep up. As the front doors hissed open, Clarissa turned back toward the deputy and raised the middle finger of her free hand. Once again, Roger turned back toward the now irate deputy, offering more apologies for his fiancée's rudeness.

If Clarissa hadn't turned around just then, she would have immediately seen Eddie walking toward her. As it was, she gave herself a bit of satisfaction by flipping the deputy off, taking her time to turn back around toward the parking lot. She'd taken five steps before she saw a man walking directly toward her from twenty feet away, her mind processing the emotion she'd just experienced before confusion first, then full recognition as she placed the man's face. Eddie.

Clarissa froze in place so quickly that Liam ran into her backside, and her hand flew to her mouth, stifling a surprised and terrified scream that rose from deep inside of her.

SIXTY-FOUR

WATCHING THE U-HAUL turn into the parking lot and seeing both the woman and child on the passenger seat, Eddie fought the temptation to stand and run along the fence. But he had to make sure it was truly her. When after several minutes he saw the woman step out, helping down a mop-haired boy of about five, Eddie knew it was really them.

Excitement flowing through him, he watched Clarissa, Roger and Liam walk into the building. Good. His plan was to intercept them on their way out. Perhaps best to hide behind the U-Haul and appear around the passenger side once Clarissa and Liam reached their door.

Clarissa, please don't scream. I'm not going to hurt anyone.

Then, no matter what happened—

Hello, Liam. I'm Eddie, your dad. I probably won't be able to see you for a long time, maybe not ever again. I want you to know I'm sorry I messed up, and that I love you. Always remember that.

Then he would raise his hands in the air and back away, waiting for the rush of officers from inside the headquarters building and elsewhere.

He judged the distance between his position and the U-Haul to be about fifty yards. Too far to sit and wait until she came out, especially in his physical condition. He would only have one chance at this. The four-foot fence ran the length of the parking lot, breaking for the driveway before continuing around the far side of the lot.

As he rose to his feet, Eddie considered Roger also going inside just might have made things better for him. Eddie knew he would have to get close enough to the U-Haul without drawing suspicion anyway. From his vantage point, the few cruisers and handful of civilian vehicles parked in the lot did not seem to be occupied. But a few of the cruisers were positioned at too odd an angle to be sure; with their dark-tinted driver-side windows facing away from the sun, a deputy could easily be behind the wheel writing a report or eating lunch. He'd just have to risk it.

He traveled along the fence line until he came to the open lot entrance. Cutting over the concrete median separating the in and out lanes, he nearly tripped over the curb as he hurriedly made his way behind the U-Haul. Feeling terribly exposed but having no other choice but to wait here, Eddie peeked around the corner of the truck at the front doors. No movement. Thirty seconds later they slid open, revealing Clarissa and Liam, hand in hand as they stepped out onto the large black entrance mat. Even better, Roger did not seem to be with them. Clarissa stopped long enough to turn and say something to someone inside the lobby.

Come on! Keep walking!

Then, from somewhere to his left, a voice. Commanding him to back away from the rear of the truck and asking him what he was doing.

Eddie looked that direction and saw a uniformed deputy standing beside the open driver's door of a parked police cruiser, one that Eddie had been unable to see inside.

Shit.

Eddie froze. The deputy pointed to an area behind the U-Haul, one hand resting on his gun.

Eddie did not hesitate. Ducking around the far corner of the U-Haul, he hobbled alongside the passenger side, clearing the front of the truck and continuing toward the front of the building as fast as his cramping legs could carry him. He heard the deputy shouting from behind him, commanding him to stop. Twenty yards. Fifteen. Clarissa turned her head toward Eddie's voice, confusion in her eyes at first as she made eye contact with him. And then a spark of recognition, and her feet cemented in place, causing Liam to bump into her backside. Still no sign of Roger. On instinct, one of Clarissa's hands rose to cover the boy's eyes as she turned protectively behind her, all while an agonized wail built in her throat that was both fearful and angry and disgusted at the same time. And Eddie, for all his suffering and unspent anticipation that had finally reached its terminus, froze in his tracks also, holding both arms out in front of him to beckon and plead for just one glance, one hint of acknowledgment from the only thing left on this earth he truly cared about.

Liam!!!

As the name passed through his mind and reached his lips, two metal darts struck him in the back. A split second later, his eyes bulged as fifty thousand volts of electricity jolted through his body. White-hot pain—like none he had ever experienced—seized him. For a curious moment he stood frozen with arms clutched at weird angles, every muscle in his body locked and unable to move. And then he felt his body falling forward, having no ability to brace for his fall, until he crashed face-first into the pavement.

Then complete and utter blackness.

SIXTY-FIVE

As State Attorney Hood ended his conversation with the sheriff, he inquired of nearby deputies what the commotion was about. An excited lieutenant, himself preparing to race to the scene, told Hood that during Grassle's capture he had gone "down for the count." Annoyed that Paolo had allowed this information to be broadcast in such a way, Hood nonetheless felt comforted that the entire affair was finally over. Grateful for his faithful associate having at last succeeded in his mission, Hood sped toward the admin building, his mood exuberant. An almost sexual electricity surged through him as he drove with the Mercedes's top down, the wind causing his tie to flutter out behind him. The fact Paolo hadn't relayed confirmation to him yet meant little. The scene of a deputy-related shooting or other deadly force incident was expected to be chaotic. Arriving supervisors would of course declare it a crime scene, and after cordoning off Grassle's corpse, they would no doubt separate Paolo to prepare for his questioning by homicide detectives. Therein lay Hood's ace up his sleeve. Being that he stood in charge of any potential clearing of law enforcement agents—and civilians as well—anyone who had taken another's life fell under his direct legal authority. Despite the sure media frenzy, few would raise serious questions anyway, Hood reasoned. Grassle had thrice been accused of murder, after all. And one of those victims had been a seasoned sheriff deputy. All that would be left would be tying up the final loose end of his arrangement with Driscoll. The fact that the sheriff had himself declared their arrangement *finis* only served to place an exclamation point on the whole situation.

He darted along the interstate, watching the waning orb in the sky paint pastels on the western horizon. After so much tediousness, a seemingly interminable amount of sand falling through one globe of the hourglass into the other, there now seemed just a few granules left. All that remained to be determined was if Paolo had been able to use the bullet Hood had given him to finish the deed—his father's bullet from so long ago.

The anticipation alone was delicious.

I have avenged you, Father...

Exiting the interstate, Hood swept along several more streets until he turned into the headquarters parking lot. Two dozen marked and unmarked cruisers sat at varying angles, their overhead lights still swirling. Spotting a crowd of deputies and detectives standing around a body lying prone on the pavement, Hood rushed toward them, gasping as he spotted Eddie Grassle's handcuffed form. It took him seconds to realize he had merely been Tasered and not shot.

"Where is Mr. Bruzzi?" Hood demanded, taking the on-scene supervisor by his uniform collar. "And why is the prisoner still alive?"

The supervisor, a squat sergeant with a bulldog head, pulled away from Hood's grasp and held out a hand to ward away the state attorney. "We have it under control, sir. Please stand back."

"I will do no such thing," Hood said, disregarding the sergeant's order. His now panicked eyes swept the group again. "Unless the sheriff informs me otherwise, Mr. Bruzzi will transport this prisoner to the county jail."

The sergeant held his ground, a fierce and prideful light in his eyes that spoke of many such past forced acts of acquiescence. Hood also stood his ground, ignoring the sergeant's rigid gaze, as well as the other eyes that bore into him from all around. "Let me assure you, sergeant, that if you do not relinquish the prisoner to Mr. Bruzzi immediately, I will have your badge. Is your family prepared for your sudden loss of employment?"

A look somewhere between resentment and naked hatred burned in the sergeant's eyes. Just as he began to speak, a vehicle skidded into the parking lot. Sheriff Driscoll and Captain Escobar both leaped from the car and hurried to where the group stood around Eddie's motionless body.

"Where is he?" the sheriff asked, breathless.

As if on cue, Eddie came to, half-rolling with an audible groan to face the sheriff's grizzly voice. Handcuffed behind his back, he moaned as the probes sticking out of his back dug in even deeper. The copper wires attached to them led to the Taser held by a severe-looking deputy. The makeshift tourniquet around Eddie's left wrist loosened with his body movement, and blood instantly seeped from his flayed-open hand. The squat sergeant seemed to notice the grisly injury for the first time and radioed for paramedics.

Huge knots already rose on Eddie's face from where he'd fallen. A fresh cut above his right eye lay in stark contrast to his fallow skin. He looked like he'd been through a war.

The sheriff approached the deputy holding the Taser and shook his hand. "Great job, son. Tell me how you captured this man while every other deputy in this agency tripped over their own feet."

The young deputy shrugged. "I was sitting in my cruiser typing a report when he walked right by me, sir. It took me a second to recognize him."

"But you did, didn't you?" said the sheriff, patting the deputy on the back.

"Yes, sir. I have his mugshot taped to my dash."

When the sheriff took a step toward Eddie, Hood held an arm out to block his path.

"Mr. Bruzzi will bring him in, Bo," Hood said. Despite this coming out as a command, an undercurrent of concern had risen in his voice. His black, usually confident eyes now contained a desperation they'd never before possessed. *Where was Paolo?*

Sheriff Driscoll swatted away Hood's arm and cast him a cautionary stare. "Mathias, this is no concern of yours. Kindly remove yourself from this scene before you poison our investigation any further."

Hood's eyes widened with naked indignation. His teeth ground together as the rage that had simmered within him for months, years, boiled over. "Mr. Bruzzi *will* take custody of the prisoner, sheriff. As head prosecutor of this circuit, I'll have to insist that—"

"Mr. Bruzzi is dead," the sheriff interjected. "Now step aside, or I will have you forcibly removed from the area."

At first, Hood did not appear to register the sheriff's words. His confused expression gave the impression that the collection of syllables had merely passed through his ears and failed to form any intelligible meaning. Looking to Captain Escobar, whose grim silence only seemed to confirm what the sheriff had just declared, Hood finally managed to speak, his voice weak and eerily childlike. "There—there must be some mistake."

Unable to contain himself any further, Captain Escobar stepped forward. "Mr. Hood, with all due respect, you have overstepped your bounds for the last time. What the sheriff said is true. Mr. Bruzzi was killed about an hour ago in a fall. I viewed the body myself."

Hood's expression went from doubt to disbelief as a sudden realization aligned within him. Certainly, Driscoll and Escobar could not both be mistaken. Still.

"You're lying." He turned and examined the collection of faces surrounding him, as if expecting any of them to morph into the one face that was unbelievably, frustratingly absent. "Paolo!" Hood shouted. His eyes widened with rising panic. "Paolo! Come take custody of your prisoner! I will see to the sheriff. You will be safe." Hood scanned the area again, his bald head whipping in all directions as madness took full hold of his being. Captain Escobar stepped to him and planted a custodial hand on his broad shoulder.

"Mr. Bruzzi fell ten stories from a building not far from the command post. He died instantly. I have pictures of his body if you wish to—"

Hood should not have been able to move so quickly for being so large a man. In an instant he stooped and seized Eddie by his shirt, yanking him upward and holding him at arm's length several feet off the ground. Gripping one hand around Eddie's throat, he squeezed with such strength that Eddie's eyes bulged from their sockets.

From somewhere behind them, pleas for Hood to put the suspect down, that it was all over now, and no need existed for this needless violence.

For a moment, Hood made no motion to oblige. Rage seething in his black eyes, his lips curled back to expose his perfectly white, veneered teeth. A sheen of sweat shone on his bald dome, lit by strange light from the post-storm sun. The full effect cast him as a modern-day Azrael, the angel of death that had now taken matters into his own hands, literally and figuratively. Perhaps the sheriff's presence on the scene prevented anyone from interceding. The group of deputies and Escobar himself stood looking on in mute shock. Not until Sheriff Driscoll calmly stepped forward, un-holstered his revolver, and placed it at the back of Hood's head did the towering state attorney take notice.

"Put him down, Mathias, or by God I'll put you down."

Instead of lowering Eddie to the ground, Hood increased his grip around his throat.

Eddie, kicking wildly at the air, felt himself begin to lose consciousness from lack of oxygen. The brightening blue sky went gray before his eyes as what little life remained in him fizzled like a candle flame between wet fingers.

"It won't be over until he's dead!" Hood bellowed. "It's my destiny!"

The sheriff cocked the hammer and nodded self-assuredly to himself. He had never killed a man in his life. Yet for many reasons (none of them being sympathy toward the man who at the moment remained the number one suspect in the killing of one of his own deputies), he felt confident he could do so now. "I am the sheriff of this county, and right now I say this is over. Put him down, Mathias, or I'll explain my use of deadly force to your replacement."

This got Hood's attention. Turning to face the sheriff, he judged the aging lawman to be resolute in his threat. Finally releasing his grip around Eddie's throat, he let the smaller man drop to the ground like a rag doll. Eddie landed on his side, one of the Taser probes tearing out of his back, its barbed end first bending against one of his ribs as he struck the ground. His throat still bearing deep indentations from Hood's vise-like fingers, he struggled to take in air through his partially crushed windpipe. Gasping for breath, Eddie felt his world swim. Panic convulsed him when after several more attempts to fill his oxygen-starved lungs, he still could not breathe. Wheezing and coughing, he finally managed to take in enough air to keep from passing out. Stunned at what had just occurred, he looked helplessly up into the equally shocked faces of the cops all around him.

"Place him under arrest," Escobar demanded of the sergeant while pointing at Hood. "Aggravated Battery. You all saw it!" Escobar had always mistrusted Hood. Personal dislike aside, he'd managed to keep a professional distance from the powerful head prosecutor whenever possible. But now with witnesses abounding, he finally had cause at minimum to embarrass the man who during this entire ordeal had insisted on wedging himself into every possible crevice of an investigation in which he did not belong.

Driscoll holstered his gun and held a hand in the air. "Last time I checked, the star on my shirt still says 'Sheriff.' And until they unpin it, I'll be the one who decides who gets arrested around here." He stared down Escobar, who stood fuming but nonetheless remained silent.

"Now, emotions have been high the past two days," the sheriff continued. "I understand that. I will assume Mr. Hood here reacted badly at the news his investigator was killed. We experienced this last night ourselves. That isn't to say I condone an assault on a hand-cuffed prisoner. Is that understood?" The sheriff looked from face to face until he received assenting nods from each. Coming toe-to-toe with Hood but forced to look up at least six inches, he shook a crooked finger at him. "And you, sir, are finished here. You will vacate this scene immediately, or so help me God I will order your arrest by whatever means necessary. Do you realize what you've done, butting in the way you have? I would think you of all people would appreciate that."

Hood adjusted the lapels on his suit coat. Indignation blanketed his reddened face. "I will respect your decision, Bo. But first I would like proof that Mr. Bruzzi is dead."

Captain Escobar didn't wait for instructions. He produced the digital camera and thumbed through the series of still photos he'd recently shown the sheriff. Hood viewed them without expression at first. But when he came to several showing close-ups of Paolo's lifeless, impaled body, he looked away, his face ashen. A strange sadness seemed to wash over him. Then, a look that had not shown itself there in years, decades even.

Fear.

Paolo *was* dead. How the resourceful and edgy professional had allowed himself to be bested by an amateur, Hood could not fathom. Questions swirled in his brain. That he was forced to confront this sudden change of events in front of the assembled group—Grassle even—seemed to him the greatest insult of all. Donning a mask of nonchalance, Hood forced himself to consider the positives of Paolo's untimely demise. First, he felt no personal loss for the man. Paolo could just as easily have quit Hood's employ without notice. Aside from any existing professional contracts Paolo may have needed to close, Hood would not have missed the man's company one bit had he simply vanished into obscurity instead of dying the way he had. In fact, the disgust Hood had felt over Paolo's romantic advances was now moot. No more need to pretend.

Searching his mind next for any legal consequences, Hood quickly concluded that nothing directly connected him to Paolo's actions. True, Paolo's silenced pistol had been found with its serial number filed away. But Hood could simply claim ignorance of having knowledge of that fact. Vicarious liability would normally have extended to his own office, since it was established fact that Hood had employed Paolo in a host of investigative duties. Normally, any connection made between Paolo and the deaths of both the deputy and woman could result in both legal and financial liability to the employer—in this case, Hood himself. But herein lay the genius of his plan. When the sheriff documented his assent that civilians could assist in the search, he had transferred liability onto himself. It was not Hood's job to vet those who had effectively been deputized. That responsibility fell solely onto the sheriff's shoulders. The Wild West may be ancient history, but many of its laws still permeated state statutes. As for any potential political fallout Hood could expect, he could simply argue that Paolo, his own employee, had gone rogue. All communication with him had occurred either in person or via burner phones. The government even had difficulty gaining access to terrorists' locked cell phones. The relatively low-level corruption case of a county official would surely not elicit such attention. In the unlikelihood of that even happening, Hood reasoned his worst-case scenario would be facing a conspiracy charge that could easily be undone by a governor's pardon.

Leverage was applied best at high places.

Staring down at the handcuffed man who had single-handedly seemed to tilt the earth on its axis, Hood instead saw a vision of his father lying dead in his coffin. He remembered that scene, played out nearly fifty years ago, in vivid detail. And since, in the absence of fatherly advice, the lack of a man's strong voice echoing throughout the halls of his home, where his younger self had brooded and stewed in his own hate—hate for whoever had been responsible for such an abomination, one that had left him a virtual orphan. Hood recalled his mother's incessant weeping after the funeral, her shutting herself in her room for months on end, eventually emerging a ghost of herself.

From his position on the ground, Eddie stared up into those soul-less black eyes. Even in his depleted state of mind, he knew Hood would have strangled the life from him then and there had the police not been present. Everything seemed to click into place. The removal of his jail privileges enacted ostensibly due to Eddie's minor rules infractions. The mysterious man who had chased him non-stop over the past twenty-four hours, threatening his life at every turn. The state attorney, who normally would exclude himself from active law enforcement matters, insisting on doing the opposite. And of course, that cryptic statement spoken just before the killer had fallen to his death.

Somewhere behind Hood's father lay a truth of some kind. Did that mean his physical grave, or something else entirely? And how sure could they be about chasing a lead uttered by a man suspended by his fingertips one hundred feet above the ground?

It was beginning to make sense now. Except that none of it made any sense at all. Despite the paradox, Eddie did know one thing— he had failed. He had come maddeningly close to achieving what at first had seemed an impossibility. Having twice come seconds away from contact with Liam felt to him like a punishment handed down from God himself. In prison, he knew time would pass vacuously, the image of Clarissa covering Liam's eyes teasing at his conscience. A part of him hated her for it because what the action had communicated had been that Eddie himself had been foul, a thing not worthy of even a glance. The stain Clarissa had once feared. But still a part of him had to acknowledge the bitter truth that spoke of never being there in the first place, and that by virtue of that, he had forfeited his right to be there in the future. Marginalized and shut away, like a bad decision never to be repeated.

The pain in Eddie's body came back in a flood as the last of his adrenalin wore off. He detected someone standing over him, bending low and grasping hold of the one Taser probe that remained embedded in his back. A pressing hand beside the probe, then a sudden pulling of it, and it was out of him just like that. With the loosened tourniquet, his hand began to pound as if it had a pulse of its own. His eyelids fluttered. He passed in and out of consciousness. All the while, his eyes sought a chance to view what he'd come here for. But Liam was nowhere to be seen. Everything Eddie had ever dreamed or wanted seemed now like a faraway star, its light gone extinct a million years ago.

SIXTY-SIX

HOLDING HIS HEAD high, Hood walked past the assembled group to his waiting car. As he turned out of the lot and sped toward the sanctuary of his home, his mind raced. How had this lone individual evaded an entire sheriff's office for the past thirty hours? How had he slipped past Paolo not once but twice, the second time resulting in Paolo's death? It was impossible to imagine, let alone believe. Hood's dream of listening firsthand to how Grassle had suffered before he died would never be. At least not in the sense he had first conjured. The time had come to improvise. Grassle would no doubt be held under heavy guard now and would most assuredly be untouchable while held in the county jail. Too risky to strike him there. State prison would be best, where Hood had many contacts, some of whom were lifers who would be all too happy to provide certain services for a fee. But it could take years for Grassle to find his way there as his case wound its way through the system. Even Hood's influence only stretched so far. Although he could still lean his hand on the scales of justice, that didn't eliminate the existence of some measure of legal protection the system provided defendants.

As he drove, his fingers gripped the steering wheel to the point they turned a ghastly white. This stood in contrast to the center-pointed stone on his finger, which glowered like a reddened, vengeful eye staring into the sky.

Detective Riggins stabbed a finger toward the windshield as Sanchez whipped the car into the admin parking lot. "There he is! That must be Eddie!"

Screeching to a stop, Sanchez threw the car into park and both he and Riggins were out running toward the group. As they arrived, a pair of newly arrived paramedics lifted Eddie onto a gurney. Riggins and Eddie stared at each other, neither saying a word. Her heart beating in her chest, Riggins looked him up and down with mixed shock and gratitude. Shock at the fact he had somehow made his way here of all places, and gratitude at the fact he hadn't been killed in the process. He looked like pure hell; but if the exhausted look on his bloodied face said anything, it confirmed that he was still very much alive. The assembled group, including Sheriff Driscoll and Captain Escobar, stood lock-still, not knowing if they should allow the paramedics to escort Eddie into the awaiting ambulance or allow Riggins an opportunity to say something. Clearly, some connection existed between her and Eddie, who for his part mouthed a half-conscious hello to her. Finally, Riggins herself broke the palpable tension by addressing the sheriff, who stood nearby with both hands planted on his slender hips and wearing a look of utter resignation.

"Sir, I know I'm not even supposed to be here," she said. "I take full responsibility for my actions so far and have nothing to say in my own defense. I disobeyed a direct order—two of them actually—and will accept whatever punishment comes my way."

All eyes moved onto the sheriff. Eddie looked up toward him as well, struggling to keep his eyes open. The sheriff pursed his lips together as if deciding against saying one thing before deciding on another. He looked Riggins squarely in the eye and said, "This here fella is suspected of killing one of our own last night, detective. I'm sure you're aware of that."

Before she could respond, another voice broke the still air that had settled over the group. Startled that the suspect would have nerve enough to speak up on the matter, all eyes moved to Eddie who lay half-dead on the gurney.

"What did you say?" Captain Escobar asked him, incredulous.

"I said I didn't kill anyone. Especially not that deputy. Why won't you people believe me?"

Riggins held out both palms to cut him off. "Eddie, this isn't the time for that. Let me handle this."

"You won't be handling anything, detective," interjected Captain Escobar, stepping forward. "We've got it all under control. And you're right, you aren't supposed to be here. If you hadn't gone running off on your own, Heinke wouldn't be laid up in the hospital with a hole in him."

Sheriff Driscoll waved his captain off. "It's over, Alice. And no one blames you for trying to help, despite the fact you were told to stand down. I don't like my people being insubordinate, but I can also appreciate a cop looking out for another cop. Lieutenant Heinke may very well be alive right now *because* of you."

The sheriff shot Escobar a reproachful glance, with the latter simply shaking his head and standing mute. "Go home to Chet," the sheriff told her. "We have this under control now." His usually friendly drawl had been replaced with something sharper, more authoritative, and barbed. For a man who alternately had seemed to have aged and grown younger a decade or more over the past two days, Sheriff Bo Driscoll wore the overall expression that suggested his days of wearing the uniform—and especially the sheriff's star—may indeed be coming to a close.

Riggins looked toward Sanchez, whose tight nod of the head confirmed to her that this truly was the end of her involvement in the Grassle saga. They'd recaptured their prisoner, after all, and had brought him in alive just as the sheriff had preferred. The question of who the mysterious man Eddie had told her about, the same one who'd shot Heinke and tried to kill her too, had still gone unanswered. The nagging sense that the Eddie Grassle saga was far from over, contrary to what the sheriff had said, continued to pull at her sensibilities. But what could she do? She felt at the end of her proverbial rope.

"Yes, sir," Riggins said, not wanting to look the sheriff in the eye but feeling she owed as much to him. "I'm sorry if I've caused any harm. I've been a cop a long time. A detective for most of it. I guess I just feel like a racehorse forced to ease back near the finish line."

The sheriff nodded, his eyes betraying disappointment and

admiration at the same time.

Riggins sighed deeply, meeting Eddie's gaze again and feeling as if some silent message of thanks had been conveyed between the two of them. Their prisoner was in rough shape, and from his condition it appeared as though he could have died had he not been captured when he was.

Detective Riggins, for her own part, nodded a silent *you're welcome* to him before walking back to her car.

SIXTY-SEVEN

BY THE SHERIFF'S order, no fewer than a dozen cruisers accompanied Eddie's ambulance to the hospital, with a pair of deputies left posted at the main entrance, another pair positioned in the emergency room waiting area, and three more remaining with him at all times. The escapee had already caused enough embarrassment. Driscoll did not mince words, declaring if another escape somehow occurred, he would personally rip the offending deputy's star from their uniform and ensure they never worked in law enforcement again.

When Eddie was wheeled into the emergency room, the attending doctor took one look at him and asked the escorting deputies how he was still alive. The gunshot wound to his shoulder and the gash on his left leg had both required multiple sutures, and aggressive antibiotics had been ordered to ward away future infection. He had a large hematoma on his head from where he'd struck the ground after being Tasered, and initial tests suggested he likely had a concussion. His feet were a mess of open blisters and micro-lacerations; his blood pressure registered dangerously low, and he was severely dehydrated. Other scrapes and assorted bruises peppered his body head to toe. But by far his worst injury, a life-threatening one, had been the knife wound to his left hand. The attending ER doctor stated Eddie had lost a quart of blood from that injury alone. How he had remained conscious long enough to traverse the two miles from the construction site to the headquarters building, the doctor did not know. As Eddie was prepared for emergency surgery, the consensus remained that had he not fashioned the makeshift tourniquet when he had, he could just as easily be lying on a metal slab in the morgue instead of on the operating table.

From the Springwood Gazette, Saturday, June 1, 2016
ESCAPED PRISONER CAPTURED
Story by Benjamin Mixer, *Gazette* staff writer

The search for escaped jail inmate Eddie Grassle ended yesterday afternoon in a dramatic scene at the sheriff headquarters building. The Springwood man had been held on robbery and murder charges when he affected a brazen daytime escape from the Calusa County Jail Thursday morning. Sheriff's deputies scoured the surrounding area for the next thirty hours until finally taking Grassle into custody in what officials described as "a forceful takedown" Friday afternoon. Following his recapture, it remained unclear whether Grassle turned himself in, due to the fact he was apprehended on Sheriff Office property. Bloodied and in what officials described as "very rough shape," Grassle was taken to Springwood Memorial Hospital where he underwent emergency surgery for an array of injuries. He remained there Saturday morning under heavy police guard.

In what officials described as possibly related to the escape, Calusa County resident Elizabeth Downing, 56, and Sheriff Deputy Erwin "Bigfoot" Hammer, 42, were both shot and killed early yesterday evening. The shooting took place at Ms. Downing's private residence in unincorporated Calusa County. Sheriff spokeswoman Diana Farrow did not provide details of Grassle's possible connection, other than stating that credible evidence had been obtained regarding his involvement. In a statement given to reporters, Sheriff Driscoll expressed relief over Grassle's capture, calling him "a scourge against humanity."

Spokeswoman Farrow offered the following account of the jail escape: Alone in an outdoor recreation yard, Grassle managed to scale a reinforced barbed wire fence before being fired upon by a tower deputy. Grazed, Grassle then defeated a perimeter fence before disappearing into an adjacent wooded area, prompting the largest manhunt in Calusa County's history. Hampered by what officials described as "operational difficulties," Sheriff's deputies did not make contact with Grassle again until Friday afternoon, when he was suspected of being at the scene of yet another shooting, one involving Sheriff's Lt. Frank Heinke. The twenty-six-year veteran underwent emergency surgery last night for a life-threatening gunshot wound. As of late Friday, he was listed in serious condition.

Additional charges against Grassle are pending.

Adding to the already confounding case was the revelation that a civilian investigator, Paolo Bruzzi, was killed Friday afternoon while attempting to apprehend Grassle. When asked why a civilian had been allowed access to the search area, Farrow declined to comment. A press conference held after Grassle's capture shed little light on this revelation, with Sheriff Driscoll also declining to comment on the issue.

In a final footnote to the day's developments, Claude Devereux, Calusa County Jail's superintendent for the past eleven years, resigned suddenly following Grassle's capture. When asked for a reason, he cited family concerns. Sheriff Driscoll is expected to announce his replacement by next week.

STATE ATTORNEY MATHIAS Hood threw the newspaper to the floor and stared at his home study wall. The French doors to the pool area stood open, a warm early summer breeze blowing in from the river. Working the red-stoned ring around his finger, the veteran prosecutor listened to the sounds of the mid-morning Saturday—birds chirping in the yard's lone cypress tree, the drone of a boat motor somewhere on the river, and the breeze rustling the fronds of the sabal palm that now shaded a portion of the pool. Hood had not slept during the night. He'd remained exactly where he was now, in his office chair, the crystal decanter of special reserve scotch within arm's reach. He'd begun the night with the decanter half full. Now it sat empty.

How had things come to this end? he wondered. Bleary-eyed, and still in shock from yesterday's events, Hood turned to face the portrait that hung behind him, its subject glaring down with eyes that spoke of vengeance, and death, and the seemingly newer expression of disappointment.

SIXTY-EIGHT

FEVERISH, EDDIE AWOKE in a fog of swirling memories and sensing a queer discomfort he had never felt before. He couldn't be sure if he'd been unconscious for an hour or a month. A vague sense of being in some sort of clinical environment enveloped him. The cloying smell of iodine filled the air. He realized he lay in some sort of bed, the pillow beneath his head soaked with his own sweat. He painfully turned his head to the left and saw a wall-mounted vital signs monitor displaying a series of digital numbers. He detected light from his right. Turning his head in that direction, he immediately squinted against bright sunlight streaming in from a window. It took his eyes a moment to adjust, after which he made out three uniformed deputies seated against the wall in front of him. Two of them thumbed their cell phone keyboards while the third sat engrossed in a hushed phone conversation. Eddie blinked, unable to remember how he'd gotten to this place, or why he was under such close guard. A ponytailed nurse in blue scrubs entered his field of vision just then and typed something on a wheeled machine's keyboard. Unable to speak due to his badly swollen throat, Eddie tried to raise his right arm to gain the nurse's attention but immediately felt it stop several inches above the bedrail, metal biting into his wrist. At first, he thought his IV had somehow entangled him, but upon closer inspection he realized his wrist was handcuffed to the bed rail. He found his left leg shackled in a similar manner.

"You should try to go back to sleep," the nurse said, turning her head to look at him. "You were in surgery for quite a while last night."

One of the deputies whispered something to his partners and all three of them leaned forward expectantly. Eddie tried again to speak but found it impossible. Pain ravaged his entire body and clouded his thoughts. He had begun raising his free arm to adjust the blanket covering him when the nurse reached down and placed her hands on him.

Memories of the previous two days filtered back to him in pieces. And lying beneath each memory, the man stalking him like death itself, until he had finally caught up with Eddie at the construction site. The man's knife, the gray blade like a razor, plunging down toward him. Jules's pocketknife, then the man falling to his death.

The nurse turned away to continue her work. Eddie, intent on moving the blanket as he had intended, caught sight of something strange then. The lower half of his left arm was heavily bandaged. Thinking back, Eddie remembered it had been his hand and not his arm that had been injured. Visions of watching the knife blade slide through it came to him. Wishing to drive the image away, he tried to pull the blanket over his eyes, anything to make that horrible image go away, but he realized an instant later that he couldn't pull the blanket upward because his entire lower left arm was missing. Holding the remainder of his arm in front of him, Eddie stared at it curiously, his mouth opening in shock and his eyes going wide as he studied the heavily bandaged stump. It seemed to him as if a magic trick had just been performed on him, one where a magician snapped his fingers and, in a puff of smoke, a person's hand disappeared before their eyes.

A low moan escaped from somewhere deep inside of him. And then his throat relaxed, the intubation swelling he'd received with his surgery wearing off, and his IV medication too, and he screamed. Even to his own ears, the sound seemed to originate from somewhere outside the room. It could have come from a different floor in the hospital for all he knew. Or a different state. Or world. The three deputies sat forward on the edge of their chairs, unsure of what to do. Eddie looked to them, wide-eyed, then back to his stump, and he screamed again. The nurse, who had just left the room to conduct other business, appeared in the doorway, a frightened look on her face. Then she saw Eddie holding what was left of his arm up in front of him, and she appeared to understand what had made him cry out. Coming to him now, she tried gently to replace his arm beneath the blanket and to calm him, but it wasn't working, because half his arm was *gone* for God's sake. Another nurse raced into the room to help, and together they pushed him down onto the bed as one of them called for the doctor to bring an injection, fast.

BACK AT SHERIFF'S HQ, a separate but no less enthralling drama was unfolding. Clarissa Fulton, fresh from a night spent tossing and turning in a motel bed, stormed down the hallway toward the conference room she'd been summoned to. Bursting through the door, she propped both hands on the edge of the table at which Detectives Grimes and Teliford sat. Ignoring their offer for her to sit down, she instead dove into an expletive-filled diatribe she had been saving for the past twelve hours. She demanded to know how Eddie had succeeded—alone and injured—in drawing her and her son here the day before.

"We're trying to figure that out, Ms. Fulton," Grimes said. "You have to understand, there are a lot of moving parts to this right now." He offered both palms in a weak attempt at diplomacy, looking to Teliford for help. His partner's only assistance was to shrug meekly.

"Moving parts?" Clarissa huffed. "How about these for moving parts?" She offered up both middle fingers to the detectives before replacing her hands back onto the table. "In my book, letting a prisoner escape a maximum-security jail and not finding him for over twenty-four hours does not constitute moving parts. Incompetence is a much better definition. And you didn't technically find him. He waltzed right into the parking lot outside."

It was Teliford's turn to hold his hands up in their defense. "We understand your concern, Ms. Fulton, and we're trying our best under—"

"You people are supposed to protect us!" she yelled. Her face and ears turned a deep red, and her breaths came so short she nearly began to hyperventilate. "I knew there was something wrong with all of this. I knew it. I should have listened to my gut. As soon as I found out Eddie escaped, I should have taken Liam out of school and packed up the car and left. But everyone told me not to panic. Roger, the principal, you people. But there's nothing like a woman's intuition. I ignored it, and it almost cost me my son. Do you know how that makes me feel?" She folded her arms across her breasts, drilling her eyes into each of them.

"Ms. Fulton, believe me when I say we understand why you're upset," Teliford said, trying his best to calm her down. "But there's no evidence that Eddie had any intention of harming your son. From what we've determined, he was merely attempting to meet with the only family he has left."

Clarissa laughed a scornful, humorless laugh. "Merely, my ass. I won't let you do this to me, *detective*." She spat the word. "I won't let you placate me like you do everyone else. I'm not an idiot. Just because you wear a badge and arrest people doesn't mean you're smarter than me. Besides, I know Eddie a lot better than you ever will. He planned the whole thing. Whoever he had call me was in on it too, so you might want to do some detecting to find out who the woman was. Eddie's been a fuck-up his whole life, but as much as it pains me to admit it, he's still the smartest person I know..."

Both detectives looked down at the notes set in front of them, unable or unwilling to respond to what she said.

"I wish I didn't have a child with him, but I do," she continued. "And right now, that child is sitting in the next room wondering why we haven't left for Ohio yet. He's wondering why his mother was such a nervous wreck last night and could barely hold herself together. Thank God Roger was there. He knew I wasn't in any shape to make the trip last night. He was afraid for me. Shit, *I'm* afraid for me."

The detectives exchanged knowing glances. This was not going swimmingly, to say the least.

"I don't know how Eddie did it, but he got me to come here yesterday," she said. "I know you said he used that dead woman's phone, so if it wasn't her who talked to me, he got someone to do it for him. I think it's pretty shitty of you people to try telling me I'm the crazy one for saying that."

Grimes held up his hand. "Ms. Fulton—Clarissa, if I may?"

She waved him on, rolling her eyes.

"Clarissa, none of us think you're any less smart than we are. In fact, I think it's pretty obvious from the events of the past two days that the entire sheriff's office has failed in many respects. We admit that failure, and it's not only embarrassing, but to a lot of us—me and Detective Teliford included—it's directly opposite of what we're hired to do." He allowed his words to settle in the air, keeping his expression neutral and tilting his head just so. An offering of empathy. Detective Grimes may not have equaled the professional acumen of his partner, but he was adept at connecting with people when he chose to.

Clarissa looked away in deep consideration, her face a splotchy canvas of a dozen pent-up emotions. Her foot tapped an impatient beat on the tiled floor. She seemed to be struggling over some promise she'd made to herself, one perhaps declared in a fit of rage and frustration over this entire mess that was coming close to consuming her. Finally calming down to the point where she could speak without yelling, she asked, "Why do you think he wasn't going to harm us?"

Teliford's turn. "For one, he was unarmed when we arrested him. And he was severely injured. You may have heard about his surgery."

"Nobody has told me anything."

"We're usually not at liberty to discuss an arrestee's medical condition with the public, but in this case, I think you deserve to know. Mr. Grassle underwent an operation last night to amputate part of his left arm. The doctors said it was a small miracle he even made it here to try meeting you and your son."

All the color drained from her face. She brought a trembling hand to her mouth, and her eyes, once flamed with rage, turned soft and glassy. "Oh, Eddie..."

"As we said, Clarissa, we don't believe he meant you or your son any harm," Detective Grimes chimed in. "It appears that Eddie was trying to arrange some sort of meeting with your son. You know him best. Do you have any idea why he would try to carry something like that out right here on our doorstep?"

But Clarissa was already a world away. Lost in thoughts that circled somewhere between her painful past and her ever-spiraling present, she mumbled an apology to the detectives. She found Roger and Liam in a reception area down the hall and beckoned them outside into the parking lot. They'd driven the U-Haul here from the motel, and after returning there now she stopped and forced back the tears that she wanted more than anything to keep away.

"Do you want to go somewhere?" Roger asked her from the edge of the bed.

"Yes," she said, not even trying anymore to keep the tears from falling. "Ohio."

SIXTY-NINE

EDDIE DREAMED OF a chase—a much different one than he had just endured. This time *he* did the chasing. Liam ran ahead of him on a dirt road, his feet seeming to float over the ground. He giggled as he looked over his shoulder, beckoning Eddie to come play with him. A sprawling playground sat a quarter mile ahead, but no matter how hard Eddie ran he seemed to lag further and further behind. At one point, Liam stopped to face him, waving Eddie on with big, looping arm circles. *Come and swing me, daddyyyyyyyy,* Liam called in his dreamy, child-voice. *Swing me before the policemen get you and take you away. Just run faster and show me how much you missed me.*

Dream-Eddie ran and ran but could never catch up. The boy was too fast. Looking down, Eddie found his feet to be mired in mud. The harder he tried to free himself the further he sank, until he was up to his waist and couldn't move his legs at all. Liam continued sprinting toward the playground when a figure appeared beside him. Roger. He extended his hand to the boy, and before taking it, Liam paused long enough to look back one more time. When he saw Eddie sunk now to his chest, he turned and took Roger's hand. Together, stepfather and stepson continued toward the playground while Eddie reached desperately out toward Liam. Deeper he went until the mud gurgled up past his neck, and then he was taking a final breath before it swallowed him completely.

Eddie bolted upright in bed. His bedsheets lay soaked with sweat. For a moment, he believed himself still mired in mud and made clawing movements upward, as if trying to climb out of the bog. But as his eyes adjusted to the dark, he understood he had been dreaming. Not only were his wrist and ankle no longer shackled, but he wasn't in a hospital room anymore. Looking to either side of him, he saw through the semi-darkness rows of single bunks, each bolted to the floor and occupied by sleeping bodies. About a dozen in all. A door lit by a meshed window stood at one end of the room, and it was then he realized he was in a jail medical ward. Intending on rubbing sleep from his eyes, he merely succeeded in knocking his stump against the left side of his head. He stared at his bandaged arm, his mind returning to the hospital scene. Memories followed like clips from an old movie. Receiving the shot meant to calm him once he'd realized half his arm was gone; the doctor describing his surgery once he'd awakened. His stab wound had been severe and would likely have resulted in an amputation regardless of the tourniquet Eddie had fashioned. Too much nerve and muscle damage to save it.

You saved your own life, Eddie remembered the hospital doctor telling him.

Now, Eddie wasn't so sure that had been a good thing.

A miserable moan escaped him as he collapsed back onto his bunk. His stump ached terribly. More moans now, these louder, as the pain seemed to come to him like a switch being flipped. A few of the figures around him stirred, one of them muttering in a sleep-filled voice, "Shut the fuck up, would you?" until finally keys clanged and a figure at the window yanked open the heavy metal door. Overhead lights blazed on, temporarily blinding him. A pair of jail deputies entering. Hands on him then, forcing him to lie back down, telling him to be quiet for God's sake, that he'd wake the dead.

"What happened?" he asked as a nurse joined them.

"You're in the jail infirmary," she said. "They brought you here from the hospital yesterday. Don't you remember?"

Reality slowly returned to him. The days following his operation, him slipping in and out of foggy consciousness, the doctors and nurses doubling or tripling in his unfocused vision as he'd struggled to remain awake for longer than thirty seconds at a time.

"I—I sort of remember. My arm—"

"It'll take some getting used to," the nurse said. "Some ampu-tees still feel their missing limbs for years afterward. It's normal. For now, it's important you don't touch it. It'll ache and itch, but that just means it's doing what it's supposed to. It's only been two days since your surgery."

Eddie moved his lips. No words came. He stared at the ceiling; his mouth was so dry he could barely swallow. His stump didn't just ache or itch, it felt like someone was holding a blowtorch to the end of it. Finally, the nurse and deputies shuffled back out of the ward, shut-ting the heavy metal door behind them. The metallic clang of a large deadbolt filled the air and a moment later the lights turned off. Eddie lay that way for the next half hour, staring at the darkened ceiling and listening to the noises of the other sleeping inmates around him. He listened for anything recognizable—Jules's haunting voice, a whisper in his ear that all of this would go away, that soon someone would appear at the door and exclaim *surprise, we really got you this time!* But Jules was never coming back to him in that way, or any other way, he knew. Eddie listened for Liam's voice to call to him from somewhere in his memory, but then he realized how ridiculous that concept was because he'd never even heard his son's voice. That thought led him to the idea of lying in a bed such as this, an old man on his deathbed, his son finally visiting him after Eddie had served fifty years behind bars. He imagined the words that might pass between them, or per-haps only awkward silence would take their place. And if words did come, perhaps they would not seem like words at all, but simply air being pushed by diaphragms, vibrations over larynxes, noises formed by tongues pressed against teeth and upper palates until the air left lips moving but not making the least bit of sense. Eddie listened for anything that could soothe him, anything that could deliver him from his waking nightmare, one seeming at this point like the first step of a thousand-mile journey.

But none came.

SEVENTY

THE NEXT DAY, in room 438 of Springwood Memorial Hospital, Alice Riggins sat in a visitor's chair beside Lieutenant Heinke's bed. Her balding boss had successfully come out of surgery immediately following his gunshot wound to repair a collapsed lung and other internal injuries. And now, just minutes after Riggins had arrived to visit him, he ended a terse phone call back to headquarters to make an official request.

"Are you sure about this, sir?" Riggins asked. She felt he may have been acting under the influence of painkillers, or from some vestige of his recent near-death experience.

"Last time I checked, I'm not dead yet," he said proudly, adjusting his hospital gown. "And I know what you're thinking. No, I'm not stoned. And I did not see the angel of death and decide to do you a favor before I met my maker. I'm doing this because it's the right thing to do."

Riggins sighed. "Thank you, sir. I don't know what to say."

Heinke scoffed. "Teliford and Grimes are good enough softball buddies, or to throw back a few beers with after work, but that doesn't make them good detectives. Not even half as good as you. I'm not asking if you want to be put back on field duty, I'm telling you. Just because the surgeons diced me up like lunchmeat doesn't mean I'm not still your boss." Tubes and wires snaking from beneath his white hospital gown, he nodded once to emphasize his point.

Riggins leaned forward in her chair and touched his arm. "It's not that I'm not grateful, sir, or that I don't want to work cases again. It's just—I feel it's my fault you're in this position, and I don't want to put you in a position where you're being forced to pick sides."

"I know whose side I'm on. Mine." He indicated his own body, which he'd had to hold at an angle due to the cumbersome bandage wrapped around the right side of his chest. "But seriously, Alice, I've always been on my detectives' side. Especially yours. When the sheriff came to see me yesterday, he asked me to call him if there was anything he could do for me. Name it, and it was mine. So right before you got here, I called him and asked him to put you back on field duty until your retirement date. You know the saying—a shot cop wants not."

Riggins squeezed his hand. "I was worried sick about you, sir. If you hadn't made it, I'm not sure I could have forgiven myself for going out there against your orders. You having my back like that means more to me than you'll ever know."

Heinke smiled, then spoke in the matter-of-fact tone of a man who'd just discovered something important. "Want to know what my new motto is going to be?"

"I can only imagine."

"Two centimeters."

Riggins frowned. "Are you sure you aren't stoned, sir?"

Heinke held two fingers close together. "That's how close I came to dying. The doctors said if my body had been turned even an inch to the right, the bullet would have pierced my heart and killed me before I hit the ground. That is what you call Providence, Alice. I believe I was meant to live for a reason. Putting you back in the field may just be it. I think you still have a lot of good to do before you leave."

Riggins looked down at her hands. "I'm not sure I deserve those kind words."

Heinke waved her off. "You know just as well as I do that I've had this coming. Twenty-six years and never been in a gunfight? How could I attend my retirement party and look everyone in the eye with that zero on my record? I should be thanking you." He added this addendum with a wink.

Riggins slapped his hand. "Don't say that. You have nothing to prove."

"The doctors say I'm going to have a long recovery," he said, his voice going from playful to resigned. "Daphne has been crying all morning, begging me to retire on a medical. Even though I've spent half my life in uniform and always swore I'd leave on my own terms, I couldn't look her in the eye and tell her no. One thing I've learned is your job doesn't cook you dinner and rub your feet at night. It doesn't have a sweet smile, and it doesn't still have an hourglass figure after twenty-five years of being married to a half-bald, ornery old bastard like me. I haven't made it official yet so don't say anything to the troops. I'd like to wait until this Grassle business is a bit more settled and my favorite detective solves her next case. No pressure, by the way."

Riggins nodded, feeling a lump grow in her throat. She hadn't come here expecting this. Just a few days ago, she'd been curled up on the couch with Chet and Gracie, peacefully watching Netflix. Heinke had undoubtedly been at home himself, doing whatever he usually did with his wife, and certainly not thinking he'd be laid up in a hospital bed talking about his sudden retirement. It amazed her how fast life could change. Work and other nonessential matters took on a whole new perspective when you came so close to dying, she supposed.

Rising, Riggins bent and kissed him on the cheek. "Thank you, sir. I'll try my best not to let you down."

He paused, glancing toward the busy corridor. "Close the door."

She did. When Heinke spoke again, his expression had darkened considerably.

"I don't like what's going on, Alice. The sheriff hasn't been himself lately. He seems...distracted. That whole business with Hood and his investigator is as shady as a gopher's ass. You be careful where you step. As in extremely."

Riggins nodded. "I understand, sir."

"And keep me updated on your new cases. I need some stimulation other than game shows and soap operas. At least we get HGTV at home, thank God."

Riggins laughed, remembering Heinke's penchant for gardening and home improvement projects.

"One more thing," he said, his eyes glazing over in fond memory. "When you started, I took you under my wing because I thought I had to protect you. Not from the bad guys out there, but from the wolves that prowl the same agency we work for. Not everyone embraced you becoming a detective. But as you proved yourself time after time, I began to realize I was no longer protecting you from them, but them from you. You could have made captain if you'd chosen to. The brass always talked of promoting you, but you never wanted it. They thought you didn't want the responsibility, but I knew it was because you wanted to continue making a real difference on the streets."

Riggins gave Heinke's hand another good squeeze. "Thank you for saying that, Lieu. I wouldn't be where I am today if it hadn't been for you believing in me."

Heinke sighed. "Yes—well, here we are then. I always pictured my last day on the job being surrounded by my squad, decorations hanging from the ceiling and someone bringing out a giant cake with some cheesy message written on it. I did *not* envision it ending with me being driven away in an ambulance, an inch from death. But none of us get to write our own endings, Alice. I guess I'll just have to get used to the one that was written for me."

The lump continued to grow in Riggins's throat. Close to tears, she looked deep into the eyes staring back at her and felt certain she'd never before felt more gratitude for another human being than she did now. "I just have a few months until I can retire. I told Chet I wouldn't stay a day longer than I had to, and I won't. But I'll promise you something, Lieu. I'm going to find out what's going on with the sheriff and Hood before I leave. I wouldn't feel right taking my retirement with this good ol' boy network still intact. I know we have Grassle back in custody, but there's still something very fishy about all of this, and I intend on finding it." She gave him another kiss on the cheek then turned to leave. She stopped when Heinke groaned even louder than before.

"You okay, Lieu?" she asked, looking back from the doorway.

He waved her off. "Yeah, I'm fine. You just reminded me of something."

"Come again?"

"They're serving fish for lunch," he said, rolling his eyes. "I despise fish."

HALF AN HOUR later, Riggins sat at her cubicle desk at HQ going over elements of the Grassle file when Sanchez poked his head in from around the corner.

"Excuse me, I'm looking for a short, light-skinned sister with a cute smile and a nasty right hook."

Riggins grinned, glad to see her field partner again. "The guy asked for it, Sanny. He tried to bite you. If it hadn't been for me, he would have eaten your face for lunch. I'd almost forgotten about that."

Sanchez approached her, sporting his trademark pretty-boy smile. He framed his face with both hands as if posing for a glamorous photograph. "No one is eating this gorgeous face for lunch!"

Riggins felt helpless but to laugh at his boyish, natural charm.

"Alright, here's what we got," she began, repeating the conversation she'd had with Heinke. When she finished, Sanchez nodded his agreement.

"When do we meet with Tweedledee and Tweedledum?" Sanchez asked.

"In about twenty minutes. They didn't sound happy at all about handing lead team duties back to us, but who cares?"

Sanchez agreed. "How's Heinke?"

"Stable." She went over his condition as best she could. Remembering that he'd asked her not to share his retirement plans with anyone, she left that part out.

"I hear Grassle lost an arm," Sanchez added.

Riggins went over everything she knew about Eddie's medical condition, and how despite her initial reservations, she had agreed to talks with a neighboring county to house Grassle in their jail. With him being a suspect in the murder of one of their own deputies, it would be impossible to continue housing him in Calusa County. Anything adverse that happened to him while incarcerated here would appear to be retaliation and would undoubtedly be grounds for a host of lawsuits.

Ten minutes later, Detectives Teliford and Grimes arrived sporting matching scowls. Teliford shook his head disapprovingly as he handed over the Grassle escape case file. Riggins had to extract information from them, pointedly mentioning to each that if they weren't going to fully cooperate with the information exchange, maybe they should go visit Lieutenant Heinke in the hospital so he could refresh them on proper detective protocol. Stuttering to explain that it wouldn't be necessary, both detectives handed over all needed information before disappearing from where they'd come.

Riggins didn't waste any time. She gave Sanchez half the file to read, saving the most pertinent half for herself. An hour later, they compared notes.

"How about forensics?" Riggins asked, satisfied she was now at least refreshed enough on the case's details to make informed decisions.

"No hits from rebar man," Sanchez replied. He had coined the nickname for the dead man, Paolo Bruzzi, known now to the sheriff's office as a former black ops agent with a hazy past. Officials in Washington would only provide basic information, the rest being sealed due to federal secrecy laws. Sanchez recited from a government teletype he'd ordered: "Active with the CIA from 2005 to 2013. Retired early due to medical reasons. The feds sometimes lump medical and psychological together, so we can't tell which one applied to him. No known relatives. No DNA or fingerprints on file. And I'm starting to doubt the name we have is even his real one. The guy was a damn ghost."

Riggins had elected to use a rarely used conference room for their discussion, out of concern that Internal Affairs had installed audio surveillance in her office area. It pained her to go to these lengths, but nothing about this case had gone through established norms. With the exception of Heinke and Sanchez, she wasn't quite sure whom to trust anymore.

"I assumed he'd had his fingerprints removed after becoming an agent, but it's weird there weren't any on file at all," she intoned. "All federal agents and police nationwide are mandated to have prints on file as a condition of their employment. If there aren't any listed, that means this guy was into some really dark shit."

Sanchez pointed to a notation in his portion of the file. "And look at this—from his state application for his concealed firearm permit. It specifies no confirmation was made concerning his criminal record. They couldn't confirm it because he never had any prints to run through AFIS. Guess who he got a special permit through?"

"Hood?" Riggins quipped.

"Think higher."

"FDLE?"

"Higher."

Riggins ruminated for a moment, her eyes widening as a burst of inspiration struck her. "The *governor*?"

"Bingo."

"So, rebar man works as an intelligence officer where he has his prints chemically removed. I can almost guarantee he changed his name. No DNA on file either, making him practically untraceable. He applies for a state CCW and gets approved without a background check, courtesy of the governor. Then he gets a private sector job for you-know-who—"

"Hood," Sanchez finished, matter-of-factly. "But we knew that. The sheriff himself announced it to the entire agency during the manhunt. I guess the conflict of interest didn't concern him."

"Yes, but the sheriff only announced it because he *had* to," Riggins said. "What he never explained, and still won't, was why he gave civilians access to the search for so long."

"Shit, it doesn't make sense even if he gives them access for a *minute*."

"Unless it makes perfect sense," Riggins said, squinting her eyes in thought.

"You're losing me, mama."

"Hear me out. Who authorized the concealed firearm waiver?"

"The governor."

"And who is the sheriff's boss?"

Sanchez had to think for a moment. "The governor."

"And who appointed State Attorney Hood to his permanent position after the former one was forced out?"

Sanchez grinned. "The governor."

"As soon as you become a detective, they teach you that one connection can be an accident. Two can be coincidence. But three is a trend, so you must pay attention to it. Not proof, but it definitely creates reasonable suspicion."

"And reasonable suspicion is just a step away from probable cause," he added.

"Exactly."

"Search warrant land."

"Sort of," Riggins cautioned. "But I don't think it's the governor himself we're looking for. He may be the lock, but I feel the key is someone much closer to the case. It has to be Hood."

"But what motive would he have to shove his nose so far into a case that isn't even close to trial yet? And why would the governor go along with it? It's not like he reports to Hood for anything."

Neither of them said anything for several moments, having long ago learned that shared silence between them was something to embrace when working through a problem. Thoughts cleared. Distractions faded. Even the ticking of the wall-mounted clock, which had just struck eleven AM, served as a sort of mental metronome, syncopating their minds.

Finally, Riggins broke the quiet. "Can you have rebar man run through forensics again?"

"Sure, but we've already done it twice. His gun was a match for the one used to kill the farm woman and Deputy Hammer. But since Eddie was spotted there and his prints were found on Hammer's OC canister, he's still implicated in the killing. Sucks for him, even though rebar man is on the hook for Heinke, according to me."

"I know. There has to be a connection we're not seeing."

"We never recovered any spent rounds from Heinke's shootout with you at the construction site."

"How about shell casings?"

"Nothing there either." Sanchez suddenly remembered something. "We did get a tip from Grassle's kid's school the day after the escape. A school secretary who saw rebar man's mug on TV. She said he and Grassle showed up to the school at the same time."

Riggins's jaw dropped. "What? Why didn't you tell me that before?" she asked, perplexed.

"I guess there was so much going on I forgot to mention it. It was an update near the end of the case file I had. I didn't think it was important at the time."

Expelling an exasperated sigh, Riggins took the part of the file Sanchez had referred to and read through it herself. "What's the first rule of detective work, Sanny?" she asked, shooting him a motherly stare.

"To question everything." He searched the wall, then the table, then the ceiling for the relevance. He shrugged. "I'm sorry, boss, I still don't get it."

"If Hood employed a special investigator, one allowed by the sheriff to assist in a manhunt for an escaped killer, and that special investigator had knowledge of Grassle's exact whereabouts not once, but twice, why didn't he call in backup as he was instructed to do?"

Sanchez thought about it. "I don't know. It doesn't make sense now that I think about it."

"No, it doesn't. He should have wanted to call in Grassle's location immediately. There's only one reason I can think of as to why he wouldn't."

Sanchez's face lit up with sudden inspiration. "Unless he had no intention of ever calling it in."

"Exactly. At first, I assumed he'd taken shots at Heinke and me because we'd both been in plain clothes and were pointing guns at him. It's raining pretty hard. He's chasing an escaped inmate on his own. But now I don't think he ever intended on catching Eddie alive. And I think he knew damn well who Heinke and I were when he shot at us."

"You think rebar man was carrying out a hit for Hood?" Sanchez asked, incredulous.

"I'm sure of it. Remember, it isn't our job to simply ask questions. We need to answer them too."

Another period of combined silence, broken by Detective Riggins's buzzing cell phone. Exchanging a few words with the caller, she hung up and said, "That was my contact from FDLE. I asked him to give rebar man a once-over, just in case we missed something."

"But I thought you wanted me to do it," Sanchez said, sounding hurt.

"I do. But I'm following the second rule of good detective work." She stood and gathered the case file envelopes, telling Sanchez to accompany her to the county jail. She wanted to see Eddie and ask if he would talk to them.

Reaching his unmarked unit, Sanchez opened the passenger side door for her then hopped behind the wheel. As he pulled out of the parking lot and began guiding them through the remnants of a morning rain shower, he said, "Okay, I'll bite. What's the second rule of good detective work?"

"I guess they stopped making new recruits memorize these things," she said, facing him. "Nothing beats good backup."

TWO HOURS LATER, after a bedside meeting with Eddie Grassle, Riggins and Sanchez were at an area restaurant to go over their interview.

"I'll hand it to him, he's one smart *hombre*," Sanchez said, sipping on his Coke. "Except for him not lawyering up. I'm not complaining, but doesn't he know a suspect should never talk to the police?"

Riggins disagreed. "I think it goes toward what he's been claiming all along. He's never *not* been cooperative. If we assume, for example, that rebar man really did kill Hammer and the woman, then it makes sense why we found Eddie's prints on the OC canister. He didn't have to admit that, because it places him directly at the scene of a deputy's murder. And it supports the theory that rebar man truly was trying to kill Eddie the entire time."

Their food came and each of them dug in greedily.

"True," Sanchez said through a mouthful of burger. "But you know how much juries love blaming a living suspect for a cop's murder."

Riggins chewed a bite of her salad, pointing her fork at Sanchez. "I can't get over what Eddie said about rebar man fooling with his gun. There you are, hanging ten stories off the side of a building, and you take the time to try reloading a single round from your pocket like that? In the context of your life in peril, it doesn't make sense."

"Maybe the guy was picky about his ammo."

"Not in that scenario," Riggins said. "You might perform a trick like that on the gun range, but not a hundred feet up with your ass in the breeze."

"So we scrap what Eddie said about it?"

"Not so fast." She chewed another bite of salad, frowning as her mind worked. "Eddie described rebar man using the side of the building to lock his pistol slide to the rear. Sort of how we're taught to use the heel of our shoe when we kneel, or another solid object if we can't use both hands to lock our slide back."

"I've used my belt buckle during training."

"Yes. What I'm saying is that's a very specific action to remember. It's not like Eddie made some vague observation that anyone could misconstrue. It's very unusual. I'm leaning toward believing what he told us is what really happened. It ended up costing the guy his life, so he had to have done it for a good reason."

"Want me to stop by the morgue and ask him?" Sanchez quipped. "I hear he's down there just chillin'."

Riggins rolled her eyes. "If you'd been a hangman, you'd tell a condemned man a rope joke."

"You mean like, 'Don't worry, dude, I'm *preeeetty* sure your head won't pop off?'"

Riggins nearly choked on her tea. "You're a sick, sick man, Sanny."

"Thank you for saying that, Rig. I work hard at it." He beamed proudly, taking a huge bite of his burger.

"I just can't shake the feeling there's something right under our noses we can't see," she said.

"We'll find it sooner or later," Sanchez responded, hopeful. "It'll probably jump right out and hit us on the head. Sort of like all your brass landing on me when I stand next to you on the range."

In mid-bite, Riggins dropped her fork, where it clanged loudly against her plate. "Sanny, you're a genius!"

Sanchez frowned. "Um, common knowledge."

Riggins scrolled through her smartphone's notepad. After reading a section she'd marked **Forensic Questions**, she slapped a hand to her forehead. "That's it!"

"What's it?"

She nodded to herself, choosing to tackle the problem from various mental angles. The method had worked for her countless times before, and even now in this convoluted situation she forced herself to be patient while working it through.

"Remember how forensics went over the construction site scene three times? Just in case we missed something?"

"Yeah, I was late for a date because of it."

"Well, we didn't know it at the time, but we missed something. There's still an unfired bullet at the scene!"

"But we found it, remember? Half stuck in the mud not far from rebar man's body. No prints, no DNA, nothing. If what Eddie said was true about rebar man trying to load a loose bullet, the one we found must have been it."

Riggins shook her head. "No, Sanny. It *could* have been it. Remember to ask every question you can."

He looked at her sideways. "You're messing with me now, aren't you? Some sort of test to see if you can confuse me?"

"No," she said, reaching across the table to grasp his hand. "Eddie told us about rebar man removing a single round from his pocket and trying to chamber it with his teeth. But Eddie swore the guy dropped it right before he fell. Naturally, we assumed that was the bullet we found in the mud."

"What other bullet could it be?"

She burned her gaze into his. "Rebar man releases his loaded magazine then uses the building ledge to lock his slide back to load that single round. What happens when you lock your slide to the rear when your gun is hot?"

Sanchez considered this for a moment, until he sat up straight in his seat. "A round is ejected! *A dios mio*, I can't believe I didn't realize that's the round we could have found!"

"It's natural to overlook something like that. Especially with so many details we've been bombarded with."

"But what makes you think there'll be anything different about a second bullet?"

She shook her head. "You can't assume, Sanny. Think back to times both of us have gone a mile further than we ever thought we had to go."

His eyes narrowed in thought. "Like the strand of hair in a vacuum cleaner we found after three days searching a landfill."

"Or that time we brought a truck to the garage and had the

mechanics take it apart, bolt by bolt. We found a drop of the victim's blood caked onto the rear axle." She squeezed his hand again. "Heinke said the sheriff gave him power to do whatever he wants with the division, saying 'a shot cop wants not.' I intend to take full advantage."

Sanchez finished his burger in two giant bites and paid their tab. "Even if it means taking the word of an escaped convicted felon?"

Riggins shoved the last forkful of salad into her mouth before sliding out of the booth. "I'd believe a suspect who's told the truth about everything else up to that point before I'd believe my best girlfriend who tells tall tales. The funny thing about the truth is that it's deaf and blind. Hell, Eddie even promised to turn himself in, and he basically did exactly that."

"Fair point," Sanchez said, holding the front door open for her. They hopped back into his car and turned back toward headquarters. Just then, Riggins's cell phone buzzed with a text message from Bert that made her frown:

> *Asked some colleagues about Hood. Corrupt but apparently untouchable. Seems to have everyone under his thumb, so be careful. May have to use unconventional methods to find a motive RE Grassle. All databases come back clean. Let me know what you find. Good luck!*

Riggins read the message to Sanchez, and he replied, "What do you think it means?"

"I don't know, but if there is some connection here, it's nothing we'll find in the places we've already checked. Bert and I have combed through just about everything this side of Mars. I'm not sure where else to turn."

Just then they came to a stoplight. Stretching her neck, she gazed out the passenger window when she saw something interesting. "Sanny, turn right here and drop me off at the curb."

"The library? Checking out a book?" he asked sarcastically, pulling around the corner and braking at the curb.

"I can't stop thinking about something Eddie said in our interview," she said, hopping out. "Something rebar man said about Hood's father. It was the last thing he ever said, a dying declaration."

"They're even admissible in court."

"Exactly. Call forensics and get a team ready with a metal detector. I'll meet you out there in a couple hours. That should give me time to satisfy my itch."

SEVENTY-ONE

Built in the 1920s, the Springwood Public Library remained a resolute edifice in the center of the downtown district, eclipsed in size only by the courthouse six blocks away. Many of its myriad tomes and reference volumes had been handled by readers born during Reconstruction; and as evidenced by a series of black and white framed photographs in the front lobby, the place boasted about having been visited by two former presidents. Riggins had spent many adolescent days here, wandering the labyrinthine aisles and plucking various selections from the shelves. As she walked now through the soaring glass doorway, she was met by the familiar smell that only a half million books could produce. On any other day she would have taken pleasure in sipping coffee while immersing herself in the many fictional worlds waiting to be explored. But today would be no ordinary visit. Gaining assistance from a library worker, she seated herself at a microform machine and studied the stack of microfiche panels before her. Having decided the answers to whatever questions she had were probably buried so far in obscurity that the average detective would unlikely take the time required to uncover them, she decided to turn over every stone available to her, no matter its size.

As she'd once read, kingdoms were not conquered by average kings. Or *queens*.

Riggins decided to focus entirely on State Attorney Hood. In her mind, it simply could not be anyone else. Applying her own principles for solid detective work, she painstakingly eliminated all other likely sources who had had the realistic capability of creating the current situation. The only person other than Hood she found to be sufficiently connected—Governor Braxton—seemed so far removed that Riggins crossed him off her list. Confident she had her man, she set forth in her search to uncover what she considered to be a proverbial needle in a haystack. Making things worse, she didn't even know where to find the haystack.

Based on Eddie's contention that Paolo had directly referred to Hood moments before his own death, her instincts told her to start from the true beginning, with Hood's father. A dying declaration was indeed considered admissible in court, so why shouldn't she too consider it? Besides, Riggins recalled several of her own homicide cases where the facts had at first seemed so muddled, she'd been unable to find any headway. Not until going back to a point in time before her initial start point had she often found a foothold.

Hood's father, and some hidden truth...

If Eddie were to be believed (since Riggins had already stepped halfway into the pool, she figured she may as well dive fully in), then Paolo had uttered these words about Hood's father moments before falling to his death. Talk about cryptic. Deeming it worthy of being explored, Riggins began with the elder Hood's birth in 1932.

Understanding the daunting nature of the task, she had begun with simple internet searches of the elder Hood and Grassle names. Finding a total of twenty-six hits, dating from the elder Hood's birth to the present day, she'd written down the excerpted article dates and selected the appropriate microfiche panels. Since the first article containing the name 'Grassle' didn't appear until April 2016 (the One-Stop robbery), she made the decision to focus entirely on Hood.

She found a short birth announcement for Mathias's father, several banking articles involving the Hood family related to county business dealings, then a 1947 article about the family inheriting a large parcel of land in the north part of the county. Moving into the next decade and the tenth article on her list, Riggins found nothing but more ho-hum information. June 1950, the elder Hood graduates high school as the salutatorian of his class. May 1954, he graduates from Florida State University. 1958, Mathias's birth announcement.

She took a break, buying a coffee from the library café and popping two Excedrin due to her burgeoning headache. She texted Sanchez. *Techs ready yet?*

He responded right away. *Still on a call, fatal H&R.*

Frustrated at the delay, but knowing the techs had been stretched thin recently, Riggins slid the first bit of film from the 1960s into the machine, a 1961 article about the Hood family home experiencing a barn fire. So far, she hadn't found anything significant with either the Hood or Grassle family. But something inside of her had perked up once realizing Mathias—even through the lens of the documented past—was now alive. A living, breathing entity, instead of simply an idea in her research. Looking back in time, she imagined Mathias sitting on his father's knee, his infant mind brewing a lifetime's worth of corruption and arrogance, both of which he'd either been known for or suspected of.

The next nine years' worth of searching resulted in nothing noteworthy. Twice more she took breaks, going outside to clear her mind and to ease her headache. When she came to a familiar story, the elder Hood's murder, she forced herself to concentrate on every word and aspect of the numerous listed articles. Having long known about the case, Riggins nonetheless felt that if anything new could be gleaned from the state attorney's past, it would likely be from here.

The year had been 1967 when the elder Hood had been cut down by a junkie robbing a drug store. Riggins had only found a brief online article about the event, devoid of the no-doubt thousands of details a murder case garners. Of course, she'd heard of the story second-hand, as many people had over the years, some of it even told by Hood himself while voicing his steadfast belief in the same justice system that had allowed his father's killer to go free due to a legal loophole. Riggins remembered hearing Hood speak of the killer having died in an automobile accident several years after his acquittal, and how as an impressionable teenager Hood had thrust his entire being into the field of law. Reading through the handful of microfiche stories covering the trial, Riggins found nothing significant. The killer, a man named Samuel Washburn, moved away from Spring-wood shortly after his acquittal and was not mentioned again in any of the articles Riggins scoured through.

Ignoring her growing headache, she forced herself to read the last three microfiche stories she'd picked out. Finding nothing of note, she switched the machine off and gathered up the panels to return to the front desk. She figured she'd given it her best shot, that searching through the archived local news stories of Hood not found on the inter-net would at least allow her to sleep well enough. Not every piece of evidence to a case could be found, she knew. Needles and haystacks...

As Riggins handed over the microfiche files, the library clerk asked her how her search had gone.

"The only thing I found was a headache," she said, offering the woman a tired smile.

"That happens a lot," the clerk said. "But sometimes people get lucky. Last week we had a woman come in looking for her long-lost father. She ended up finding him under a different name. Can you imagine that?" She laughed, as did Riggins, until something struck the detective. Seizing on an idea, she asked the clerk if she could re-check something in one of the files she'd just returned.

Flipping through them, Riggins found the panel containing the final news story from the Hood murder case. She'd grown especially tired while reading it, her head feeling as though it would split open. But thinking of the clerk's story about the woman searching for her father made Riggins recall something she'd read. A detail that had seemed so innocuous at the time that it hadn't truly registered as important until now.

The final story to the Hood murder case detailed the suspect's acquittal, as well as a brief biographical note of the man, the editors apparently preferring to wait until the case's end to humanize the defendant. Riggins carefully re-read the article. Samuel Washburn, a drifter with a checkered past. And the killer's common-law wife and young child, both of whom had attended the trial. The article's writer had chosen to name the live-in girlfriend, perhaps to force the family to leave the area due to their now-publicized notoriety:

Helen Grassle.

Snatching up her phone, Riggins made several calls and quickly got the answer she suspected she would find. Not only had Helen never married Samuel, but she'd given their son her maiden name of Grassle. And state records had confirmed that the son would grow to have a son of his own—Edward Grassle, same birthdate and same social security number as the one Riggins had charged with the One-Stop murder.

Riggins called Sanchez. "I connected them!" she said, breathless.

"Talk to me, mama," he said, excited.

"Eddie's grandfather killed Hood's father then got acquitted in trial. Back in 1967. I have it all in black and white. Do you know what this means?"

"That Hood knows about this?"

"More than that," she said. "He's on the record as being obsessed with the case his entire life."

"Then why hasn't he ever said anything about it?"

"Don't you get it, Sanny? If he wanted to unfairly punish Eddie as retribution, he *wouldn't* say anything. It would establish a clear motive. He had to hide knowledge of it."

"All of this buried in some old newspaper article nobody would ever bother to go back and read."

"Until today," she finished.

Twenty minutes later the two were at the construction site where the forensic team had just arrived with the equipment Riggins had requested. The area had since been cleared, but since construction crews hadn't worked on the premises since the incident due to heavy rains in the area, it was reasonable to presume nobody had visited the area since.

Asking the techs to cordon their search area into marked grids, Riggins grabbed a trowel from the forensics van and told Sanchez to do the same. Together with the two techs, they would become archaeologists of sorts, digging for treasure. In their case, a missing bullet.

Rolling up her pants legs, Riggins took her turn working behind the tech who swept the ground with the metal detector. On each hit, Riggins bent and dug into the mud, unearthing everything from coins to rusty nails to aluminum soda cans. Not caring that her shoes and hands got covered in mud, she postulated something as small as a single round could easily have bounced far from the building or drifted in the swirling wind. She had probably overdone it by ordering a fifty-foot search radius, but as with the microfiche article search, she refused to lay awake at night wondering if she hadn't done enough to uncover some missed piece of vital evidence.

The first two grids produced nothing of note. In the third, in an area ten yards away from where rebar man had fallen, the tech stopped and raised her hand to indicate she had a hit. It was Sanchez's turn to dig, and since he'd gotten his pants full of mud long ago, he didn't bother trying to keep them clean now. He knelt over the square foot area the tech indicated and looked skeptically up toward the building.

"That's a long way for a bullet to travel," he said.

"They proved the magic bullet theory, Sanny. Start digging," Riggins said from her position just outside the grid area.

Sanchez obeyed, driving his trowel into the spot of muddy ground the tech had indicated. He scooped mud into his meshed pan and worked his fingers carefully through it. Nothing. The same with the second scoop. On the third, he shook away the mud and fine sand particles and stared at a small cylindrical object covered in thick brown slime. Not wanting to touch it, Sanchez called excitedly to Riggins. Stamping through the muck, she bent over Sanchez's shoulder and carefully eyed the item in the pan.

"Casey, do you have a bottle of water on you?" Riggins asked the pony-tailed, dark-haired tech. The young woman dug into her backpack and produced a plastic water bottle. Riggins carefully poured water over the object, washing the mud away to expose a gleaming, unspent .45 caliber bullet.

"A different make from the others we found on rebar man," Sanchez said, holding the pan at eye level. "Doesn't look like it's been out here long."

"Casey, bag this and have it printed at the lab right away," Riggins instructed the tech.

The tech placed the bullet into a paper evidence bag and had Sanchez sign a chain of custody form. Riggins and Sanchez tramped back to their vehicles, cleaned themselves off the best they could, then followed the tech back to headquarters. Once there, they anxiously watched Casey conduct a preliminary examination under a magnifying glass.

"I'm not sure I want to risk taping it," she said, frowning. "It looks like there may at least be a partial on it and I don't want it getting degraded." After quick consideration, Casey nodded to herself. "I'll glue it."

They watched as Casey prepared the two-by-two-foot fuming tank. She first placed a small plastic cup of water inside. Next, she uncapped a tube of standard superglue and squeezed ten drops into a small foil container before setting this inside as well. A wire, much like a clothesline, stretched from one end of the chamber to the other. Several needle-nosed clamps hung from the wire at spaced intervals. Using a tweezer-like instrument, Casey carefully removed the bullet from the paper bag and attached one of the clamps to it, nose to primer. The bullet now hung about twelve inches above the cup and foil container. Closing the chamber's glass door, Casey flipped a switch on the control panel then stood back to watch the process with both detectives.

"I've heard of this process, but I've never actually seen it," Sanchez said, moving his position to more closely eye Casey's profiled face.

"The element heats the water to provide humidity," Casey said. "Once the glue vaporizes, it adheres to whatever surface you have suspended in the tank. The bullet, in our case."

For the next ten minutes the three of them watched the tank with rapt attention. Satisfied enough time had gone by to provide an accurate read, Casey flipped another switch and opened the glass door. Carefully removing the bullet with the tweezers, she hovered it over a backlit table while holding a magnifying glass over it. Inspecting the bullet on all sides, she turned to both detectives and sighed. "Well, I was hoping we'd get at least a partial." A second later, she grinned and said, "But I didn't think we'd get a full print!"

Riggins and Sanchez crowded close to view the bullet beneath the magnifying glass. There, across the side of the brass casing, was the perfectly defined white ridgeline of a thumbprint.

"If I didn't see it, I wouldn't believe it," Riggins said, shaking her head in awe.

"We're not done," Casey said, transferring the bullet into a plastic, liquid-filled tray. "I necd to dye it now."

"What for?" Sanchez asked.

"Forensic light. The print gets visualized under electromagnetic radiation at about 500 nanometers." When she noticed the detectives staring at her, she added, "500 billionths of a meter. I'll photograph the print from different angles then run it through AFIS. If the owner of that print has ever had theirs placed in the system, I'll know who it is in about five minutes."

Riggins grabbed Sanchez by the arm, excitement in her eyes. But when Casey returned several minutes later wearing a confused expression, Riggins felt a touch of anxiety.

"Don't tell me you didn't get a hit," she said.

Casey stared at them both, disbelief in her eyes. "Oh, I got a confirmed match. Right thumbprint. Confirmed through AFIS, re-confirmed through the FDLE database since I found it there too. Normally, I don't cross-check AFIS, but I knew this was important and—"

"Casey, we get it," Riggins blurted. "Just tell us."

"Mathias Thurston Hood. Age 58. Current address, 1389 Swooping Wallow Drive."

Thinking, Riggins said, "I'm trying to think of a plausible scenario where Hood handles just one round." She looked at Sanchez. "What do you think?"

"I can picture Hood rolling the round between his fingers. Maybe it has some special meaning or something, like WWII airmen who used to paint messages on bombs they dropped on the enemy. He's trying the case personally out of some perverted sense of justice, and he clearly wanted Eddie dead."

"I'm inclined to agree," Riggins said. "It makes sense from a psychological viewpoint. Eddie is approaching the prime of his life, similar enough in age to Hood's father when he died. Hood already had rebar man on his payroll, who was valued enough to receive a background waiver through the governor. Then rebar man receives privilege from the sheriff to assist in a manhunt under the umbrella that all civilians have the same access. To top it off, Hood's print is found on the bullet rebar man tried to kill Eddie with. It reeks of a high-level murder-for-hire. There are too many connections for it to be anything else."

"So where do we go from here?"

Riggins shot Sanchez a concerned look. "We'll never get a warrant with what we have. We need something specific to tie it all back to."

Sanchez shook his head and chuckled to himself. "If only Hood could be nice enough to paint us a picture of what happened."

Riggins smiled at the joke, then suddenly opened her eyes wide. "That's it, Sanny!" Commandeering Casey's computer, she Googled "Mathias Hood interviews" then checked out several YouTube videos. In one from two years ago, Hood sat in his home office, pontificating on the tenets of crime and punishment. But it wasn't his words that interested Riggins. Twice, when reaching a point in his speech that concerned appropriate punishment for violent offenders, Hood turned to show the camera his father's portrait that hung behind him. Deep hatred, or some long-burning suffering, boiled over in the prosecutor's features as he spoke. To the casual observer, it seemed to be nothing other than an impassioned state attorney intent on prosecuting dangerous criminals. But watching it again now, knowing the added elements of the more recent Grassle case, Riggins felt even more sure something personal connected all the dots.

She paused the video at the point where Hood swung the portrait wide and removed a vintage gun from a safe mounted behind it. She pressed play again, and together they listened as Hood talked about the gun having been owned by the first sheriff of Calusa County. Briefly visible inside the safe were a stack of files.

"I'm ninety-nine percent positive the safe is what rebar man was talking about," Riggins said, tapping the screen with her finger. "But we can't use Eddie's statement. It's hearsay, and he's the defendant. We'll have to use Hood's proven connections to the sheriff, the governor, and to rebar man. With video evidence that a firearm was at one point stored in the safe, the files there, and along with Hood's print on the bullet, we may have enough probable cause for a warrant."

"I don't know, boss," Sanchez said. "That video is two years old. There may not be a safe there anymore. And even if we did get a warrant, we'd have to find solid evidence of his involvement. You have to be right."

Riggins stared at them both for several moments, unsure of what to say. Chet's voice echoed inside her, that same resounding source of reason that for nearly two decades had been her saving grace more times than she could count.

After another moment of thought, she set her lips in a line and nodded emphatically. "I am right. Let's type up that warrant."

As predicted, the case judge was not particularly persuaded by Riggins's argument. He finished reading her typed warrant request, which Riggins had just completed. A scowl creased the judge's aging face as he flipped the warrant packet onto his desk. He stared long and hard at the detective duo.

"All of this because of a muddy bullet and some wild theory about wall safes behind portraits?"

"At the crime scene, your honor," Riggins added pointedly. "The bullet, I mean. And video evidence that Hood stores weapons inside that safe." She gave Sanchez a nervous glance. The two of them sat side-by-side across from the judge's desk, each of them sitting perfectly straight in their chairs and feeling very much like children in the principal's office.

"I'll agree with some of your points," the judge conceded. "But you'd previously cleared the crime scene. For all we know, Mr. Hood could have taken a stroll afterward and accidentally dropped a bullet out of his pocket. This is conjecture, of course, but it goes heavily toward exclusion. You're walking on thin ice, detective."

Judge Rooney, a well-respected jurist and one Riggins held a personal affinity toward, had ruled both for and against her in past cases. As she sat biting her lip, Riggins realized she would have to make a stronger impression on him to get even half of what she now sought.

"The construction site is fenced, your honor. It's outside the realm of reason that Hood would take a walk inside that area, especially after Mr. Bruzzi's death. The man was under his employ, and it's extremely suspicious how a bullet with Hood's thumbprint on it would end up there," she added.

The judge eyed her. "He can hire whomever he wants as an investigator. It's his reputation at risk."

"True. But this is someone who had not gone through a formal background investigation. Fingerprints are needed to make it legitimate. His prints were chemically erased."

"The governor has executive discretion on whom he gives licenses to. Try again."

Riggins bit her lip but pressed on. "A man matching Mr. Bruzzi's description was seen at the farmhouse where the Downing woman and Deputy Hammer were killed. I testified that he shot Lieutenant Heinke and narrowly missed me. I've reviewed the courthouse tapes and have proof he visited Hood's office recently on at least three occasions."

The judge removed his glasses and rubbed his eyes. "Ask me for a warrant on Bruzzi's vehicle or computer and you'll have it," he said simply.

Riggins began to object that point then decided to change course. "There is some vicarious liability involving Hood's business arrangement with Bruzzi, your honor. As a public servant, he is expected to remain above the shadow of doubt. He requested and was granted a background check waiver for Mr. Bruzzi. That has occurred only once before in the past two years. In tens of thousands of background checks. As head of the twenty-first circuit, Mr. Hood should be an example of following legal precedent, not being one of only two exceptions."

The judge stared hard at her. "I could argue you are barking up the wrong tree here, detective. You very well may have grounds for Hood's removal from office, should you take this issue up with the state ethics board. But your criminal argument is weak at best. I am willing to speculate a grand jury won't be any more impressed with your argument than I am."

"Fair enough," Riggins conceded, trying her best to contain her frustration. "But this is only exploratory evidence. I don't need to prove whether he handled that bullet beforehand or dropped it during a stroll afterward. As you know, probable cause is strengthened when you add intent and motive. His special investigator was essentially deputized by the sheriff. I am willing to call witnesses who can verify the sheriff had never done that before, during any of his three terms."

The judge leveled his gaze on her. "And I'm sure those same witnesses would also verify a hundred other solitary acts the sheriff has performed during his terms, as is his duly elected right. I'm sorry, detective. Although it does appear that Mr. Hood is on a path to potential recall, I cannot grant your request."

Having wished to keep the information about Hood's father in reserve, Riggins now felt compelled to expend the last of her ammunition. She'd preferred to withhold it not out of any respect for Hood or his office, but out of hesitation to throw the court system into the disarray such an accusation would surely create. She held great respect for Judge Rooney. Knowing how this information would confound him both personally and professionally, Riggins had preferred to gain her warrant without it. But she felt left with no choice.

"Hood had motive to want Grassle dead," she said flatly.

The judge looked sideways at Riggins before pointing a bony finger at her. "You're playing with fire saying something like that. Are you willing to risk your entire career on mere speculation?"

Riggins gave a firm nod. "Yes, your honor. I'd even risk my pension on it, which I understand is a possibility since the state considers slander of a public official grounds for a civil lawsuit. Hood's father was murdered by Eddie Grassle's grandfather in 1967. I found it in library records earlier today. I have reason to believe Hood withheld that information while insisting on personally prosecuting the Grassle case."

The judge leaned back in his chair, his eyes widening.

"If I can produce documents proving he knew this, the entire case against Grassle is at risk. That safe is proven to exist. We have video evidence he at one time stored a weapon there, and of course we now have his print on a bullet found at the construction site crime scene. I believe we have sufficient probable cause enabling us to eliminate it as a storage source of evidence to Hood's established involvement. Not to mention Hood's own criminal implication."

Riggins removed a file from her briefcase and slid it across the desk to Judge Rooney. He stared at it for several moments, wishing not to touch it for some reason, as if it were something poisonous. Finally, and with great reservation, he opened it and read through its contents. When he finished reading, he set it down and sighed heavily.

"You say you found this in library records?"

"Yes, judge. Microfiche. It took me two hours and half a dozen Excedrin to find it."

The judge turned his gaze out his chamber's tall window. He didn't speak for a full minute. When he did, his voice carried the tone of resignation and studied appreciation.

"My granddaughter told me the other day that in this day and age, people can find anything on Google. She's eleven, so of course she knows everything. I bet her a trip to Disney World she couldn't find three local legal cases on the internet that were each over a hundred years old. She found ten."

He sighed again, rubbing his temples with his bony fingers. "As I sit here, I realize two things, detective. One is that I am going to have to cancel my golf trip this weekend to take my granddaughter to Disney World." He stared hard at Riggins. "The other is I feel forced to grant you your warrant request."

Riggins felt herself go flush. Never had she felt so nervous and relieved at the same time. Her throat felt hot and her tongue seemed like it had grown to twice its size in her amazement. "Thank you, judge," she blurted, trying her best to keep the excitement from her voice.

"I congratulate you on finding something even Google couldn't find," the judge said, nodding. "Your search will be limited to the wall safe only. I don't care if you find a cannon in that mud."

Remaining circumspect, Riggins again thanked the judge and exited the chambers with Sanchez in tow. As soon as the door shut behind them, she mouthed a silent *"Yes!"* and high-fived him in celebration.

Signed warrant in hand, she called Captain Escobar, who despite her wishes insisted on informing his boss immediately. The sheriff took the news with grim resignation, offering the metaphor of "a train barreling out of control." Assembling a tactical search team, Riggins took a final moment to reflect with Sanchez on their coming task. They discussed the ramifications of them failing to uncover any solid evidence implicating Hood in Eddie Grassle's case.

"At this point, we're going to have to fire our guns dry," she said.

"What am I going to tell the ladies when I say I'm shooting blanks?" Sanchez joked. Despite her growing anxiety, Riggins laughed, saying she needed to change and grab her ballistic vest.

An hour later the two of them, accompanied by a six-man search team, pulled up to Hood's private residence. They'd arranged for an acetylene torch to be placed on standby in the event Hood refused to allow them access to the safe. Two tactical team members covered the rear corners of the home, their M4 rifles slung across their vests. Two others covered each side of the front door, while another pair cordoned off each end of the street to pedestrian and vehicle traffic. Until Hood was detained and the home deemed clear, everyone would be on high alert.

A surveillance squad deployed earlier had already verified Hood to be home. He appeared to be alone. The plan was to knock and announce, affording Hood the added courtesy of being escorted to his bedroom where he would be allowed to dress before being escorted from his home. If after two minutes he did not open the front door, Riggins had ordered it to be broken down.

But after ringing the chiming doorbell, she'd only counted twenty seconds before a looming shadow appeared behind the bezel glass door. The sound of the lock disengaging came to them, and the door cracked open before the shadow quickly receded back into the house. Holding an arm out in front of Riggins, Sanchez indicated he would be the one to first make entry. Un-holstering his Glock, he pushed the door open to reveal an empty hallway. Motioning to the other tactical team members to follow him, he stepped cautiously through the doorway.

SEVENTY-TWO

HEARING THE INSISTENT knocking at the front door, Mathias Hood knew what was coming.

Although mildly surprised, he had reasoned that somewhere along the line he must have overlooked some crucial detail. None of it mattered now. With Paolo's death had come the end of his first crusade against Grassle. The newly incarcerated escapee had somehow lived through his ordeal and sat now under protective custody in jail. Hood knew not even he could expedite the case, given the likelihood that the defense would insist on waiving their right to a speedy trial. Since Grassle's capture, Hood had brooded over his current conundrum, sitting in his office chair as he did now, quietly drinking scotch and staring out at the sparkling river.

Hearing the insistent knocks at the front door and realizing it was a Sunday, he switched on the monitors to his home surveillance system and watched two uniformed figures position themselves at the rear corners of the house. Detectives Riggins and Sanchez and a pair of tactical team members carrying a battering ram stood at the front door. They had not come for tea. Hood's mind went to the small armory he kept locked away in the next room, but he decided against utilizing it. For everything the home represented to him, he felt it an affront to be forced to use violence in this, his ultimate retreat, his refuge. He knew that if no answer came to their knocks, they'd break the door down. So much violence. So much disruption to the order he'd worked his entire life to gain. Everything in his world had settled into its own pocket of reason. Now they wished to tear down the empire of righteousness he had struggled his entire career to build.

Deciding on how he would end it, Hood stood and swung his father's portrait aside, revealing the reinforced built-in safe. Dialing the combination and unlatching the heavy door, he removed a silver-plated Colt .45 caliber handgun. His father's gun. Over the years, Hood had performed the solemn duty of cleaning it, along with the ammunition it held. If Paolo had failed to finish Grassle with it, Hood would provide a fitting terminus to his own life while including his father the best way he knew how.

As his fingers wrapped around the gun's grip, he paused. No, he would not use the gun. The corners of his mouth crept upward in a macabre facsimile of a smile as the idea blossomed in his mind. An even better way, one that while sending him into the netherworld to be reunited with his father, would also ensure unworthy eyes would never fall upon that embodiment of his life's inspiration.

Hood placed the gun back inside the safe and strode to the front door. He unlocked the heavy deadbolt, cracking the door open before ducking away into a connecting room. If they would violate his home, he would not allow them to break its sanctity any further by forcing entry. Let them come and witness a thing they had not expected.

Moving through the adjoining room, Hood slipped back into his office. He faced his father's portrait, looking deep into those resolute eyes that seemed to relay an urgency he had never seen.

"I tried, Father," Hood said, his voice thick with pained regret. He could hear them moving through the house now, no doubt clearing rooms as they went. They would be here soon. And once they found what they'd come for, the official end for him would swiftly follow. The collection of files he had refused to dispose of—volumes of them—had served as constant reminders that his father's death had not been in vain. The dozens of imprisoned persons, some of them guilty, some innocent, had had their fates sealed by Paolo's secret work. Others, their faces now lost to memory, had had their careers ended prematurely. A judge; a rising star in politics; an arrogant athlete prone to getting his way in matters that disgusted Hood. An endless list. Most had not deserved their ends but still had endured them, as Hood watched quietly from his perch atop the legal peak he had so carefully constructed. And never losing a minute's sleep. Not even for those killed and disposed of so that not even their families had the closure of burying a body, the photos of their mangled corpses kept hidden away behind the portrait all these years, solemn payment for a life lost much too soon, a life greater than all those others combined. Since not even Lady Justice could correct this perversion with her scales, Hood had chosen to lean his full weight against them. No longer would he cry out in the night and wake to a pillow wet with tears. No longer would his bedsheets be turned to shreds in his somnolence—images of a lost life lingering like a ghost at the edges of his dreams.

Sweeping the files and photos onto the floor, Hood reached for his cigar humidor and opened the lid. His fingers caressed the collection of expensive cigars there, passing over the array of lighters he'd collected over the years, until they came to the row of liquid butane re-fill containers. Removing them one by one, he depressed their pointed metallic spouts, dousing the stack of files and photos at his feet, as well as his own clothing. He used the final container to douse the portrait itself. Those painted eyes, appearing to grow wide with rapt approval.

Yes, my son...

"I have failed you, Father," Hood croaked, reaching for one of his favorite cigar lighters. Flipping it open, he watched the flame dance in his hand, teasing, goading, promising an ending the lips in the portrait themselves now seemed to command, their model likely bones now after fifty years lying still and cold in his grave.

If not avenge me, join me.

Hood's eyes widened. His mouth flared up at its corners. Standing before his father's portrait, he resembled the painted image so closely that any casual observer would not have been able to tell who was who anymore.

He could hear them in the next room, no doubt pointing into the study and readying to take him down. Except they never would, because with a gasp that he knew would be his last in the form he now held, he let the lighter fall from his fingers.

Riggins smelled burning. Having just cleared the front of the house and knowing there to be only one floor, she knew it had to be coming from the study just ahead. A second later she eyed smoke curling from around the corner, snaking along the ceiling in long, gray tendrils. She glanced at Sanchez, who stood across from her against the opposite wall. The six tactical team members, despite their heavier armaments, stood to their rear per her order. This went against normal practice, but then again nothing about this entire case seemed to be normal. Feeling there was no time to second guess or regroup, she waved her extended gun barrel toward the open study door and rushed ahead for fear Hood had begun to burn evidence.

She vaguely heard Sanchez shouting for her to wait. Ignoring him, she flattened herself against the study's opposing doorframe, sweeping her pistol to cover as much of the room as possible. What she saw in the middle of the office was unexpected. Hood, or some version of him, stood before the wall-mounted portrait of his father, engulfed in flames. The fire began at a pile of folders and scattered paperwork at his feet and consumed his giant frame. The effect was such that he appeared to be glowing, his face and other exposed skin just beginning to heat to the point it still retained its normal elasticity and color. But as Riggins stood open-mouthed, that began to change. The fire's chemical process—the combination of heat and rising gases mixed with the combustion of the clothing around him—progressed by the second, and as Riggins called out in shock and horror, yelling for the others to do something for God's sake, that he was burning, Hood turned his head to look at her. His expression was one she had never seen before from another human being. His eyes bulged to the point they could have fallen from his face had they still not been attached by muscles and tendons. His lips pulled back against his unnaturally white teeth, and together with the contorting muscles of his face he seemed to Riggins like a sideshow freak, one who by some form of magic had enabled himself to be a normal human one moment, and a living conflagration the next. And just as it seemed he may magically return to his old form, that this horrible scene had just been an illusion, a soul-tearing scream of agony grew from somewhere deep inside him as the exposed skin of his face and head began to darken and crinkle, the muscles beneath spasming in such a way that his entire face seemed to move in an undulating wave of expressed misery. Amazingly, he retained enough of his senses to reach out with one hand, his fingers splayed, and touch the hand in the portrait. A final sentiment conveyed as thousands of nerve endings in his body began to burn at over five hundred degrees.

An instant later the portrait burst into flames.

As the first hint of burned flesh struck her senses, Riggins turned her head and vomited involuntarily. Wiping her mouth clean, she recovered just as the others burst into the room behind her after what had seemed like minutes, but in reality had been mere seconds. Looking frantically around for something, anything, to put the burning man out with, Riggins saw the study to be mostly barren save for a bookcase, desk and chair and a bar cart against the far wall. Beyond the open French doors sat a large swimming pool, but without anything in sight which could have been used to transfer water, the twenty feet may as well have been twenty miles. Just when Riggins considered removing her tactical vest to use in a desperate attempt to try putting out the flames, a white cloud suddenly burst from behind her. Nearly falling toward the screaming, burning man, Riggins watched in dismay as Sanchez stepped forward with a fire extinguisher. Pointing the nozzle at the burning pile at Hood's feet, he worked the cloud upward from the pile to Hood's lower body when suddenly the canister ran out of material. Yelling for the other team members to get more extinguishers from their cruisers, Sanchez did the only thing he could think of and kicked Hood's still burning form to the floor. An area rug covered this part of the office, and he used half of it to cover Hood's upper body. This only succeeded in tamping down most of the fire, as smaller licks of flame and puffs of flesh-smelling smoke emanated from beneath the folded carpet. Moments later, two members returned with extinguishers. Sanchez directed one to finish putting out Hood's smoldering body, while Riggins told the other to put out the pile of still-burning files. Each quickly did as instructed. Kneeling over Hood's smoking body, Sanchez tried to find his carotid pulse but drew his hand away due to the heat still coming off the man's skin.

"Forget about him, he's gone," Riggins announced, kicking away heavily charred portions of the files. Standing to look down upon the body, Sanchez could see she was right. Hood's clothing had melted into his charred skin. Despite his naked and protruding eyeballs, he very clearly was not breathing. His mouth hung open in a half-formed scream, the echo of which seemed to ring in the eerie silence pervading the scene. The sickening stench of burned flesh lingered in the air, overpowering the smell of burned clothing and paperwork. Riggins instructed one of the team members to summon Captain Escobar and forensics, that they'd need special containers to bag the evidence. She called Fire Rescue and an ambulance as part of procedure. Ten minutes after they had arrived, and after consulting with a physician by phone, they officially pronounced Hood dead at the scene.

While waiting for Captain Escobar and the forensics team to arrive, Riggins walked out to the backyard pool deck to clear her head. She had to escape the overpowering stench that still lingered inside the house. She stood as far from the house as possible, watching the river's dark water lap against the sea wall. Clouds obscured the sun. Rain seemed near again. After a minute, Sanchez came out to stand with her. Neither of them spoke for some time, until finally they went back inside and stood looking down at Hood's smoldering corpse.

"You mind if I order a pizza?" Sanchez deadpanned. "All this cooking has me starving."

Riggins surprised herself by letting out a dry laugh. It was either that or cry.

EVEN THOUGH THEY found a treasure trove of evidence Hood had tried to burn, they torched the safe anyway. It took them an hour, partly because they'd initially been unable to find the secret latch to unlock the portrait itself. In his haste, Hood hadn't removed everything, they discovered. Damning files and other records seemed, at first glance, to suggest the many rumors of his corruption to be wholly accurate.

The medical examiner took his notes, completed his initial inspection of the body, then duly ordered it bagged and returned to the "shop." Meanwhile, with forensics' assistance, Riggins and Sanchez sifted through the dozens of charred file folders. The ones on top had been partially destroyed, half of their contents burned beyond recognition. But the ones beneath had gone largely untouched by the flames. Included in these mostly intact files was one marked **GRASSLE**. Riggins determined that in his haste, Hood must have swept the safe's contents to the floor without taking the time to determine which ones would burn fastest. As such, the Grassle file had escaped with only a few charred ends to several pages.

As soon as she began reading the Grassle file, Riggins knew they'd struck gold. It contained a treasure trove of damning information. Handwritten and typed notes, newspaper clippings of his father's murder attached to those of the convenience store killing, a collection of suspicious-looking invoices. And much more. On the surface, it appeared clear that Hood had been embroiled in some sort of criminal enterprise, all of it detailing a sweeping plot to first ensure that Eddie's rights were violated once incarcerated, and then killed following his escape. It amazed her that someone so acutely aware of law had bothered to leave such evidence behind. As she flipped through the file and moved on to several others, Riggins began to realize the true scope of Hood's apparent actions. She began to feel queasy. The ease with which he had manipulated the legal system and managed to insert himself into so many people's lives frightened her. She came to a file labeled **BO**. Wincing, Riggins opened it, taking several minutes to thumb through its pages and shaking her head as she went. Using her well-honed discretion, she tucked the file under her arm, determined to share the information she'd discovered with the only person she felt it her business to tell. Excusing herself, she walked past the arriving rush of administration officials and called the sheriff's direct line. Normal protocol called for detectives to go through the chain-of-command before notifying him directly. But this situation was far from normal. Besides, she'd already broken enough rules to last a career. She figured one more wouldn't hurt.

Riggins had met Mrs. Driscoll a handful of times before, most of them during one agency ceremony or another. She remembered one meeting at a formal gala, where the pair had shared a laugh while zipping one another in and out of their dresses in the ladies' room. Riggins had found Mrs. Driscoll to be a perfectly charming woman, one she discovered newfound respect for after learning she'd once taken part in a civil rights march in college. For those reasons and many more, telling the sheriff what she'd found wouldn't be easy.

She started by apologizing for jumping the chain-of-command, but the sheriff seemed disinterested with regulations. "I just watched my wife throw up for a half hour straight," he said resignedly. "Hope you never have to deal with someone on chemotherapy. And now I get to deal with a burned state attorney. Whatever you're going to tell me can't possibly be worse than that."

He quickly found out how wrong he was. When she finished telling him what she'd discovered—that Hood appeared to have evidence of the sheriff's extra-marital, illegitimate daughter that the lawman had never before disclosed—he grew quiet on the other end of the phone. Sighing, he asked her in his no-nonsense manner what she planned to do with the information.

"It's really not my place to say anything, sir. Your wife—she's going through a lot already. If it's the same to you, I'd just as soon build a fire in the hearth when I get home and accidentally drop this file into it."

Nothing from the other end. When his voice came again, the sheriff sounded even older than the ten years he seemed to have recently aged.

"Although I don't reckon I deserve it, I'm thinking a fire would be a mighty fine idea," he said.

SEVENTY-THREE

Five months later

EDDIE LAY STARING at his isolation cell ceiling, lost in a daydream, when the deputy rapped his keys against the metal door. Keying open the trap, the gruff-sounding deputy summoned Eddie to witness the inspection of a large manila envelope marked Legal Mail. Sliding into his jail-issued pants (he'd learned fairly quickly to do so one-handed, getting both legs in together as he always had before the amputation), he stood dutifully at the trap while the deputy opened the sealed envelope and searched it for contraband. Finding none, the deputy slapped the envelope on the trap, had Eddie sign for it, then walked away without uttering a word.

Plopping onto his bunk, Eddie pressed down on the envelope with his stump and removed the contents. After a court hearing the week before, he'd anxiously awaited confirmation concerning the state's position on his most serious charges. The state attorney's office, having endured the humiliating effects of the late Mathias Hood's revealed crimes and multiple ethics violations, had felt compelled to concede on the heaviest of Eddie's charges. Eddie had sat dumbfounded beside his attorney, absently rubbing his now-healed stump. Afterward, Mr. Passmore had explained to him the meaning of the hearing. "You could still receive life if they change their mind, so don't go celebrating anything until you get official word."

Eddie removed an official-looking two-page letter from the

envelope, noting the familiar public defender letterhead along the top of the page, with *Philip Passmore, Esq.* below that. Since his recapture, Eddie had received dozens of pieces of such correspondence from his court-appointed attorney. Most had been hearing and arraignment notices. But this letter carried a particular weight to it none of the others had. Understanding his entire future lay in the two printed pages he held, Eddie took a moment to look around his tiny one-man cell. Would he reside in a prison cell such as this forever, living out perhaps the next fifty years in interminable regret? Or would he receive some respite, even a shred, something on which he could glimpse the smallest pinhole of hope through the blanket of misery he'd found himself in?

Feeling sick to his stomach, he waited a full ten minutes until he finally convinced himself that nothing would be gained by being afraid to read it. When he finally steeled himself to read it, he could barely keep the pages from trembling in his hand.

November 8, 2016
Mr. Grassle,

As you know, the 21st Circuit Public Defender's Office has continued to represent you in your current case. Since your initial arrest in April of this year, and including the additional charges placed against you as a result of your alleged escape, you have been arraigned on the following charges: Four (4) counts of (1st) Degree Murder; One (1) count of Armed Robbery/Principle; One (1) count of Escape; One (1) count of Aggravated Fleeing and Eluding; One (1) count of Felony Impersonation of a Law Enforcement Officer; and One (1) count of Violation of Felony Probation.

In accordance with your written and signed wishes as they relate to these charges, and in conjunction with those of the court, I hereby inform you in writing of your case's disposition: The State of Florida has agreed to withdraw all four (4) counts of (1st) Degree Murder, and the one (1) count of Armed Robbery/Principle, in exchange for guilty pleas on all remaining charges. The state attorney's office acknowledges the official misconduct of an officer under their jurisdiction. As a result, the state concedes your constitutional rights under the 4th Amendment were likely violated.

You are under no obligation to accept the terms of this plea agreement. You may elect to stand trial on all charges until such time you effect official signature.

As your attorney, it is my responsibility to advise you as to what may be in your best interest. In essence, the removal of your murder and armed robbery (principle) charges would also remove the statutory requirement of life imprisonment, should you be convicted of those charges. Circuit Court Judge Raymond McCarthy, upon agreement by the State, has pre-calculated your sentence on the three lesser charges. Each carried a cumulative sentence of seventy-eight (78) months. His Honor agreed to have the sentences run concurrently. This would amend your sentence to sixty (60) months, with seven months counted as time served. You are reminded of the state's 85% sentence rule. Should you formally accept this sentence agreement, you will be transported to the Florida State Reception Center to be processed. From there you will be assigned to an institution to complete your sentence. This office will mail you a copy of all court findings pursuant to your case at that time. You may consult with prison officials regarding your projected release date once you arrive.

Furthermore, your ACLU attorney, Mr. Van Buren, has begun civil litigation on your behalf regarding your pending lawsuit against the State of Florida. You may contact him for further details. Be reminded of the statutory award limit of $200,000 regarding municipal, county, and state governments. Attorneys are remitted a rate of 33⅓% for services rendered. If you have any questions concerning your criminal case, I can be reached at the number listed above. Written correspondence should be mailed to the return address provided.

Signed,
Philip Passmore, Esq.

Eddie read the letter a dozen times over, not quite sure how to feel. He recalled his pre-sentencing hearing several days ago. The letter was confirmation that it had indeed taken place, and not been a dream. And the days and nights afterward spent in a fog, his sleep fitful, his appetite nil. So, the new state attorney truly had told the judge of the state's unenviable position, that the case had been degraded to such a point that it seemed untenable as it was. That Eddie had over the past five months begun to slowly accept his fate was something a psychologist might consider a final stage of grief. Facing not just the end of his life as he'd known it, but to mire and stew in the constant reminder of the fact—clanging cell gates, the collective groans of those tortured souls around him, the walls and barbed wire and the general *sameness* assigned to everyone else, the stripping of individuality—had been the most difficult prospect of them all. Up until now, the State opting not to seek the death penalty had served him little solace. Florida did not provide parole. Life meant life.

Even as the evidence against him had begun to unravel, clouds of doubt lifting over the case, he had refused to believe today would ever happen. He had kept the attitude that hope was a dangerous thing to keep close to one's heart. It was best glanced at, touched briefly, tasted like a bit of honey on the tip of a finger before being placed back on the shelf. In the end, the attorneys and trial judge had conferred and agreed the case against him would likely fall apart during trial. The signed letter in his hands was now proof that all of it had been real, that sometimes life did throw you curveballs, but if you kept your eye on the ball, you could hit it just the same.

SEVENTY-FOUR

Three years later

IN A SMALL town twenty miles east of Akron, Ohio, Clarissa Fulton and her son sat at the kitchen table of their modest home. In the next room, Roger fiddled with a new television cable box, cursing as he tried unsuccessfully to make a proper connection. Clarissa had just served breakfast, which Liam now only poked at. The boy's glum expression mirrored the dreary December sky.

"Momma, what's a jailbird?" Liam asked, seemingly out of nowhere.

So, now the questions. Clarissa leaned her elbows onto the table and glanced toward the living room where Roger remained distracted with the cable box.

"Did you hear that from someone at school?"

Liam nodded, looking out the large kitchen window to where the early winter wind blew swirling circles of snow down the sidewalk. They had been in Ohio for over three years and yet the place still seemed foreign, a universe removed from Florida.

"Your father—your birth father—" Clarissa began, "Is in prison because that's where people go when they break the law. It has *nothing* to do with you. Don't let those kids at school tell you any different."

She had taken great pains to keep the information surrounding Eddie's case from her son's ears. Kids would always be kids, and with practically every one of them over the age of five having a computer in their back pocket, it was no real surprise to her that news of the case had sprouted among Liam's classmates. One overheard conversation from a teacher, or a quick Google search after Liam became evasive about his birth father, and the entire story could have popped up on a cell phone screen in mere seconds.

"Will I ever get to see him?" Liam asked, looking back to his mother.

Okay. So, there it was. She had expected questions, but not this one. She winced, feeling as though someone had punched her in the stomach. "Why would you want to see him?" She instantly regretted her choice of words. "I mean, I just don't know if that would be a good idea, honey. Isn't Roger a good dad to you?"

Liam cast a wary glance toward the other room where Roger had just thrown the cable box to the floor in frustration. "He's okay, I guess. But he never has time to play with me."

Clarissa put a hand to her mouth and swallowed hard. A thousand miles and three years had dissolved in the span of the past thirty seconds. "Roger works hard to help both of us, honey. And I understand how mean kids can be, what they can put into your head. When I was a little girl, I got teased because I wore glasses and had crooked teeth. I looked like this—" She made circles with her fingers and put them over her eyes then twisted her mouth.

Liam tried not to laugh but couldn't help it. "You're crazy, Momma."

"I know I am, baby. But what I'm crazy about is *you*."

The two listened to the sound of Roger's movements and occasional curses that floated from the other room. Clarissa watched Liam seem to consider something. When his next words came, she had the impression many parents get when they realize their children are much smarter than they seemed.

"Jimmy said my daddy was a bad person, but I didn't believe him."

Clarissa took Liam's hands in hers. Seeing a new fire in his eyes, she felt compelled to speak her true mind. She figured she'd lied to herself enough already, and that sometimes speaking a truth just felt good for the soul.

"Your father may not have been there for you, but he's not a murderer. Don't believe anyone who tells you different."

"Then why did he escape from jail? Jimmy showed me the story on the internet."

"I don't know why he escaped, honey," she said, taking a moment to look him over before glancing away.

But deep down, she knew.

ON A CLOUDLESS February afternoon six weeks later, Clarissa stopped at the mailbox after picking Liam up at his bus stop. Sorting through the usual junk mail at the kitchen table, she came upon a white envelope with a familiar return address—*Florida Department of Corrections.* Believing it to be another trite update, she opened it and read the letter with ever-widening eyes. When she finished reading, she sent Liam to his room and called Roger at work.

"He's getting out," she blurted before Roger could even say hello. "What? Who?"

"Eddie. I just got a letter from the prison. He's due to get out next week."

Silence then from the other end. She could hear Roger's breathing coming harder.

"You're not thinking of letting him see Liam, are you? He didn't sign the paperwork for the adoption, so I hope not."

Now it was her turn to remain quiet. The clock on the wall ticked away the seconds. Each of them could have been ticking an eternity, for all she knew.

"Of course not," she said.

But not even she believed that.

THE BARBED WIRE fence yawned open, expelling the figure dressed in donated Salvation Army clothing. The figure looked up into the pale sky, letting his eyes adjust to the first natural light he'd seen since arriving here over three years before. Prison administrators had been fearful of a similar incident from his stay in the county jail; their answer to preventing another escape had been to limit his thrice-weekly, hour-long recreation periods to a solid concrete box with only a four-by-four-foot metal wall grate to provide the mandated fresh air allowance. A highlight from his pacing the featureless box had been once sighting a small airplane through the grated opening, the pilot doing acrobatic loops with his plane before moving out of Eddie's view. And after recreation had been completed, back to the six-by-nine, windowless isolation cell, complete with its own toilet and sink. He had had no visitors during his time there. Only once had he viewed a television—a several-second glimpse of a football game broadcast from a population pod, while returning from a sick call visit. His days, just over eleven hundred in all, had passed by one at a time. Each being one fewer to live in freedom. Each being one closer to simply living.

Now, the sky in its full wonder. It seemed almost too much to take in at once. Eddie dared only take small peeks at it for fear staring too long would somehow create metallic lattices across the sky, a gigantic grate through which he would forever be forced to view the world. He made his way down the paved pathway toward the guard house serving as the main entry and exit point to the facility. All released inmates took this route when they left the prison proper, but most other inmates were not so well-known. The pair of guards manning the gatehouse regarded him with quiet, searching eyes. The tableau must have been striking for them—Eddie, having not only affected such a well-publicized escape but somehow managing to have four murder charges against him dropped, now walking out the front gates a free man. And having taken down such a well-respected pillar of the criminal justice system in the process, no less. There remained some who still believed Mathias Hood had been framed, and that he'd taken his own life out of some deep-seated ignominy that for a man of his stature may have seemed a fate worse even than death. But, as Eddie had learned in a prison psychology book, there were people who still believed the earth to be flat and that the moon was made of cheese.

For his part in the entire episode, Eddie had served just under four years in total. Along with the five years he'd served taking the rap for Jules, he'd lived a third of his life behind bars. During one of his final talks with Mr. Passmore, Eddie had learned a few interesting tidbits of his case. The new state attorney, under immense pressure from the governor and media alike, had had a vested interest in seeing Eddie's case resolved quickly. Prosecutors had shared a collective embarrassment unlike any seen before in the circuit's history. Two judges and several other high-ranking local politicians had been forced to resign their posts, having been dragged into the legal quagmire Hood's files had created. Within six months of his death, twenty-eight men and women proven to be falsely imprisoned by his nefarious methods had had their sentences vacated or greatly reduced. Several dozen more cases, including five involving life sentences, had recently been sent to the appellate courts for further review.

Eddie even learned about a sex-trafficking ring that Hood had been involved with. Having the sordid details left to his own imagination, he'd found added comfort in his own plight with the knowledge that more than a few of the rescued girls in the underground business had been underage. He supposed others had been through worse, as difficult as that had seemed.

The last thing Passmore had done before his release had been to assist Eddie sign the paperwork for the agreed-upon settlement process to begin. Although Passmore hadn't agreed with Eddie's decision to forgo a full-fledged lawsuit (the potential for millions on the table, providing of course the state legislature agreed), he'd voiced his respect for Eddie having the final say. A two-hundred-thousand-dollar settlement sounded like a lot, but after attorney fees and other fiduciary responsibilities, Eddie would be left with just over half of that. Four years of his life, his reputation, and even one of his limbs had been the price for the blatant disregard of his civil rights. In signing the settlement, Eddie had relinquished all future claims against the State in the matter. What would more money bring, anyway?

With just over four hundred dollars cash in his pocket that he had saved from his prison work assignment (he'd made two dollars a day, working sometimes ten-hour days), Eddie waved at the gate guards and made his way to the prison's public parking lot, his feet touching free ground for the first time since the day of his recapture. He took a moment to reflect on the significance. Freedom. Not just a dream anymore. It was no longer a distant ideal, one dreamed of while play-ing basketball under the watchful glare of Officer Schultz or imagined while evading that stalking figure with the knife. His life was now his own to live. Whatever version of reality had fallen upon him, he had no choice but to confront it. The prison counselor had helped arrange him a temporary residence of sorts—an extended-stay motel a few miles from the prison's front gate. At a hundred fifty a week, Eddie figured he'd be able to stretch two weeks as long as he ate cheaply. Civilian jobs had been available, but regulations had forbidden inmates from applying until officially released from custody. And even though a handful of unfilled jobs existed in the small town adjacent to the prison, most of them had seemed to involve picking fruit in the fields or some other form of two-handed required labor. Worse coming to worst, he figured he would just have to pick twice as fast as everyone else, assuming he would even be hired. He would even clean toilets if he had to. Anything to scratch together an honest living.

But first things first.

Adjusting the bag over his right shoulder, Eddie walked toward the road and turned east into the rising sun. After two miles he reached the highway and followed it another mile north until he came to his extended-stay motel. A short, barbed-wire fence stretched around the property, and an old junk car sat propped on blocks in the park-ing lot. A pair of shady-looking fellows exchanged something near the back corner of the building, turning to check if anyone had been watching them. Eddie pretended not to notice them. He looked up to the motel's marquee which read, 'Home is what you make it.'

It wasn't much, he figured, but it was a start.

EPILOGUE

CHARLES NADY OPENED his home's front door and looked skeptically at the delivery man standing on the stoop. Or more specifically, at the pair of new bicycles—one adult and one youth—standing in the driveway behind him.

"You must have the wrong address," Nady said, refusing to take the electronic sign pad.

The driver verified Nady to be the correct recipient, and that his address matched the one on the invoice. Still skeptical, Nady asked if there was a sender's name listed on the invoice.

"Nope," the delivery man said, checking his hand-held device. "It's marked private. But there's this that came with it." He handed Nady a small manila envelope. Written on it was his name, with the sender's section containing the words "An old friend."

Intrigued, Nady tore open the envelope and began reading the note there.

Dear Officer Nady,

I hope I got the right address. There's a website that lists people's home addresses, and this was the most recent one under your name. I figured I'd take a chance sending you a little something to say thank you for treating me like an actual person while I was at your jail. I got a settlement from the state. Please accept the bikes as a gift. I remembered that you never learned how to ride. Well, now's your chance. Then you can teach your boy. I never got the chance to teach mine, so maybe me having gone to prison can do some good for other people in a small way.

Prison isn't fun, but I managed okay. After I got there, I finally got a job in the prison motor pool fixing cars. It took me over a year to convince them to let me work twice a week, and even though it didn't let me see the sky like I'd wanted, it was better than rotting in my cell all day. You'd be proud of me. I even learned to rebuild a transmission. After I got released, I thought I was going to have to work the fields, but there are programs for people like me to find work. As long as you're willing to work long hours and do jobs most people don't want to do, you can make it just fine. My probation officer calls it "sweat equity." Funny sounding name, but it makes sense. I decided to settle down for now in a town outside of Springwood. I have a lot of good memories there, but some real bad ones too. It just felt right to make a start somewhere new.

I heard you got suspended because of what happened that day on the rec yard. I feel bad about that. The last thing I wanted was to get you in trouble for something I did. You were one of the few deputies there who treated me like a real person. Good luck with everything, and enjoy the bikes. I made the purchase as anonymous just in case someone questions who they came from. If it's a problem keeping them, I understand. But I hope not.

Eddie

P.S. I heard Officer Schultz got fired a while back for bringing cigarettes in for inmates. Glad you don't have to work with him anymore.

As Nady slipped the letter into his pocket and signed for the bicycles, his wife joined him on the stoop.

"What in the world are *those*?"

Nady watched the delivery truck pull away, then straddled the adult bike's seat. "What do they look like to you?" he said excitedly, footing up the kickstand.

"But you don't even know how to *ride* a bike!" his wife exclaimed.

"Go get Junior," he said, ignoring her statement and grinning over the handlebars. He pedaled down the driveway several feet before crashing to the pavement. Rubbing a skinned knee, he climbed back on to try again.

"And bring some Band-Aids too..."

As Nady and his son tested out their new bicycles, two hundred miles to the northwest another package was being delivered to a small beachside condominium overlooking the Gulf of Mexico. The delivery man rang the doorbell, and soon a large black man, barrel-chested and wearing a good-natured smile, answered the door.

Chet Riggins signed for the package, addressed to his wife, and entered the living room where she busied herself with a new sewing project that she'd begun that morning.

"For me?" she said as Chet extended the oversized envelope to her. The return address read *Calusa County Sheriff's Office.*

She opened the envelope and was surprised to see a handwritten Post-it Note from Detective Sanchez stuck on a pocket folder. In the note he said he'd received the envelope's contents from someone in her past and had wanted to pass it along to her. Inside the folder, Riggins found several sheets of paper—an itinerary of some sort, a voucher, and a folded, handwritten note. The itinerary had been made out for both her and Chet, with the destination being Florence, Italy. A voucher for two round-trip, first-class airline tickets and a seven-night hotel reservation for the Villa Medici in the heart of the city had been included. According to the voucher and ticket information, each was good for up to one year. Riggins frowned, feeling this surely to be a mistake. She wondered why anyone from the sheriff's office would have given her such an expensive and meaningful gift. She'd retired on schedule, but not without first going through a taxing internal affairs investigation. A written reprimand had been quietly slipped into her personnel file—a relatively minor blemish on her resume, but still enough of a reminder of how close she'd come to dismantling everything she'd ever worked for during her entire career. Adding to her confusion was the fact that her fiftieth birthday was still a few years away. She'd been dead set on waiting until then to withdraw a substantial amount from one of their retirement accounts to pay for the trip, something that would allow them to avoid an early withdrawal penalty.

Unfolding the note, her frown disappeared. Her already expressive eyes widened as she began reading. One hand to her mouth, she read the note once to herself then repeated it aloud as Chet came up behind her and placed his giant hands on her shoulders.

Dear Detective Riggins,

I never got a chance to thank you in person. I tried looking you up, but your address was unlisted. Detective Sanchez was pretty cool on the phone—he said he'd mail this to you. He told me you and your husband moved to the beach not long after I went away. I'm happy for you, and hope you're enjoying your retirement. I know men aren't supposed to talk about a woman's age, but you're not even fifty yet. Most people can't leave their jobs that early, so you're fortunate.

I had the chance to give you something as a token for risking so much for me. You saw me for who I was—a person. I've felt sorry for myself my whole life. I don't know how much my childhood had to do with that, but the last four years taught me that no one can help you as much as you can yourself. After losing my arm, I thought my life would be over. Then some disabled veterans came into the prison one day to talk to us and I met one of them who had lost both legs and arms in an explosion. He had such a good attitude that I told myself afterward I'd never feel sorry for myself again. And I won't. You were a big reason for that too, and I'll never be able to repay you.

The first time we spoke, you told me about wanting to go to Florence, Italy with your husband after you retired. Over time,

I forgot the name. Then one day after I got released, I went to a diner here in town and my waitress was named Florence. Then it hit me!

The money from my settlement is pretty much gone. I wanted it that way, so I won't depend on it. I figured I got it by messing up and not taking care of the people who should have mattered most, so spending it on myself wouldn't feel right. Like blood money. I put most of it into a trust for my son's college. I had to pay for someone to handle it, but figured it was worth it.

I'm saving to buy my own place someday. A real home. And I found a program that helps disabled people like me take college classes. But not before I take a trip next week. It's something I need to do before I get my life back in order. I already arranged it, and even though it's something I really want to do, it makes me nervous at the same time. Twenty-four hours on a Greyhound bus isn't bad when I consider I thought I'd never have the chance at all.

Thank you again. I'm sorry for things ending up the way they did, but my mother used to tell me God has a plan for everyone. Maybe this was ours.

Your old pal,
Eddie

Husband and wife made their way out the sliding glass door to the balcony, the Gulf breeze blowing warm and salty air. Chet brought the acoustic guitar Riggins had bought him several years before as an anniversary present and picked out a smooth rendition of 'Ain't No Sunshine' as waves broke, and scattered beachgoers roamed the shore several stories below them. Gracie padded out the still-open sliding door and jumped up onto the wicker loveseat, curling up between her human companions. Riggins stroked the butterscotch colored Maltipoo's head and received a series of loving licks in return.

"I'm not sure what to even say," she said, placing the letter onto the table next to her.

Chet touched her chin and turned her face toward him. "I think that letter says it all."

Riggins shook her head, her eyes clouding with doubt. "But I wasn't the one running for my life. I didn't get shot, or stabbed, or chased by dogs. Eddie went through so much more than I did, and look what happened—he still went to prison. Hood may be dead, but that means he isn't around to feel the damage he caused. How is any of that justice?"

Chet raised his eyebrows. "I don't know. But I do know you're a fighter. You lasted twenty-five years doing a job most people couldn't last twenty-five days at. And there's something else I know."

Her eyes did all the asking.

"I know that people get help from the last place they think, sometimes," he said. "Eddie may have lost some years of his life, but he wouldn't be walking around a free man right now if it hadn't been for you. And you wouldn't have stopped having those nightmares without *him*."

She looked at him, her eyes flashing surprise at first, then with the growing knowledge that her husband knew things she had never suspected he did. He'd done it before, and each time it had amazed her. She could almost feel her love for him grow inside her like a living thing containing its own soul.

"Do you think we should give the gift back?" she asked, resting her head on Chet's massive shoulder. "It's a sweet gesture, but I'm not sure I deserve it."

Chet Riggins kissed the top of his wife's head.

"Who in the world really *deserves* anything?"

Fifty-three dollars...

Eddie looked at the wrinkled bills and realized it was all he had left of his settlement after securing his apartment, some used furniture, and of course his two-night stay at the motel. That's the way he felt it had to be, not wanting the settlement money to fall back on. The bulk of it—one hundred thousand dollars—had been safely tucked away into a college trust for Liam. Not a replacement for not being in his son's life, he knew, but at least a token of what Eddie was willing to do to truly start fresh.

He'd already bought enough cans of chili and tuna fish to last him the entire trip. The front office had a drinking fountain, as did the many bus stops between here and Florida. He was due to get paid from his new factory job this coming Friday, six days from now, so he didn't feel panicked. His return bus ticket sat safely tucked inside his backpack in the motel room, so the only concern he had was having enough money to buy the several items he needed for his visit.

Today marked the farthest he had ever been from Florida. As a child, his mother had taken him to North Carolina for the funeral of a family member, and once as a teenager, he and Jules had hitchhiked their way to Georgia and back. But Ohio seemed a world away from those other places. The sky looked paler; the grass felt softer. Chirping birds celebrated their return from their winter homes, welcoming by the thousands summer's early arrival.

The motel clerk gave him directions to the town Walmart two miles away. Walking along the road's shoulder, Eddie tried his best to contain his anxiety. How would the boy act around him? Would it be awkward, and would they have nothing to talk about? What if he asked Eddie a question that he didn't know the answer to? He ran through countless possibilities, finally settling on the notion he would just have to let things happen as they were meant to.

He made the trip in a half hour. Finding what he'd come for and relieved at having enough money to pay for them, he removed a folded scrap of paper from his pocket and consulted the hand-drawn map he'd made before coming here. His destination looked to be about a mile to the northeast. Slinging the plastic shopping bag over his shoulder, he dug his heels into the pavement and started walking at a quickened pace. His heart hammered inside his chest. Despite the dry air, sweat glistened on his brow. To keep his growing anxiety from overtaking him, he recited lyrics from some of his favorite tunes. He stopped singing once he realized all of them contained lines that could easily transpose into his current situation.

When he arrived at the address, he stood looking at the simple clapboard house for several minutes, his feet seemingly glued to the pavement. He contemplated turning around and forgetting the whole thing. The sounds of suburbia seemed so alien to him; he wondered for a moment if all of it hadn't been some giant production, and he the unwitting actor playing a part doomed to fail. He vaguely remembered watching a movie like that. Somewhere close by a dog barked; a mother scolded her child for running barefoot in the street; a car passed lazily by. When at last he found the courage to approach and knock on the front door, he steeled himself for whatever reaction he may receive.

When a blond-haired woman answered the door, Eddie felt the sickening feeling that Clarissa had given him the wrong address. Maybe she'd changed her mind and hadn't had the guts to tell him. Or worse, that Liam had told her he no longer wished to meet him. But the woman had opened the door with her head turned, saying something to someone else inside the house. When she closed the door behind her and turned to face him, he relaxed. Clarissa. He'd only known her as a natural brunette. Everything else about her seemed the same. That slightly equine nose, her pouty lips, those piercing green eyes.

"Oh—" she said, running a hand self-consciously through her hair. "I dyed it a few weeks ago. Roger already hates it."

That's when he noticed the wedding band on her finger. She caught his surprised expression and instinctively covered it with her other hand. But just as quickly as she'd done that, she uncovered it, her face settling into a softer expression even from the one she'd greeted him with. Nostalgic even. Then seamlessly her eyes shifted from nostalgic to sad as she glanced at the stump of his left arm.

"I'm so sorry, Eddie. How are you doing with it?"

Eddie looked down at it and shrugged. "It still tingles off and on. And I wake up some days and forget it isn't there. Talk about a rude awakening when you go to rub sleep from your eyes. But I'm getting used to it. The doctors say there are prosthetics that look like real limbs, and have fingers that grab things."

She nodded, unable to take her eyes from the stump. "Roger says I'm making a mistake letting you see him. I can't blame him. But Liam turned nine last week, so he isn't a baby anymore."

Eddie shook his head. "Nine. Wow."

"I've let a lot of things go," she said to him, fighting back tears. "I had so many issues with you. I talked with someone too and figured some things out. At the end of the day, life must go on. I always wanted that life to include you, but I got to the point where I was going nowhere. Like treading water. You can do it for hours but when you get out of the water you hadn't made any progress."

Eddie smiled. "I'm happy for you. Really. I beat myself up for a long time about losing you. If I learned anything in prison, it was that you really can't be happy until you learn to forgive yourself."

Their eyes locked. Time itself seemed to halt. One moment in the history of the universe, a grain of sand in an hourglass with no end; and then as quickly as it had come it passed, each of them seeming to have transitioned to another place, one more secure and peaceful than the place they had vacated. Like ships finding calm seas after a storm.

Then Clarissa did something he didn't expect. Rising on her tiptoes, she kissed him gently on the cheek. "I'll always love you, Eddie Grassle." Her voice came wistful, happy. Yes, she was definitely happy saying it, Eddie felt. And then the mood broke, and they returned to the business at hand.

"He's excited to see you," she said, wiping away a tear. "He could barely sleep last night."

"Me either," Eddie said with a laugh. "I even called my probation officer and checked in early. He told me I'd woken him up and promised to revoke my out-of-state pass if I called again."

She laughed. "What's in the bag?"

"Just a little something I thought Liam would appreciate," he said with a shrug.

Clarissa smiled, turning to crack open the door. "There's a park a few blocks down the street. Try to have him back by five. He has chores he needs to finish."

"Five it is," Eddie said, feeling his stomach flutter when he heard a boy's voice grow near.

"If he responds well, I'll see about you visiting him again. The counselor I had him talk to said it should be his choice."

"Of course," he said, and then the door opened wide and a dark-haired boy of medium height stood before him. The resemblance was so sharp Eddie took a step backward. Before Eddie could make a move, the boy offered his right hand. Eddie shook it, and after the two made awkward introductions, Clarissa ruffled Liam's hair.

"Have fun—your father came a long way to see you. But make sure you're back by five, or there won't be a next time."

Grinning, Liam ducked under his mother's parting hug and stood next to his father. Eddie mouthed the words *thank you* to her then turned down the walk, side-by-side with his son. As they walked, Eddie asked Liam a litany of questions. How did he like Ohio? What was school like? What were his favorite TV shows, and were there any girls he liked? At first, Liam seemed bent on giving short answers (too cold—Ohio, it's okay—school, action shows—TV, and, predictably, they were dumb—girls). But as the park came into view, its large playground and sprawling grass field like a beckoning oasis, Liam began to offer more than just a few words at a time. He grew more relaxed, and he even laughed when Eddie made a spot-on voice impression of Roger. Eddie had him promise not to tell his mother about it. They fist-bumped to seal the deal.

They came to an empty row of swings. When Liam went to climb onto one of them, figuring that's what they'd come here for, Eddie pointed instead to the grassy field that sat just beyond where they stood. Opening the oversized plastic shopping bag, he removed a wooden bat.

"You play baseball?"

"A little," Liam answered, accepting the bat his father extended toward him.

"That's okay, we'll get you coached up. Know how to hit?"

"Yes, sir. I can even hit a curveball."

"Excellent."

Eddie tossed the one glove he'd purchased onto the ground. "We'll use that for home plate. I'll pitch to you for a while, then we can play catch."

Eddie dug out the baseball he'd bought and paced off forty feet. He stood for a moment staring at the sky. The air seemed more alive than it had just moments before, as if electricity flowed through it. It seemed as if all the elements of the earth had combined just then, reassembling inside his own body to create a new version of himself.

It wasn't until a smile creased his lips that he realized the sensation he felt was more than just the taste of true freedom. It was the sense that his past had finally fallen into its proper place, like a marble settling into a gameboard hole after years of rolling and searching for its home. And now that his past felt sufficiently closed, the air around him seemed lighter and less constricting. A clearer present. A brighter future.

Leaning in toward home plate, the ball behind his back, Eddie gripped a curveball. As he began his windup, he spied a hawk circling high above—majestic in its silent flight—and then he made his delivery, the ball leaving his hand, where it spun and tumbled toward the single greatest thing he had left in his life.

ACKNOWLEDGEMENTS

Many people have assisted me in the completion of this book. If I do not name them all here, I hope they won't be offended. I am confident my appreciation will be properly conveyed privately, as much of this creation would not have been possible without them. First, to my entire family network, who raised and supported me to even make this journey possible. My late-aunt Barbara Andersen, a writer herself, encouraged me and expressed genuine interest in my writings when I first put pen to paper long ago. She provided early inspiration for me—needed fertilizer for the seed of my muse. Close personal friends helped encourage and support me throughout this book's process, assisting with reading early samples and making informed suggestions. Their help has been invaluable. Business professionals helped as well, providing medical, legal and other assistance that supplemented my own technical know-how. And taking it back to my army days, where my NCOs and officers taught me self-discipline and helped forge me into manhood—I both hated and loved them for it. My fellow soldiers shared with me an uncommon brotherhood that remains today—*hooah!*

I wish to specially thank my developmental editor Jennifer Collins, who challenged me to look deeply into the story itself and to flesh out my characters for who they truly are. Her shrewd eye for these details was essential in transforming this work into so much more than it had been before. Jason Pettus, my line and copy editor, applied his surgical attention to detail adding to and trimming the manuscript where it was needed most. His readiness to share his vast knowledge of the publication process is greatly appreciated. Chris Egner, my proofreader, proved an invaluable resource as well. Her meticulous eye for catching errors and making sound last-minute suggestions smoothed out the remaining edges to the manuscript. My thanks also to Lorie DeWorken, my cover designer and formatter, who lent her patience and creativity to the physical aspect of the overall book design. Without these consummate professionals, this book would not have the life it now has.

Lastly, to all who have read and shared this journey with me, I hope you enjoyed the story. I ask for an honest on-line review from your site of choice, if you have the time. Much thanks.

Made in the USA
Monee, IL
26 February 2021